EXTRATERRITORIALITY AND CLIMATE CHANGE JURISDICTION

This book builds on the scholarship of the law of state jurisdiction, engaging with fundamental questions about states' legislative competence to respond to climate change. Considering general theory, the author advocates for a systemic analytical framework for the contested issue of 'extraterritoriality' in international law.

Exploring the crystallisation of 'climate change jurisdiction', the book provides a comprehensive exploration of the jurisdictional bases and limitations for unilateral climate protection measures. In doing so, crosscutting issues of world trade law, international civil aviation law, the law of the sea, and importantly, the customary international law of state jurisdiction are considered.

Amidst the myriad of developing norms, a novel 'considerate design' tool is introduced to assist policymakers in finding a better balance between regulatory autonomy, development needs and the protection of common concerns.

Volume 83 in the series Studies in International Law

Studies in International Law

Recent titles in this series

Predictability and Flexibility in the Law of Maritime Delimitation, 2nd edition
Yoshifumi Tanaka

Feminist Engagement with International Criminal Law: Norm Transfer, Complementarity, Rape and Consent
Eithne Dowds

Asylum Control and Access to Protection: Admission, Readmission and Human Rights
Mariagiulia Giuffré

Intertemporal Linguistics in International Law: Beyond Contemporaneous and Evolutionary Treaty Interpretation
Julian Wyatt

The Responsibility to Protect and the Failures of the United Nations Security Council
P M Butchard

The Role of Multilateral Environmental Agreements: A Reconciliatory Approach to Environmental Protection in Armed Conflict
Britta Sjostedt

Prosecutorial Discretion at the International Criminal Court
Anni Pues

Judicial Deference in International Adjudication: A Comparative Analysis
Johannes Hendrik Fahner

Human Rights Commitments of Islamic States: Sharia, Treaties and Consensus
Paul McDonough

Intervention in Civil Wars: Effectiveness, Legitimacy, and Human Rights
Chiara Redaelli

General Principles as a Source of International Law: Art 38(1)(c) of the Statute of the International Court of Justice
Imogen Saunders

The Law of Humanity Project: A Story of International Law Reform and State-making
Ukri Soirila

Extraterritoriality and Climate Change Jurisdiction: Exploring EU Climate Protection under International Law
Natalie L Dobson

For a complete list of titles in this series, see www.bloomsburyprofessional.com/uk/series/studies-in-international-law

Extraterritoriality and Climate Change Jurisdiction

Exploring EU Climate Protection under International Law

Natalie L Dobson

•HART•
OXFORD • LONDON • NEW YORK • NEW DELHI • SYDNEY

HART PUBLISHING

Bloomsbury Publishing Plc

Kemp House, Chawley Park, Cumnor Hill, Oxford, OX2 9PH, UK

1385 Broadway, New York, NY 10018, USA

29 Earlsfort Terrace, Dublin 2, Ireland

HART PUBLISHING, the Hart/Stag logo, BLOOMSBURY and the Diana logo are trademarks of Bloomsbury Publishing Plc

First published in Great Britain 2021

A catalogue record for this book is available from the British Library.

Library of Congress Cataloging-in-Publication data

Names: Dobson, Natalie L., author.

Title: Extraterritoriality and climate change jurisdiction : exploring EU climate protection under international law / Natalie L. Dobson.

Description: Oxford, UK ; New York, NY : Hart Publishing, an imprint of Bloomsbury Publishing, 2021. | Series: Studies in international law ; volume 83 | Includes bibliographical references and index.

Identifiers: LCCN 2021022804 (print) | LCCN 2021022805 (ebook) | ISBN 9781509935826 (hardback) | ISBN 9781509951086 (paperback) | ISBN 9781509935840 (pdf) | ISBN 9781509935833 (Epub)

Subjects: LCSH: Climatic changes—Law and legislation—European Union countries. | Emissions trading—Law and legislation—European Union countries. | Climate change mitigation—International cooperation. | Exterritoriality.

Classification: LCC KJE6246 .D63 2021 (print) | LCC KJE6246 (ebook) | DDC 344.2404/633—dc23

LC record available at https://lccn.loc.gov/2021022804

LC ebook record available at https://lccn.loc.gov/2021022805

ISBN: HB: 978-1-50993-582-6
ePDF: 978-1-50993-584-0
ePub: 978-1-50993-583-3

Typeset by Compuscript Ltd, Shannon

Acknowledgements

THIS MONOGRAPH WOULD not have been possible without the generous helping hands and minds of many. A first thanks goes to Professors Cedric Ryngaert and Seline Trevisanut, my PhD supervisors, whose open-minded approach and insightful feedback were invaluable for the doctoral dissertation, defended at Utrecht University in 2018. I am also most grateful to the PhD reading committee, Professors Joanne Scott, Catherine Redgwell, Thomas Cottier, Marleen van Rijswick and Chris Backes. Their diverse comments and reflections laid the foundation for the further development of the doctoral research into the present monograph.

Cutting across various legal fields, this project is only one piece of the greater UNIJURIS project on global values and unilateral jurisdiction. It has been wonderful be part of the warm 'Unilaterals' family, tirelessly testing concepts and broader world views. I am also grateful to my colleagues at the Utrecht Center for Water Oceans and Sustainability Law and Utrecht Center for Regulation and Enforcement Europe. The variety of initiatives and exchange of ideas made Utrecht University an inspiring and supportive place to be. A special thanks to Marieke Koekkoek and Dr Imelda Tappeiner for being there at the very beginning, even when I was not.

Many thanks also to the team at Hart Publishing, in particular Sinead Moloney and Sasha Jawed, for their wonderful assistance with the development of this book. I am also very grateful to the anonymous reviewers for their helpful feedback.

Finally, thank you to my family and friends for your patient support and consistent curiosity over the years. For Freek, my partner and Archimedes, thank you for sitting steadfast through all weather, with a listening ear, sharp eyes and good dose of humour. In many ways you were my wings even though we all know that, of course, humans cannot fly. This book is dedicated to you and Ila Louise.

"The best thing for disturbances of the spirit is to learn … Learn why the world wags and what wags it. That is the only thing which the poor mind can never exhaust, never alienate, never be tortured by, never fear or distrust, and never dream of regretting." – T H White, The Sword in the Stone

Contents

PART II
JURISDICTIONAL BASES AND LIMITATIONS
IN *LEX SPECIALIS* REGIMES

PART III
LEX GENERALIS: THE CRYSTALLISATION OF 'CLIMATE CHANGE JURISDICTION' UNDER CUSTOMARY INTERNATIONAL LAW

Abbreviations

AB	Appellate Body
AG	Advocate General
ALI	American Law Institute
ASIL	American Society of International Law
BCA	border carbon adjustment
BTA	border tax adjustment
CBDRRC	Principle of Common But Differentiated Responsibilities and Respective Capabilities
CJEU	Court of Justice of the European Union
COP	Conference of the Parties
CORSIA	Carbon Offsetting and Reduction Scheme for International Aviation
DSB	Dispute Settlement Body
DSU	Dispute Settlement Understanding
EC	European Community
ECHR	European Convention on Human Rights
ECtHR	European Court of Human Rights
ECJ	European Court of Justice
EEA	European Economic Area
EEC	European Economic Community
EEZ	Exclusive Economic Zone
EU ETS	EU Emission Trading System
FLEGT	Forest Law Enforcement, Governance and Trade
GATS	General Agreement on Trade in Services
GATT	General Agreement on Tariffs and Trade

GSP	Generalized System of Preference
IBA	International Bar Association
ICAO	International Civil Aviation Organization
ICJ	International Court of Justice
ILA	International Law Association
ILC	International Law Commission
IMO	International Maritime Organization
IPCC	Intergovernmental Panel on Climate Change
LOSC	United Nations Convention on the Law of the Sea
MEA	multilateral environmental agreement
MFN	most-favoured nation
NGO	non-governmental organization
NT	national treatment
PCIJ	Permanent Court of International Justice
PPM	process and production method (measure)
SPS	Agreement on the Application of Sanitary and Phytosanitary
TBT	Agreement on Technical Barriers to Trade
TEU	Treaty on the European Union
TFEU	Treaty on the Functioning of the European Union
UN	United Nations
UNCED	United Nations Conference on Environment and Development
UNEP	United Nations Environment Programme
UNGA	United Nations General Assembly
UNFCCC	United Nations Framework Convention on Climate Change
VCLT	Vienna Convention on the Law of Treaties
VPA	Voluntary Partnership Agreement
WTO	World Trade Organization

Table of Cases

Permanent Court of International Justice (PCIJ)

International Court of Justice (ICJ)

Permanent Court of Arbitration

Ad hoc Arbitration

International Criminal Tribunal for the former Yugoslavia

International Trubunal for the Law of the Sea

General Agreement on Tariffs and Trade (GATT)/ World Trade Organisation (WTO)

GATT Panel Reports

WTO Cases

Court of Justice of the European Union / European Court of Justice

European Court of Human Rights

United Nations Human Rights Council

Inter-America Court of Human Rights

National Case Law

Belgium

Canada

Germany

Ireland

Israel

Netherlands

New Zealand

Pakistan

United Kingdom

United States

1

Introduction

A point has been reached in history when we must shape our actions throughout the world with a more prudent care for their environmental consequences. Through ignorance or indifference we can do massive and irreversible harm to the earthly environment on which our life and wellbeing depend.*

1. INTRODUCTORY REMARKS: THE DILEMMA OF AMBITIOUS UNILATERAL CLIMATE PROTECTION

IN 1988, PROMPTED by an initiative of Malta, the United Nations General Assembly (UNGA) passed resolution 43/53 on the protection of the global climate for present and future generations of mankind.[1] The resolution recognised the climate as an 'essential condition which sustains life on earth', and expressed concern 'that certain human activities could change global climate patterns, threatening present and future generations'.[2] The resolution went on to declare climate change 'a common concern of mankind', calling upon states to 'treat climate change as a priority issue' and 'collaborate in making every effort to prevent [its] detrimental effects'.[3] Initially, the 1992 United Nations Framework Convention on Climate Change (UNFCCC) seemed to promise a swift international response, yet further progress soon stalled due to the complex conflict of interests that continues to plague multilateral efforts today.[4] As a result, even after the 2015 Paris Agreement on Climate Change, we are left with a persistent 'emissions gap' between the reductions of greenhouse gas (GHG) emissions pledged by states and the overall reductions needed to prevent a 'dangerous' increase in global temperature calculated by scientists as a rise beyond 2°C above pre-industrial levels.[5]

*UNGA, Declaration of the United Nations Conference on the Human Environment (16 June 1972) UN Doc A/Conf48/14/Rev 1 ('Stockholm Declaration') rec 6.

1 UNGA Res 43/53 (6 December 1988) UN Doc A/RES/43/53.

2 ibid rec 2.

3 ibid [1], [6], [9].

4 United Nations Framework Convention on Climate Change (adopted 9 May 1992, entered into force 21 March 1994) 1771 UNTS 107 (UNFCCC).

5 This ambition gap has been recognised in the decision to adopt the 2015 Paris Agreement, UNFCCC, Draft Decision -/CP.21 'Paris Agreement' (2015) 7 FCCC/CP/2015/L.9/Rev.1 (Decision to Adopt the Paris Agreement), rec 10. See also 'The Emissions Gap Report 2017: A UN Environment

With their different policy priorities, not all states, or groups of states, share the same level of climate ambition, with some taking a far more proactive approach than others. For proactive states, a key means of mitigating anthropogenic climate change is to regulate the production processes of goods and services to limit the GHGs emitted throughout their lifecycle.[6] Importantly, in doing so, individual regulators have strong incentives to engage actors beyond their territory. From an environmental perspective, this is because climate change responses will achieve more effective results when they reduce the greatest possible amount of GHGs, all over the world.[7] At the same time, regulators also have a strong economic motive to apply their legislation to foreign products and services so as to level the playing field, ensuring that their higher standards of climate protection do not disadvantage the competitive position of domestic producers.[8] Although potentially more effective, such measures risk infringing the regulatory freedom of other states, which have, for their own reasons, chosen either not to regulate a certain issue or to do so in a different way. This creates tensions with the principle of sovereign equality, and raises important issues regarding the equitable distribution of climate change burdens.

It is within this context that questions then arise as to the limits of state competence to target GHG-emitting activities outside of their territories. In the face of fast-evolving policy and fragmented legal developments, this book seeks to provide a comprehensive exploration of the jurisdictional bases and limitations for unilateral climate protection measures.[9] The overall picture of jurisdictional rules makes up what is termed here as 'climate change jurisdiction'. Section 2 of this introductory chapter first turns to this book's main case study, the European Union. With its consistently outward-reaching and ambitious policy, the EU is catalysing questions of climate change jurisdiction in the legal arena. Section 3 then defines the key conceptual parameters as they are employed in this study. Subsequently, the structure and approach to the jurisdictional analysis are briefly set out in section 4.

Synthesis Report' (UNEP, 2017) ('UNEP Emissions Gap Report 2017') www.wedocs.unep.org/bitstream/handle/20.500.11822/22070/EGR_2017.pdf?sequence=1&isAllowed=y.

[6] This is because climate change is the result of cumulative GHG emissions. For further information on the science of climate change, see 'IPCC, 2013: Summary for Policymakers' in Stocker et al, *Climate Change 2013: The Physical Science Basis, Contribution of Working Group I to the Fifth Assessment Report of the Intergovernmental Panel on Climate Change* (Cambridge, Cambridge University Press, 2013) 1–30.

[7] As noted by Bodansky, the mitigation of climate change requires an 'aggregate effort' for effective results. See D Bodansky, 'What's in a Concept? Global Public Goods, International Law and Legitimacy' (2012) 23 *European Journal of International Law* 651.

[8] See further on this issue, G Marceau, 'The Interface Between the Trade Rules and Climate Change Actions' in DY Park (ed), *Legal Issues on Climate Change and International Trade Law* (Basel, Springer International, 2016).

[9] This research is part of the Utrecht University UNIJURIS project on unilateral jurisdiction and the protection of shared values, with funding from the European Research Council under the European Union's Seventh Framework Programme (FP7/2007-2013)/ERC grant agreement no 336230 and the Dutch Organization for Scientific Research ('NWO VIDI scheme').

2. FOCUS OF THIS STUDY: THE EU AS A PROVOCATIVE CLIMATE LEADER

Over the past decade the EU has emerged as a global environmental actor and a self-proclaimed leader in the field of climate change.[10] Its initial 40 per cent reduction target for 2030 under the Paris Agreement, has been surpassed by even greater ambition in the proposed European Climate Law.[11] As will be seen in this book, the EU continues to take unilateral action, 'integrated' across various policy fields, which effectively seeks to engage actors beyond its territory.[12] The EU Green Deal expresses explicit concern that 'efforts to go climate-neutral by 2050 could be undermined by lack of ambition by our international partners', necessitating, among other policies, a carbon border adjustment mechanism for goods from outside the EU.[13]

The EU's extension of its measures beyond its borders has not been without controversy, a key example being the EU Aviation Directive 2008/101/EC, which extended the EU's Emission Trading Scheme (ETS) to cover international aviation emissions for flights to and from EU territory.[14] This led to the well-known *Air Transport Association of America (ATAA)* case before the Court of Justice of the European Union (CJEU), where appellants argued that the Aviation Directive was an extraterritorial measure for which the EU lacked jurisdiction under international law.[15] The CJEU did not agree, finding that the EU had 'unlimited jurisdiction' to require the submission of emissions allowances for carbon dioxide (CO_2) emitted outside its territory from aircraft landing in or departing from EU aerodromes.[16]

[10] For further discussion, see eg E Morgera and G Marín Durán, *Environmental Integration in the EU's External Relations – Beyond Multilateral Dimensions* (Oxford, Hart Publishing, 2012); T Delreux, 'The EU as an Actor in Global Environmental Politics' in A Jordan and C Adelle (eds), *Environmental Policy in the EU. Actors, institutions and processes*, 3rd edn (Abingdon, Routledge, 2013).

[11] This is compared to 1990 levels. See 'Submission by Latvia and the European Commission on Behalf of the European Union and its Member States – Intended Nationally Determined Contribution of the EU and its Member States' (Riga, 6 March 2015) www.ec.europa.eu/clima/sites/clima/files/docs/2015030601_eu_indc_en.pdf. For increasing ambitions, see Commission (EU) 'Amended proposal for a Regulation of the European Parliament and of the Council on establishing the framework for achieving climate neutrality and amending Regulation (EU) 2018/1999 (European Climate Law)' (Communication) COM(2020) 563 final, 17 September 2020.

[12] The integration of environmental protection across EU policy is mandated by Art 11 of the Consolidated version of the Treaty on European Union [2012] OJ C326/01 (TEU).

[13] This can be found in the Inception impact assessment – Ares (2020)1350037 on the website 'EU Green Deal (carbon border adjustment mechanism' (European Commission) www.ec.europa.eu/info/law/better-regulation/have-your-say/initiatives/12228-Carbon-Border-Adjustment-Mechanism.

[14] Parliament and Council (EC) Directive 2008/101 amending Directive 2003/87/EC so as to include aviation activities in the scheme for greenhouse gas emission allowance trading within the Community [2008] OJ L8/3 (Aviation Directive); Parliament and Council (EU) Directive 2003/87/EC establishing a scheme for greenhouse gas emission allowance trading within the Community and amending Council Directive 96/61/EC [2003] OJ L275 ('ETS Directive').

[15] Case C-366/10 *Air Transport Association of America, American Airlines, Inc, Continental Airlines, Inc, United Airlines, Inc v The Secretary of State for Energy and Climate Change* [2011] ECR I-0000 (*ATAA* case).

[16] ibid [124]–[125].

This finding did little to still the political controversy. Indeed, ultimately, threats of economic sanctions from other states pressured the EU to issue Regulation 421/2014 restricting the scope of the Aviation Directive to flights within the European Economic Area, 'in view' of the implementation of an international agreement on aviation emissions by 2020.[17] Importantly, from a legal perspective the reasoning of the CJEU was also heavily criticised.[18] Indeed, the ensuing reactions illustrate a lack of clarity in legal discourse on the jurisdictional framework applicable to unilateral measures seeking to target GHGs emitted abroad.

With its ample and explicit examples of unilateral climate protection measures, the EU is the central case study of this book. As the Union is not a state, it is necessary at the outset to address the question of the applicable jurisdictional rules. This study takes an international law perspective, conceiving of the EU as an international organisation, based on multilateral constituent treaties, and endowed with legal personality by virtue of the conferral of sovereignty from its member states.[19] As noted by the International Court of Justice (ICJ), international organisations 'are subjects of international law and, as such, are bound by any obligations incumbent upon them under general rules of international law'.[20] This will clearly be the case where the EU is itself a party to a treaty, as it is for example to the UNFCCC and the Paris Agreement. Rules of another international organisation will further be 'incumbent' upon the EU when it becomes a member, as is the case with the World Trade Organization (WTO).[21]

Matters are more complex, however, when the EU is not a party to a treaty, or member of another international organisation, while all or most of its Member States are. This is, for example, evident in the case of the International Civil Aviation Organization (ICAO) and the International Maritime Organization (IMO), which are developing concurrent regulatory frameworks for international transport emissions. The applicability and jurisdictional implications of

[17] Parliament and Council Regulation (EU) 421/2014 establishing a scheme for greenhouse gas emission allowance trading within the Community, in view of the implementation by 2020 of an international agreement applying a single global market-based measure to international aviation emissions [2014] OJ L129/1-4.

[18] For a pointed critique. see eg B Havel and J Mulligan, 'The Triumph of Politics: Reflections on the Judgment of the Court of Justice of the European Union Validating the Inclusion of Non-EU Airlines in the Emissions Trading Scheme' (2012) 37 *Air and Space Law* 3.

[19] These are the EU primary treaties: the Treaty on European Union (TEU), and the Treaty on the Functioning of the European Union [2012] OJ C326/47 (TFEU). Ziegler described the EU as having 'derived' legal personality (codified in Art 47 TEU): K Ziegler, 'The Relationship between EU Law and International Law' (2015) University of Leicester School of Law research paper 15-04, 3.

[20] *Interpretation of the Agreement of 25 March 1951 between the WHO and Egypt*, Advisory Opinion [1980] ICJ Rep 73, 90.

[21] 'Members and Observers' (World Trade Organization) www.wto.org/english/thewto_e/whatis_e/tif_e/org6_e.html.

these competing multilateral schemes will be discussed further in part III of this book on the *lex specialis* regimes, and part IV on jurisdictional conditions.

Notably, there is also heated discussion as to whether customary international law binds international organisations, particularly given the latter's lack of involvement in its formation.[22] This relates to the broader debate on whether being a *subject* of international law with separate legal personality necessarily entails that one is bound by 'general rules' – itself a contested category.[23] In this regard, Reinisch appealingly argues that 'if the functionally limited personality of international organizations develops over time … they are in fact subject to [custom] when they act in a way capable of infringing it'.[24] This aligns with 'the legal premise that "subjects of international law" are usually "subject to international law"'.[25] For its part, the CJEU has unequivocally recognised that custom binds the EU, and has indeed applied customary jurisdictional rules.[26] In light of the forgoing, and the fact that the customary rules are binding upon all of the EU Member States, customary rules are considered here as being very relevant to the delimitation of EU jurisdictional competences.

3. CONCEPTUAL PARAMETERS: UNILATERAL JURISDICTION AND 'EXTRATERRITORIALITY'

At the outset, it is valuable to briefly clarify the conceptual parameters central to this book. The first is that of unilateralism and 'unilateral prescriptive jurisdiction', discussed further in section 3.1. Where unilateral measures take into account foreign conduct or circumstances, they are likely to raise issues of 'extraterritoriality', introduced briefly in section 3.2. As will be explained, this is particularly relevant in the context of climate change, where measures are more effective when they target the full 'carbon footprint' of goods and services consumed at home.

[22] See eg H Schermers and N Blokker, *International Institutional Law: Unity Within Diversity* (Brill, Leiden, 2011) 1004; J Klabbers, 'The Sources of International Organizations Law' in J d'Aspremont and Besson S (eds), *The Oxford Handbook of the Sources of International Law* (Oxford University Press 2017) 997; K Daugirdas, 'How and Why International Law Binds International Organizations' (2016) 57 *Harvard International Law Journal* 325.

[23] Klabbers (n 22) 998–99, argues that 'general rules' refers to secondary rules and not to custom and general principles. See for an opposing view, A Reinisch, 'Sources of International Organizations' Law: Why Custom and General Principles Are Crucial' in J d'Aspremont and S Besson (eds), *The Oxford Handbook of the Sources of International Law* (Oxford, Oxford University Press, 2017) 1016–19.

[24] ibid 1021.

[25] ibid 1019.

[26] Case C-162/96 *Racke v Hauptzollamt Mainz* [1998] ECR I–3655 [45]-[56]; *ATAA* case (n 15) [101].

3.1. Unilateral Jurisdiction

This study approaches 'unilateralism' and 'unilateral acts' in a legally neutral manner.[27] 'Unilateralism' can be defined as a 'generally individualistic' approach to foreign affairs.[28] As noted by Nollkaemper, this approach may encompass both decisions to act, and decisions not to act, an example of the latter being the US decision not to become a party to the Kyoto Protocol.[29] Within the broader concept of unilateralism, a narrower category of acts is distinguished with a strict legal meaning: unilateral acts of states. These are acts, 'formulated by a State with the intent of producing certain legal effects under international law'.[30] Such acts can be *individual*, expressing the will of only one legal person, or *collective*, expressing the will of a group of subjects endowed with a single legal personality.[31] The latter is notably the case for the EU, comprising (currently) 27 Member States and now explicitly endowed with its own legal personality in Article 47 of the Treaty on European Union (TEU).

The core characteristic of unilateral acts is that they are taken without recourse to international procedure.[32] Their permissibility thus depends on the legal framework within which they are taken.[33] The focus of the present research is on the law of state jurisdiction, the conditions of which are found in both customary international law, and specifically applicable regimes, such as those discussed below in section 4. *Jurisdiction* pertains to the limits of state competence to regulate the conduct and consequences of an event.[34] A state, or group of states, exercises *unilateral jurisdiction* when it asserts jurisdiction on its own, or collectively through a single supranational regulator. Throughout this research, references to state jurisdiction are also considered to apply to the EU.

This book further focuses on prescriptive jurisdiction, ie 'the authority of a state to make its law applicable to particular persons or circumstances, usually

[27] On the use of a 'neutral' definition, see R Bilder, 'The Role of Unilateral Action in Preventing International Environmental Injury' (1981) 14 *Vanderbilt Journal of Transnational Law* 51, 54. Bilder notes, '[t]he phrase implies neither approval nor disapproval, nor any judgment as to the consistency or inconsistency of unilateral action with international law or international community interests'.

[28] A Nollkaemper, 'Unilateralism/Multilateralism' in R Wolfrum (ed), *Max Planck Encyclopaedia of Public International Law* (online ed) (Oxford, Oxford University Press, 2011) 1.

[29] ibid.

[30] ibid 2, citing *Nuclear Tests (Australia v France)* [1974] ICJ Rep 253.

[31] PM Dupuy, 'The Place and Role of Unilateralism in Contemporary International Law' (2000) 11 *European Journal of International Law* 19, 20.

[32] M Hakimi, 'Unfriendly Unilateralism' (2014) 55 *Harvard Journal of International Law* 111. See also P Sands et al, *Principles of International Environmental Law*, 3rd edn (Cambridge, Cambridge University Press, 2012) 292, who define unilateral acts of states as acts taken without recourse to international or multilateral *authority*.

[33] See further, Hakimi (n 32) 112. The increase in international agreements and organisations has led to an increase in formal legal alternatives, making unilateral acts more 'suspect'.

[34] V Lowe and C Staker, 'Jurisdiction' in M Evans (ed), *International Law* (Oxford, Oxford University Press, 2010) 313.

through adopting legislation'.[35] This must be distinguished from a state's enforcement jurisdiction 'to ensure compliance with its laws', which is subject to very different legal conditions.[36] In the absence of explicit permission, states may only enforce measures territorially. This book focuses on prescriptive jurisdiction, the application of which in the field of climate change is currently far from clear.

3.2. 'Extraterritoriality' and the Foreign Carbon Footprint

Like 'unilateralism', the term 'extraterritoriality' is used neutrally here, referring simply to that 'beyond the territory' of the regulating state.[37] The term 'extraterritorial' is then employed loosely to denote measures seeking to regulate conduct or circumstances abroad.[38] Stepping away from the concept's pejorative connotation, this contribution does not consider a finding of extraterritoriality to pre-empt a measure's legality under international law. Rather, it indicates, as a preliminary matter, that there is a 'potential interference' in the sovereignty of other states so as to give rise to questions of jurisdiction.[39] The fact that a measure is enforced territorially or only addresses actors present in the regulator's territory is not determinative.[40] The acting state must then be able to justify the interference by demonstrating a basis of jurisdiction under international law. This approach is explained in further detail in chapter 3.

Measures are likely to contain an 'extraterritorial element' when they seek to regulate lifecycle emissions of a product or service generated outside the territory of the acting state. Together, these lifecycle emissions constitute their 'carbon footprint', which, in addition to CO_2 includes all GHGs emitted during sourcing, production, transport and disposal.[41] The carbon footprint also includes

[35] International Bar Association, 'Report of the Taskforce on Extraterritorial Jurisdiction' (2009) (IBA Report on Extraterritorial Jurisdiction) 7.

[36] M Kamminga, 'Extraterritoriality' in R Wolfrum (ed), *Max Planck Encyclopaedia of Public International Law* (Oxford, Oxford University Press, 2011) [1].

[37] Report of the International Law Commission on the Work of its 58th Session (1 May–9 June and 3 July–11 August 2006), UN Doc A/61/10, Annex E (Report on Extraterritorial Jurisdiction) 518.

[38] 'Extraterritorial jurisdiction' then concerns 'the competence of a State to make, apply and enforce rules of conduct in respect of persons, property or events beyond its territory' – see Kamminga (n 36) [1].

[39] For the use of 'interference' as an indicator that jurisdictional issues arise, see eg International Law Commission, 'Fragmentation of International Law: Difficulties Arising from the Diversification and Expansion of International Law', Report of the Study Group of the International Law Commission (13 April 2006), A/CN.4/L.682 (ILC Report on Fragmentation).

[40] Notably, this is a point of much discussion in the literature, with many eminent commentators taking the opposite view. See eg R Howse and D Regan, 'The Product/process Distinction – An Illusory Basis for Disciplining "unilateralism" in Trade Policy' (2000) 11 *European Journal of International Law* 249.

[41] International Organization for Standardization (ISO), 'Environmental Management – Lifecycle Assessment: Principles and Framework' (2006) ISO 141040:2006. See further, M Berners-Lee, *How Bad Are Bananas? The Carbon Footprint of Everything* (London, Profile Books, 2011) 6. Other important GHGs include nitrous oxide and methane.

'indirect' emissions from the sourcing of energy used to manufacture products, as well as land-use change.[42] The latter contributes to climate change when land that originally functioned as a carbon 'sink', removing GHGs from the atmosphere, is impacted by human activities, altering the 'carbon cycle' between the terrestrial atmosphere and the biosphere.[43] Attempts to regulate lifecycle emissions beyond the regulator's territory are referred to throughout this book as measures targeting the 'foreign carbon footprint'

4. STRUCTURE AND APPROACH OF THIS BOOK

In exploring the emerging contours of climate change jurisdiction, this book takes a largely doctrinal approach. It thus draws on the traditional sources of public international law: international conventions, international custom, general principles of law, and subsidiarily, judicial decisions and teachings of qualified publicists.[44] Importantly, it also considers other sources relevant to international law making, including resolutions of UN bodies, reports and studies of the International Law Commission (ILC), soft law agreements in the field of international environmental law, and policy documents of specialised international organisations.[45] Relevant national and supranational legal sources are also examined.

Also of importance to this book's approach is the emphasis placed on the function of jurisdiction as a means of balancing the affected interests, both of states and of the international community. The interests of private actors are considered as an extension of the regulatory choices of different states. Thus, where a home state has chosen not to burden its producers with certain environmental regulations, foreign state measures imposing costs on these actors raise issues of jurisdiction. In principle, the law of jurisdiction serves a formal function, aimed at safeguarding legal procedure rather than guaranteeing the protection of certain values or outcomes. Nevertheless, this safeguard has normative underpinnings, as it is assumed that the procedure should facilitate a 'fair' balancing of state and community interests.

[42] For a widely accepted definition, see International Organization for Standardization (ISO), 'Greenhouse Gases – Carbon Footprint of Products – Requirements and Guidelines for Quantification' (2018) ISO 14067:2018.

[43] See further, UNFCCC, 'Land Use, Land-Use Change and Forestry (LULUCF)' (UNFCCC 2017) www.unfccc.int/land_use_and _climate_change/lulucf/items/1084.php.

[44] For the traditional sources of international law, see Statute of the International Court of Justice (adopted 28 June 1945, entered into force 24 September 1945) 891, UNTS 119, Art 38.

[45] For further analysis of the literature and theory on soft law, see FA Cárdenas Castañeda, 'A Call for Rethinking the Sources of International Law: Soft Law and the Other Side of the Coin' (2013) XIII *Anuario Mexicano de Derecho International* 355; A Boyle, 'Soft Law in International Law Making' in MD Evans (ed), *International Law*, 4th edn (Oxford, Oxford University Press, 2014).

In light of the legal fragmentation in the field of climate change, distilling the applicable rules is no straightforward task.[46] This book seeks to analyse and, where relevant, connect the overarching jurisdictional frameworks found in certain key legal regimes. This is done following the constitutional rule of *lex specialis derogat lex generali*, whereby more specific rules take precedence over general rules when they both apply to the same subject matter.[47] Specific rules may be part of 'self-contained regimes', loosely defined as a 'cluster' of rules laying down substantive rights and obligations (primary rules), and secondary rules relating to their 'administration' in a certain field.[48] Importantly, the special law does not 'extinguish' the relevant general law, which remains valid and may 'continue to give direction for the interpretation and application of the relevant special law'.[49] In particular, general law may fill gaps within special law regimes.[50]

Underlying this approach is the assumption that, in view of the nascent state of jurisdictional rules in the field of climate change, it is possible and desirable to base the legal analysis on the principle of harmonisation. According to this principle, concurrently applicable norms should to the greatest extent possible, 'be interpreted so as to give rise to a single set of compatible obligations'.[51] As such, this book supports the objective of systemic integration as defined by the ILC, whereby parties to a treaty are considered to 'refer to customary international law and general principles of law for all questions which the treaty does not itself resolve in express terms', where it is assumed that they 'do not intend to act inconsistently with generally recognized principles of international law'.[52]

However desirable, systemic integration is not currently a reality. Part I of this book therefore foregrounds the analysis by examining the problematic gap

[46] See further H van Asselt, F Sindico and MA Mehling, 'Global Climate Change and the Fragmentation of International Law' (2008) 30 *Law & Policy* 423; M Koskenniemi, 'Fragmentation of International Law – Topic (a): The Function and Scope of the Lex Specialis Rule and the Question of "Self-Contained Regimes": An Outline', legal.un.org/ilc/sessions/55/pdfs/fragmentation_outline.pdf, 2.

[47] For recognition of this maxim as a generally accepted principle, see the *Southern Bluefin Tuna Cases (No 3 and 4) (New Zealand v Japan; Australia v Japan)*, (Provisional Measures, Order of 27 August 1999) ITLOS Reports 1999, 280 (*Southern Bluefin Tuna* cases), [123]. Importantly Koskenniemi (n 46) 4 further notes that the *lex specialis* maxim need not only apply in situations of conflict.

[48] Koskenniemi (n 46) 8.

[49] 2006 ILC Report on the Fragmentation of International Law (n 39) [14(9)].

[50] ibid [14(15)], referring to *Bankovic v Belgium and others* (App no 52207/99) ECHR 2001-XII, 12 December 2001, 351, [57].

[51] 2006 ILC Report on the Fragmentation of International Law (n 39) [14(4)]. For an opposing view, see, however, PS Berman, 'Global Legal Pluralism' (2007) 80 *Southern California Law Review* 1155, 1165, arguing that the universal, harmonisation approach is not entirely realistic.

[52] ILC Report on Fragmentation (n 39) [14 (19)], referring to the *Georges Pinson Case (France/United Mexican States)* (1928) 5 RIAA 327, 422; and the *Case Concerning the Right of Passage over Indian Territory (Portugal v India)* (Preliminary Objections) [1957] ICJ Rep 125, 142.

between states' obligations and competences to act in response to the climate change. Chapter 2 first briefly sketches states' open-natured obligations to mitigate climate change, focusing on the international climate change treaties and relevant principles of international environmental law. Chapter 3 then turns to the theoretical foundations of state jurisdiction, as the field of law governing states' regulatory competence to respond. Engaging with the lively conceptual debates in legal discourse, it sets out and defends a sequential approach to the jurisdictional analysis, which is subsequentially carried out in parts II–IV. Concrete examples of EU measures with an 'extraterritorial element' are also introduced and categorised.

Part II of this book focuses on three *lex specialis* regimes chosen for their pertinence to unilateral trade measures targeting lifecycle emissions. These are WTO law,[53] the United Nations Law of the Sea Convention (LOSC) and the Convention on International Civil Aviation ('the Chicago Convention').[54] As will be discussed in chapter 4, WTO law is of general relevance to measures which risk unlawfully restricting international trade. This is likely to be the case for measures setting unilateral conditions on foreign production processes. For maritime emissions, the LOSC sets important parameters on port state jurisdiction to regulate foreign-flagged vessels within the different maritime zones. Also of relevance here is the International Convention for the Prevention of Pollution from Ships (MARPOL) and its Annex VI, the latter which was amended to incorporate the IMO's Global Data Collection Scheme (DCS) for shipping emissions. The Chicago Convention contains the basic multilateral framework for the regulation of international civil aviation, in particular the imposition of taxes and charges for aircraft emissions. A key amendment is the adoption of the Carbon Offsetting and Reduction Scheme for International Aviation (CORSIA) in Annex 16.

At this junction it is important to note that while the EU is a party to the LOSC, this is not the case for MARPOL and its Annex VI, the latter of which contains the IMO's DCS.[55] The EU is further not a formal party to the Chicago Convention, although all of its Member States are. As alluded to above, it is nonetheless argued that these international agreements are of relevance to the Union's unilateral competence to regulate international transport emissions. The role of each agreement is different, and will be explored further in chapters 5 and 6. Even in the absence of clear hierarchical rules, the EU, as an international

[53] See generally, the Marrakesh Agreement Establishing the World Trade Organization (adopted 15 April 1994, entered into force 1 January 1995) 1869 UNTS 401.

[54] United Nations Convention on the Law of the Sea (adopted 10 December 1982, entered into force 16 November 1994) 1833 UNTS 3 (LOSC); Chicago Convention on International Civil Aviation (adopted 7 December 1944, entered into force 4 April 1947) 15 UNTS 295.

[55] The International Convention for the Prevention of Pollution from Ships (adopted 2 November 1973, entered into force 2 October 1083) 2 ILM 1319 as supplemented by the Protocol of 17 February 1978 (MARPOL); The Protocol of 1997 amending the International Convention of 1973 for the Prevention of Pollution from Ships, as amended by the Protocol of 1978 relating thereto (signed 26 September 1997) adding Annex VI, 'Prevention of Air Pollution from Ships'.

organisation, is arguably under an intrinsic duty to respect the obligations of its Member States. As the exercise of Union competences is an extension of its Member States' sovereignty, it seems logical that the EU must not place the latter in a stranglehold with their other obligations.

As will be seen, within the *lex specialis* regimes the territorial limits of climate change jurisdiction are often far from clear. There is no overarching codification of the rules of state jurisdiction, Ryngaert noting the 'near total absence of useful treaty law in the field of jurisdiction' outside the field of criminal law.[56] This leaves an important role for customary international law, discussed further in part III. Laying the groundwork, chapter 7 sets out the general rules of prescriptive jurisdiction in the fields of criminal and economic law where they have evolved most clearly. Chapter 8 then draws on the established doctrinal openings and developments in state practice to explore the application of these prescriptive jurisdictional bases in the field of climate change.

Due to the global nature of the causes and effects of climate change, it is likely that multiple states will be able to demonstrate a jurisdictional basis to regulate the same subject matter. Even in the absence of concurrent legislation, measures with an 'extraterritorial element' may well interfere with other states' choices *not* to regulate certain activities. Against this backdrop, part IV discusses important questions regarding possible limitations on the exercise of unilateral jurisdiction. In this regard, chapter 9 examines the continuing debate on the existence, in law or international comity, of an obligation of jurisdictional self-restraint. Particular attention is paid to the reconstructed role of 'reasonableness' in the US Fourth Restatement of Foreign Relations Law.[57] Reflecting on legal discourse, this chapter proposes the 'considerate design' approach as a tool to assist regulators to take into account the interests of extraterritorial actors affected by their laws. Chapter 10 then considerskey challenges and opportunities when applying the considerate design approach to climate-protection measures. In doing so it first explores possible 'negative' conditions to respect the regulatory autonomy of other states, flowing from sovereign equality and non-intervention. It then focuses on the operationalisation of the principle of common but differentiated responsibilities and respective capabilities as a 'positive' condition for the realisation of equitable burden sharing in a jurisdictional context. The latter is of growing importance in light of the increasing regulatory burdens across supply chains, which often fall on actors in developing countries.

[56] See C Ryngaert, *Jurisdiction in International Law,* 2nd edn (Oxford, Oxford University Press, 2015) 4.

[57] *Restatement (Fourth) of the Foreign Relations Law of the United States* (St Paul MN, American Law Institute Publishers, 2018).

Part I

Regulating to Protect the Global Climate: Obligations and Rights

2

The Obligation to Regulate: The Open International Legal Framework for Climate Protection

1. INTRODUCTION

ALTHOUGH IT NOW has a prominent place on the global agenda, climate change did not gain broad political recognition until relatively recently.[1] Indeed, in the 1972 Stockholm Declaration, the word 'climate' does not appear anywhere in the document, and little was known about its scientific background. Nevertheless, the Stockholm Declaration laid important foundations for the current international approach, emphasising the equitable use and distribution of resources, and the link between environment and economic development. Chapter 2 will now discuss this framework, setting out the key sources and basic structure of states' obligations to respond to climate change.

Climate-related obligations can be found across variety of international agreements. This chapter will focus on the agreements primarily directed at climate change, namely the UNFCCC, the Kyoto Protocol and the Paris Agreement.[2] It will also consider the more general environmental law norms of prevention and precaution, which are widely accepted as informing states' climate change obligations, both within and beyond the climate change treaties.[3] This book refers to these climate change agreements and related instruments and norms as the 'climate change regime'.[4]

[1] The first multilateral agreement primarily aimed at protecting the environment in general was the International Convention on the Prevention of Pollution of the Sea by Oil (adopted 12 May 1954, entered into force 26 July 1958) 327 UNTS 3. The real proliferation of multilateral environmental agreements began in the 1980s.

[2] United Nations Framework Convention on Climate Change (adopted 9 May 1992, entered into force 21 March 1994) 1771 UNTS 107, (UNFCCC); Kyoto Protocol to the United Nations Framework Convention on Climate Change (adopted 11 December 1997, entered into force 16 February 2005) UN Doc FCCC/CP/1997/7/Add.1, 10 December 1997 ('Kyoto Protocol'); Paris Agreement (adopted 15 December 2015, entered into force 4 November 2016) (2016) 55 ILM 740 ('Paris Agreement').

[3] However, for discussion on the applicability of general customary norms to the climate change agreements, see eg B Mayer, 'The Place of Customary Norms in Climate Law: A Reply to Zahar' (2018) 8 *Climate Law* 261.

[4] For a comparable approach, see D Bodansky, J Brunnée and L Rajamani, *International Climate Change Law* (Oxford, Oxford University Press, 2017) 11, referring to the 'UN climate regime'.

Importantly, this chapter does not attempt to provide a comprehensive analysis of states' climate-protective obligations.[5] Rather, the aim here is to set out the legal context needed to understand the policies and types of climate-protective measures developed by states. It is essential to sketch these parameters, as these motivate the regulatory action which gives rise to the *jurisdictional* questions at issue in this book.

Section 2 starts by examining the meaning and legal implications of the UNFCCC's recognition of climate change as a 'common concern of humankind'. It argues that, placed in a broader legal context, such a characterisation has a signalling function that creates an imperative for states to act. Section 3 then briefly sketches the core international legal framework for climate protection, illustrating its open and developing nature. Section 3.1 sets out the basic framework of the UNFCCC, Kyoto Protocol and Paris Agreement, with a focus on mitigation obligations. Section 3.2 examines the more general norms of prevention and precaution as they apply to climate change. Finally, section 3.3 considers the continuing discussion on the existence and challenges of a binding collective target for global warming mitigation.

2. AN IMPERATIVE TO ACT: CLIMATE CHANGE AS A 'COMMON CONCERN OF HUMANKIND'

The first recital of the UNFCCC recognises the 'change in the Earth's climate and its adverse effects' as 'a common concern of humankind'.[6] There is ongoing discussion in the literature as to the meaning of this prominent characterisation and its implications for the framing of parties' obligations.[7] A clear definition is provided by Hey, who considers that the common concern 'deals with issues that are of concern to all of humanity and that no one state can address on its own'.[8] Cottier et al define it as 'a proposition of a shared problem and shared responsibility, and for an issue which reaches beyond the bounds of a single community and state as a subject of international law'.[9] Indeed, in line with the reference to

[5] For more comprehensive literature, see eg ibid; KR Gray, R Tarasofsky and C Carlarne (eds), *The Oxford Handbook of International Climate Change Law* (Oxford, Oxford University Press, 2016).

[6] UNFCCC (n 2) rec 1.

[7] For a more comprehensive study, see T Cottier et al, 'The Principle of Common Concern and Climate Change' (2014) 52 *Archiv des Völkerrechts* 293. Jutta Brunnée further argues that some treaties that predate the rise of the concept in the early 1990s 'circumscribe legal consequences that closely resemble those now associated with common concern regimes'. Examples include the 1972 Convention for the Protection of World Cultural and Natural Heritage, and the 1987 Montreal Protocol on Substances that Deplete the Ozone Layer. See J Brunnée, 'Common Areas, Common Heritage and Common Concern' in D Bodansky, J Brunnée and E Hey (eds), *The Oxford Handbook of International Environmental Law* (Oxford, University Press, 2008) 550, 565.

[8] E Hey, 'Global Environmental Law: Common Interests and the Reconstruction of Public Space' (2009) 1 *Iustum Aequum Salutare* 41.

[9] Cottier et al (n 7) 302.

'humanity', it would seem appropriate to consider concerns as 'common' when they 'transcend the interests of single states and instead correspond to needs, hopes and fears of all human beings'.[10] While not all individuals share the same values and interests, there are arguably some matters of such a fundamental nature that they can be considered 'common', the primary one being collective survival.[11] Where a concern has been recognised in a near-universal treaty such as the UNFCCC, it would seem sufficiently 'shared'.

Common concerns are typically issues of environmental law, as ecosystems are not neatly delineated according to state territory.[12] The need to 'bridge the discrepancy between ecological unity and administrative separation' creates collective action issues in which several states have an interest.[13] Conceptually speaking, the 'common concern' must then be distinguished from the linked concepts of the 'common heritage of humankind' and the 'global commons'. Global commons are areas outside of the jurisdiction of any state, such as the high seas, outer space and the atmosphere.[14] The common heritage of humankind is a broader concept, referring to shared ownership or control over resources of the 'common heritage', including those within the territory of individual states.[15] This differs from common concerns in that the latter do not pertain to equal ownership or use of certain spaces or resources.[16] Rather, as mentioned, common concerns relate to common *problems*. Anthropogenic climate *change* is illustrative of this. This is defined under the UNFCCC as 'a change of climate which is attributed directly or indirectly to human activity that alters the composition of the global atmosphere and which is in addition to natural climate variability observed over comparable time periods'.[17]

At first glance, common concerns also bear considerable resemblance to obligations *erga omnes*, which are obligations owed by all states to the international community as a whole.[18] In the *Barcelona Traction* case the ICJ found

[10] See D Shelton, 'Common Concern of Humanity' (2009) 1 *Iustum Aequum Salutare* 33. See also C Voigt, 'Delineating the Common Interest in International Law' in W Benedek et al (eds), *The Common Interest in International Law* (Cambridge, Intersentia, 2014) 9.

[11] Voigt argues that collective survival is '*the* primary common concern' (Voigt (n 10) 17).

[12] Notably, it has also been suggested that the common concern may also include other areas such as human rights and exchange rates, see further ibid 6. See also Shelton (n 10) 33.

[13] J Brunnée, '"Common Interest" – Echoes from an Empty Shell? Some Thoughts on Common Interests and International Environment Law' (1989) 49 *Zeitschrift für Ausländisches Öffentliches Recht und Völkerrecht* 791.

[14] E Clancy, 'The Tragedy of the Global Commons' (1998) 5 *Indiana Journal of Global Legal Studies* 601.

[15] Cottier et al (n 7) 306.

[16] See further Hey (n 8) 43. Thus, as noted by Cottier et al (n 7) 298, unlike the common heritage of mankind, climate change does not 'fundamentally alter the paradigms of permanent sovereignty over natural resources and territoriality'. For an in-depth discussion on the common heritage of mankind, see K Baslar, *The Concept of the Common Heritage of Mankind in International Law* (Leiden, Martinus Nijhoff, 1998).

[17] UNFCCC (n 2) Art 1(2) (emphasis added).

[18] *Case Concerning Barcelona Traction, Light and Power Co Ltd, Belgium v Spain*, (Merits) [1970] ICJ Rep 3 (*Barcelona Traction*) [33].

that such obligations arise in relation to certain rights of such importance that all *states* have a 'legal interest' in their protection.[19] Crawford suggests that obligations *erga omnes* are owed to the 'international community' made up not only of states, but also international organisations and natural legal persons.[20] This view would further align the concept with common concerns. There is, however, a difference in emphasis. *Erga omnes* obligations are generally related to issues of state responsibility. They become relevant when one state's responsibility is invoked by another state that is not directly injured by a violation but has an interest in compliance.[21]

A key issue in the discussion on common concerns is whether they trigger a duty for states to respond and if so, what type of duty. Intuitively, it seems logical that common concerns should trigger obligations *erga omnes* to react in some way. This would align with the ICJ's finding in *Belgium v Senegal* that 'the common interest implies that the obligations in question are owed by any State party to all the other States parties to the Convention'.[22] In the context of climate change, the link between common concern and common obligation is also underscored in the commentary of the International Law Association's *Legal Principles Relating to Climate Change*, which notes that there is universal acceptance for both 'the idea that climate change is a common' and 'the proposition that all states have a *common responsibility* to take appropriate measures to address the concern'.[23] In this vein, Cottier et al argue that recognising a 'common concern principle' with 'more precise operational contours' could assist in overcoming existing collective action problems'.[24]

Logic notwithstanding, the dominant view in the literature is that at this stage the common concern 'does not entail specific rules governing the conduct of states'.[25] Nevertheless, while the common concern may not be an autonomous source of specific legal obligations, it is argued here that it does have an important signalling function in relation to more general state duties. Of particular relevance here are the duty to cooperate and to consider others out of respect

[19] ibid [33].

[20] J Crawford, 'Articles on Responsibility of States for Internationally Wrongful Acts' (United Nations Audiovisual Library of International Law, 2012) www.legal.un.org/avl/pdf/ha/rsiwa/rsiwa_e.pdf. See further E de Wet, 'Invoking Obligations *Erga Omnes* in the Twenty-First Century: Progressive Developments Since Barcelona Traction' (2013) 37 *South African Yearbook of International Law* 1.

[21] *Draft Articles on Responsibility of States for Internationally Wrongful Acts* (November 2001) UN Doc A/56/10 (DARS), Art 19(d)) and Art 48.

[22] *Questions Relating to the Obligation to Prosecute or Extradite, Belgium v Senegal* (Merits) [2012] ICJ Rep 422 (*Belgium v Senegal*) [38].

[23] Committee on Legal Principles Relating to Climate Change, 'Resolution 2/2014: Declaration of Legal Principles Relating to Climate Change', Seventy-Sixth Conference of the International Law Association (Washington DC, 2014) ('ILA Principles Relating to Climate Change'), Commentary to principle 2 (emphasis added, references omitted).

[24] Cottier et al (n 7) 298.

[25] D Bodansky, J Brunnée and L Rajamani (n 4) 51. Indeed, in another contribution, Brunnée argues that it is no more than a 'potential frame of reference for limited areas' (Brunnée (n 13) 791).

for sovereign equality and fundamental human rights.[26] In this way, as noted by Shelton, while the common concern 'does not connote specific rules and obligations' it does 'establish … the general basis for the concerned community to act'.[27] Indeed there is wide support for the notion that states have a general duty under international law to cooperate 'for the purposes of development to increase the social welfare of the world community'.[28] According to Perrez, this duty is inherent to sovereignty itself, which today is generally accepted to include certain responsibilities as well as state powers.[29] That the common concern may signal a specific instance where cooperation is required, aligns with the shift in the function of international law from a law of 'coexistence' to a law of 'cooperation'.[30]

It is further argued that the signalling function of the common concern extends beyond cooperation to state action on a *national* level likely to exacerbate the concern beyond its borders. This flows from the fundamental principle of sovereign equality, according to which a state's sovereign rights are inherently limited by the equal sovereignty of other states.[31] As such, '[t]he existence of a number of sovereignties side by side places limits on the freedom of each State to act as if the others did not exist'.[32] In this regard, the rationale is largely analogous to the general principle of prevention, discussed further below. This premise can arguably be further expanded, to include consideration of the interests of the 'higher' international community.[33] As famously noted by ICJ Judge Weeramantry in the *Gabčikovo-Nagymaros* case, 'we have entered an era … in which international law subserves not only the interests of individual States,

[26] See further on the duty to consider others based on the right to self-determination, E Benvenisti, 'Sovereigns as Trustees of Humanity: On the Accountability of Sovereigns to Foreign Stakeholders' (2013) 107 *AJIL* 295, discussed further below.

[27] Shelton (n 10) 37.

[28] See further, R Wolfrum, 'International Law of Cooperation' in R Wolfrum (ed), *Max Planck Encyclopaedia of Public International Law* (online edn) (Oxford, Oxford University Press, 2008) [7]. In the context of marine environmental pollution, this duty was found by the International Tribunal for the Law of the Sea (ITLOS) in the *MOX Plant* case to be a 'fundamental principle' of general international law. See *The MOX Plant Case (Ireland v United Kingdom)* (Provisional Measures, Order of 3 December 2001) ITLOS Reports 2001 [82].

[29] F Perrez, *Cooperative Sovereignty: From Independence to Interdependence in the Structure of International Environmental Law* (The Hague, Springer, 2000) 332. Indeed, in the words of Jackson, 'almost no perceptive observer or practitioner is prepared to sign on the full import of the traditional Westphalian notion of sovereignty'. JH Jackson, 'Sovereignty-Modern: A New Approach to an Outdated Concept' (2003) 97 *African Journal of International Law* 782, 789.

[30] For an older contribution, see W Friedmann, *The Changing Structure of International Law* (New York, Columbia University Press, 1964).

[31] Charter of the United Nations (adopted 26 June 1945; entered into force 24 October 1945) UNTS XVI, Art 2(1).

[32] *Legality of the Threat or Use of Nuclear Weapons* (Advisory Opinion) [1996] ICJ Rep 226 (*Nuclear Weapons* case) 393–94, Dissenting Opinion of Judge Shahabuddeen. This is discussed further in chapter 6 on jurisdictional limitations.

[33] For a discussion on the hierarchy between state and humanitarian interests, see S Stec, 'Humanitarian Limits to Sovereignty: Common Concern and Common Heritage Approaches to Natural Resources and Environment' (2010) 12 *International Community Law Review* 361, 364.

but looks beyond them and their parochial concerns to the greater interests of humanity and planetary welfare'.[34] From a practical perspective, this is the result of an increasing interdependence between states, which defies the theoretical premise of a 'perfect or almost perfect fit' between a sovereign and its citizens who are affected by its actions.[35] Such a view aligns with the more 'humanity-oriented' perspective put forward by Benvenisti that national regulators have sovereign 'other-regarding' obligations towards foreign individuals, where this may impact their right to self-determination.[36]

To conclude, the recognition of climate change as a 'common concern of humankind' is not without relevance. While not containing its own specific legal obligations, the common concern signals an imperative to act, through cooperation and prevention of activities that may exacerbate the common concern beyond a state or regulator's territory.

3. THE OPEN INTERNATIONAL LEGAL FRAMEWORK FOR CLIMATE PROTECTION

After recognising climate change as a common concern in the late 1980s, the international community swiftly set out to develop a multilateral agreement on the reduction of global emissions. Over the past decades, this has grown, though not without difficulties, into a more comprehensive international climate change regime.[37] Section 3.1 will briefly sketch the contours of states' core obligations in today's climate change agreements, namely the UNFCCC, the Kyoto Protocol and the Paris Agreement.[38] Particularly given their open nature, these provisions are appropriately understood in light of more general norms of international environmental law. Section 3.2 will therefore consider these further, with a focus on prevention and precaution, which are widely accepted as informing the architecture of states' broader climate-protection obligations. Drawing together the discussed norms, Section 3.3 touches upon the question of whether states have a collective binding mitigation obligation to prevent 'dangerous' climate change.

3.1. The International Climate Change Agreements

At the basis of today's multilateral climate regime lies the 1992 UNFCCC, the 'ultimate objective' of which is to achieve the 'stabilization of greenhouse

[34] *Case concerning the Gabčikovo-Nagymaros Project, Hungary v Slovakia* [1997] ICJ Rep 88, Separate Opinion of Vice-President Weeramantry, 115.

[35] Benvenisti (n 26) 297.

[36] ibid 316. The precise form of these obligations will depend on the applicable law.

[37] For a more detailed analysis of the lengthy political trajectory leading up to the Paris Agreement, see L Rajamani, 'The Warsaw Climate Negotiations: Emerging Understandings and Battle Lines on the Road to the 2015 Climate Agreement' (2014) 63 *ICLQ* 721; and L Rajamani, 'The Durban Platform for Enhanced Action and the Future of the Climate Regime' (2012) 61 *ICLQ* 501.

[38] UNFCCC (n 2); Kyoto Protocol (n 2); Paris Agreement (n 2).

gas concentrations in the atmosphere at a level that would prevent dangerous anthropogenic interference with the climate system'.[39] As a compromise between a traditional 'framework' and a substantive agreement, the UNFCCC contains the broad contours of both binding and non-binding obligations which underlie the more specific 1997 Kyoto Protocol and 2015 Paris Agreement.[40] Some of the most important commitments can be found in Article 4, paragraph 1 of which provides that all Parties:

> … taking into account their common but differentiated responsibilities and their specific national and regional development priorities, objectives and circumstances, shall:
>
> …
>
> (b) Formulate, implement, publish and regularly update national and, where appropriate, regional programmes containing measures to mitigate climate change by addressing anthropogenic emissions by sources and removals by sinks of all greenhouse gases not controlled by the Montreal Protocol, and measures to facilitate adequate adaptation to climate change.[41]

In line with the sovereign obligation to respect the common interest discussed above, it also requires parties to '[t]ake climate change considerations into account, to the extent feasible, in their relevant social, economic and environmental policies and actions'.[42]

Complementing these binding 'bottom-up' obligations, paragraph 2 contains the non-binding 'top-down' requirement that each of the 'developed country Parties and other Parties included in Annex I' are to 'adopt national policies and take corresponding measures on the mitigation of climate change, by limiting its anthropogenic emissions of greenhouse gases and protecting and enhancing its greenhouse gas sinks and reservoirs'.[43] Annex I Parties must communicate these policies 'with the aim of returning individually or jointly to their 1990 levels these anthropogenic emissions of carbon dioxide and other greenhouse gases not controlled by the Montreal Protocol'.[44]

The UNFCCC thus created a clear division between Annex I parties with concrete reduction commitments, and 'non-Annex I' parties with no binding commitments. Within this group, a further division is drawn between members of the Organisation of Economic Cooperation and Development (OECD), included as a sub-group in Annex II, and Economies in Transition (EITs).

[39] UNFCCC (n 2) Art 2.

[40] Bodansky, Brunnée and Rajamani (n 4) 119–20, noting that the UNFCCC 'lies somewhere between a framework and a substantive agreement'. Both the Paris Agreement and the Kyoto Protocol are based on the UNFCCC, though this link was a topic of debate during negotiations because it risked implying that the Annex I division would retain relevance in the later agreements.

[41] UNFCCC (n 2) Art 4(1)(b).

[42] ibid Art 4(1)(f).

[43] ibid Art 4(2)(a). The division between 'bottom-up' and 'top-down' climate change obligations was a source of considerable discussion in the lead-up to the Paris Agreement. For an interesting analysis of the political developments, see Rajamani (n 37) 725–27.

[44] UNFCCC (n 2) Art 4(2)(b).

Annex II countries are further required to provide developing countries with the financial assistance needed to meet their obligations under Article 4(1) (Article 4(3)), and to cover the costs of adaptation for particularly vulnerable countries (Article 4(4)). They must also participate in the transfer of environmentally sound technologies and know-how (Article 4(5)).

Notably, while it created a clear mandate for emission reduction policies, the UNFCCC did not specify binding reduction targets for individual parties. This was left to the Kyoto Protocol, which, five years later, laid down a system of quantified CO_2 emission reduction targets for developed countries listed in Annex I.[45] Article 3(1) instructs Annex I Parties to:

> individually or jointly, ensure that their aggregate anthropogenic carbon dioxide equivalent emissions of the greenhouse gases listed in Annex A do not exceed their assigned amounts, calculated pursuant to their quantified emission limitation and reduction commitments inscribed in Annex B … with a view to reducing their overall emissions of such gases by at least 5 per cent below 1990 levels in the commitment period 2008 to 2012.

More generally, Article 2 instructs Annex I parties to 'implement and/or further elaborate policies and measures in accordance with [their] national circumstances', providing a list of possibilities, including the enhancement of energy efficiency and the reduction of GHGs in the transport sector.[46]

Article 6 foresees the possibility of joint implementation between Annex I parties, provided that the joint project creates 'additional' emission reductions to those that 'would otherwise occur'.[47] The requirement of additionality also appears in the Clean Development Mechanism (CDM), established in Article 12. According to this mechanism, Annex I parties may use 'certified emission reductions' (CERs) generated from projects based in non-Annex I states to meet their own reduction targets, provided that these are 'additional to any that would occur in the absence of the certified project activity'.[48]

The rigid, static distinction between Annex I and non-Annex I parties created a stumbling block for further negotiations. Unable to reach an agreement on a successive climate change treaty, states resorted, through the Doha Amendment, to an extension of the Kyoto Protocol for a second commitment period up to 2020.[49] After the failure of the highly anticipated Copenhagen Conference of the Parties (COP) in 2009,[50] an attempt was made to break the stalemate

[45] Kyoto Protocol (n 2) Art 3.

[46] ibid Art 2.1 (a)(i), (iv).

[47] UNFCCC (n 2) Art 6(1)b.

[48] See in particular, Kyoto Protocol (n 2) Arts 12(3)b and 12(5)b.

[49] See *Marrakesh Accord* (FCCC/CP/2001/13/Add.2 21 (2002)); and *Doha Amendment to the Kyoto Protocol*, (C.N.718.2012. TREATIES-XXVII.7.c).

[50] Fifteenth Session of the Conference of the Parties (COP 15), Copenhagen, 7–18 December 2009. For a contemporary news analysis of the failure, see 'Why Did Copenhagen Fail to Deliver a Climate Deal?', *BBC News* (22 December 2009) www.news.bbc.co.uk/2/hi /8426835.stm.

through reliance on bottom-up 'nationally determined contributions' (NDCs) to GHG reductions.[51] What resulted was the 2015 Paris Agreement, which operates through a system of 'bound self-differentiation', including less-developed countries in the overall mitigation efforts.[52] In doing so it requires all participating countries to specify a nationally determined contribution (NDC) which they 'intend to achieve' through domestic mitigation measures.[53] These contribute to the overall objective of keeping the average global temperature increase 'to *well below* 2°C above pre-industrial levels and to pursue efforts to limit the temperature increase to 1.5°C above pre-industrial levels'.[54]

As aptly noted by Rajamani, the Paris Agreement is a 'curious instrument', 'littered with provisions that either have weak normative content or seem to be wholly lacking in it'.[55] Often cited as one of its stronger features is the 'ratcheting-up' approach, requiring states to increase their voluntary targets every five years, with the 'highest possible ambition'.[56] The first 'global stocktake' of NDCs takes place in 2023, and is intended to 'inform parties in updating and enhancing their action'.[57] It is hoped that in this way total global emissions will peak 'as soon as possible', although the agreement recognises that developing countries need more time to make substantial emission reductions.[58] In terms of scope, the NDCs pertain only to mitigation,[59] that is, to human activities causing climate change.[60] At the same time, Article 3 requires broader 'ambitious efforts' in relation to other responses including adaptation to the effects of climate change, finance and technology transfer.[61]

As a whole, the Paris Agreement 'recasts' differentiated burden-sharing in a more flexible, tailored manner than its predecessor.[62] Rajamani suggests that to the extent that the principle's 'operationalization' under the Paris Agreement differs from that under the UNFCCC, the former may arguably constitute a

[51] For further analysis on how key negotiation milestones influenced the legal form of the Paris Agreement, see L Rajamani, 'The 2015 Paris Agreement: Interplay Between Hard, Soft and Non-Obligations' (2016) 28 *Journal of Environmental Law* 337, 338.

[52] Paris Agreement (n 2). See further on bound self-differentiation, Bodansky, Brunnée and Rajamani (n 4) 223.

[53] Paris Agreement (n 2) Arts 4.2 and 4.3. For a detailed analysis of the 'many treasures to be mined in this carefully negotiated text', see L Rajamani, 'Ambition and Differentiation in the 2015 Paris Agreement: Interpretative Possibilities and Underlying Politics' (2016) 65 *ICLQ* 493, 497.

[54] Paris Agreement (n 2) Art 2.1(a) (emphasis added).

[55] Rajamani (n 51) 337.

[56] Paris Agreement (n 2) Art 4.3.

[57] ibid Art 14.

[58] ibid Art 4.3.

[59] ibid Art 4.2.

[60] UNFCCC, 'Introduction to Mitigation', unfccc.int/topics/mitigation/the-big-picture/introduction-to-mitigation.

[61] Paris Agreement (n 2) Art 3 does so through direct reference to more specific provisions: Arts 4, 7, 9, 10, 11 and 13. For further analysis regarding adaptation, see eg A. Lesnikowski 'What Does the Paris Agreement Mean for Adaptation?' (2017) 17 *Climate Policy* 825.

[62] Bodansky, Brunnée and Rajamani (n 4) 220.

'distinct rather than derivative version of the principle'.[63] This operationalisation is reflected across several provisions.[64] One important reference to the CBDRRC principle can be found in Article 2, according to which the Paris Agreement 'will be implemented to reflect equity and the principle of common but differentiated responsibilities and respective capabilities (CBDDRC), in the light of different national circumstances'. There was much controversy behind the precise wording of this provision, as developed states were reluctant to include imperative language into an operative paragraphs which 'frames the implementation of the entire Agreement'.[65] The agreed phrase 'will be implemented to reflect' 'preserves the range of interpretative possibilities of CBDDRC for developing countries yet stops short of prescribing equity and CBDDRC in the implementation of the agreement'.[66]

Another key provision is Article 4(4), which instructs developed-country parties to 'continue taking the lead by undertaking economy-wide absolute emission reduction targets', while developing-country parties should 'continue enhancing their mitigation efforts'. Notably, however, this principle is intended to confirm the UNFCCC approach without creating new obligations, which was a *conditio sine qua non* for the United States during negotiations.[67]

The Paris Agreement represents a tenuous compromise between state autonomy and binding obligations.[68] As such, many of the finer details on how the objectives should be achieved were left to domestic policy, or were to be coordinated later. The subsequent 2018 Paris Rulebook provides essential guidelines on the further implementation of specific focus areas.[69] Of particular importance is its additional guidance for the Paris Agreement's transparency framework. Transparency was considered to provide more stringent procedural requirements to bolster the voluntary targets.[70] This was an important issue for

[63] ibid. See also on the debated scope of the CBDRRC under Art 3 UNFCCC, C Redgwell, 'Principles and Emerging Norms in International Law: Intra- and Intergenerational Equity' in Gray, Tarasofsky, and Carlarne (n 5) 185, 194.

[64] Paris Agreement (n 2) rec 3 (emphasis added). See further A Savaresi, 'The Paris Agreement: A Rejoinder', *European Journal of International Law Talk!* (16 February 2016) www.ejiltalk.org/the-paris-agreement-a-rejoinder/. The CBDRRC principle is discussed further in Chapter 10.

[65] Rajamani (n 51) 508.

[66] ibid.

[67] Bodansky, Brunnée and Rajamani (n 4) 224, noting that in order to save the French 'take it or leave it' text from dissolution in its final hours, the word 'shall' in relation to developed country leadership was declared a typographical error, and altered to 'should'.

[68] See further R Falkner, 'The Paris Agreement and the New Logic of International Climate Politics' (2016) 92 *International Affairs* 1107. See also Rajamani (n 51) 358, noting that '[t]he Paris Agreement is arguably an exemplar of the "brave new world of international law" in which forms of law and lawmaking have "mutated into fascinating hybrid forms"'.

[69] Also referred to as the 'Katowice Climate Package' adopted at the COP24 in Katowice Poland. See further UNFCCC, 'Report of the Conference of the Parties on its twenty-fourth session, held in Katowice from 2 to 15 December 2018' (19 March 2019) FCCC/CP/2018/10/Add.1.

[70] For further analysis, see L Rajamani and D Bodansky, 'The Paris Rulebook: Balancing International Prescriptiveness with National Discretion' (2019) 68 *ICLQ* 1023.

the United States and the European Union which wanted to ensure that other states, particularly China, would be properly and equally scrutinised in their implementation.[71] At the same time, the mechanism has a 'built in flexibility which takes into account Parties' different capacities', differentiating reporting requirements according to the type of action concerned.[72] Neverthless, even with the Rulebook's more detailed 'information to facilitate clarity, transparency and understanding' of NDCs, there remains considerable discretion for parties. The informational requirements must be provided 'as appropriate' to each NDC, and there were no specific indicators for how they address the 'fairness and ambition' of their targets.[73]

Another issue is the development of a market mechanism to enable 'cooperative implementation' through Internationally Transferred Mitigation Outcomes (ITMOs) (Article 6).[74] This area was too contentious to be included in the Paris Rulebook, and at the time of writing remains under negotiation by the parties, through the Subsidiary Body for Scientific and Technological Advice (SBTA).[75]

A weaker area under the Paris Agreement is 'loss and damage associated with the adverse effects of climate change, including extreme weather events and slow onset events'.[76] Whereas Article 8 encourages parties to enhance their understanding and cooperation, the Decision to adopt the Paris Agreement explicitly excludes liability and compensation for damage suffered.[77]

Finally, and importantly for this study, neither the Kyoto Protocol nor the Paris Agreement reduction targets cover international aviation and maritime emissions, which remain under the remit of the ICAO and the IMO.[78] However, over the past decades, both organisations have been quite slow in reaching inclusive emissions reduction agreements. The lack of results has been an impetus for the EU to include both areas in a unilateral reduction policy applicable also

[71] See further Rajamani (n 51) 357. See also S Evans and S Yeo, 'Analysis: The Final Paris Deal' (12 December 2015) www.carbonbrief.org/analysis-the-final-paris-climate-deal.

[72] See in particular Paris Agreement (n 2) Art 13(1), (9) and (10).

[73] See further Rajamani and Bodansky (n 70) 1013, referring to Decision 4/CMA.1, Annex I.

[74] See Paris Agreement (n 2) Art 6(4), establishing a 'mechanism to contribute to the mitigation of greenhouse gas emissions and support sustainable development … under the authority and guidance of the Conference of the Parties serving as the meeting of the Parties to the Paris Agreement for use by Parties on a voluntary basis'.

[75] On recent developments, see UNFCCC, 'Cooperative Implementation', unfccc.int/process/the-paris-agreement/cooperative-implementation. Key issues under negotiation are how to avoid double counting and ensure environmental integrity of the mechanism. See further B Müller and A Michaelowa, 'How to Operationalize Accounting under Article 6 Market Mechanisms of the Paris Agreement' (2019) 19 *Climate Policy* 812.

[76] Paris Agreement (n 2) Art 8.

[77] Decision to Adopt the Paris Agreement (n 2) rec 52.

[78] Kyoto Protocol (n 2) Art 2(2). The Paris Agreement was silent on this matter, implicitly confirming the exclusion under the Kyoto Protocol. See further T Bäuerle, 'Integrating Shipping into the EU Emissions Trading Scheme?' in HJ Koch, D König and J Sanden (eds), *Climate Change and Environmental Hazards Related to Shipping: An International Legal Framework; Proceedings of the Hamburg International Environmental Law Conference 2011* (The Hague, Martinus Nijhoff, 2013).

to foreign operators.[79] Catalysed, at least in part, by this provocative action, in 2016 the ICAO reached an agreement, CORSIA, on carbon offsetting and reduction. In the same year, the IMO also adopted a mandatory global data collection system for CO_2 emissions as an amendment to Annex VI of the MARPOL Convention.[80] At the time of writing, the EU is consistently refusing to align with these multilateral measures, raising interesting jurisdictional dilemmas, discussed further in chapter 5.

3.2. Prevention and Precaution in Relation to Climate Change

In addition to the open-textured climate change agreements, more general norms of environmental law also steer state action in relation to the climate. This section will consider the two key norms of prevention and precaution. While some argue that the climate change regime is completely 'self-contained' to exclude general norms,[81] the widely accepted view is that the general norms inform the more specific treaty provisions.[82]

3.2.1. Prevention

The roots of the harm prevention principle can be found in the 1941 *Trail Smelter Arbitration* between the United States and Canada.[83] This case concerned the spread of air pollution caused by a smelter in Trail, Canada to the territory of the United States.[84] There the arbitral tribunal found that:

> [U]nder the principles of international law … no State has the right to use or permit the use of its territory in such a manner as to cause injury by fumes in or to the territory of another or the properties or persons therein, when the case is of serious consequence and the injury is established by clear and convincing evidence.[85]

[79] See in particular the controversial Parliament and Council (EC) Directive 2008/101 amending Directive 2003/87/EC so as to include aviation activities in the scheme for greenhouse gas emission allowance trading within the Community [2008] OJ L8/3 ('Aviation Directive').

[80] Resolution MEPC.278(70), 'Amendments to the Annex of the Protocol of 1997 to amend the International Convention for the Prevention of Pollution from Ships, 1973, as modified by the Protocol of 1978 relating thereto – Data Collection System for Fuel Oil Consumption of Ships' (adopted 28 October 2016), MEPC 70/18/Add.1, Annex 3 (Resolution MEPC.278(70)).

[81] A Zahar, 'The Contested Core of Climate Law', (2018) 8 *Climate Law* 244.

[82] See specifically B Mayer (n 3); R Verheyen, *Climate Change Damage and International Law: Prevention Duties and State Responsibility* (Leiden, Brill, 2005) 138. See further on the concretisation of states' climate obligations eg J Peel, 'The Practice of Shared Responsibility in Relation to Climate Change' in A Nollkaemper and I Plakokefalos (eds), *The Practice of Shared Responsibility in International Law* (Cambridge, Cambridge University Press, 2016) 1009.

[83] *Trail Smelter Arbitration (United States v Canada)* (1938 and 1941) RIAA 1905 (*Trail Smelter*) 1917.

[84] ibid.

[85] ibid 1965.

A more general obligation was subsequently formulated in Principle 21 of the 1972 Stockholm Declaration, which provides that:

> States have … the sovereign right to exploit their own resources pursuant to their own environmental policies, and the responsibility to ensure that activities within their jurisdiction or control do not cause damage to the environment of other States or of areas beyond the limits of national jurisdiction.

Today, the duty to prevent transboundary harm has been widely recognised as having the status of customary international law. This was confirmed by the ICJ in its Advisory Opinion on the *Legality of the Threat or Use of Nuclear Weapons* where the Court recognised that:

> [T]he existence of the general obligation of States to ensure that activities within their jurisdiction and control respect the environment of other States or of areas beyond national control is now part of the corpus of international law relating to the environment.[86]

In terms of substance, the prevention principle is a due-diligence obligation of a state within its territory.[87] It pertains not only to the adoption of certain rules, but also to a 'certain level of vigilance over their enforcement'.[88] As noted in the 2012 International Tribunal the Law of the Sea (ITLOS) Advisory Opinion on *Responsibilities in the Area*, the due-diligence standard is a contextual one, which 'may change over time', particularly in light of scientific developments.[89] Carrying out procedural obligations may help to prove the due-diligence standard has been met. Thus in the 2015 *Costa Rica/Nicaragua* cases, the Court noted that:

> [T]o fulfil its obligation to exercise due diligence in preventing significant transboundary environmental harm, a State must, before embarking on an activity having the potential adversely to affect the environment of another State, ascertain if there is a risk of significant transboundary harm, which would trigger the requirement to carry out an environmental impact assessment.[90]

In the 2010 *Pulp Mills* case, the requirement to carry out an environmental impact assessment 'where there is a risk that the proposed industrial activity may have a significant adverse impact in a transboundary context, in particular,

[86] *Legality of the Threat or Use of Nuclear Weapons* (Advisory Opinion) [1996] ICJ Rep 226 (*Nuclear Weapons* case) [28].

[87] *Pulp Mills on the River Uruguay (Argentina v Uruguay)* (Judgment) [2010] ICJ Rep 2010 (*Pulp Mills*) 55; Bodansky, Brunnée and Rajamani (n 4) 41.

[88] Bodansky, Brunnée and Rajamani (n 4) 41.

[89] ibid, citing *Responsibilities and obligations of States sponsoring persons and entities with respect to activities in the Area* (Advisory Opinion, Order of 1 February 2011), ITLOS Reports 2011 ('*Responsibilities in the Area*') [115].

[90] *Certain Activities Carried Out by Nicaragua in the Border Area (Costa Rica v Nicaragua)* and *Construction of a Road in Costa Rica along the San Juan River (Nicaragua v Costa Rica)* (Judgment) [2015] ICJ Rep 665 [104].

on a shared resource' was also recognised as constituting customary international law.[91]

Notably there is some discussion as to whether the prevention principle actually applies in the context of the indirect, cumulative harm caused by climate change.[92] The prevention principle has traditionally been applied in cases of direct transboundary harm across a border.[93] Neverthless, there is considerable support for a broader understanding of this principle. As noted by Mayer, customary international law, as evidenced for example by Article 21 of the Stockholm Convention and Article 2 of the Rio Declaration on Environment and Development, recognise the principle's applicability to 'areas beyond the limits of national jurisdiction', which are protected under international law in order to prevent indirect cumulative damage.[94] This recognition can also be found in recital 8 of the preamble of the UNFCCC itself, which refers to states' 'sovereign right to exploit their own resources pursuant to their own environmental and developmental policies', and the 'responsibility to ensure that activities within their jurisdiction or control do not cause damage to the environment of other States or of areas beyond the limits of national jurisdiction'. Accepting this, the prevention principle occupies an important position in shaping states' climate protective obligations.

3.2.2. *Precaution*

Of particular relevance for climate change is the norm of precaution. There is, however, no single agreed definition of this norm, and while some argue that it is a principle, others consider it better characterized as an 'approach' or 'general posture for policy-making'.[95] An authoritative formulation can be found in Principle 15 of the Rio Declaration, which provides that: 'Where there are threats of serious irreversible damage, lack of full scientific certainty shall not be used as a reason for postponing cost-effective measures to prevent environmental degradation.' As noted by Wiener, this formulation takes a permissive approach, and is helpful 'as a rebuttal to the mistaken claim that uncertainty

[91] *Pulp Mills* (n 87) [204].

[92] See, in particular, A Zahar, 'Mediated versus Cumulative Environmental Damage and the International Law Association's Legal Principles on Climate Change' (2014) 4 *Climate Law* 217. For further discussion by the present author, see N Dobson, 'Exploring the Crystallization of "Climate Change Jurisdiction": A Role for Precaution?' (2018) 8 *Climate Law* 207.

[93] ibid, analysing among others, the *Trail Smelter Arbitration* (n 83), and *Pulp Mills* (n 87).

[94] B Mayer, 'The Applicability of the Principle of Prevention to Climate Change: A Response to Zahar' (2015) 5 *Climate Law* 1, 9–10, noting that the prevention principle has been internationally recognised as applying in the context of cumulative damage, eg in the 1985 Vienna Convention for the Protection of the Ozone Layer, rec 2 and Art 2(1).

[95] On the debates surrounding the substance and legal status of precaution, see JB Wiener, 'Precaution', and U Beyerlin, 'Policies, Principles and Rules', in Bodansky, Brunnée and Hey (n 7) 597 and 425, respectively. See also JB Wiener, 'Precaution and Climate Change' in Gray, Tarasofsky and Carlarne (n 5) 168.

warrants inaction'.[96] An alternative version goes a step further, providing that uncertainty not only removes a defence for inaction, but positively mandates action.[97] This is based on the risk of grave and 'irreversible' harm.[98]

Another interpretative possibility is to consider precaution as part of the prevention principle.[99] An example of this is again *Responsibilities in the Area*, where ITLOS used due diligence to 'build a bridge' between prevention and precaution.[100] Considering the obligations states sponsoring exploration and exploitation activities in the Area, it considered the precautionary approach to be

> an integral part of the general obligation of due diligence of sponsoring States, which is applicable even outside the scope of the Regulations [at issue]. The due diligence obligation of the sponsoring States requires them to take all appropriate measures to prevent damage that might result from the activities of contractors that they sponsor. This obligation applies in situations where scientific evidence concerning the scope and potential negative impact of the activity in question is insufficient but where there are plausible indications of potential risks.[101]

As noted by Wiener, while 'sharply controversial', 'if there is any sensible form of precaution to apply to any problem, then climate change seems an especially apt and urgent case'.[102] Article 3(3) of the UNFCCC lends support for the norm's applicability in general terms, providing that the 'Parties should take precautionary measures to anticipate, prevent or minimize the causes of climate change and mitigate its adverse effects'. De Sadeleer points out that this language is 'less forceful' than in other multilateral environmental agreements, using the term 'should' rather than 'shall', and 'encapsulating a right to take preventative measures and not an obligation to act'.[103] As will be argued later in chapter 8, this permissive approach, where precaution is seen to legitimise but not require state action, is relevant for the interpretation of the permissive principles of prescriptive jurisdiction.

3.3. A Binding Collective Mitigation Obligation to Prevent 'Dangerous' Climate Change?

Considering the norms discussed above, a key point of contention is whether they may, together or separately, contain a legally binding collective obligation

[96] Wiener, 'Precaution' (n 95) 610.
[97] ibid 604.
[98] ibid, referring among others to Art 5 of the 2004 the French Environment Charter.
[99] ibid 603.
[100] Bodansky, Brunnée and Rajamani (n 4) 44.
[101] *Responsibilities and obligations of States sponsoring persons and entities with respect to activities in the Area* (Advisory Opinion, Order of 1 February 2011), ITLOS Reports 2011, 131.
[102] Wiener (n 95) 164.
[103] Nicolas de Sadeleer, 'Climate Change, Uncertainties and the Precautionary Principle' (2016) 1 Jean Monnet Working Paper Series, Environment and Internal Market 5.

to keep the global temperature rise below 2°C.[104] Indeed, some would argue that this goal should in fact be 'well below' 2°C and closer to 1.5°C, in line with the wording of the Paris Agreement and the 2018 Report of the Intergovernmental Panel on Climate Change (IPCC).[105] In Voigt's view, 'the position is defendable that the ultimate objective of the UNFCCC is to provide a duty of prevention with regard to dangerous climate change'.[106] Voigt focuses on Annex I parties, which according to Article 2(1) UNFCCC 'shall adopt national policies and take corresponding measures on the mitigation of climate change' demonstrating 'that developed countries are taking the lead in modifying longer-term trends in anthropogenic emissions consistent with the objective of the Convention'.[107]

The Paris Agreement invites a broader approach, focusing on all states' NDCs. Zahar argues that while the Paris Agreement and UNFCCC may contain a binding collective obligation, clearer language would be needed to give such a 'new and consequential' obligation effect.[108] An important issue which then arises is how to divide obligations (and responsibility) equitably, in line with the CBDRRC principle. Here, the ambiguous language 'plaguing' the treaty provisions provides little in the way of definitive answers on how these obligations should concretely be shared.[109] As noted by Zahar, this is complicated by the fact that empirical calculations necessarily exclude unquantifiable yet relevant factors.[110] They could, however, provide an 'informational basis' to inform the political processes.

Interestingly, some authors suggest that the due-diligence threshold for harm prevention and precaution may go beyond the obligations contained in the Kyoto (and Paris) frameworks, as neither is currently sufficient to prevent a dangerous rise in the global temperature.[111] Indeed, the 2015 Oslo Principles go so far as to argue that states have a legal obligation to achieve set, per capita emission reductions.[112] This 'permissible GHG quantum' is calculated based on scientific data on the maximum amount of GHGs that can 'safely' be emitted

[104] This is, for example, considered by R Verheyen, *Climate Change Damage and International Law* (Leiden, Martinus Nijhoff, 2005) 66. J Peel, 'Climate Change, in A Nollkaemper and I Plakokefalos, *The Practice of Shared Responsibility in International Law* Cambridge, Cambridge University Press) 1024.

[105] See Art 2(1)a Paris Agreement (n 2); V Masson-Delmotte et al, 'Special Report: Global Warming of 1.5°C. Summary for Policymakers' (IPCC 2018) www.ipcc.ch/site/assets/uploads/sites/2/2019/05/SR15_SPM_version_report_LR.pdf.

[106] C Voigt, 'State Responsibility for Climate Change Damages' (2008) 77 *Nordic Journal of International Law* 5.

[107] ibid 6.

[108] A Zahar, 'Collective Obligation and Individual Ambition in the Paris Agreement' (2019) 9 *Transnational Environmental Law* 165.

[109] Peel (n 104) 1025.

[110] Zahar (n 108) 168, 182.

[111] Peel (n 104) 1009; Voigt (n 106) 5.

[112] *Oslo Principles on Global Climate Change Obligations*, 1 March 2015 ('Oslo Principles') www.osloprinciples.org/principles, Principles 1, 14.

over a period of time.[113] Importantly, states' respective obligations are to be adjusted according to the CBDRRC principle so that more developed states shoulder a financial burden proportionate to their capabilities and historical contributions.[114] Notably, while the Oslo Principles purport to clarify existing legal obligations, they have not in themselves been incorporated into positive law.[115]

4. CONCLUSION

Unilateral responses to climate change as a common concern occupy a tenuous position between state obligations and state competences under international law. This chapter has considered the core framework of states' obligations, with a focus on mitigation. As a common concern of humankind, climate change creates an imperative for states to act and has an important signalling function in relation to existing obligations to cooperate and prevent the exacerbation of the concern beyond their territories. The multilateral climate change regime impresses upon the international community the need for ambitious emission reduction targets, to be undertaken in line with the principle of common but differentiated responsibilities and respective capabilities.

Nevertheless, as we have seen, the climate change regimes leaves states with considerable discretion as to the attainment of their individual emission reduction targets. In the face of the collective 'ambition-gap' this leaves us with difficult questions about how far more ambitious states may go in attempting to reduce global anthropogenic greenhouse gas emissions. To what extent do states' jurisdictional rights accommodate their environmental obligations? Chapter 3 will now set out the core jurisdictional issues at play in this context, illustrated with examples from EU practice.

[113] ibid Art 3.

[114] ibid Principle 14. This principle has been codified in the UNCED, 'Declaration of the United Nations Conference on the Human Environment' (1973) UN Doc A/Conf.48/14/Rev. 1, Principle 12.

[115] The Oslo Principles have been drafted by legal experts who seek to 'identify and articulate a set of Principles' that comprise states' 'essential obligations' to 'avert the critical level of global warming' (Oslo Principles (n 112) rec 1).

3

The Right to Regulate: Jurisdiction and Extraterritoriality in Theory and Practice

1. INTRODUCTION

THE PREVIOUS CHAPTER considered the open-natured obligations of the climate change regime that steer the design of states' climate-protective measures. While these obligations promote ambition, such measures must not exceed states' competence to regulate. This chapter now explores the foundations of the *right* of states to regulate. This is a question of state jurisdiction, which 'concerns essentially the extent of each State's right to regulate the conduct or consequences of events'.[1]

In sketching the theoretical foundations, section 2 first defines 'unilateral jurisdiction' as an extension of state sovereignty. Filling out the conceptual parameters, section 3 then considers the 'types' and 'bases' of jurisdiction available to states. Section 4 turns to the contested issue of 'extraterritoriality', and its appropriate situation within the jurisdictional analysis. As will be seen, the conceptual core of the law of state jurisdiction is heavily debated. This chapter therefore takes time to explore the various debates, and set out the approach employed in this book. Section 5 considers extraterritoriality in practice, focusing on the EU as the primary case study of this book. Briefly sketching policy trends, it analyses the drive towards extraterritoriality arising from the combination of high climate-protection standards, competitiveness concerns and the desire the prevent carbon leakage. Drawing on select examples, it then considers various mechanisms through which an extraterritorial element is incorporated into EU climate-protection measures.

[1] R Jennings and A Watts, *Oppenheim's International Law*, 9th edn (Oxford, Oxford University Press, 2008) 456. Oxman describes jurisdiction more generally, as referring to a state's 'lawful power to act'. B Oxman, 'Jurisdiction of States', *Max Planck Encyclopaedia of Public International Law*, online edn (Oxford, Oxford University Press, 2007) 1. See also, FA Mann, 'The Doctrine of Jurisdiction in International Law' (1964) 111 *Collected Courses of the Hague Academy of International Law* 9: 'Jurisdiction involves a State's *right* to exercise certain of its powers' (emphasis added).

2. UNILATERAL JURISDICTION

An essential starting point when defining jurisdiction is its relationship with sovereignty. In the words of Mann, 'Jurisdiction is an aspect of sovereignty, it is coextensive with and, indeed, incidental to, but also limited by, the State's sovereignty.'[2] Jurisdiction thus 'describes the limits of the legal competence of a State or other regulatory authority to make, apply and enforce rules of conduct upon other persons'.[3] The primary limit of state jurisdiction derives from sovereign equality, which aims to ensure the equal legal representation of states and, as a corollary, safeguard the stability of the international system.[4] Traditionally, sovereign equality is conceptualised in terms of independence. As famously held by Judge Huber in the *Island of Palmas* case:

> Sovereignty in the relations between States signifies independence. Independence in regard to a portion of the globe is the right to exercise therein, to the exclusion of any other State, the functions of a State.[5]

Today, as noted by Oxman, the law of jurisdiction also serves to recognise *inter*-dependence by 'ensuring effective jurisdiction exists to achieve common goals', and to harmonise the rights of states with concurrent jurisdiction.[6]

As the term suggests, a state exercises 'unilateral jurisdiction' when it acts alone. The EU exercises unilateral jurisdiction when it acts as a supranational organisation, using the legislative competences conferred on it by the EU Member States.[7] This can be contrasted with 'multilateral jurisdiction', which is exercised in agreement with more than one legislature. Unilateralism and unilateral acts have a decisively negative connotation in legal discourse, and are sometimes used to imply the illegitimate use of power by a state.[8] However, the right to act

[2] Mann (n 1) 30.

[3] V Lowe and C Staker, 'Jurisdiction' in MD Evans (ed), *International Law*, 3rd edn (Oxford, Oxford University Press, 2010) 313.

[4] However, for a more critical analysis of the principle's evolution, see J Kokott, 'States, Sovereign Equality' in R Wolfrum (ed), *Max Planck Encyclopaedia of Public International Law*, online edn (Oxford, Oxford University Press, 2011).

[5] *Island of Palmas, United States v The Netherlands* (1928) II RIAA 829 (*Island of Palmas*), 838.

[6] Oxman (n 1) 9.

[7] See Consolidated version of the Treaty on European Union [2012] OJ C326/01 (TEU) Art 5 (2): 'Under the principle of conferral, the Union shall act only within the limits of the competences conferred upon it by the Member States in the Treaties to attain the objectives set out therein.' See Oxman (n 1) 12, who notes: 'Substantial competences – particularly with regard to legislative jurisdiction – have been transferred by the Member States of the European Union. … Although it is not a State as such, the same principles regarding jurisdiction also apply to the competences exercised by the EU that affect non-members and their nationals.'

[8] See eg M Reisman, 'Unilateral Action and the Transformations of the World Constitutive Process: The Special Problem of Humanitarian Intervention' (2000) 11 *European Journal of International Law* 3. See eg P Dupuy, 'The Place and Role of Unilateralism in Contemporary Law' (2000) 11 *European Journal of International Law* 19, 20 who writes: 'Unilateralism includes recourse to juridical unilateral acts but may also denote the general tendency prevailing among some powerful states or groups of states to act without regard to respect for the equal sovereignty of their partners.'

unilaterally is part of 'the essence of sovereignty', and states do it every day.[9] A unilateral assertion of jurisdiction will only be problematic if it is in violation of a binding international rule. An important question, then, is how a potential violation should be determined. In the 1927 *Lotus* case the Permanent Court of International Justice (PCIJ), famously held that:

> International law governs relations between independent States. The rules of law binding upon States therefore emanate from their own free will as expressed in conventions or by usages generally accepted as expressing principles of law and established in order to regulate the relations between these co-existing independent communities or with a view to the achievement of common aims. Restrictions upon the independence of States cannot therefore be presumed.[10]

According to this so-called '*Lotus*-approach', jurisdictional assertions are '*prima facie* lawful' in the absence of a specific prohibitive rule.[11] Today, it has been observed state practice appears to turn *Lotus* 'upside down'.[12] A regulator must instead be able demonstrate a *permissive* legal basis to support jurisdictional assertions.[13]

The sources of such jurisdictional bases – and limitations – can be found across the fragmented landscape of public international law.[14] They are often connected to the regulation of substantive issues within certain regimes, which have evolved through functional differentiation to address their own respective problems.[15] In the context of climate change measures, these more specific legal regimes form important *lex specialis* sources of states' regulatory competence, which must be considered first.[16] As discussed, this study will focus on WTO

[9] D Bodansky, 'What's so Bad about Unilateral Action to Protect the Environment?' (2000) 11 *European Journal of International Law* 339, 341. See further P Sands, '"Unilateralism", Values, and International Law' (2000) 11 *European Journal of International Law* 291, 292.

[10] *The S S Lotus (France v Turkey)* 1927 PCIJ Series A, No 10 (*Lotus* case) 18.

[11] C Ryngaert, *Jurisdiction in International Law*, 2nd edn (Oxford, Oxford University Press, 2015) 44. The *Lotus* case will be discussed further in chapter 7 on customary international law.

[12] For further discussion, see Ryngaert (n 11) 35. Although note Oxman (n 1), who argues that it is 'unclear' what the current state of affairs is in relation to the *Lotus* case finding [10].

[13] Ryngaert (n 11) 35.

[14] See further H van Asselt, F Sindico and MA Mehling, 'Global Climate Change and the Fragmentation of International Law' (2008) 30 *Law & Policy* 423.

[15] See ILC, 'Report of the Study Group of the International Law Commission: Fragmentation of International Law – Difficulties arising from the Diversification and Expansion of International Law' (13 April 2006) UN Doc A/CN.4/L.682 ('ILC Report on Legal Fragmentation') 5: '[T]his expansion [of the scope of international law] has taken place in an uncoordinated fashion, within specific regional or functional groups of States. Focus has been on solving specific problems rather than attaining general, law-like regulation. This reflects what sociologists have called "functional differentiation", the increasing specialization of parts of society and the related autonomization of those parts.'

[16] See further DM Banaszewska, 'Lex Specialis' in R Wolfrum (ed), *Max Planck Encyclopaedia of Public International Law*, online edn (Oxford, Oxford University Press, 2015) [2], noting that: 'The maxim "*in toto iure generi per speciem derogatur et illud potissimum habetur, quod ad speciem*

law, the law of the sea and international civil aviation law as three specific regimes of particular relevance to climate change measures.[17] The customary international law of state jurisdiction will then be analysed as the supplementary *lex generalis*.

3. TYPES AND BASES OF JURISDICTION

In balancing sovereign powers, the law of jurisdiction distinguishes between different 'types' of jurisdiction that have different degrees of invasiveness on the regulatory competence of other states.[18] To start with, a state's 'enforcement' jurisdiction 'to ensure compliance with its laws' interferes greatly with the sovereignty of other states, and, according to customary international law, may only be exercised within its own territory.[19] A state's 'adjudicative jurisdiction' to subject cases to be tried and determined by its courts may also cause considerable interference.[20] By contrast, a state's 'legislative' or 'prescriptive' jurisdiction to 'adopt legislation governing persons, property and conduct' is considered comparatively less intrusive, and in addition to territory, may be based on a number of recognised 'extraterritorial' principles, discussed briefly below.[21] Importantly, though, it is a prerequisite for the validity of both adjudicative and enforcement measures that they also be based on a valid act of prescriptive jurisdiction.[22] Each jurisdictional act must thus have its own independent legal basis in international law.[23] This study focuses on prescriptive jurisdiction, looking at the competence of states (and the EU) to legislate in the interest of common concerns.

derectum est" ("in the whole of law, special takes precedence over genus, and anything that relates to species is regarded as most important") was already to be found in Papinian's Digest in the *Corpus Iuris Civilis*.'

[17] See part II of this book.

[18] M Kamminga, 'Extraterritoriality' in R Wolfrum (ed), *Max Planck Encyclopaedia of Public International Law*, online edn (Oxford, Oxford University Press, 2011) 1: 'these distinctions are important because some methods of exercising extraterritorial jurisdiction of States are more likely to conflict with the competence of other States and therefore more likely to raise questions as to their compatibility with international law'.

[19] ILC, 'Report of the International Law Commission on the Work of its 58th Session' (1 May–9 June and 3 July–11 August 2006) UN Doc A/61/10, Annex E: Extraterritorial Jurisdiction ('ILC Report on Extraterritorial Jurisdiction') 518; Kamminga (n 18) 8.

[20] ILC Report on Extraterritorial Jurisdiction (n 19) 518.

[21] See further on the prescriptive principles eg Mann (n 1); Lowe and Staker, 'Jurisdiction' (2010) 317; J Crawford, *Brownlie's Principles of Public International Law*, 8th edn (Oxford, Oxford University Press, 2012) 447; Ryngaert (n 11) 101. See also, International Bar Association, 'Report of the Task Force on Extraterritorial Jurisdiction' (2009) ('IBA Report on Extraterritorial Jurisdiction').

[22] ILC Report on Extraterritorial Jurisdiction (n 19) 518.

[23] ibid 521.

Turning to the bases of prescriptive jurisdiction, territory and territorial sovereignty continue to play a central role. As Judge Huber noted in the *Island of Palmas* case:

> The development of the national organization of States during the last few centuries and, as a corollary, the development of international law, have established this principle of the exclusive competence of the State in regard to its own territory in such a way as to make it the point of departure in settling most questions that concern international relations.[24]

Indeed, territory remains the primary, most well-established basis of jurisdiction. This principle extends to both conduct initiated within a state's *territory* ('subjective' territoriality), and to 'persons, property or acts outside its territory when a constitutive element of the conduct sought to be regulated occurred in the territory of the State' ('objective' territoriality).[25]

However, as noted by Mann, 'the complications of modern life are responsible for the steadily increasing reluctance to "localise" facts, events or relationships'.[26] Over time, several other principles have thus continued to develop, providing permissive bases for states to regulate conduct or circumstances outside of their territory. The most well-recognised principle is that of *nationality*, according to which states may exercise jurisdiction over foreign conduct relating to their citizens (and sometimes residents).[27] Again this principle consists of two subcategories, extending to both conduct of nationals occurring abroad ('active' nationality principle), and situations where a state's national is injured by conduct committed by an actor abroad ('passive' nationality principle).[28] In addition, the *protective principle* provides a basis for jurisdiction over foreign conduct that threatens 'vital state interests'.[29] The *universality principle* requires no individual connection with the regulating state and has traditionally been based on the recognised gravity of certain crimes that violate the fundamental values of the international community.[30] Finally, the *effects doctrine* provides a basis for jurisdiction over foreign conduct that produces direct and substantial effects within a state's territory.[31] Closely related to the objective territoriality

[24] *Island of Palmas* (n 5) 838.

[25] IBA Report on Extraterritorial Jurisdiction (n 21) 143, citing *US v Pasquantino*, 544 US 349 (2005), *DPP v Stonehouse* (1978) AC 55, and *Treacy v DPP* (1971) AC 537 (HL) which concerned adjudicative jurisdiction over a blackmail case where demands were sent by post from England to Germany. See also ILC Report on Extraterritorial Jurisdiction (n 19) 521.

[26] Mann (n 1) 37.

[27] Oxman (n 1) 18.

[28] IBA Report on Extraterritorial Jurisdiction (n 21) 143; ILC Report on Extraterritorial Jurisdiction (n 19) 522–23.

[29] ILC Report on Extraterritorial Jurisdiction (n 19) 522.

[30] S Yee, 'Universal Jurisdiction: Concept, Logic, and Reality' (2011) 10 *Chicago Journal of International Law* 503, 505, noting: 'Behind the "absence" façade however, rests the basis for such an assertion of jurisdiction, normally formulated this way: The alleged crime is an attack on the fundamental values of the international community as a whole.'

[31] Restatement of the Law Fourth – The Foreign Relations Law of the United States (St Paul, MN, American Law Institute Publishers, 2018) ('US Fourth Restatement').

principle, this last doctrine has traditionally been more controversial, although it has received increasing recognition over the past decades.[32] These bases of prescriptive jurisdiction will be discussed in more detail in chapter 7.

Importantly, in practice these principles are not equally well-recognised, and their application varies across different fields of law.[33] Rather than serving as delineated rules, the classical jurisdictional bases are generally accepted as initial indicators with which to evidence the overarching requirement of a 'significant connection' or 'nexus' between the state and the regulated subject matter.[34] This connection pertains to the relationship between the state and the 'persons, property or acts concerned', and can be seen as the 'common element underlying the various principles'.[35] Where such a connection exists, states may, under certain conditions, regulate the relevant conduct or circumstances outside of their territory. As demonstrated by the *ATAA* case discussed in chapter 1, such regulation may give rise to tensions, as states are perceived to have overstepped the limits of their sovereign power.[36] This raises questions of 'extraterritoriality' and 'extraterritorial jurisdiction', which are now discussed further.

4. 'EXTRATERRITORIALITY' AND THE LAW OF STATE JURISDICTION

Extraterritorial jurisdiction pertains to 'the competence of a State to make, apply and enforce rules of conduct in respect of persons, property or events beyond its territory'.[37] According to the 2006 International Law Commission Report on Extraterritorial Jurisdiction (2006 ILC Report):

> The assertion of extraterritorial jurisdiction by a State is an attempt to regulate by means of national legislation, adjudication or enforcement the conduct of persons, property or acts beyond its borders which affect the interests of the State in the absence of such regulation under international law.[38]

There are, however, quite strongly diverging views on when a jurisdictional assertion should be characterised as 'extraterritorial', and what legal implications this then has. As these are essential threshold questions for the present study, the following section will now explore the lively discussion in the literature, and set out the conceptual framework employed in this book.

[32] A development reflected in the US Fourth Restatement (n 31), §409 of which recognises the effects-doctrine under its own heading, rather than as part of the territoriality principle. This will be discussed further in chapter 7.

[33] Kamminga (n 18) [10].

[34] ibid, noting that 'it should immediately be pointed out that these principles must be employed with great caution'.

[35] ILC Report on Extraterritorial Jurisdiction (n 19) 521.

[36] Case C-366/10 *Air Transport Association of America, American Airlines, Inc, Continental Airlines, Inc, United Airlines, Inc v The Secretary of State for Energy and Climate Change* (201)] ECR I-0000 (*ATAA* case).

[37] Kamminga (n 18) [1].

[38] ILC Report on Extraterritorial Jurisdiction (n 19) 516.

4.1. Situating 'Extraterritoriality' within the Jurisdictional Analysis

Due in part to its pejorative connotation, the concept of extraterritoriality remains a contested one.[39] Broadly speaking, the definitions in legal discourse can be placed on a spectrum from expansive to narrower, more suspicious approaches. As will now be shown, this has implications for the overarching analysis of a measure's legality. This section will briefly sketch the key approaches, arguing for a decoupling of 'extraterritoriality' from immediate legal conclusions.

On the one end of the spectrum, the more traditional approach is less suspicious, characterising extraterritoriality according to the classical bases of jurisdiction. On this view, the customary bases of nationality, protection and universality are seen as 'extraterritorial' bases or principles, supporting jurisdictional assertions. The 2006 ILC Report, for example, refers to the 'various principles for the extraterritorial exercise of jurisdiction'.[40] The Report of the International Bar Association Taskforce on Extraterritoriality ('IBA Report on Extraterritoriality') also employs the terminology of 'extraterritorial bases' of jurisdiction.[41] There, however, a distinction is drawn between the 'extended territoriality' bases (objective territoriality and effects) and 'pure' extraterritorial jurisdiction which is based on the nationality, protective and universality principles.[42] Used in this way, characterising a measure as extraterritorial need not suggest illegality.

Seeking distance from extraterritoriality's pejorative label, Joanne Scott proposes an alternative conceptualisation, distinguishing between extraterritorial measures and exercises of 'territorial extension'.[43] Extraterritorial measures are more narrowly defined as those which 'impose an obligation on persons who do not enjoy a relevant territorial connection with the regulating state'.[44] By contrast, exercises of territorial *extension* occur where the application of a measure is dependent on a territorial connection, but the 'relevant regulatory determination' is formed, 'as a matter of law, by conduct or circumstances abroad'. Territorial connections or triggers giving rise to territorial extension may take the form of (a) conduct that occurs within a territory, (b) nationality and (c) the presence of persons within a state's territory.[45] Scott also observes a

[39] Indeed, according to Ryngaert, 'while '"extraterritorial" may … be useful as shorthand for "not *exclusively* territorial", the term might best be avoided, because it is tainted by the pejorative connotation it has acquired over the years'. Ryngaert (n 11) 8.

[40] ILC Report on Extraterritorial Jurisdiction (n 19) 520.

[41] IBA Report on Extraterritorial Jurisdiction (n 21) 142.

[42] ibid. For its part, the Committee of Ministers for the Council of Europe Model Plan recognised four different categories of 'extra-territorial exercise of jurisdiction', namely consular jurisdiction, jurisdiction over military personnel abroad and 'others' (artificial islands, terra nullius etc), Council of Europe Model Plan, Recommendation No R (97) 11, Part 8.

[43] J Scott, 'Extraterritoriality and Territorial Extension in EU Law' (2014) 62 *American Journal of International Law* 87, 89–90.

[44] ibid.

[45] ibid 90.

new wave of 'extraterritorial' triggers emerging in the context of EU antitrust law, which instead give rise to extraterritorial measures. These are (i) effects, (ii) anti-evasion and (iii) transacting with EU persons or property.[46] Importantly, according to the author, a measure's characterisation as extraterritorial need not render it illegal; however, exercises of 'territorial extension' are considered less suspect.

On the other end of the spectrum, a narrower view entirely rules out the label of extraterritoriality when there is an element of territorial presence. For example, in their Separate Opinion to the *Arrest Warrant* case Judges Higgins, Kooijmans and Buergenthal defined the obligation to establish universal jurisdiction over persons present in a state's territory as the 'jurisdiction to establish territorial jurisdiction over extraterritorial events'.[47] Here the judges appear to consider the territorial presence of the accused to render the assertion of jurisdiction territorial, even if the act for which the accused is charged occurred abroad. However, as noted by O'Keefe, this approach does not sufficiently distinguish between prescriptive and enforcement jurisdiction.[48] The fact that a rule is enforced within a state's territory does not alter the nature of the rule itself as being concerned with extraterritorial conduct. This need not be problematic, as the very essence of universal jurisdiction is that it grants a basis to regulate such extraterritorial conduct.

A similar discussion can be found with regard to import and export restrictions which are imposed at the border, and therefore enforced territorially. As will be seen in section 5, this is of particular relevance for climate-protection measures. Several commentators take the view that as such trade measures are concerned with a product's entry into sale in the territory of a state, the corresponding legislative competence can be based on the territoriality principle.[49] Nollkaemper frames the issue in terms of sovereignty, arguing that 'under general international law, import policies and corresponding measures at the border or in the national market are a prerogative of sovereign states, and as such lawful'.[50] A similar reasoning can be found in the *ATAA* case, concerning the legality of the EU Aviation Directive 2008/101 EC. This directive extended

[46] J Scott, 'The New EU Extraterritoriality' (2014) 51 *CML Rev* 1343.

[47] *Case Concerning the Arrest Warrant of 11 April 2000, Democratic Republic of the Congo v Belgium*, ICJ Reports 2002 (*Arrest Warrant* case) Separate Opinion Judges Higgins, Kooijmans, Buergethnal [41]–[42].

[48] See further R O'Keefe, 'Universal Jurisdiction Clarifying the Basic Concept' (2004) 2 *Journal of International Criminal Justice* 735, 755, who finds the terminology used 'unhelpful and, with respect, a trifle silly'.

[49] EU Petersmann, 'International Trade Law and International Environmental Law' (1993) 27 *Journal of World Trade* 34, 69; A Nollkaemper, ''Rethinking States'' Rights to Promote Extra-Territorial Environmental Values' in F Weiss, E Denters and P de Waart (eds), *International Economic Law with a Human Face* (The Hague, Kluwer Law International, 1998) 188.

[50] Nollkaemper (n 49)) 188. For a similar argument, see S Charnovitz, 'The Moral Exception in Trade Policy' (1997) 38 *Virginia Journal of International Law* 689, 179, referring to the term 'extrajurisidictional' rather than extraterritorial.

the scope of the EU Emission Trading Scheme (ETS) to include emissions from aircraft throughout the entire duration of their flights to and from EU airfields.[51] There the CJEU found that as the aircraft were physically present in EU airfields, the Union had 'unlimited jurisdiction' to require the submission of emission credits for CO_2 emitted outside its territory.[52]

It is argued here that this approach also blurs the distinction between prescriptive and enforcement jurisdiction. Measures which condition the import or export of goods and services on conduct and circumstances abroad are concerned with extraterritorial circumstances. The legislation itself requires a basis under international law, the absence of which can constitute an international wrong.[53] The fact that such measures are only imposed at the border is a question of enforcement, which requires its own valid basis under international law (generally territory), as well as a valid act of prescriptive jurisdiction.[54]

In line with the realities of globalisation, this book prefers a loose definition of extraterritoriality, closer to the term's plain meaning, which is simply that 'beyond the territory' of the regulating state.[55] A measure can then be characterised as 'extraterritorial' when it seeks to regulate conduct or circumstances outside of the territory of the acting state.[56] It is argued that identifying a measure as 'extraterritorial' serves as a *preliminary threshold* only, indicating that the acting state must be able to demonstrate a valid jurisdictional basis under international law. It is then not in itself an immediate legal qualification. Used in this context, this book will describe such measures as having an *extraterritorial element*. In an increasingly integrated world, extraterritoriality is an inescapable reality of states' policy measures, and need not always be negative. The underlying question at issue is how to delineate regulatory spheres. This is indeed the core function of the law of state jurisdiction.[57] The applicable rules are those in the relevant *lex specialis* regimes and *lex generalis* of customary law.

[51] The controversial Parliament and Council (EC) Directive 2008/101 amending Directive 2003/87/EC so as to include aviation activities in the scheme for greenhouse gas emission allowance trading within the Community [2008] OJ L8/3 ('Aviation Directive').

[52] *ATAA* case (n 36) 124–25.

[53] See eg L Bartels, 'Article XX of GATT and the Problem of Extraterritorial Jurisdiction – The Case of Trade Measures for the Protection of Human Rights' (2002) 36 *Journal of World Trade* 353, 378; C Ryngaert and H Ringbom, 'Introduction: Port State Jurisdiction: Challenges and Potential' (2016) 31 *International Journal of Marine and Coastal Law* 379, 382–83.

[54] Ryngaert and Ringbom (n 53) 382–83.

[55] ILC Report on Extraterritorial Jurisdiction (n 19) 518.

[56] This approach finds considerable support in the literature. See eg F Francioni, 'Extraterritorial Application of Environment Law' in KM Meessen (ed), *Extraterritorial Jurisdiction in Theory and Practice* (Leiden, Brill, 1996) 122: 'when legislation extends to production processes and technologies abroad, an issue of extraterritorial jurisdiction arises'. See also, International Committee, 'International Committee on the Legal Aspect of Extraterritorial Jurisdiction' (1990) 64 *International Law Association Report of Conferences* 312, 318. The Committee defines extraterritoriality 'as meaning the adoption of rules of law [including their adjudication and enforcement] that control conduct abroad, thereby undercutting or purporting to override the control exercised or exercisable by the foreign territorial sovereign'.

[57] On interest-balancing in a jurisdictional context, see further Ryngaert (n 11) 145.

Before investigating these rules further, it is necessary to further delineate the category of 'suspect' measures with an extraterritorial element, in need of jurisdictional justification. Section 4.2 will now set out the approach supported here.

4.2. Defining 'Relevant' Extraterritoriality: Potential Interference with States' Regulatory Freedom

At what point is it necessary that a state be able to prove it has a 'substantial connection' or legitimate interest in regulating particular subject matter? From an international law perspective, it is argued that this is when a measure 'potentially interferes' with the regulatory freedom of other states.[58] Theoretically speaking, the differing degrees of 'potential interference' form a key rationale for the distinction between the different types of jurisdiction (see section 3 above). It then seems logical and doctrinally consistent to employ the same criterion *within* the analysis of prescriptive jurisdiction. In practical terms, it is also at this point that the acting state may be called upon by other affected states to demonstrate its basis for regulating that subject matter. Importantly, this need not be difficult to do, and states will often have little problem justifying their jurisdictional assertions.

When, then, does a measure potentially interfere with the sovereignty of other states requiring justification beyond that of territoriality? Is it enough that a measure 'takes into account', 'relates to' or 'considers' foreign conduct, or should it actively seek to coerce actors outside of the state's territory? This issue is especially important for expansive trade measures, which do not, strictly speaking, force foreign actors to comply, but rather provide a (strong) incentive for them to do so.[59] Again various views can be found across legal discourse. These must be distilled with caution, as they are embedded within differing approaches to the jurisdictional analysis. They nonetheless provide valuable insights for comparison and analysis here.

To start with, according to Meng, the defining factor of extraterritorial measures is that they intend to have coercive effects (*Persuasionswirkung*) abroad.[60] Such measures must be distinguished from those with 'mere foreign links' (*Auslandsanknüpfungen*), or other factual effects.[61] In his view, trade measures

[58] For the use of 'interference' as an indicator that jurisdictional issues arise, see eg ILC Report on Extraterritorial Jurisdiction (n 19) 518. 'The potential interference resulting from the extraterritorial exercise of prescriptive jurisdiction is less than that resulting from either adjudicative or enforcement jurisdiction.'

[59] See eg L Ankersmit, J Lawrence and G Davies, 'Diverging EU and WTO Perspectives on Extraterritorial Process Regulation' (2012) 21 *Minnesota Journal of International Law* 14, 25. 'PPMs [production process measures] occupy a middle ground. Because PPMs incentivize, but do not mandate, certain behavior in other states, it is not clear to what extent these types of measures should be considered truly "extraterritorial".'

[60] W Meng, *Extraterritoriale Jurisdiktion im öffentlichen Wirtschaftsrecht* (Heidelberg, Springer-Verlag, 1994) 86.

[61] ibid.

would fall into the latter category, the foreign effects of which are merely the result of factual realities of international commerce.[62] A similar reasoning is also used by Anderson, who distinguishes between extraterritorial measures, which 'command or compel results beyond a nation state's borders', and trade measures, which 'merely induce or influence results beyond its borders'.[63]

For Howse and Regan, what is important is whether measures 'directly regulate any behaviour occurring outside the border'.[64] This will only occur when what 'has happened outside the border attracts, by itself, [a] criminal or civil sanction'.[65] While the authors do not deny that certain trade measures may be dependent on prior conduct or circumstances, such measures are not extraterritorial in the 'core sense', as the only thing forbidden to foreign producers is that they 'bring products produced with certain processes into the country'.[66] The requirement of explicit regulation is also reflected in the Opinion of Advocate General Kokott in the *ATAA* case, which notes that it is 'undoubtedly true that, to some extent, account is … taken of events that take place over the high seas or on the territory of third countries', which might 'indirectly give airlines an incentive to conduct themselves in a particular way'.[67] However, the fact that the 'calculation of emission allowances to be surrendered is based on the whole flight … does not bestow upon Directive 2008/101 any extraterritorial effect' as it contained 'no concrete rule' regarding the conduct of foreign aircraft outside of EU airspace.[68]

Taking the 'middle ground', Ankersmit, Lawrence and Davies consider that where certain (trade) measures 'incentivize but do not mandate' behaviour occurring 'entirely in other jurisdictions', 'it is not clear to what extent these measures should be considered "truly" extraterritorial'.[69] Proposing a possible threshold, Churchill considers a measure to be extraterritorial when its 'primary purpose' is the regulation of extraterritorial circumstances.[70] These must be distinguished from measures that aim to regulate domestic situations, which are 'purely an exercise in territorial jurisdiction'.[71] On this view, 'incentivising' port entry conditions *could* then be extraterritorial if these effects are the primary

[62] ibid 77.

[63] B Anderson, 'Unilateral Trade Measures and Environmental Policy' (1993) 66 *Temple Law Review* 751, 755.

[64] R Howse and D Regan, 'The Product/process Distinction – An Illusory Basis for Disciplining "Unilateralism" in Trade Policy' (2000) 11 *European Journal of International Law* 249, 274.

[65] ibid.

[66] ibid.

[67] Opinion of Advocate General Kokott in the *ATAA* case (n 36) 147.

[68] ibid 145–48, continuing: 'It is by no means unusual for a State or an international organisation also to take into account in the exercise of its sovereignty circumstances that occur or have occurred outside its territorial jurisdiction.'

[69] Ankersmit, Lawrence and Davies (n 59) 24.

[70] R Churchill, 'Port State Jurisdiction Relating to the Safety of Shipping and Pollution from Ships – What Degree of Extra-Territoriality?' (2016) 31 *International Journal of Marine and Coastal Law* 442, 454.

[71] ibid.

purpose of a measure. Cooreman formulates the issue slightly differently, arguing that measures imposed to protect 'outward-looking' physical concerns, such as animal welfare abroad, may raise jurisdictional tensions.[72] 'Inward-looking' measures regulating domestic concerns do not raise such tensions as they are based upon a strong (territorial) nexus with the regulating state.[73]

Rather than focusing on a measure's intent, Bartels argues that 'what is relevant is whether the legislation has an impermissible practical *effect* on persons abroad'.[74] This approach is preferred here, as it is a more appropriate indicator of whether there is a potential interference with the sovereignty of *other* states. Such interference may occur even when a measure is 'inwardly focused', and irrespective of its explicit purpose. Furthermore, as noted by Bartels, the use of intent 'steers dangerously close' to the assumption that an extraterritorial measure is 'only problematic when it is enforced (or at least enforceable) by civil or criminal sanctions'.[75] As already discussed, this is not consistent with the distinction between enforcement and prescriptive jurisdiction in customary legal theory.

Clearly, some minimum threshold must be set for the intensity of the extraterritorial effects. Focusing more on how a measure functions, Bartels suggests that 'relevant' extraterritoriality should be identified according to the '*legal* connection between the legislation and the extraterritorial subject-matter', and whether this amounts to a 'denial of opportunities normally open to the person against whom enforcement is directed'.[76] With regards to the first criterion, the author argues that there is a legal connection not only when legislation 'specifically applies to a particular action or thing, but also when that action or thing is an essential element in the *definition* of some other action or thing to which the legislation applies'.[77] With regards to the second aspect, while admitting that there is no right to trade under customary international law, Bartels notes that such a right does exist within the established framework of WTO law, whereby denial of the opportunity to trade would constitute a 'denial of opportunities normally open' to foreign actors.[78]

Reflecting on this, the 'denial of opportunities' criterion does offer one reason why a measure's extraterritoriality may be *problematic*, and is certainly relevant from a WTO perspective. However, a measure may interfere with affected states' regulatory competence whether or not it denies certain actors specific rights in

[72] This is particularly true where there are no direct effects in the territory of the regulating state. B Cooreman, 'Addressing Environmental Concerns through Trade? A Case for Extraterritoriality' (2015) 65 *ICLQ* 229, 235.

[73] ibid. This will be discussed in more detail in a WTO context in chapter 4.

[74] Bartels (n 53) 380.

[75] ibid.

[76] ibid 381. This last-mentioned aspect is based on the commentary to the US Third Restatement; 'Restatement of the law, Third, Foreign Relations of the United States', vol 1 (St Paul, MN, American Law Institute Publishers, 1986) §431, comment (c).

[77] Bartels (n 53) 381.

[78] ibid 382–83.

other areas of law. Arguably, the 'legal connection' criterion alone would appear enough. This criterion is attractive because it provides a clear indication of when a measure is engaging foreign actors so as to raise questions of jurisdiction. From an evidentiary perspective, it can be identified quite easily with less of a discretionary margin than thresholds such as whether a measure 'coerces' or 'commands and compels' foreign conduct. It further cannot be sidestepped by 'territorialising' a rule so as only to address domestic conduct, such as a failure to produce a required certificate of conformity.[79] As will be seen in section 5, this is a common mechanism in EU unilateral policy.

More important, perhaps, is the substantive argument that implicit economic 'incentives' may seriously affect the independence of the states upon whose territories compliance is dependent. As noted by Ankersmit et al, economic '"incentives" can skirt very close to coercion where the regulating state or trade bloc is a large and powerful economic force'.[80] As will be discussed in chapter 4, the power of economic incentives is also well recognised in WTO law. This was in fact the reason why trade measures regulating production processes that left no visible trace in the final product were initially considered a violation of the General Agreement on Tariffs and Trade (GATT).[81] According to the Panel in the 1994 *Tuna–Dolphin* dispute, interpreting the general exemptions provision, Article XX GATT, to allow such measures would 'permit contracting parties to take trade measures so as to force other contracting parties to change their policies within their jurisdiction'.[82] In practice, the economic cost of denied market access, or even administrative compliance conditions,[83] may then greatly resemble that of financial sanctions, and can be just as 'compelling' as physical pressure in shaping the behaviour of foreign actors.

Based on these arguments, this book considers a measure to have an 'extraterritorial element' when its application is de facto dependent on conduct or circumstances abroad. The emphasis on effects rather than intent facilitates recognition of the interests of other equal sovereign states, which must then – in the subsequent inquiry into the existence of a jurisdictional basis – be balanced against the interests of the acting state. Notably, the interests of private actors are considered as an extension of the regulatory choices of different states.

[79] See Ryngaert and Ringbom (n 53) 384, noting that 'port states have found ingenious ways to *territorialize* extraterritorial offenses'.

[80] ibid.

[81] See *United States – Restrictions on Import of Tuna* (1991) DS21/R, (*US–Tuna I*), and *United States – Restrictions on Imports of Tuna* (1994) DS29/R, (*US–Tuna II*), relating to the General Agreement on Tariffs and Trade 1994 (Marrakesh, 15 April 1994; in force 1 January 1995) 1867 UNTS 187 (GATT).

[82] *US–Tuna II* (n 81) [5.26].

[83] See further, WTO, *US – Certain Country of Origin Labelling (COOL) Requirements* (23 July 2012) WT/DS384/AB/R, WT/DS386/AB/R, where the administrative burden on upstream producers not visible in the required labelling was considered 'less favourable treatment' under Art 2.1 of the Agreement on Technical Barriers to Trade (adopted 15 April 1994, entered into force 1 January 1995) 1868 UNTS 120 ('TBT Agreement').

Thus, where a home state has chosen not to burden its producers with certain environmental regulations, foreign state measures imposing costs on these actors raise issues of jurisdiction.

Section 5 will now consider how extraterritoriality looks in practice, taking a closer look at the EU as the primary case study.

5. EXTRATERRITORIALITY IN PRACTICE: THE EU'S AMBITIOUS CLIMATE POLICY

Over the past decade the EU has emerged as a global environmental actor and a self-proclaimed leader in the field of climate change.[84] In doing so, it has also consistently forged ahead with its unilateral policy, seeking to implement its ambitious reduction commitment under the second phase of the Kyoto Protocol.[85] Having taken on an even greater 40 per cent reduction target under the Paris Agreement, it has not appeared to slow down.[86] A key element of this policy is the reduction of negative environmental externalities beyond EU borders, caused by domestic consumption of industrialised goods and services.[87] As will be demonstrated, the EU does this through targeting the whole carbon footprint of goods and services present in its territory, including those originating abroad. This is an explicit policy objective – the European Green Deal, for example, endorses the EU's capacity to 'set standards that apply across global value chains'.[88] This has not been without controversy, and it is no coincidence that it was EU policy at the heart of the *ATAA* dispute as the first (and to date only) case before a multinational tribunal concerned with the territorial limits of unilateral climate change jurisdiction under international law. To contextualise

[84] For further discussion, see eg E Morgera and G Marín Durán, *Environmental Integration in the EU's External Relations – Beyond Multilateral Dimensions* (Oxford, Hart Publishing, 2012); AR Zito, 'The European Union as an Environmental Leader in a Global Environment' (2005) 2 *Globalizations* 363. The EU's growth as an environmental actor has been developing for some time. See eg J Vogler and HR Stephan, 'The European Union in Global Environmental Governance: Leadership in the Making?' (2007) 7 *International Environmental Agreements: Politics Law and Economics* 389.

[85] Kyoto Protocol to the United Nations Framework Convention on Climate Change (adopted 11 December 1997, entered into force 16 February 2005) UN Doc FCCC/CP/1997/7/Add.1 ('Kyoto Protocol'). See further Council (EC) Decision 2002/358 concerning the approval, on behalf of the European Community, of the Kyoto Protocol to the United Nations Framework Convention on Climate Change and the joint fulfilment of commitments thereunder [2002] OJ L130/1.

[86] 'Submission by Latvia and the European Commission on Behalf of the European Union and its Member States – Intended Nationally Determined Contribution of the EU and its Member States' (Riga, 6 March 2015) www4.unfccc.int/sites/ndcstaging/PublishedDocuments/European%20Union%20First/LV-03-06-EU%20INDC.pdf.

[87] This is not new, see eg Decision of the Parliament and Council (EU) 1386/2013 on a General Union Environment Action Programme to 2020 'Living well, within the limits of our planet' [2013] OJ L354 ('7th EAP').

[88] Commission (EU) 'The European Green Deal' (Communication) COM(2019) 640 final, 11 December 2019, 22.

the concrete examples discussed below, Section 5.1 will first briefly sketch the contours of the EU's ambitious climate and energy policy.

5.1. The EU as a Global Climate Leader

The EU has been keen to profile itself as an ambitious climate leader on the global stage.[89] This was particularly visible in the run-up to the 2015 Paris climate summit, where it engaged in self-appointed 'climate diplomacy' strategy.[90] The hope was to 'help frame national debates, in particular in [the] strategic partners as well as other key emerging and developing countries'.[91] Bäckstrand and Elgström describe the EU as a 'leadiator', a 'leader-cum-mediator', attempting to secure multilateral agreement prior to the Paris climate summit.[92] This was part of an effort to avoid a repeat of the 2009 Copenhagen summit, where the normative agenda and unrealistic expectations prevented parties from reaching an inclusive agreement.[93]

In addition to securing agreement, the Union's efforts are clearly directed at shaping the design and substance of the climate change regime, a tactic coined in the literature as 'policy forging unilateralism'.[94] Through initiating strategic cooperation 'with countries sharing its vision about the overall level of ambition', the EU steered the formation of the 'High Ambition Coalition'. This was described by Miguel Arias Cañete (EU Climate Action and Energy Commissioner) as 'the masterplan of Europe and its allies'.[95] The strategy 'managed to put pressure on the big emitters' which 'changed the game in Paris'.[96] Since the conclusion of the Paris Agreement, EU policy has explicitly promoted the use of the Union's 'economic weight', 'to shape international standards that are in line with EU environmental and climate ambitions'.[97] This is particularly visible in the field of international transport emissions, where the EU continued to engage in an 'ultimatum strategy', putting pressure on the IMO and the ICAO. These emissions were excluded from the scope of states'

[89] ibid, ch 3: 'The EU as Global Leader'.

[90] European Commission, 'EU Climate Diplomacy for 2015 and Beyond' (Europa website, 11 April 2015) www.ec.europa.eu/clima/sites/clima/files/international/negotiations/docs/eeas_26062013_en.pdf.

[91] ibid.

[92] K Bäckstrand and P Elgström, 'The EU's Role in Climate Change Negotiations: From Leader to "Leadiator"' (2013) 20 *Journal of European Public Policy* 1369.

[93] ibid.

[94] L Boisson de Chazournes, 'Unilateralism and Environmental Protection: Issues of Perception and Reality of Issues' (2000) 11 *European Journal International Law* 315, 317.

[95] M Arias Cañete, 'Historic Climate Deal in Paris: Speech at the Press Conference on the Results of COP21 Climate Conference in Paris' (speech 15/6320, Europa website 2015) www.ec.europa.eu/commission/presscorner/detail/en/SPEECH_15_6320.

[96] ibid.

[97] European Green Deal (n 88) 22.

mandatory reduction commitments under the Kyoto Protocol, an arrangement on which the Paris Agreement remained silent. This will be discussed further in chapters 5 and 6.

Alongside its lobbying efforts, the EU seeks to 'set an example through robust policy making at home'.[98] This finds support in – and is arguably driven by – the primary EU treaties, which contain outward-looking normative objectives.[99] Article 5(3) TEU, for example, states that the Union, '[i]n its relations with the wider world … shall contribute to peace, security, the sustainable development of the Earth, solidarity and mutual respect among peoples, [and] free and fair trade' to name but a few objectives.[100] Article 191(1) TFEU, is particularly relevant here, providing that EU environmental policy must contribute to 'promoting measures at international level to deal with regional or worldwide environmental problems, and in particular combating climate change'.[101] Paragraph 2 further provides that:

> Union policy on the environment shall aim at a high level of protection taking into account the diversity of situations in the various regions of the Union. It shall be based on the precautionary principle and on the principles that preventive action should be taken, that environmental damage should as a priority be rectified at source and that the polluter should pay.

In line with these goals, the EU has adopted a phased approached with increasingly ambitious climate targets over time. Key to its policy strategy is that emission reductions be achieved through integrating all sectors of the economy.[102] This aligns with the requirement in Article 11 TEU that 'environmental protection requirements … be integrated into the definition and implementation of the Union's policies and activities'.[103] As a first milestone, the 2020 Climate and Energy Package aimed for a 20 per cent cut in greenhouse gases compared with 1990 levels, a 20 per cent share of EU energy from renewables and a 20 per cent improvement in energy efficiency.[104] These targets are built upon by the 2030 Climate and Energy Framework, which at the time of writing aims for 40 per cent GHG reductions, and at least a 32 per cent share of renewable energy and 32.5 per cent improvement in energy efficiency, although the

[98] European Commission, 'European Climate Change Programme' (Europa website, 2017) www.ec.europa.eu/clima/policies/eccp_en.

[99] See I Manners, 'Normative Power Europe: A Contradiction in Terms?' (2002) 40 *Journal of Common Market Studies* 235, 242, arguing that the Union's 'elite-driven, treaty based legal order' forms a 'normative basis' for the EU that predisposes it to act as a 'normative power'.

[100] Consolidated version of the Treaty on European Union [2012] OJ C326/01 (TEU), Art 3(5).

[101] Consolidated version of the Treaty on the Functioning of the European Union [2012] OJ C326/47 (TFEU), Art 191.

[102] 7th EAP (n 87) rec 24.

[103] For further analysis of the integration requirement, see Morgera and Marín Durán (n 84) 5.

[104] European Commission, '2020 Climate and Energy Package' (Europa website, 2020) www.ec.europa.eu/clima/policies/strategies/2020_en.

overall target is envisioned to increase.[105] For 2050, the European Green Deal sets out a 'roadmap' for a 'modern, resource-efficient and competitive economy where there are no net emissions of greenhouse gases'.[106] Using strong wording, the Green Deal purports to 'reset[] the Commission's commitment to tackling climate and environmental-related challenges that is this generation's defining task'.[107]

To facilitate the realisation of zero net emissions by 2050, in 2020 the Commission proposed a new European Climate Law.[108] The Commission proposal considers the 'fixed long-term objective' to be 'crucial' 'to move in a fair and cost-effective manner towards the temperature goal of the 2015 Paris Agreement'.[109] This open formulation treads carefully around the issue of defining individual and collective obligations under the climate change regime. The proposal envisages increasing the ambition for the 2030 Climate and Energy Framework, 'in light of the climate-neutrality objective'. The Commission is instructed to 'explore options for a new 2030 target of 50 to 55% emission reductions compared with 1990 levels'.[110] Starting from the established 2030 target, the Commission is then 'empowered' to set out and continuously review a Union-level trajectory towards the 2050 objective.[111] Member States' collective progress and the 'consistency' of Union measures will be regularly assessed every five years by the Commission. Notably, adaptation is also a focus point of the proposed European Climate Law, with explicit reference to Article 7 of the Paris Agreement. The collective progress of Member States and 'adequacy' of Union adaptation measures will be assessed by the Commission together with mitigation policy.[112] Focusing on concrete examples, the following section will now consider how the realisation of these high ambitions creates a drive towards extraterritoriality in EU climate policy.

5.2. The Drive Towards Extraterritoriality in (EU) Climate Policy

From a jurisdictional perspective, EU policy documents have been quite explicit about the Union's intention to steer conduct and circumstances beyond its territory. Thus, '[i]n order to increase the Union's effectiveness in addressing international

[105] A policy framework for climate and energy in the period from 2020 to 2030, COM(2014) 15 final.

[106] European Green Deal (n 88) 2.

[107] ibid.

[108] Proposal of the Parliament and Council (EU) for a Regulation of the European Parliament establishing the framework for achieving climate neutrality and amending Regulation COM(2020) 80 final ('European Climate Law').

[109] ibid rec 3.

[110] ibid rec 17 and Art 2(3). See further Commission (EU), 'Stepping up Europe's 2030 climate ambition – Investing in a climate-neutral future for the benefit of our people' (Communication) COM(2020) 562 final, 17 September 2020, 16.

[111] ibid art 3(1).

[112] ibid art 5(1), (2).

environmental and climate related challenges', the 7th Environmental Action Programme to 2020 was to 'ensure' that by 2020 '*the impact of consumption in the Union on the environment beyond the Union's borders is reduced*'.[113] Going further, the 2019 European Green Deal notes that 'as the world's largest single market, the EU can *set standards that apply across global value chains*'.[114] Considering that '[t]he drivers of climate change and biodiversity loss are global and are not limited by national borders' the Green Deal states that the 'EU can *use its influence*, expertise and financial resources *to mobilise its neighbours* and partners to join it on a sustainable path'.[115] At the same time, it 'recognises the need to maintain its security of supply and competitiveness even when others are unwilling to act'.[116] This hints at the trade-off between the EU's own competitiveness and the shared value of environmental protection. Seeking a level playing field as a means to navigate this tension, climate-protection standards are then applied to the production processes of products and services abroad. In this way, competitiveness concerns and ambitious climate goals create an incentive to legislate with an extraterritorial element.

An exacerbating factor here is that of carbon leakage, whereby production is moved to – or centred in – states with less stringent climate-protection standards in order to lower costs. The Green Deal points to the risk of carbon leakage to support the steering of conduct where 'international partners do not share the same ambition as the EU'.[117] Indeed, '[s]hould differences in levels of ambition worldwide persist', the Green Deal envisions a carbon border adjustment mechanism to 'ensure that the price of imports reflect more accurately their carbon content'.[118] This would be an 'alternative' to the current carbon leakage measures under the EU's cornerstone ETS.

It is worth noting that, where production processes are not rationally divisible, foreign producers may choose to apply the required higher standards for the production of goods destined for other markets as well. Where private actors across the globe voluntarily adopt higher standards, this may drive a form of 'unilateral regulatory globalisation'.[119] Bradford observes that the EU, with its market power, regulatory capacity and propensity for strict regulatory standards, generates such a 'Brussels Effect', particularly evident in the field of climate change.[120] In this way the EU is indeed capable setting standards 'across global value chains'.

[113] 7th EAP (n 87) Annex, (106 (C)) (emphasis added).
[114] European Green Deal (n 88) 22.
[115] ibid 5.
[116] ibid.
[117] ibid.
[118] ibid. The Green Deal is quick to note that this would be designed to comply with WTO rules and other international obligations of the EU.
[119] A Bradford, 'The Brussels Effect' (2012) 107 *Northwestern University Law Review* 1, 3; for a more extensive reflection, see A Bradford, *The Brussels Effect: How the European Union Rules the World* (Oxford, Oxford University Press, 2020).
[120] Bradford, *The Brussels Effect* (n 120) 3.

5.3. Key Examples of EU Measures with an 'Extraterritorial Element'

Across EU policy, we see a wealth of climate-protection measures with an extraterritorial element. It goes beyond the scope of this book to present a comprehensive overview, and measures are notably subject to regular amendment. Rather, this section identifies three 'mechanisms' by which a measure's application is made de facto dependent on conduct or circumstances abroad. These mechanisms are illustrated using selected examples found in measures in force at the time of writing. Notably, the mechanisms are merely intended as a supportive analytical matrix, without any immediate legal weight.

The first mechanism through which an extraterritorial element is woven into a measure is where market access is made conditional on conduct of foreign actors. These conditions impose a *cost* on production. The second mechanism is the offering of a voluntary *benefit* to foreign operators or suppliers for products or services, who comply with certain climate-protective conditions. Unlike the first category, here market access is not strictly dependent on compliance. The third type of extraterritorial element can be found in measures whose application is dependent on policy choices of third states. This has been referred to in the literature as 'contingent unilateralism'.[121] These mechanisms are now considered below.

5.3.1. *Measures Conditioning Market Access on Foreign Conduct or Circumstances*

The first and most prominent mechanism for incorporating an extraterritorial element is to make market access conditional, directly or indirectly, on the conduct of foreign actors. A key example here is the well-known Directive 2008/101/EC (Aviation Directive), amending the ETS. The Directive aims to 'contribute to fulfilling the [Kyoto] commitments of the European Community and its Member States more effectively, through an efficient European market in greenhouse gas emission allowances, with the least possible diminution of economic development and employment'.[122] Essentially, the ETS places a price on carbon emissions, allotting a set amount of carbon credits to operators. This creates a market for carbon credits between operators, where those whose emissions exceed their quota are obliged to buy excess credits from more efficient operators which emit below their target.

At the time of writing, the ETS applies to operators of stationary installations engaging in GHG-intensive activities, such as fuel combustion, refining

[121] J Scott and L Rajamani, 'EU Climate Change Unilateralism' (2012) 23 *European Journal of International Law* 469.

[122] Directive 2003/87 establishing a scheme for greenhouse gas emission allowance trading within the Community and amending Council Directive 96/61/EC [2003] OJ L275 ('ETS Directive') rec 5 and Art 1.

mineral oil and production of nitric acid.[123] In addition, the Aviation Directive extended the scope of the ETS to include 'aircraft operators', which originally included operators of aircraft engaged in international commercial flights to and from the EU.[124] By requiring the monitoring of CO_2 emitted abroad and submission of corresponding carbon credits, the original Aviation Directive set indirect conduct requirements on foreign actors outside EU territory as a condition of market access. As discussed, Regulation 421/2014 amended the Aviation Directive to include only operators of aircraft flying within the EEA.[125]

Despite subsequent international push-back, the threat of this extraterritorial element has been kept alive. The restriction of the ETS to intra-EEA flights was maintained by Regulation 2017/2392, which purports to 'prepare to implement a global market-based measure from 2021'.[126] Rather than opting for immediate alignment, the Commission is instructed to present a report considering ways to implement the 'relevant ICAO instruments' through a *revision* of the ETS.[127] This revision is not unconditional. Based on its report, the Commission must propose an amendment that is 'consistent with the Union economy-wide greenhouse gas emission reduction commitment for 2030 with the aim of preserving the environmental integrity and effectiveness of Union climate action'.[128] In the absence of a new amendment, the Commission has stated that 'the EU ETS would revert back to its original full scope from 2024'.[129]

Another prime example in the making is the envisioned carbon border adjustment mechanism under the Green Deal, which seeks to 'counteract' the risks of carbon leakage 'by putting a carbon price on imports of certain goods from outside the EU'.[130] Other examples in this category of extraterritorial element include Regulation 757/2015 laying out a monitoring, reporting and verification scheme (MRV) for large ships (above 5,000 gross tonnage) involved

[123] ibid Annex 1.

[124] Aviation Directive (n 51), inserting Art 3a and Annex I, [2].

[125] Parliament and Council Regulation (EU) 421/2014 establishing a scheme for greenhouse gas emission allowance trading within the Community, in view of the implementation by 2020 of an international agreement applying a single global market-based measure to international aviation emissions [2014] OJ L129/1–4, regulates the interim period ('Regulation 421/2014') Art 1.

[126] Parliament and Council (EU) Regulation 2017/2392 of 13 December 2017 amending Directive 2003/87/EC to continue current limitations of scope for aviation activities and to prepare to implement a global market-based measure from 2021 [2017] OJ L350/7.

[127] ibid art 7.

[128] ibid. See further A van Velzen, 'CORSIA, EU ETS and the EU2030 Aviation Emissions Target' (Transport and Environment, report no 18-13, 2018) www.transportenvironment.org/sites/te/files/publications/2018_09_Study_CORSIA_EU_ETS_and_EU2030_aviation_emissions_target_Final.pdf.

[129] European Commission, 'Reducing emissions from aviation' (Europa website 2020) www.ec.europa.eu/clima/policies/transport/aviation_en.

[130] At the time of writing the initiative was under public consultation. European Commission, 'EU Green Deal (carbon border adjustment mechanism)' (Europa website, 2020) www.ec.europa.eu/info/law/better-regulation/have-your-say/initiatives/12228-Carbon-Border-Adjustment-Mechanism.

in commercial transportation 'regardless of their flag'.[131] 'Companies' responsible for the ships' operation are required to monitor the CO_2 emitted during voyages to, between and from ports under the jurisdiction of an EU Member State as of 2018.[132]

One can also think of the EU Timber Regulation 995/2010, which seeks to combat illegal deforestation and also mitigate climate change.[133] To place timber on the EU market, foreign suppliers must employ extensive due-diligence systems.[134] Traders of timber products have an obligation of traceability throughout the supply chain, to prove that timber is harvested legally, where 'illegal logging' is defined by the state of origin.[135] These are conduct requirements for market access addressed to timber suppliers outside the EU subject to active enforcement, with Commission reports on practices and risks in leading timber-exporting countries.[136] For example, in 2020 The Hague District Court of the Netherlands found that operators placing teak from Myanmar on the EU market had violated the due-diligence standard through insufficient risk assessment and reporting.[137]

5.3.2. *Measures Offering Benefits Dependent on Foreign Conduct or Circumstances*

The second mechanism for incorporating an extraterritorial element is to offer a *benefit* within an obligatory scheme that is dependent on conduct or circumstances abroad. Such measures do not in themselves bar market access in the case of non-compliance. They do, however, offer a strong incentive to meet the climate-protection standards. A clear example of this type of mechanism is the sustainability criteria for biofuels in the recast EU Renewable Energy Directive 2018/2001 (RED II).

RED II sets a binding EU collective target for the share of energy consumed from renewable sources (at the time of writing this was 32 per cent by 2030).[138] To meet this collective target, Member States must each make a national

[131] Parliament and Council (EU) Regulation 2015/757 on the monitoring, reporting and verification of carbon dioxide emissions from maritime transport, and amending Directive 2009/16/EC [2015] OJ L123/55 ('EU Maritime MRV') rec 13 and Arts 1, 3(d).

[132] ibid Arts 2, 4, 8, 9.

[133] Parliament and Council (EU) Regulation 995/2010 laying down the obligations of operators who place timber and timber products on the market [2010] OJ L295/23 ('Timber Regulation') rec 3.

[134] ibid Art 4(2).

[135] ibid Art 5 and rec 14.

[136] For an interesting overview of implementation developments at the time of writing, see UNEP-WCMC, 'Briefing Note for the Competent Authorities (CA) implementing the EU Timber Regulation: December 2019–January 2020' (Europa website, 2019) www.ec.europa.eu/environment/forests/pdf/EUTR_Briefing_note_Dec_2019-Jan_2020.pdf.

[137] Case SGR 18/6466 and SGR 18/6467 (anonymised), (9 January 2020) The Hague District Court, ECLI:NL:RBDHA:2020:473.

[138] Parliament and Council (EU) Directive 2018/2001 on the promotion of the use of energy from renewable sources [2018] OJ L328/82 ('RED II'), Art 3(1).

contribution, which they may achieve with the aid of support schemes.[139] The transport sector notably has its own sub-target of a 'minimum share' of 14 per cent consumption of renewable energy that Member States must oblige fuel suppliers to ensure (Article 25(1)).

The sustainability criteria for biofuels, bioliquids and biomass fuels are a requirement for the latter to be taken into account for: (a) the Union's collective target, (b) the renewable energy obligations in the transport sector and (c) eligibility for financial support (Article 29). This offers attractive benefits for energy suppliers. The sustainability criteria include requirements on sourcing and land-use change which are clearly dependent on extraterritorial conduct or circumstances. Specifically, biofuels may not be made from raw material obtained from land which in 2008 had a 'high biodiversity value', namely 'primary' and 'high-biodiverse' forest and other wooded land.[140] Nor may biofuels be produced from raw material obtained from land with high-carbon stock or land that was peatland in 2008.[141]

The sustainability criteria also include increasing GHG savings requirements (Article 29(10)). Installations starting operations from 2021 must achieve at least 70 per cent GHG savings for 'electricity, heating and cooling production from biomass fuels' used, a figure raised to 80 per cent for installations starting operation from 2026.[142] In the transport sector, biofuels and biogas consumed must achieve GHG savings of at least 65 per cent as of January 2021.[143] GHG savings are calculated according to the method in Article 31, together with the more complex values specified in Annexe V. The GHG savings requirements have an exterritorial element because emissions calculations include gases emitted during the whole lifecycle. Thus 'emissions from the production and use of biofuels', include: 'extraction or cultivation of raw materials', 'transport and distribution' and 'emission savings from soil carbon accumulation via improved agricultural management' (Annex V). For imported biofuels, these requirements clearly target activities occurring outside the EU.

Additional extraterritorial elements can be found in the quite controversial limitations on indirect land use change (ILUC) for biofuels produced from food and feed crops. ILUC occurs where the production of biofuels on land originally used for agriculture displaces essential crops onto non-crop land. Displacement is particularly problematic when it occurs on land with high carbon stock. The EU was concerned that the resulting release of CO_2 stored in these areas would 'negate' the intended GHG savings from increased consumption of biofuels.[144]

[139] ibid Arts 3(2) and 4.
[140] ibid Art 29(23). Notably, this is based on the land's status in January 2008, 'whether or not the land continues to have that status'.
[141] ibid Art 29(4) and (5).
[142] ibid Art 29(10)d.
[143] ibid Art 29 (1)(c).
[144] European Commission, 'Renewable Energy – Recast to 2030 (RED II)' (Europa website, 2020) www.ec.europa.eu/jrc/en/jec/renewable-energy-recast-2030-red-ii.

To remedy this issue, RED II introduced a 'freeze' of high ILUC-risk biofuels at 2019 levels from 2021 to 2023, with a 'phase out' to zero by 2030 (Article 26(2)). An exception was, however, carved out for 'low' ILUC biofuels, bioliquids or biomass fuels, although the definition of these categories was only later defined by the Commission in Delegated Regulation 2019/807.[145]

According to Article 3, high ILUC-risk feedstock is to be determined based on the 'average annual expansion of the global production area of the feedstock since 2008' and 'the share of such expansion into land with high-carbon stock'. This effectively banned palm oil-based biofuels as of 2030, leading Indonesia to immediately initiate a complaint at the WTO.[146] In addition to steering other states' policy, the EU measure incentivises foreign producers to switch to other crops, or where possible, to pursue qualification of a 'low ILUC-risk' biofuel.

To qualify as 'low risk' and be exempted from the phase-out, fuels must comply with the aforementioned RED II sustainability and GHG savings criteria (Article 4). Furthermore, however, they must be 'produced from additional feedstock obtained through additionality measures' which must be 'thoroughly documented'. Additionality measures are defined as:

> any *improvement of agricultural practices* leading, in a sustainable manner, to an increase in yields of food and feed crops on land that is already used for the cultivation of food and feed crops; and *any action* that enables the cultivation of food and feed crops on unused land, including abandoned land, for the production of biofuels, bioliquids and biomass fuels.[147]

While this definition alone clearly includes foreign conduct and circumstances, the additionality measures must also meet at least one of three conditions. A first option is that 'they become financially attractive or face no barrier preventing their implementation *only* because the biofuels, bioliquids and biomass fuels produced from the additional feedstock can be counted towards the [EU] targets for renewable energy'.[148] This underscores the very real steering pressure EU unilateral regulation has – and is *intended* to have – on foreign conduct. Additionality measures will alternatively meet the conditions if they 'allow for cultivation of food and feed crops on abandoned land or severely degraded land' or 'are applied by small holders'.[149] As such, those wishing to reap the benefits granted to 'low ILUC-risk' biofuels must jump through considerable hurdles.

[145] RED II (n 138) Art 26(2); Commission (EU) Delegated Regulation (EU) 2019/807 of 13 March 2019 supplementing Parliament and Council (EU) Directive 2018/2001 as regards the determination of high indirect land-use change-risk feedstock for which a significant expansion of the production area into land with high carbon stock is observed and the certification of low indirect land-use change-risk biofuels, bioliquids and biomass fuels [2019] OJ L133/1.

[146] European Union, 'Certain Measures concerning Palm Oil and Oil Palm Crop-Based Biofuels – Request for consultations by Indonesia' (Communication from the Delegation of Indonesia and the European Union 2019) WT/DS593/1, G/L/1348G/TBT/D/52, G/SCM/D128/).

[147] Delegated Regulation 2019/807 (n 145) Art 2(5).

[148] ibid Art 5(1)a(i).

[149] ibid Art 5(1)a(ii), (iii).

5.3.3. *Measures Dependent on Policy Choices of Other States*

As an extension of the previous categories, the third type of extraterritorial element concerns measures whose application is dependent on the *policy choices* of other countries. Such measures 'potentially interfere' with the autonomy of other sovereign states because they seek to influence states' regulatory choices in favour of EU preferences.

One strand of this has been described by Scott and Rajamani as 'contingent unilateralism', where the EU 'may agree to waive the external application of its climate change law if adequate international or third country climate change regulation has been put in place'.[150] A key example is again the Aviation Directive, Article 25a of which makes the measure's application dependent on policy choices of third countries, providing that:

> Where a third country adopts measures for reducing the climate change impact of flights departing from that country which land in the Community, the Commission, after consulting with that third country, and with Member States …, shall consider options available in order to provide for optimal interaction between the Community scheme and that country's measures.

While the provision does not explicitly mention equivalent protection, this is nonetheless reflected in recital 17 of the preamble, which states that:

> The Community and its Member States should continue to be in contact with third parties during the implementation of this Directive and to encourage third countries to take equivalent measures. If a third country adopts measures, *which have an environmental effect at least equivalent to that of this Directive*, to reduce the climate impact of flights to the Community, the Commission should consider the options available in order to provide for optimal interaction between the Community scheme and that country's measures, after consulting with that country. (emphasis added).

As noted by Scott and Rajamani, 'ultimately it is for the EU to determine what is to count as "good enough" when measures to tackle the climate change impact of aviation are agreed or adopted elsewhere'.[151] As will be discussed further in chapter 10, the authors argue that flexibility is needed to ensure that this measure respects the principle of common but differentiated responsibility and respective capabilities.[152]

The EU Timber Regulation also contains an element of contingent unilateralism, as it deems timber 'legally harvested' when covered by the EU Forest Law Enforcement, Governance and Trade (FLEGT) scheme and the Convention on International Trade in Endangered Species of Wild Fauna and Flora (CITES).[153]

[150] Scott and Rajamani (n 121) 469.
[151] Ibid 475.
[152] ibid 482.
[153] Timber Regulation (n 133) Art 3; Regulation 2173/2005 on the establishment of a FLEGT licensing scheme for imports of timber into the European Community [2005] OJ L347/1; Convention on International Trade in Endangered Species of Wild Fauna and Flora (adopted 3 March 1973, entered into force 1 July 1975) 993 UNTS 243 (CITES).

Such legally harvested timber is exempted from the due-diligence standards that otherwise form a condition of entry into the EU market.

A further example is again RED II, where a voluntary benefit is conferred based on states' policy choices. Thus in order for biofuels produced from forest biomass to be counted towards the renewable energy targets, the country of origin must have 'national and sub-national laws' and 'monitoring and enforcement systems in place' to ensure, among other things, forest regeneration and the legality of harvesting operations.[154]

In addition, the land-use, land-use change and forestry (LULUCF) criteria for biofuels from forest biomass also include the requirement that 'the country or regional economic integration organisation of origin of the forest biomass

> (i) is a Party to the Paris Agreement;
> (ii) has submitted a nationally determined contribution (NDC) to the United Nations Framework Convention on Climate Change (UNFCCC), covering emissions and removals from agriculture, forestry and land use which ensures that changes in carbon stock associated with biomass harvest are accounted towards the country's commitment to reduce or limit greenhouse gas emissions as specified in the NDC; or
>
> has national or sub-national laws in place, in accordance with Article 5 of the Paris Agreement, applicable in the area of harvest, to conserve and enhance carbon stocks and sinks, and providing evidence that reported LULUCF-sector emissions do not exceed removals.[155]

This is a powerful example of the EU putting pressure on sovereign policy choices of other states, which in practice may limit their regulatory autonomy, raising tensions with the principle of sovereign equality.

6. CONCLUSION

Unilateral responses to climate change occupy a tenuous position between state obligations and state competences under international law. On the one hand, the multilateral climate change regime departs from a premise of interdependence, impressing upon the international community the need for ambitious emission reduction targets and adaptation efforts. On the other hand, the law of state jurisdiction is more concerned with preserving sovereign equality, traditionally understood in terms of independence. As seen in this chapter, there is a great focus on territorial sovereignty, and measures with 'extraterritorial' effects are treated as 'suspect'.

Looking first at theory, this chapter has analysed the legal debates on the definition of 'extraterritoriality' and its appropriate situation within the legal

[154] RED II (n 138) Art 29(6).
[155] ibid Art 29(7).

analysis. Here, a legally neutral approach to extraterritoriality is supported, as simply referring to that 'beyond the territory' of the regulating state. As jurisdiction is concerned with delineating the regulatory competence *between* states, the analysis of a measure's legality must consider both the acting and the effected states. This book therefore proposes an approach that first assesses whether a measure may potentially 'interfere' with the regulatory autonomy of *other* states. Drawing on legal discourse, the suggested threshold is whether a measure's operation is de facto dependent on foreign conduct or circumstances. Such measures are referred to here as having 'extraterritorial element', signalling that the *acting* state must be able to demonstrate a valid jurisdictional basis.

Turning to practice, this chapter has considered the EU as a self-proclaimed global climate leader. Over time the Union has becoming increasingly explicit about its desire to shape the behaviour of public and private actors abroad using its powerful single market. A first means of doing so is to set market-entry conditions based on conduct or circumstances abroad, as exemplified by the Aviation Directive and the Timber Regulation. A second mechanism identified here is to attach a voluntary benefit to extraterritorial conduct or circumstances. This is illustrated by the sustainability and GHG savings requirements for biofuels under the recast Renewable Energy Directive. Finally, sometimes the EU makes market-entry conditions of benefits dependent on policy choices of other states. From a jurisdictional perspective, such measures are particularly relevant as they directly seek to limit the regulatory autonomy of other states, raising tensions with the *Grundnorm* of sovereign equality.

In exploring the bases and limitations for measures with an extraterritorial element in international law, Part II will now turn to the *lex specialis* regimes. Given that the discussed measures all affect trade in goods and services, the next chapter will first focus on the existence and nature of jurisdictional conditions under the law of the WTO.

Part II

Jurisdictional Bases and Limitations in *Lex Specialis* Regimes

4

Regulating Emissions from Foreign Production Processes under WTO Law

1. INTRODUCTION

PART I HAS examined the unique place of unilateral climate change responses under international law, exploring the tensions arising when a state or supranational organisation seeks to regulate conduct and circumstances beyond its territory. Focusing on the EU, it has identified a number of measures giving rise to such issues of 'extraterritoriality'. Part II now seeks to identify the jurisdictional conditions on these unilateral climate-related measures in the applicable *lex specialis* regimes. Here, the law of the WTO has an essential role to play, imposing a complex web of requirements on unilateral measures regulating products, production methods and the provision of services with a cross-border element. Importantly, WTO law does not pursue free trade alone, but rather seeks to facilitate a predictable, non-discriminatory trading system that allows equal opportunity for economic development.[1] As such, states retain the competence to set fiscal and non-fiscal requirements for imports of goods and cross-border services, as long as they do so even-handedly. States are, however, prohibited from imposing quantitative restrictions on products under the GATT.[2] This will be discussed further below.

Over the past years, climate change has clearly emerged as a trade issue, given its close nexus with the production and consumption of industrialised goods and services. WTO law is concerned with the trade impacts of climate-protection measures, and in particular their means of addressing competitiveness issues and carbon leakage.[3] Within this regime, there has been much debate on how to balance states' regulatory autonomy to protect the environment at their chosen level of protection, against the resulting trade-restrictive effects. An important

[1] P Williams, 'Law and Lawyers in the Multilateral Trading System: Back to the Future' in G Marceau (ed), *A History of Law and Lawyers in the GTT/WTO* (Cambridge, Cambridge University Press, 2015) 85.

[2] General Agreement on Tariffs and Trade 1994 (adopted 15 April 1994, entered into force 1 January 1995) 1867 UNTS 154 (GATT) Art XI.

[3] G Marceau, 'The Interface Between the Trade Rules and Climate Change Actions' in Park DY (ed), *Legal Issues on Climate Change and International Trade Law* (New York, Springer 2016) 4.

concern is that states will use environmental product and production requirements as a means of protecting domestic industry.[4] With this trade-oriented focus, WTO law does not directly address the question of state jurisdiction, and the relevant Agreements contain no explicit territorial limits.[5] It is therefore necessary to distil the jurisdictional limitations from the applicable rules.

In exploring the trade law conditions, this chapter will concentrate on the GATT, the Technical Barriers to Trade (TBT) Agreement and the General Agreement on Trade in Services (GATS).[6] The EU measures discussed in chapter 3 all pertain, either directly or indirectly, to the sale of products, and as such in principle fall under the GATT.[7] Climate-related product and production process requirements may also fall under the TBT Agreement, which is a *lex specialis* in relation to the GATT.[8] There is, however, considerable discussion on whether all process-based measures can be considered to be 'technical regulations' so as to fall within the scope of the TBT Agreement, an issue left undecided in the 2014 *EC–Seals* case.[9] In so far as the EU measures may affect trade in services, they may also fall within the scope of the GATS.[10] The applicability of the national treatment requirement is, however, dependent on whether a WTO member has included the service in its schedule of commitments.[11] Two key measures affecting trade in services are the EU Aviation Directive, and the monitoring, reporting and verification scheme (MRV) for international maritime transport.[12]

[4] ibid.

[5] H Horn and P Mavroidis, 'The Permissible Reach of National Environmental Policies' (2008) 42 *Journal of World Trade* 1107, 1113–14, referring to 'an implicit notion of jurisdiction' in the GATT. As a notable exception, the Agreement on the Application of Sanitary and Phytosanitary Measures (adopted 15 April 1994, entered into force 1 January 1995) 1867 UNTS 493 ('SPS Agreement') does contain express territorial limits in the types of SPS measures covered.

[6] GATT (n 2); General Agreement on Trade in Services (adopted 15 April 1994, entered into force 1 January 1995) 1869 UNTS 183 (GATS); Agreement on Technical Barriers to Trade (adopted 15 April 1994, entered into force 1 January 1995) 1868 UNTS 120 ('TBT Agreement').

[7] See further section 3.1.1.

[8] *European Communities – Measures Affecting Asbestos and Asbestos-Containing Products*, Panel Report (18 September 2000) WT/DS135/R [8.16]; *European Communities – Regime for the Importation, Sale and Distribution of Bananas*, Appellate Body Report (9 September 1997) WT/DS27/AB/R (*EC–Bananas III (AB)*) [204].

[9] *European Communities – Measures Prohibiting the Importation and Marketing of Seal Products*, Appellate Body Report (18 June 2014) WT/DS401/AB/R (*EC–Seals*). See further G Marceau, 'A Comment on the Appellate Body Report in EC–Seal Products in the Context of the Trade and Environment Debate' (2014) 23 *Review of European Comparative & International Environmental Law* 318.

[10] GATS (n 6).

[11] ibid Art XVII.

[12] Parliament and Council (EC) Directive 2008/101 of 19 November 2008 amending Directive 2003/87/EC so as to include aviation activities in the scheme for greenhouse gas emission allowance trading within the Community [2008] OJ L8/3 ('Aviation Directive'); Parliament and Council (EU) Regulation 2015/757 of 29 April 2015 on the monitoring, reporting and verification of carbon dioxide emissions from maritime transport, and amending Directive 2009/16/EC [2015] OJ L123/55 ('EU Maritime MRV').

Applying a jurisdictional lens, this chapter will not examine all of the applicable WTO rules in a detailed compatibility assessment. Rather, it focuses on how WTO law regulates the 'extraterritorial element' of climate-protection measures more generally. This is, of course, a highly contextual question because much depends on the way in which the environmental condition is woven into a measure. Section 2 starts by coupling the conceptual framework set out in chapter 3 with the terminology used in WTO law.[13] Section 3 then considers the non-discrimination requirements contained in the 'most favoured nation' and 'national treatment' provisions of the relevant Agreements. As will be seen, according to the current case law, measures targeting extraterritorial production processes that leave no physical trace in the end product are likely to constitute discrimination. They will therefore require justification under the general exemptions provisions. Here there is considerable discussion as to the existence of an implied jurisdictional limitation, particularly under Article XX GATT. This issue is of particular relevance to the present study and will be discussed further in section 4.

2. LOCATING THE 'EXTRATERRITORIAL ELEMENT' IN A TRADE LAW CONTEXT: FOREIGN PRODUCTION PROCESS REQUIREMENTS

As discussed in Chapter 3, a measure is considered to have a relevant 'extraterritorial element' when its application is de facto dependent on conduct or circumstances abroad. In trade law discourse, a category of measures falling squarely within this definition are measures relating to process or production methods (PPMs).[14] When applied to imports, PPMs contain an extraterritorial element as they direct foreign producers to comply with set conduct requirements prior to the arrival of a good in the territory of the regulating state.[15] Notably, this can also have an effect on the provision of services, transport being of particular relevance here. As the conceptualisation and permissibility of PPMs is a topic of considerable discussion, it is helpful to briefly set out

[13] This issue has been discussed more comprehensively in an article based on the present doctoral research, NL Dobson, 'The EU's Conditioning of the "Extraterritorial" Carbon Footprint: A Call for an Integrated Approach in Trade Law Discourse' (2018) 27 *Review of European, Comparative & International Environmental Law* 75.

[14] See further N Bernasconi-Osterwalder et al, *Environment and Trade: A Guide to WTO Jurisprudence* (London, Earthscan, 2006) 238.

[15] See M Marceau and JP Trachtman, 'The Technical Barriers to Trade Agreement, the Sanitary and Phytosanitary Measures Agreement, and the General Agreement on Tariffs and Trade: A Map of the World Trade Organization Law of Domestic Regulation of Goods' (2002) 36 *Journal of World Trade* 811, 858: 'the product-process distinction serves as a clear and simple rule on territorial–extraterritorial regulatory distinctions in the main GATT market access rules: production processes occur in the exporting Member. Policies effected in the other Members are not under the jurisdiction of the importing Member'. See further also L Ankersmit, *Green Trade and Fair Trade in and with the EU: Process-Based Measures within the EU Legal Order* (Cambridge, Cambridge University Press, 2017) 8.

the key concepts and consider their manifestation in different climate change instruments.

Measures regulating PPMs set conditions on the *way* in which products are produced, and as such are directly contingent on specific extraterritorial conduct or circumstances. Such PPM measures are generally distinguished from product requirements, which set conditions on the physical 'characteristics' of products placed on a market, including imports. In *EC–Asbestos*, the WTO Appellate Body (AB) found that such characteristics included the 'objectively definable "features", "qualities", "attributes", or other "distinguishing mark" of a product'.[16] These are typically found in the first 'type' of extraterritorial element discussed in the previous chapter, namely as a binding condition on market entry. A key example is the EU Ecodesign Directive which, together with the implementing regulations, lays out a framework for a host of energy-efficiency requirements for 'energy-related products'.[17] 'Energy-related products' are defined quite broadly as 'any good that has an impact on energy consumption during use which is placed on the market and/or put into service' including 'individual parts for end-users and of which the environmental performance can be assessed independently'.[18] Product requirements are not controversial under WTO law, as long as they are applied even-handedly. From a jurisdictional perspective, they do indirectly influence or 'steer' the prior conduct of foreign producers to manufacture products with certain characteristics. Whether or not product requirements contain an 'extraterritorial element' will depend on the extent to which they leave foreign producers with discretion on *how* they meet the product requirements. If a product requirement can only be met through specific prior conduct, then the measure's operation is still de facto dependent on such foreign conduct (eg made from materials that in practice can only be acquired according to a specific sourcing or production method). This chapter will focus on PPMs that more directly target the conduct itself.

Trade law discourse generally draws a distinction between PPM requirements that leave a physical trace in the end product ('incorporated' or 'product-related' PPMs) and those that leave no physical trace in the end product ('unincorporated' or 'non-product-related' PPMs).[19] The Conceptual Guidelines of the OECD

[16] *European Communities – Measures Affecting Asbestos and Asbestos-Containing Products*, Appellate Body Report (12 March 2001) WT/DS135/AB/R [169–175] (*EC–Asbestos (AB)*) [67]. See also the AB in *EC–Seals* (n 9) [5.11] confirming *EC–Asbestos* in its consideration of Annex 1.1 of the TBT Agreement.

[17] See Parliament and Council (EC) Directive 2009/125 of 21 October 2009 establishing a framework for the setting of ecodesign requirements for energy-related products [2009] OJ L285/10 ('Ecodesign Directive') Arts 1, 2(1), and Annex 1 – Method for Setting Generic Ecodesign Requirements.

[18] ibid Art 2(1).

[19] See further D Regan, 'How to Think about PPMs (and Climate Change)' in T Cottier, O Nartova and SZ Bigdeli (eds), *International Trade Regulation and the Mitigation of Climate Change: World Trade Forum* (Cambridge, Cambridge University Press 2009) 97; H Horn and P Mavroidis, 'To B(TA) or Not to B(TA)? On the Legality and Desirability of Border Tax Adjustments from a Trade Perspective' (2011) 34 *World Economy* 1911; R Howse and D Regan, 'The Product/Process Distinction – An Illusory Basis for Disciplining "Unilateralism" in Trade Policy' (2000) 11

provide helpful clarification, noting that incorporated PPM measures bear upon the consumption externalities of a product. Such externalities manifest themselves when the goods are consumed and disposed of during the 'downstream' phases of the lifecycle.[20] One can think, for example, of the Ecodesign requirement that manufacturers must supply certain information 'which may influence the way the product is handled, used or recycled by parties other than the manufacturer'.[21] Incorporated PPM measures need not be problematic under WTO law, as the regime recognises states' competence to regulate territorial consumption externalities, even where this has trade-restrictive effects.[22]

The second category of measures is more controversial, namely 'unincorporated' or 'non-product-related' production process measures (npr-PPMs). These measures set requirements for the 'upstream' production process that are not visible in the physical characteristics of the end product.[23] Arguably, however, this definition renders the phrase 'non-product-related' something of a misnomer, as PPMs are technically 'related' to a product, even if this is not visible in its *physical* characteristics. For the purposes of the present discussion, it is therefore preferable to refer to 'incorporated' or 'unincorporated' PPMs.[24]

PPM requirements provide particularly effective means of protecting common environmental concerns beyond the territory of the legislating state.[25] As discussed, this has become an increasingly explicit policy tool of the EU, which under the Green Deal proposed a controversial border carbon adjustment on imports. Key trading partners, including the Russian Federation, China and the United States, expressed concern at the WTO Council for Trade in goods, seeking increased transparency and assurances that this would be consistent with WTO non-discrimination rules.[26]

Notably, the carbon footprint includes not only CO_2, but also other GHGs emitted during the entire lifecycle of a product or service, and also covers

European Journal of International Law 249; B Jansen and M Lugard, 'Some Considerations on Trade Barriers Erected for Non-Economic Reasons and WTO Obligations' (1999) 2 *Journal of International Economic Law* 530.

[20] 'Processes and Production Methods (PPMs): Conceptual Framework and Considerations on Use of PPM-Based Trade Measures' (Organisation for Economic Co-operation and Development 1997) OCDE/GD (97)137 ('Conceptual Framework PPMs') 10.

[21] ibid; Ecodesign Directive (n 17) Annex 1, Part 2.

[22] This is evident in the case law regarding Art XX GATT discussed in section 4, although the AB noted that any discriminatory effects of the measure must be 'explained by a rationale that bears … [a] relationship to the objective of a measure'. *Brazil – Measures Affecting Imports of Retreaded Tyres*, Appellate Body Report (17 December 2007) WT/DS332/AB/R (*Brazil – Retreaded Tyres*) [232].

[23] See further 'Conceptual Framework PPMs' (n 20) 10; B Cooreman, 'Addressing Global Environmental Concerns through Trade: Extraterritoriality under WTO Law from a Comparative Perspective' (PhD dissertation, Leiden University 2016) 34.

[24] This is particularly true given the threshold discussed on 'related' PPMs under the TBT Agreement, which is not necessarily dependent on physical characteristics.

[25] Marceau (n 9) 326.

[26] 'Goods Council Considers EU Plans for Carbon Taxes on Certain Imports' (WTO, 11 June 2020) www.wto.org/english/news_e/news20_e/good_11jun20_e.htm.

emissions from land-use change.[27] This last-mentioned criterion is relevant for the EU's deforestation measures, as well as the sourcing requirements for biofuels under the Fuel Quality and Renewable Energy Directives.[28] In addition to explicit conditions on foreign conduct, PPM requirements may be embedded in other measures such as an import ban on or a tax exemption for certain products.[29] A classic example here is the *US–Shrimp* case, concerning a US import ban on tuna from countries it had listed as failing to use US-mandated dolphin-friendly fishing nets.[30]

In terms of design, under WTO law, 'product-based' distinctions and 'country-based' or 'origin-based' distinctions are treated differently. Product-based distinctions pertain to measures which grant differential treatment based on the characteristics or production process of a product or service.[31] Country- or origin-based distinctions base their application on the country of origin, raising issues of de jure discrimination.[32] This was, for example, the case for the import ban in *US–Shrimp*, which, in practice at least, was based on country of origin.[33] The overarching requirement of non-discrimination forms the central condition on WTO members' regulatory competence in relation to climate-protective measures, and will now be considered in more detail.

3. NON-DISCRIMINATION AND THE FOREIGN CARBON FOOTPRINT: A DE FACTO LIMITATION

The non-discrimination principle forms one of the foundations of WTO law, 'the essence' of which, according to the AB in *EC–Bananas III*, 'is that like

[27] See eg ISO, 'Environmental Management – Lifecycle Assessment: Principles and Framework' (2006) ISO 141040 ('2006 ISO Lifecycle Assessment Principles'). While land-use change is not explicitly mentioned in the ISO Framework it is consistent with other ISO guidelines, including: 'Carbon Footprint of Products – Requirements and Guidelines for Quantification and Communication' (2013) ISO/TS 14067; and the 2001 Greenhouse Gas Protocol of the World Resources Institute and World Business Council for Sustainable Development; see www.wri.org/sites/default/files/ pdf/ghg_protocol_2001.pdf.

[28] Directive (EU) 2018/2001 of the European Parliament and of the Council of 11 December 2018 on the promotion of the use of energy from renewable sources [2018] OJ L328/82 (RED) Art 7b; Council and Parliament (EC) Directive 98/70 relating to the quality of petrol and diesel fuels and amending Council Directive 93/12/EEC [1998] OJ L350/58 ('Fuel Quality Directive') Art 17.

[29] For a helpful taxonomy of PPM measures, see J Potts, 'The Legality of PPMs under the GATT: Challenges and Opportunities for Sustainable Trade Policy' (International Institute for Sustainable Development 2008) 8.

[30] This gave rise to the well-known 'Tuna/Dolphin' cases, discussed later in this chapter: *United States – Restrictions on Import of Tuna* (1991) BISD 39S/155 (*US–Tuna I*) and *United States – Restrictions on Imports of Tuna* (1994) DS29/R (*US–Tuna II*).

[31] See further eg Horn and Mavroidis (n 5) 62; Howes and Regan (n 19) 102.

[32] Horn and Mavroidis (n 5) 61.

[33] WTO, *United States – Import Prohibition of Certain Shrimp and Shrimp Products*, Appellate Body Report (6 November 1998) WT/DS58/AB/R (*US–Shrimp*).

products should be treated equally'.[34] This requirement finds expression in two key norms, namely through the 'most-favoured nation' (MFN) and 'national treatment' (NT) principles. According to the NT principle, imports must be granted 'treatment no less favourable' than 'like' domestic products.[35] This requirement can be found in Article III GATT, Article 2.1 of the TBT Agreement and Article XVII GATS. The MFN principle extends this benefit to all other WTO members, requiring that all products be granted the 'same advantage', irrespective of their origin.[36] This finds expression in Article I GATT, Article 2.1 of the TBT Agreement and Article II GATS. Importantly, the precise application of these principles varies per provision, with the AB having introduced complex and technical interpretative nuances. There also remains considerable discussion as to which provisions apply to the different types of trade measures, particularly in relation to unincorporated PPMs. The following section therefore briefly considers the applicability of these provisions (section 3.1), before proceeding to the substance of the non-discrimination requirement (section 3.2).

3.1. The Non-discrimination Requirement under the WTO Agreements

In order to sketch out the jurisdictional conditions under WTO law, the first step is to identify which requirements apply to the different kinds of measures. This is no simple task, as considerable uncertainty remains regarding the precise delineation of the different provisions. The following section will briefly outline the contours of these debates, seeking to provide a working framework for the remaining analysis.

3.1.1. Measures Relating to Products under the GATT

The GATT sets a variety of limitations on measures relating to products. To start with, Article XI proscribes

> prohibitions or restrictions other than duties, taxes or other charges, whether made effective through quotas, import or export licences or other measures … on the exportation or sale for export of any product destined for the territory of any other contracting party.

[34] *EC–Bananas III (AB)* (n 8) [190]. See further on the role of this norm, J Weiler, 'Law, Culture, and Values in the WTO – Gazing into the Crystal Ball' in D Bethlehem et al (eds), *The Oxford Handbook of International Trade Law* (Oxford, Oxford University Press, 2009) 758.

[35] Notably, fiscal measures under Art III:2 GATT may not charge internal taxes on 'like' imported goods, 'in excess of' those applied to domestic products. Products in a 'directly competitive or substitutable' relationship may not be taxed 'dissimilarly' (see the GATT Note *Ad* III).

[36] This includes de jure and de facto discrimination; see *Canada – Certain Measures Affecting the Automotive Industry*, Appellate Body Report (31 May 2000) WT/DS139/AB/R, WT/DS142/AB/R (*Canada-Autos (AB)*), [78].

This is essentially a prohibition on non-tariff barriers for imports. Members remain, however, competent to set certain requirements on product characteristics or production processes as long as they are applied uniformly.

This brings us to Article III GATT on NT.[37] Article III:2 regulates 'internal taxes or other internal charges of any kind' (fiscal measures) 'applied directly or indirectly to like domestic products'. Excise tax benefits granted under EU Member State support schemes to biofuels and bioliquids that have met the revised Renewable Energy Directive (RED II) sustainability criteria would fall under Article III:2 GATT.[38] Article III:4 covers 'all laws, regulations and requirements' affecting the 'internal sale, offering for sale, purchase, transportation, distribution or use of a product' (non-fiscal measures). Key examples in EU policy include the Ecodesign requirements for energy-related products, and the due-diligence requirements for imported timber under the Timber Regulation.[39] Importantly, in *US–Tobacco* the Panel also found that financial penalty provisions for failing to comply with domestic laws should not be assessed as separate fiscal requirements, where the underlying measure is an 'internal regulation' under Article III:4.[40] For the EU, this means that its climate regulations do not qualify as fiscal measures simply because they contain financial compliance mechanisms.[41]

While Article III is in principle permissive of even-handed internal measures, the story is different for charges imposed at the border, which fall under Article II GATT and may not exceed states' respective tariff schedules (Article II:1(b)). In *China–Autos*, the AB clarified the distinction between 'internal measures' (*in casu* a tax) and 'border measures', finding that for a measure to qualify as the former, the obligation to pay must 'accrue due to an internal event, such as the distribution, sale, use or transportation of the imported product', where the national characterisation or the legislative intent are not dispositive.[42]

[37] The NT provision covers 'internal taxes and other internal charges, and laws, regulations and requirements' (Art III:1 GATT) applied to 'products of the territory of any contracting party imported into the territory of any other contracting party'.

[38] Parliament and Council (EU) Directive 2018/2001 on the promotion of the use of energy from renewable sources [2018] OJ L328/82 (RED II) Art 29(1).

[39] See Ecodesign Directive (n 17), Annex I; Parliament and Council (EU) Regulation 995/2010 laying down the obligations of operators who place timber and timber products on the market [2010] OJ L295/23 ('Timber Regulation') Arts 4, 6.

[40] *United States – Measures Affecting the Importation, Internal Sale and Use of Tobacco*, Panel Report (4 October 1994) DS44/R (*US–Tobacco*) [80].

[41] The distinction between fiscal and non-fiscal measures is not always clear cut, a relevant example being the EU ETS. Pauwelyn considered that the ETS could in fact be a border tax adjustment under Art II:2a GATT, an 'internal tax' under Art III:2 tax or an internal regulation under Art III:4 on internal regulations. See J Pauwelyn, 'Carbon Leakage Measures and Border Tax Adjustments under WTO Law' in D Prévost and G van Calster (eds), *Research Handbook on Environment, Health and the WTO* (Cheltenham, Edward Elgar, 2012) 37.

[42] *China – Measures Affecting Imports of Automobile Parts*, Appellate Body Report (12 January 2009) WT/DS339,340,342/AB/R (*China–Autos*) [139], [162].

Notably, according to the Note *ad* Article III, an internal measure (either fiscal or non-fiscal)

> which applies to an imported product and to the like domestic product and is collected or enforced in the case of the imported product at the time or point of importation, is nevertheless to be regarded as an internal tax or other internal charge, or a law, regulation or requirement ... and is accordingly subject to the provisions of Article III.[43]

In addition to the non-discrimination requirement of Article III, PPM measures must also comply with the MFN requirement in Article I:1 GATT, which applies to both internal measures and border measures. In terms of scope, Article I GATT concerns 'any advantage, favour, privilege or immunity' 'granted by any party to any product', and is therefore broader than Article III.[44] In *EC–Bananas III (Guatemala and Honduras)* the Panel found that an 'advantage' creates 'more favourable competitive opportunities' or 'affects the competitive relationship' between products of different origins.[45] Hence, PPM measures (both incorporated and unincorporated), which generate such an advantage, must accord it 'immediately and unconditionally' to like products originating from or destined for all origins. This will be discussed further in section 3.2.

When determining the applicability of these provisions to different types of measures, there are two discussions of particular relevance. The first is whether unincorporated PPMs fall under Article III as measures 'affecting the internal sale, offering for sale, purchase, transportation, distribution or use' of products. This discussion stems from the (unadopted) finding of the Panel in *US–Tuna I*, concerning a US import ban on tuna from states which it had listed as failing to comply with its requirements on the use of dolphin-safe purse seine nets to catch tuna.[46] There the Panel held that the US measure, as an unincorporated PPM, did not fall under Article III:4 GATT, which only applies to 'measures affecting products as such'.[47] This finding has received much attention in the literature, and has been heavily criticised as an incorrect reading of the text of Article III:4.[48] This critique appears supported by other case law where

[43] Notably, in *India – Measures Affecting the Automotive Sector*, Panel Report (21 December 2001) WT/DS146/R; WT/DS175/R, the Panel found that different parts of the same measure could fall under Arts III and XI GATT depending on whether the competitive opportunities for entering the market (Art XI) or for those on the market (Art III) are affected by a measure [7.224].

[44] Explicit reference is made to 'all matters referred to in paragraphs 2 and 4 of article III' in Art I:1 GATT. See further *Canada–Autos (AB)* (n 36) [79].

[45] WTO, *European Communities – Regime for the Importation, Sale and Distribution of Bananas*, Panel Report (25 September 1997) WT/DS27/R/GTM [7.239].

[46] Imports of tuna from those countries as well as 'intermediaries' were prohibited according to the US Marine Mammal Protection Act *US–Tuna I* (n 30) [2.7].

[47] ibid [5.11].

[48] Howse and Regan (n 19) 253. See also Conrad, noting that: 'Not only the verb "to affect", but the remainder of the sentence is an indication for an indirect rather than direct relationship between the aspect affected by the measure and the product. Measures embraced by both paragraphs may affect any of several listed stages of the product life cycle rather than the product in terms of physical properties.' CR Conrad, *Processes and Production Methods (PPMs) in WTO Law: Interfacing Trade*

Article III GATT has been found to apply to process-based measures, including, for example, the older *Italian Discrimination Against Imported Agricultural Machinery* and WTO, *United States – Tax Treatment for 'Foreign Sales Corporation' (Recourse to Article 21.5 EC)* (2002).[49]

The second debate pertains to whether charges on unincorporated carbon emissions may be adjusted at the border in line with Articles III:2 and II:2(a) GATT, or whether they then risk violating Article II:1(b) limiting charges to those in tariff schedules.[50] This is of particular relevance for the EU's proposed carbon border adjustment under the Green Deal. At the time of writing, the EU is considering various instruments, including a carbon tax on selected imported and domestic products and extending its ETS to imports'.[51] In line with the Note *Ad* III, charges on a good's equivalent carbon tax liability would constitute an internal measure because they are applied at the border as an 'adjustment' to equal internal taxes.[52] The question is then whether they 'apply directly or indirectly to products' in the sense of Article III:2.[53] In the *US–Superfund* dispute, a GATT Panel came close to answering this question, finding a US measure imposing a domestic tax on products that had used certain chemicals, including imports, to be permissible.[54] There, the chemicals constituted 'materials in the manufacture or production' of the imported product in the sense of Article II:2(a).[55]

and Social Goals (Cambridge, Cambridge University Press, 2011) 150. See further S Charnovitz, 'The Law of Environmental PPMs in the WTO: Debunking the Myth of Illegality' (2002) 27 *Yale Journal of International Law* 59; Potts (n 29); L Ankersmit, J Lawrence and G Davies, 'Diverging EU and WTO Perspectives on Extraterritorial Process Regulation' (2012) 21 *Minnesota Journal of International Law online* 14. For criticism of this approach to Art III GATT, see JH Jackson, 'Comments on Shrimp/Turtle and the Product/Process Distinction' (2000) 11 *European Journal of International Law* 303.

[49] *Italian Discrimination Against Imported Agricultural Machinery* (1958) GATT BISD 7S/60, [12]: 'The selection of the word "affecting" [implies] … that the drafters of the Article intended to cover in paragraph 4 not only the laws and regulations which directly governed the conditions of sale or purchase but also any laws or regulations which might adversely modify the conditions of competition between the domestic and imported products on the internal market'. *United States – Tax Treatment for 'Foreign Sales Corporation' (Recourse to Article 21.5 of the DSU by the European Communities)*, Appellate Body Report (29 January 2002) WT/DS108/AB/RW. See also *United States – Measures Affecting Alcoholic and Malt Beverages* (1992) BISD 39S/206 (*US–Malt Beverages*).

[50] *India – Additional and Extra-Additional Duties on Imports from the United States*, Appellate Body Report (20 October 2008) WT/DS360/AB/R [214]: 'Art II:2(a), subject to the conditions stated therein exempts a charge from the coverage of Art II:1(b)'. According to Horn and (n 19) 1914, this confirms that Art II does not restrict the scope of Art III GATT. See also MA Mehling et al, 'Designing Border Carbon Adjustments for Enhanced Climate Action' (2019) 113 *American Journal of International Law* 433, 442.

[51] Commission (EU) 'Inception Impact Assessment', Directorate-General for Taxation and Customs Union (4 March 2020) COM Ares(2020)1350037, 1.

[52] E Vranes, 'Carbon Taxes, PPMs and the GATT' in P Delimatsis (ed), *Research Handbook on Climate Change and Trade Law* (Cheltenham, Edward Elgar, 2016) 83.

[53] ibid.

[54] *United States – Taxes on Petroleum and Certain Imported Substances* (1987) GATT BISD 34S/136 (*US–Superfund*) [2.5], [5.2.4].

[55] ibid [2.5].

However, the Panel did not clarify whether these materials need to be incorporated in the end product.[56]

As noted by Mehling et al, 'the jury is still out' on whether Article II:2(a) includes taxes on unincorporated carbon emissions.[57] More generally, Vranes points to the findings of the Panels in *Argentina – Hides and Leather* and *Mexico Soft Drinks* as possible support for the inclusion of unincorporated PPMs in Article III:2.[58] There, the Panel found that '[t]axes *directly* imposed on finished products can *indirectly* affect the conditions of competition between imported and like domestic inputs and therefore come within the scope of Article III:2, first sentence'.[59] Also persuasive is the argument that the Agreement on Subsidies and Countervailing Measures (SCM) does allow border tax adjustments for *exports* based on product inputs, including energy used in production.[60] The SCM Agreement provides relevant contextual support when interpreting Article III:2 because it concerns the symmetric issue of tax adjustments for exports.[61] Vranes argues that the two should be interpreted in the same way so as to enable the coherent application of the destination principle, under which taxes are levied at the place where a commodity is consumed.[62] For the present purposes, it is therefore considered possible that charges on unincorporated carbon equivalent to an internal tax may be adjusted at the border.

To conclude this section, it is worth noting the warning of Howse and Regan not to 'fall into the trap' of 'treating Article III as if its function were to authorize measures which would otherwise be illegal'.[63] There is no general right of access for foreign goods, and Article III merely conditions state competence to set discriminatory entry requirements. Of course, there is a clear benefit in being found to fall within the scope of Article III, as even-handed measures need not constitute a prima facie violation, saving a state from having to prove compliance with the more stringent requirements of Article XX GATT.

[56] See further P Demaret and R Stewardson, 'Border Tax Adjustments under GATT and EC Law and General Implications for Environmental Taxes' (1994) 28 *Journal of World Trade* 5, 59. F Biermann and R Brohm, 'Implementing the Kyoto Protocol Without the United States: The Strategic Role of Energy Tax Adjustments at the Border' (2005) 4 *Climate Policy* 289, 295.

[57] Mehling et (n 50) 459. See further F Deane, *Emissions Trading and WTO Law: A Global Analysis* (Cheltenham, Edward Elgar, 2015) 178, 183; Pauwelyn (n 41) 128.

[58] Vranes (n 52) 77, 84. *Argentina – Measures Affecting the Export of Bovine Hides and the Import of Finished Leather*, Panel Report (16 February 2001) WT/DS155/R (*Argentina Hides and Leather*) [11.183]; WTO, *Mexico – Tax Measures on Soft Drinks and Other Beverages – Report of the Panel* (24 March 2006) WT/DS308/R (*Mexico Soft Drinks*) [8.44].

[59] *Mexico Soft Drinks* (n 58) [8.44] (references omitted).

[60] Vranes (n 52) 85; Deane (n 57) 183.

[61] Vranes (n 52) 85.

[62] ibid.

[63] Howse and Regan (n 19) 256–57. See further Charnovitz (n 48) 81, discussing the AB in WTO, *Japan – Taxes on Alcoholic Beverages*, Appellate Body Report (4 October 1996) WT/DS8/AB/R (*Japan–Alcoholic Beverages II (AB)*), [102]: 'The broad purpose of Article III of avoiding protectionism must be remembered when considering the relationship between Article III and other provisions of the WTO Agreement.'

3.1.2. *Technical Regulations under the TBT Agreement*

Import requirements may also qualify as 'technical regulations' under the TBT Agreement, which is a more specific, *lex specialis* agreement that must be considered before the GATT.[64] This is important as the TBT Agreement is in some ways more stringent than the GATT, requiring that a measure be no more trade restrictive than necessary to fulfil a legitimate objective at a preliminary phase, even in the absence of discrimination.[65] Where a measure is found to comply with the TBT Agreement, it must also meet the requirements of the GATT which may apply simultaneously (*EC–Asbestos*).[66] Annex 1.1 defines a 'technical regulation' as a:

> Document which lays down product characteristics *or their related* processes and production methods, including the applicable administrative provisions, with which compliance is mandatory. It may also include or deal exclusively with terminology, symbols, packaging, marking or labelling requirements as they apply to a product, process or production method.[67]

These must be distinguished from non-mandatory 'standards' as defined in Annex 1.2 of the TBT Agreement.[68] Whether a measure constitutes a 'technical regulation' will depend on its 'integral and essential' aspects, where a measure must be assessed as a whole.[69]

An important issue of considerable discussion is whether unincorporated PPMs are 'related to' product characteristics so as to fall within the scope of the TBT Agreement.[70] This was a matter on which the negotiators did not appear to agree.[71] The AB came to answering this question in the *EC–Seals* case,

[64] *European Communities – Measures Affecting Asbestos and Asbestos-Containing Products –* Report of the Panel (5 April 2001) WT/DS135/R and Add.1 (*EC–Asbestos (Panel)*) [8.16]; *EC–Bananas III (AB)* (n 8) [204].

[65] Art 2.1 and 2.2 TBT Agreement. See further S Hartmann, 'Comparing the National Treatment Obligations of the GATT and the TBT: Lessons Learned from the EC-Seal Products Dispute' (2014) 40 *North Carolina Journal of International Law and Commercial Regulation* 629, 638.

[66] *EC–Asbestos (AB)* (n 16) [80]. See further MJ Trebilcock and R Howse, *The Regulation of International Trade*, 3rd edn (Abingdon, Routledge, 2005) 309.

[67] Annex 1.1 TBT Agreement (emphasis added). See further, *European Communities – Trade Description of Sardines*, Appellate Body Report (23 October 2002) WT/DS231/AB/R (*EC–Sardines*) 176.

[68] The TBT Agreement also covers 'conformity assessments', defined as 'any procedure used, directly or indirectly, to determine that the relevant requirements in technical regulations or standards are fulfilled' (Annex 1.3).

[69] *EC–Seals* (n 9) [5.18]; *EC–Asbestos (AB)* (n 18) [72].

[70] See further eg Cooreman (n 23) 58; Conrad (n 48) 377; Hartmann (n 66) 644; LDO Silveira and T Obersteiner, 'The Scope of the TBT Agreement in Light of Recent WTO Case Law' (2013) 8 *Global Trade and Customs J* 112; Marceau and Trachtman (n 15) 861. Notably, the definition of standards in Annex I.2 TBT refers to products or related characteristics, whereas Annex 1.1 includes the possessive, products or their related characteristics which may arguably make a difference for unincorporated PPMs.

[71] See Committee on Technical Barriers to Trade, 'Negotiating History of the Coverage of the Agreements with Regards to Labelling Requirements, Voluntary Standards and Processes and Production Methods Unrelated to Product Characteristics', Note by the Secretariat (29 August 1995)

concerning the EU measures prohibiting, with limited exemptions, the import and sale of seals and seal products.[72] In interpreting Annex 1.1, the AB first defined product 'characteristics' as including 'objectively definable "features", "qualities", "attributes", or other "distinguishing mark" of a product', which may 'relate *inter alia*, to "a product's composition, size, shape, colour, texture, hardness, tensile strength, flammability, conductivity, density, or viscosity"'.[73] In addition to features and qualities intrinsic to the product itself, 'related characteristics' are also included, such as the means of identification, the presentation and the appearance of a product.[74] 'In order to determine whether a measure lays down related PPMs, the AB found that a panel 'will have to examine whether the processes and production methods prescribed by the measure have a *sufficient nexus* to the characteristics of a product in order to be considered related to those characteristics'.[75]

What exactly constitutes such a 'sufficient nexus' was, however, left unanswered by the AB. Marceau convincingly argues that if the words 'relating to' were interpreted to mean 'physically affecting' – the defining characteristic of incorporated PPMs – there would be little point in distinguishing between such 'product-related' PPMs and the product characteristics themselves.[76] Rather, according to Marceau, the required examination of whether the PPM in question is 'related', 'connected' or has a sufficient 'nexus' with a product 'seems to open the door for a broader meaning of PR PPM than has been understood in the literature thus far'.[77] Pauwelyn also supports this conclusion, noting that 'nothing in the text of the definition of "technical regulation" requires that product characteristics or their related process or production methods must be intrinsic or physically incorporated in the end product'.[78] Given the present uncertainty, this chapter will consider the role of the TBT Agreement in setting conditions on both incorporated and unincorporated PPMs.

G/TBT/W/11, 131. Notably, the absence of the words 'in relation to' in the second sentence arguably implies that labelling requirements in respect of unincorporated PPMs are covered by the TBT Agreement. This was not contested in the cases *US–COOL* (2012) and *US–Tuna (Mexico) II* (2012), which both concerned labelling requirements for unincorporated PPMs, and further appears supported in the 2014 *EC–Seals* Case. See *US – Certain Country of Origin Labelling (COOL) Requirements*, Appellate Body Report (23 July 2012) WT/DS384/AB/R, WT/DS386/AB/R (*US-COOL*); *United States – Measures Concerning the Importation, Marketing and Sale of Tuna and Tuna Products*, Appellate Body Report (13 June 2012) WT/DS381/AB/R (*US–Tuna II (Mexico)*); *EC–Seals* (n 9) [5.14].

[72] *EC–Seals* (n 9).

[73] *EC–Seals* (n 9) [5.11].

[74] *EC–Asbestos (AB)* (n 16) [67].

[75] *EC–Seals* (n 9) [5.12] (emphasis added).

[76] Marceau (n 9) 327.

[77] ibid. See for a more detailed analysis of the applicability of the TBT Agreement to the EU Aviation Directive (n 12), see SR Sánchez-Tabernero, 'For Whom the Bell Tolls: The EU ETS in Aviation under the TBT Agreement' (2015) 49 *Journal of World Trade* 781.

[78] Pauwelyn (n 41) 33.

3.1.3. Measures Affecting Trade in Services under the GATS

While primarily aimed at regulating products, PPM requirements may well affect trade in services, bringing them within the purview of the GATS. Indeed in *EC–Bananas III*, the AB held that measures involving 'a service relating to a particular good or a service supplied in conjunction with a particular good' fall under a special category governed by both the GATT and the GATS.[79] Notably, however, the object of the enquiry under each agreement remains different, the GATS being focused on 'how the measure affects the supply of the service or the service suppliers involved'.[80] What is determinative is whether, as stipulated by Article I:1 GATS, the requirement in question constitutes a measure by a member 'affecting trade in services'.[81]

In terms of scope, a defining issue here is what constitutes a 'service' that is the object of transboundary trade. The GATS remains obtuse, Article I:3(b) providing more generally that '"services" includes any service in any sector except services supplied in the exercise of governmental authority'.[82] Considering the failure of the negotiators to agree on a more precise definition, Zacharias proposes a useful 'working formula', defining services as 'commercial activities which are not embodied directly in tradeable, tangible products'.[83] In *Argentina-Financial Services* the AB referred to the Services Sectoral Classification List and the UN Central Product Classification (CPC) as important sources for the classification and description of services.[84] To be an object of transboundary trade, a service must fall under one of the four modes of supply provided in Article I:2, the most relevant here being the supply of a service 'from the territory of one Member into the territory of any other Member' (Article I:2(a)).[85] Notably, 'services supplied in the exercise of governmental authority' (Article I:3(b)) are exempt from the GATS. The Annex on Air Services (ATS) also exempts 'measures affecting air

[79] *EC–Bananas III (AB)* (n 8) [221].

[80] *Canada–Autos (AB)* (n 36) [160].

[81] This is a threshold question which must be determined first, see ibid [150]–[152]. Notably, the phrase 'measures by members' is very broad in scope, defined in Art XXVIII(a) as 'any measure by a Member, whether in the form of a law, regulation, rule, procedure, decision, administrative action, or any other form'. See also Art I:3(a) GATS. In *EC–Bananas III (AB)* (n 8) [220], the AB held that the word 'affecting' also reflects the intent of drafters for a broad reach of the GATS, being wider in scope than the terms 'regulating' or 'governing'. This includes de facto restrictions.

[82] According to Zacharias, the provision is modelled according to the 'comprehensive approach', whereby 'in principle any service which is either demanded or consumed is capable of being an object of trade', D Zacharias, 'Part I Scope and Definition' in R Wolfrum, PT Stoll and C Feinäugle (eds), *Max Planck Commentaries on World Trade Law – General Agreement on Trade in Services (GATS)* (Leiden, Brill, 2008) 31, 43.

[83] ibid. In the contribution the author notes, however, the limitations of this approach.

[84] *Argentina – Measures Relating to Trade in Goods and Services*, Appellate Body Report (9 May 2016) WT/DS453/AB/R (*Argentina Financial Services*) [6.27], referring to the Note by the Secretariat, 'Services Sectoral Classification List' (10 July 1991) MTN.GNS/W/120 (1991 Services Sectoral Classification List); and the 'Provisional Central Product Classification', UNSP Series M, No 77 (1991) 189.

[85] The service supplier need not be present in the territory in which the service is supplied, *Mexico – Measures Affecting Telecommunications Services*, Panel Report (1 June 2004) WT/DS204/R [7.30].

traffic rights' (paragraph 2(a)) and 'services directly related to the exercise of air traffic rights' (paragraph 2(b)). As argued by Bartels, however, neither of these exemptions appears to definitively preclude the applicability of the GATS to the EU Aviation Directive.[86]

In addition to the air transport sector, maritime transport is also likely to be affected by EU policy, namely the EU maritime MRV and potential future market-based measure (MBM).[87] Wholesale trade services would also be affected by EU measures setting product requirements for wholesale goods such as energy-related products (eg air heating systems and cooking appliances) or timber and timber products.[88] In *EC–Bananas III*, which, as the name implies, concerned banana imports, the EU (then EC), questioned whether 'operators within the meaning of the relevant EC regulations are, in fact, service suppliers in the sense of the GATS, in that what they actually do is buy and import bananas'.[89] The AB answered in the affirmative, finding that the 'operators' in question were suppliers of 'wholesale trade services' within the definition set out in the UN CPC.[90] That a service-focused analysis is then necessary was demonstrated in *Canada-Autos* (2000).[91] There the AB corrected the Panel for a failure to examine the effect of the relevant measure on wholesale trade services in a certain product as 'services', or on wholesale suppliers in their capacity as 'service suppliers'.[92]

An area in which there is more discussion is the supply of energy, which is not comprehensively regulated under the WTO agreements.[93] The GATT Note on the Classification of Services Sectors includes 'services incidental to energy

[86] L Bartels, 'The Inclusion of Aviation in the EU ETS: WTO Law Considerations' (International Centre for Trade and Sustainable Development 2012) Issue Paper No 6, 23. In support of this conclusion, see also S Hiesinger and P Mavroidis, 'Planes, Trains, and Automobiles: The EU Legislation on Climate Change and the Question of Consistency with WTO Law' in C Bakker and F Francioni (eds), *The EU, the US and Global Climate Governance* (Abingdon, Routledge, 2014).

[87] Both air and maritime transport services are included in the 1991 Services Sectoral Classification List (n 84) no 11A and B.

[88] See eg Commission (EU) Regulation 2016/2281 of 30 November 2016 implementing Directive 2009/125/EC of the European Parliament and of the Council establishing a framework for the setting of ecodesign requirements for energy-related products, with regard to ecodesign requirements for air heating products, cooling products, high temperature process chillers and fan coil units [2016] OJ L346 /1.

[89] *EC–Bananas III (AB)* (n 8) [224].

[90] ibid [225]. Wholesale trade services are also listed under the 1991 Services Sectoral Classification List (n 84) no 4(b).

[91] *Canada–Autos (AB)* (n 36).

[92] ibid [165], concerning the wholesale supply of motor vehicles, where the AB held that: 'A proper analysis of whether the measure is one "affecting trade in services" under art I:1 would have required the Panel to show that the import duty exemption "affects" wholesale trade services in motor vehicles as services, or wholesale trade service suppliers of motor vehicles in their capacity as service suppliers.'

[93] See further T Cottier et al, 'Energy in WTO Law and Policy' (WTI 2010) Individual Project No 6, www.wto.org /english/res_e/publications_e/wtr10_7may10_e.pdf; R Leal-Arcas, A Filis and ES Abu Gosh (eds), *International Energy Governance* (Cheltenham, Edward Elgar, 2014).

distribution' (no 1F(j)); however, it provides little further clarification. In this regard, a distinction must be drawn between the distribution and transmission of coal, oil and gas and that of electricity. While the first three are generally understood to fall under the GATS, electricity has been classified as a 'good', in the Harmonized System Nomenclature on the codification of commodities, which is followed by the WTO tariff schedules.[94] As noted by Cottier and others, this illustrates the inadequacy of 'the fundamental divide between goods and services' as 'an appropriate basis for addressing and regulating energy in an integrated manner'.[95] Electricity is a physical process that cannot be stored and must be generated, transmitted and supplied at the time of consumption. Its classification as a 'good' appears to be something of an 'artificial determination', and stems rather from the original lack of regulation on services under the GATT 1947.[96]

Finally, it is worth noting that there is also discussion on whether certified emission reductions (CERs) recognised under the EU ETS may constitute 'financial instruments' in the sense of the GATS Annex on Financial Services.[97] A detailed consideration of this issue goes beyond the scope of the present chapter, however, which focuses on the way in which world trade law governs the 'extraterritorial elements' of measures more specifically.

With regard to the applicable GATS conditions, two further limitations on the scope of the agreement must be observed. Firstly, until the date of the entry into force of the WTO Agreement, members could exempt certain measures from the scope of the MFN treatment provision in Article II GATS.[98] For the EU, these can be found in the European Communities Final List of Article II (MFN) Exemptions.[99] While, according to paragraph 6 of the Annex on Article II Exemptions, these should be phased out after a period of ten years, this has not always occurred in practice.[100] Secondly, and importantly, the NT obligation in Article XVII only applies to states in respect of service sectors for which they have made specific commitments.[101] The EU's original commitments can be found in the 1994 Schedule of Specific Commitments,[102] which has since been

[94] See further Cottier et al (n 93) 4.

[95] ibid.

[96] Leal-Arcas, Filis and Abu Gosh (n 93) 111; Cottier et al (n 93) 4.

[97] See further P Delimatsis and D Mavromati, 'GATS, Financial Services and Trade in Emission Reduction Certificates (RECs) – Just Another Market-Based Solution to Cope with the Tragedy of the Commons?' in T Cottier, O Nartova and SZ Bigdeli (eds), *International Trade Regulation and the Mitigation of Climate Change* (Cambridge, Cambridge University Press, 2009) 231.

[98] GATS 'Annex on Article II Exemptions' [1].

[99] 'European Communities and their Member States: Final List of Article II (MFN) Exemptions' (15 April 1994) GATS/EL/31.

[100] P van den Bossche and W Zdouc, *The Law and Policy of the World Trade Organization* (Cambridge, Cambridge University Press, 2013) 342.

[101] See *China – Measures Affecting Trading Rights and Distribution Services for Certain Publications and Audiovisual Entertainment Products*, Appellate Body Report (19 January 2010) WT/DS363/AB/R (*China – Publications and Audiovisual Products*) [396]–[7].

[102] 'European Communities and their Member States: EU Schedule of Specific Commitments' (15 April 2994) GATS/SC/31 (EU Schedule of Specific Commitments).

subject to several revisions, with certain differences for later EU members.[103] While this may be an issue in specific cases, the EU has made commitments for the sectors affected by its key climate-related measures discussed above.

Having examined the network of provisions applicable to the EU's climate-related measures, the following section now turns to the substance of the non-discrimination requirement, which, as will be shown, strictly regulates WTO members' policy autonomy in relation to climate protection.

3.2. Unpacking Non-discrimination: 'Like' Products and 'Less Favourable Treatment'

Under WTO law, the non-discrimination requirement essentially entails that 'like' products and services are to be 'accorded the same advantage' as or 'treated no less favourably' than their counterparts of different origins, including the home state.[104] Broadly speaking this can then be broken down into two key elements: 'likeness' and 'less favourable treatment', both of which may pose a particular obstacle to unincorporated PPMs. Two key issues are of particular relevance here. The first is whether products are 'like' irrespective of their carbon footprint. The second is whether a measure's climate-protection objective has any role in determining whether there is discrimination between like products or services. Due to their common core, the following sections will consider the MFN and NT requirements together through the lens of these two elements. As these principles are interpreted differently across the various agreements, context remains important in individual cases.

3.2.1. Different Size Shoes: To What Extent May the Carbon Footprint Define the Final Product or Service?

Are products and services 'like' irrespective of their carbon footprint? In *Japan–Alcoholic Beverages II* the AB stressed the relative nature of 'likeness' as a context-dependent criterion, which, like an accordion, 'stretches and squeezes in different places as the different provisions of the WTO Agreements are applied'.[105] According to the AB, 'likeness' 'is, fundamentally, a determination about the nature and extent of a competitive relationship between and among products'.[106] A merely economic analysis of cross-price elasticity of demand

[103] These can be found on the WTO website: 'Schedules of specific commitments and lists of Article II exemptions', www.wto.org/english/tratop_e/serv_e/serv_commitments_e.htm.

[104] See further Conrad (n 48) 163.

[105] 'Report of the Working Party on Border Tax Adjustments' (2 December 1970) BISD 18S/97 ('BTA Report'). See *Japan–Alcoholic Beverages II (AB)* (n 63) 21.

[106] In the context of Art III:4 GATT, see *EC–Asbestos (AB)* (n 16) [99]. In the context of Art III:2 GATT, see *Philippines – Taxes on Distilled Spirits*, Appellate Body Report (20 January 2012) WT/DS396/AB/R, WT/DS403/AB/R (*Philippines–Distilled Spirits*) [170].

is not sufficient here, as the requirement is both qualitative and quantitative, depending on the context in which it appears.[107] The determination of likeness thus contains an 'unavoidable element of individual, discretionary judgment' and has to be made on a case-by-case basis.[108]

In making such determinations, the AB generally relies on the criteria in the Report of the Working Party on Border Tax Adjustments ('the BTA Report').[109] These essentially 'comprise four categories of "characteristics" that the products involved might share', namely:

> (i) the physical properties of the products; (ii) the extent to which the products are capable of serving the same or similar end-uses; (iii) the extent to which consumers perceive and treat the products as alternative means of performing particular functions in order to satisfy a particular want or demand; and (iv) the international classification of the products for tariff purposes.[110]

Notably, this list is not a closed one, rather the criteria are 'simply tools to assist in the task of sorting and examining the relevant evidence'.[111]

Within the individual provisions, the AB has introduced somewhat complex nuances to the way in which the 'accordion of likeness' 'stretches and squeezes'.[112] Of particular relevance here is the distinction under the GATT between 'likeness' for fiscal and non-fiscal measures in Article III:2 and III:4. This stems from the fact that Article III:2 GATT contains two routes of enquiry, distinguishing between 'like' products in the first sentence and 'directly competitive or substitutable products' in the second sentence.[113] 'Likeness' in the first sentence of Article III:2 GATT is 'meant to be narrowly squeezed', as a more restricted category than 'directly competitive or substitutable products'.[114] Products are competitive or substitutable when they are 'interchangeable' or offer 'alternative ways of satisfying a particular need or taste'.[115] While products may not

[107] van den Bossche and Zdouc (n 100) 388; *Japan–Alcoholic Beverages II (AB)* (n 63) 18–19, 21.

[108] *EC–Asbestos (AB)* (n 16) [101]. That being said, the AB noted that 'not all products that are in some competitive relationship are "like products"', and 'it is difficult, if not impossible, in the abstract, to indicate precisely where on this spectrum the word "like" falls' [99].

[109] BTA Report (n 105). This has been explicitly embraced in several cases, including *EC–Asbestos (AB)* (n 16) [101]; *Japan–Alcoholic Beverages II (AB)* (n 63); *Philippines–Distilled Spirits* (n 106) [161].

[110] *EC–Asbestos (AB)* (n 16) [101].

[111] ibid [102]. Where measures make a 'distinction based exclusively on the origin of a product', 'likenesses' may be presumed. It will be for the complainant to establish that this is indeed the case.

[112] For use of this famous analogy, see *EC–Asbestos (AB)* (n 16) [96], [99].

[113] Art III:2 GATT reads: 'The products of the territory of any contracting party imported into the territory of any other contracting party shall not be subject, directly or indirectly, to internal taxes or other internal charges of any kind in excess of those applied, directly or indirectly, to like domestic products. Moreover, no contracting party shall otherwise apply internal taxes or other internal charges to imported or domestic products in a manner contrary to the principles set forth in paragraph 1.'

[114] See *EC–Asbestos* (n 16) [99].

[115] *Korea – Taxes on Alcoholic Beverages*, Appellate Body Report (17 February 1999) WT/DS75/AB/R, WT/DS84/AB/R (*Korea–Alcoholic Beverages*) [115]. See further S Switzer and JA McMahon, 'EU Biofuels Policy – Raising the Question of WTO Compatibility' (2011) 60 *ICLQ* 713, 726.

be taxed 'in excess of' their 'like' domestic counterparts, products in a 'directly competitive or substitutable' relationship may not be taxed 'dissimilarly'.[116] The latter threshold is lower, although its precise location must be assessed on a case-by-case basis.[117] Importantly, a violation of Article III:2 second sentence also requires a third criterion, namely that dissimilar taxation be 'applied so as to afford protection to domestic products'.[118] This has implications for the role of a measure's objective, and will be discussed further in section 3.2.2. As Article III:4 GATT does distinguish between 'like' and 'directly competitive or substitutable products', the reference to 'like products' in Article III:4 is broader than that in Article III:2 GATT. It is, however, 'certainly *not* broader than the *combined* scope of the two sentences of Article III:2'.[119]

In the context of the GATS, the AB found that '[w]hile what is being compared is different in the context of trade in goods and trade in services, we consider that, in the context of both trade in goods and trade in services, "likeness" refers to something that is similar'.[120] Consonant with the approach in the ambit of trade in goods, 'the concept of "likeness" of services and service suppliers under Articles II:1 and XVII:1 of the GATS is concerned with the competitive relationship of services and service suppliers'.[121] Use of the BTA criteria must, however, be 'adapted as appropriate to account for the specific characteristics of trade in services', in particular 'these criteria may be applied both in regard to the service and in regard to the service supplier'.[122] These criteria also form the cornerstone for determining likeness under the TBT Agreement (*US–Clove Cigarettes*).[123]

A point of discussion and inconsistency in WTO case law has been the inclusion of the 'aims-and-effects' or 'regulatory intent' of a measure in determining 'likeness', particularly in the context of Article III GATT. According

[116] See GATT Note *Ad* III: measures conforming with the first sentence of para 2 only violate the second sentence 'where competition was involved between, on the one hand, the taxed product and, on the other hand, a directly competitive or substitutable product which was not similarly taxed'.

[117] *Japan–Alcoholic Beverages II (AB)* (n 63) 24. With regard to the intensity of the competitive relationship required for 'likeness', products must be 'closely' but need not be 'perfectly' substitutable, as this would be 'too narrow an interpretation and would reduce the scope of the first sentence essentially to identical products'. *Philippines–Distilled Spirits* (n 106) [149].

[118] *Japan–Alcoholic Beverages II (AB)* (n 63) 24.

[119] *EC–Asbestos (AB)* (n 16) [96], [99]. Art III:4, by contrast, articulates the 'general principle' in Art III:1 'through a single obligation that applies solely to "like products"'.

[120] *Argentina Financial Services* (n 84) [6.21], [6.31]. For earlier cases, see WTO, China – Certain Measures Affecting Electronic Payment Services – Panel Report (31 August 2012) WT/DS413/R (*China–Electronic Payment Services*) [7.705]–[7.709].

[121] *Argentina Financial Services* (n 84) [6.25]. The phrase 'like services *and* service suppliers' was seen as an 'integrated element' for the analysis, making separate findings of likeness in respect of 'services' and 'service suppliers' unnecessary [6.29].

[122] ibid [6.31]. This may 'require additional considerations of whether or how this analysis is affected by the mode(s) of service supply' [6.33].

[123] *United States – Measures Affecting the Production and Sale of Clove Cigarettes*, Appellate Body Report (24 April 2012) WT/DS406/AB/R (*US–Clove Cigarettes*).

to the 'aims-and-effects' test, the ultimate determinant of likeness is whether a measure is applied 'so as to afford protection to domestic industry' (*US–Taxes on Automobiles*).[124] The test would thus allow for 'legitimate regulatory distinctions' based on non-protectionist objectives. This would have positive implications for carbon footprint measures which aim to protect the climate. Yet despite persuasive arguments to the contrary,[125] this approach was rejected by the Panel in *Japan–Alcoholic Beverages II*.[126] It has similarly been excluded from 'likeness' under the TBT Agreement (*US–Clove Cigarettes*), although the AB did note that '[t]o the extent that they are relevant to the examination of certain "likeness" criteria and are reflected in the products' competitive relationship, regulatory concerns underlying technical regulations may play a role in the determination of likeness'. Finally, in *EC–Bananas III*, the AB rejected the 'aims-and-effects' test in relation to the NT and MFN requirements in Articles XVII and II GATS as a whole.[127] This issue will be discussed further in section 3.2.2.

Applying the 'likeness' criterion to different climate-related measures, it is unincorporated PPMs that predictably face the most difficulties. The BTA criteria emphasise physical characteristics of the end product, which are generally not the target of carbon footprint measures.[128] Consumer preferences then seem the key remaining window through which 'invisible' lifecycle emissions could have a role to play. Indeed, as noted in *EC–Asbestos*, 'consumer perceptions may similarly influence – modify or even render obsolete – traditional uses of the products'.[129] The ultimate question is therefore whether a product or service's unincorporated or 'embodied' carbon alters the relevant competitive relationship, the most likely reason for this being consumer preferences for 'climate-friendly' goods or services.[130] If consumers

[124] *United States – Taxes on Automobiles* (1994) DS31/R [5.10]. This test was developed in *US–Malt Beverages* (n 49) [5.25]. See further A Porges and JP Trachtman, 'Robert Hudec and Domestic Regulation: The Resurrection of Aim and Effects' (2003) 37 *Journal of World Trade* 783.

[125] See eg D Regan, 'Regulatory Purpose and Like Products in Article III: 4 of the GATT (With Additional Remarks on Article III: 2)' (2002) 36 *Journal of World Trade* 443.

[126] *Japan – Taxes on Alcoholic Beverages*, Panel Report (11 July 1996) WT/DS8/R, WT/DS10/R, WT/DS11/R [6.16], considering Art III:2 GATT, accepted by the AB in *Japan–Alcoholic Beverages II (AB)* (n 63) 18, 19. It also appears implicitly excluded from Art III:4 GATT by the AB in *EC–Seals* (n 9) [5.83], discussed below.

[127] *EC–Bananas III (AB)* (n 8) [132]. This was because, unlike the GATT, the GATS has no provision comparable to Art III:1 GATT, which was the basis of the original 'aims-and-effects' theory.

[128] For a detailed analysis of biofuels under RED II, see A Mitchell and D Merriman, 'Indonesia's WTO Challenge to the European Union's Renewable Energy Directive: Palm Oil & Indirect Land-Use Change' (2020) 12(2) *Trade, Law and Development* (forthcoming) https://papers.ssrn.com/sol3/papers.cfm?abstract_id=3665463.

[129] *EC–Asbestos (AB)* (n 16) [102].

[130] Notably, in the context of BTAs, it has been suggested that, were carbon inputs to be eligible for BTAs, this may implicitly do away with the need for a likeness analysis between the two end-products. However, given the remaining lack of clarity, this section considers BTAs under the AB's traditional 'likeness' criteria. See further J Pauwelyn, 'US Federal Climate Policy and Competitiveness Concerns: The Limits and Options of International Trade Law' (Nicholas Institute for Environmental Policy Solutions, Duke University, 2007) Working Paper NI WP 07-02 28; K Holzer, *Carbon-Related Border Adjustment and WTO Law* (Cheltenham, Edward Elgar, 2014) 108.

make sufficient difference between 'green' and other goods and services, 'so can the government'.[131]

In analysing consumer preferences, one possible lens is that of perceived health concerns. This finds support in *EC–Asbestos* where the AB recognised that known health risks (carcinogenic fibres) may be assumed to affect consumer preferences, while in *EC-Biotech* it was not ruled out that *perceived* health concerns may also have an effect.[132] As noted by Horn and Mavroidis, climate protection measures may be considered as public health measures, because 'absent their adoption, life on the planet is threatened'.[133] Nevertheless, the health implications of embodied carbon are far less direct than in the above-mentioned cases.[134] Indeed, as the authors point out, the negligible environmental impact of an individual's purchasing decision is the cause of the negative externalities in the first place.[135]

An alternative argument is that the 'climate-friendliness' of a product or service itself affects consumer preferences. In this regard McAusland and Najjar cite some studies in support of consumer 'willingness-to-pay' considerable premiums for low-carbon goods, 'suggesting that tastes for high- and low-carbon goods are distinct (for some consumers at least)'.[136] However, willingness to pay for diffuse environmental externalities is unlikely to be uniform throughout the EU market as a whole. Importantly here, as noted by Cooreman, individuals' voting preferences may not reflect their consumption preferences.[137] Consumer information is another factor, as lifecycle emissions are not clearly visible in the end products and services. The great variety of production steps is simply not detected by most individual consumers, and is often not transparently available.

Interesting questions then remain for the role of governments in steering the conditions of the likeness analysis. As recognised in *US–Clove Cigarettes*, 'regulatory concerns and considerations' may affect consumer preferences.[138] Where a measure presumes goods or services are not like, and treats them differently, this

[131] J Pauwelyn, 'Recent Books on Trade and Environment: GATT Phantoms Still Haunt the WTO' (2004) 15 *European Journal of International Law* 575, 586, referring as an example to electricity.

[132] *EC–Asbestos (AB)* (n 16) [115]. *European Communities – Measures Affecting the Approval and Marketing of Biotech Products*, Panel Report(21 November 2006) WT/DS291/R, WT/DS292/R, WT/DS293/R (*EC–Biotech*) [7.2514].

[133] Horn and Mavroidis (n 19) 1913.

[134] C McAusland and N Najjar, 'The WTO Consistency of Carbon Footprint Taxes' (2014) 46 *Georgetown Journal of International Law* 765, 778.

[135] Horn and Mavroidis (n 19) 1917.

[136] McAusland and Najjar (n 134) 777, referring also to C Michaud, D Llerena and I Joly, 'Willingness to Pay for Environmental Attributes of Non-Food Agricultural Products: A Real Choice Experiment' (2013) 40 *European Review of Agricultural Economics* 313, 325.

[137] Cooreman (n 23) 41.

[138] *US–Clove Cigarettes* (n 123) [117]. According to Ming Du, here one can distinguish between a measure's concrete objective and the underlying regulatory concerns, such as healthcare or environmental protection. M Du, 'Taking Stock: What Do We Know, and Do Not Know, about the National Treatment Obligation in the GATT/WTO Legal System?' (2015) 1 *Chinese Journal of Global Governance* 67, 80, referring to *US–Clove Cigarettes* [123].

may already affect consumer behaviour. A subsequent determination of 'likeness' based on contemporary consumer preferences may then be complicated.

Also of relevance is the case *Canada-Renewable Energy*, concerning Canadian domestic content requirements for wind and solar electricity generators eligible for feed-in-tariffs (FITs), which were challenged under the SCM Agreement.[139] In determining whether the FIT contracts conferred a 'benefit to the recipients' as required for the existence of a 'subsidy' in the sense of Article 1 SCM, the AB overturned the Panel's finding that the relevant market was the wholesale market for all electricity from any source.[140] The Panel had based this on a lack of consumer differentiation and the like physical properties of electricity irrespective of its generation process.[141] However, the AB found that the Panel's approach did not sufficiently consider the role of the government in creating a distinct market for renewables. Such government action may be aimed at 'addressing the negative and positive externalities that are associated with conventional and renewable electricity production'.[142]

According to McAusland and Najjar, the AB in *Canada-Renewable Energy*

> essentially approved of creating a separate market on the grounds that renewable sources generate fewer negative externalities. ... If we allow the corollary that goods with separate markets cannot be like, then the AB has set an indirect precedent for treating goods as un-like based on their npr-PPMs.[143]

While this would certainly be an interesting precedent, the case was focused on the SCM Agreement, where government intervention is a 'supply-side factor' that may influence the determination of the relevant market for the purpose of finding a subsidy.[144] It remains to be seen whether this rationale stretches to the 'likeness' of products and services, particularly as it would effectively import regulatory objectives back into the analysis which, as will now be seen, has been clearly rejected in case law.

3.2.2. Honest Intentions: Regulatory Objectives and Differential Treatment

According to the MFN and NT principles, a measure will constitute discrimination when it grants 'less favourable treatment' to imports, or 'fails to accord the same advantage' to like products of different origins. Given the aforementioned conclusion that products and services will generally be considered 'like' irrespective of their carbon footprint, any difference in treatment then risks being

[139] *Canada – Certain Measures Affecting the Renewable Energy Generation Sector/Canada – Measures Relating to the Feed-In Tariff Program*, Appellate Body Report (24 May 2013) WT/DS412/AB/R, WT/DS426/AB/R (*Canada–Renewable Energy*).
[140] ibid [5.167] et seq.
[141] ibid [5.168].
[142] ibid [5.177].
[143] McAusland and Najjar (n 134) 780.
[144] *Canada–Renewable Energy* (n 139) [5.171].

qualified as discrimination. This section will briefly set out this second step in the discrimination analysis, considering the regulatory space for states to steer the relevant markets.

Under the NT principle, WTO members must grant 'treatment no less favourable' to imports compared with like national products (Articles III:4 GATT, 2.1 TBT and XVII GATS). In the context of Article III:4 GATT, the AB has clarified that this consists of: (1) 'effective equality of opportunities for imported products to compete with like domestic products', where (2) 'a formal difference in treatment between imported and domestic like products is neither necessary, nor sufficient, to establish that imported products are accorded less favourable treatment than that accorded to like domestic products'.[145] This (3) 'involves an assessment of the implications of the contested measure for the equality of competitive conditions between imported and like domestic products', where 'detrimental impact will amount to treatment that is "less favourable"'. As a final matter, (4), measures modifying the conditions of competition must be in a 'genuine relationship' with the adverse impact on competitive opportunities for imported products.[146]

In *US–Clove Cigarettes* the AB held that the interpretative rules in relation to Article III:4 GATT were also 'instructive' in relation to determining 'treatment no less favourable' under Article 2.1 of the TBT Agreement, although they must be read in light of the specific TBT context.[147] There remains an important difference for the role of legislative intent, discussed further below.[148] With regard to scheduled services, Article XVII:2 GATS uses different wording, providing that 'treatment no less favourable' may be achieved through both formally identical or formally different treatment. According to Article XVII:3 GATS, treatment 'shall be considered to be less favourable if it modifies the conditions of competition in favour of services or service suppliers of the Member compared to like services or service suppliers of any other Member'.[149]

Under the MFN principle, measures must 'afford the same advantage' 'immediately and unconditionally' to like products of all contracting parties. Generally speaking, a measure will 'grant an advantage' under Article I:1 GATT when it 'creates more favourable competitive opportunities' or influences the commercial relationship between products of different members.[150] For services, treatment must again be 'no less favourable' (Article II:1 GATS). Unlike the NT provision in Article XVII GATS, the MFN clause contains no explanation of this threshold. As noted by Howse and Zdouc, however, the same general rule

[145] See *EC–Seals* (n 9) [5.101], referring inter alia to *US–Clove Cigarettes* (n 123) [176]; *China–Publications and Audiovisual Products* (n 107) [305].

[146] ibid.

[147] *US–Clove Cigarettes* (n 123) [180]. See further van den Bossche and Zdouc (n 100) 686.

[148] *US–COOL* (n 71) [269] [271].

[149] For application, see eg *China–Electronic Payment Services* (n 120) [7.705].

[150] See *Belgium – Family Allowances* (1952) GATT BISD 1S/59 [3].

applies, whereby a measure grants less favourable treatment when it 'modifies the conditions of competition' between like products of different origins.[151]

A key debate for carbon-footprint requirements is whether or not measures that differentiate between products based on a 'legitimate regulatory distinction' fail to grant 'treatment no less favourable', or 'accord the same advantage', to like foreign products. The answer to this question depends on the Agreement at issue. In the context of the GATS, *EC–Bananas III* rejected the consideration of regulatory intent during the discrimination analysis of both the MFN and NT principles some time ago.[152] By contrast, detrimental impact which results from a 'legitimate regulatory distinction' does not constitute 'less favourable treatment' under Article 2.1 of the TBT Agreement.[153]

Under the GATT, the debate persisted somewhat longer, and was explicitly raised by the EU in the *EC–Seals* case.[154] *EC–Seals* concerned the WTO consistency of the EU's 'Seal Regime', banning the placing on the market of seals and seal products except those hunted by indigenous communities (IC exemption), for the purposes of maritime resource management (MRM exemption) or taken by travellers into the EU under limited circumstances.[155] The somewhat controversial policy objective of this ban was to protect EU citizens' public morals on animal welfare. Norway and Canada claimed that the IC and MRM exemptions violated Articles I:1 and III:4 GATT.[156] Considering this claim, the AB unequivocally shot down the EU's argument that its differentiation was based on legitimate regulatory distinctions.[157] In addition to the lack of textual basis, the AB held that a measure's public policy objective should only be considered in the independent general exemptions provision of Article XX.[158] The GATT structure differs from that of the TBT Agreement where the non-discrimination requirement in the first paragraph of Article 2, is immediately followed by paragraph 2, requiring that technical regulations 'not be more trade-restrictive than necessary to *fulfil a legitimate objective*'. According to the AB, reading Article 2.1 as prohibiting '*a priori* any obstacle to international trade' would deprive Article 2.2 of its *effet utile*.[159] A different approach is therefore merited.

Perhaps unsurprisingly, *EC–Seals* has been heavily criticised, and some speculation remains as to the remaining role for the right to regulate. In addition to placing the burden of proof on the appellant, Article 2.1 TBT looks more

[151] van den Bossche and Zdouc (n 100) 344, noting the caution of the AB in *EC–Bananas III* that the guidance in Art XVII:3 GATS does not necessarily equally apply to Art II:1 GATS.

[152] *EC–Bananas III (AB)* (n 8) [132].

[153] *US–COOL* (n 71) [271].

[154] *EC–Seals* (n 9) [5.83].

[155] ibid [1.4].

[156] They also claimed a violation of Arts 2.1 and 2.2 of the TBT Agreement, but these were held not to apply to the measure as it did not constitute a 'technical regulation' under Annex 1.1 TBT (*EC–Seals* (n 9) [5.58]).

[157] ibid.

[158] AB *EC–Seals* (n 9) [5.90], [5.125].

[159] *US–Clove Cigarettes* (n 123) [171].

narrowly at 'legitimate regulatory distinctions', considering only whether they are the sole cause of the established 'detrimental effect'. The Article XX standard of 'arbitrary and unjustifiable discrimination' entails a broader balancing exercise of the regulatory autonomy of the acting state with the WTO rights of the other members. This means that the objective of reducing extraterritorial externalities may alone be enough to prevent a violation of Article 2.1 TBT, but not enough to prevent a violation of the more extensive Article XX GATT. That being said, as measures must comply with both the TBT and the GATT, they will always need to be able to pass the hurdles set by Article XX GATT.[160] As noted by Ming Du, this means that a 'large universe of laws and regulations is now *prima facie* illegal under WTO law', which is an extreme outcome, 'hard to reconcile with the intent and text of the GATT'.[161]

Notably, regulatory objectives may be relevant under the GATT for products in a 'directly competitive or substitutable relationship' under Article III:2, second sentence. The second sentence namely refers to Article III:1, containing the general principle not to apply measures 'so as to afford protection' to domestic products. A determination of protectionism must be based on a measure's 'design, architecture and structure', where the legislator's subjective intent is not relevant (*Chile-Alcoholic Beverages*).[162] Applying, *a contrario*, the reasoning in *EC–Seals*, the textual reference to Article III:1 appears to legitimise an inquiry into whether the dissimilar taxation is based exclusively on a legitimate regulatory distinction under Article III:2. This may be particularly relevant for the different types of biofuels under national support schemes of the RED II, which may be considered 'directly competitive and substitutable'.

Practical issues of consistency would seem to arise from the fact that Article III:2 second sentence does consider regulatory objectives by reference to Article III:1, whereas Article III:4 does not. As 'likeness' in Article III:4 may cover goods in a 'directly competitive and substitutable' relationship under Article III:2, there is essentially less policy autonomy for states when using regulations than when using fiscal measures. Such a difference in protection is precisely what the AB wanted to avoid in its analysis of 'likeness' in *EC–Asbestos*, where it found it to be

> incongruous if, due to a significant difference in the product scope of these two provisions, Members were prevented from using one form of regulation – for instance, fiscal – to protect domestic production of certain products, but were able to use another form of regulation – for instance, non-fiscal – to achieve those ends.[163]

[160] As such, the AB's finding that there is no 'imbalance' between Arts XX GATT and 2.1 TBT remains difficult to square with its holding in the same case that the two provisions have a different legal standard, scope and function (*EC–eals* (n 9) [5.311]–[5.312]).

[161] Du (n 138) 92. See also R Howse, J Langille and K Sykes, 'Sealing the Deal: The WTO Appellate Body's Report in EC – Seal Products' [2014] 18(2) *ASIL Insights*.

[162] *Chile – Taxes on Alcoholic Beverages*, Appellate Body Report (12 January 2000) WT/DS87/AB/R, WT/DS110/AB/R [71].

[163] *EC–Asbestos (AB)* (n 16) [99].

The reasoning in *EC–Seals* also appears to contradict the AB's finding in the same case that:

> The scope and meaning of Article III:4 should not be broadened or restricted beyond what is required by the normal customary international law rules of treaty interpretation, simply because Article XX(b) exists and may be available to justify measures inconsistent with Article III:4.[164]

Despite critique in legal discourse, there seems little space for a measure's climate-protection objective under the substantive non-discrimination provisions of the GATT and GATS. As such, measures conditioning the foreign carbon footprint will more than likely need to be justified under these agreements.[165] As will now be discussed in section 4, it is at this stage of the legal analysis that questions of extraterritoriality and jurisdiction have arisen more explicitly.

4. JUSTIFYING PRIMA FACIE VIOLATIONS: AN IMPLIED JURISDICTIONAL LIMITATION?

Where foreign carbon footprint conditions are found to constitute prima facie violations of the GATT or GATS, they may nonetheless be justified under the general exemptions provisions of Article XX GATT and Article XIV GATS. Qualifying for such exemptions is no simple task, as these provisions contain a host of strict requirements both in relation to the design and application of public policy measures.

The general exemptions contain no explicit jurisdictional conditions, and there remains considerable debate as to the existence of an implied territorial limitation, particularly under Article XX GATT. While opportunities have arisen, most notably in *US–Shrimp* and *EC–Seals*, the AB has remained consciously silent on this question, refusing to rule on whether this provision contains an implied jurisdictional limitation.[166] Notably, given their textual and functional resemblance, the AB has found that case law on Article XX GATT may be relevant for its analysis of Article XIV GATS (*US–Gambling*).[167] The case law on Article XX GATT is therefore considered here as relevant for the GATS as well.

Sections 4.1.1 and 4.1.2 first briefly outline the basic conditions for provisional justification under the environmental exemptions in the sub-paragraphs of Article XX GATT. Section 4.2 then explores the debate surrounding a possible

[164] ibid [115].

[165] See C Ryngaert, *Selfless Intervention: The Exercise of Jurisdiction in the Common Interest* (Oxford, Oxford University Press, 2020) 165.

[166] *US–Shrimp* (n 33) [121]; *EC–Seals* (n 9) [5.173].

[167] *United States – Measures Affecting the Cross-Border Supply of Gambling and Betting Services*, Appellate Body Report (20 April 2005) WT/DS285/AB/R (*US–Gambling*) [291]. Notably, Art XIV GATS does not contain a paragraph similar to Art XX(g) GATT.

implied jurisdictional limitation in this first tier of the analysis. Building on the discussion in the literature, it proposes an integrated approach to the 'sufficient nexus' requirement alluded to by the AB. Finally, section 4.3 considers the further limitations in the 'chapeau' of Article XX GATT, which as the second tier of the analysis conditions the way a measure is applied in concrete cases.

4.1. Provisional Justification of Environmental Measures

Under the two-tiered analysis of Article XX GATT, a prima facie violation must first be 'provisionally justified' under at least one of the limited and conditional exceptions contained in the sub-paragraphs.[168] The application of such measures must then meet the requirements of the chapeau. Climate protection measures most plausibly fall under Article XX(b) on the 'protection of human, animal or plant life or health' and Article XX(g) on the 'conservation of exhaustible resources'. Given the environmental and human rights implications, it could well be argued that they are also defensible under Article XX(a) on 'public morals'. In *EC–Seals* the protection of animal welfare was accepted as a public moral of EU citizens.[169] In climate change context, the RED explicitly justifies its land-use change limitations for biofuels on the basis that '[c]onsumers in the Community would … find it morally unacceptable that their increased use of biofuels and bioliquids could have the effect of destroying biodiverse land'.[170] However, as sub-paragraphs (b) and (g) provide more direct avenues for climate protection, this section will focus on these exemptions.[171]

4.1.1. *Article XX(b): Measures 'Necessary to Protect Human, Animal or Plant Life or Health'*

To provisionally qualify under Article XX(b), state measures must pursue the objective of protecting human, plant and animal life or health, and be 'necessary' for its achievement.[172] In *Brazil-Retreaded Tyres* the Panel noted that Members must do more than 'establish the existence of 'risks to "the environment" generally', but rather establish more specifically risks to animal or plant life or health.[173] This need not pose a great hurdle in the present context, as the risks posed by climate change to the protection of human and animal life

[168] *US–Shrimp* (n 33) [157].
[169] *EC-Seals* (n 9) AB [5.198]–[5.200].
[170] RED (n 28) rec 69.
[171] This was a topic of considerable discussion in *EC–Seals* (n 9), see in particular from [5.192].
[172] See eg *United States – Standards for Reformulated and Conventional Gasoline*, Appellate Body Report (20 May 1996) WT/DS2/AB/R, (*US–Gasoline (AB)*) [6.21], where the AB found that reducing air pollution is a policy objective aimed at protecting life or health.
[173] ibid [7.46].

and health have been repeatedly recognised by the EU and the international community.[174]

Importantly, it is a 'fundamental principle' that WTO Members retain the authority both to set the environmental or public health objective and the 'level of protection that they consider appropriate in a given context'.[175] A distinction is, however, drawn between members' freedom to define their objective and desired level of protection, and the limitations on the measure itself, which must be 'necessary'.[176]

The assessment of a measure's necessity entails a holistic 'weighing and balancing' of 'the importance of the interests or values at stake, the extent of the contribution to the achievement of the measure's objective, and its trade restrictiveness'.[177] A measure will make a contribution to the achievement of the objective, where 'there is a genuine relationship of ends and means between the objective pursued and the measure at issue'.[178] The contribution need not be immediately observable, and both quantitative and qualitative factors may be used in its assessment.[179]

In *Brazil-Retreaded Tyres* it was recognised that

> certain complex public health or environmental problems may be tackled only with a comprehensive policy comprising a multiplicity of interacting measures. … Moreover, the results obtained from certain actions – for instance, measures adopted in order to *attenuate global warming and climate change*, … – can only be evaluated with the benefit of time'.[180]

This finding is particularly relevant in the context of the EU's cap and phase-out of high ILUC-risk biofuels under RED II.[181] In its complaint before the WTO, Indonesia argued that the EU has offered 'no adequate scientific basis' for its criteria, and recognises in its own policy that 'ILUC cannot be observed or measured'.[182] As an additional obstacle for the necessity requirement, Mitchell

[174] See IPCC, 'Climate Change 2014 Synthesis Report Summary for Policymakers: Future Risks and Impacts Caused by a Changing Climate' (2014) Fifth Assessment Report (AR5) www.ipcc.ch/report/ar5/wg1/.

[175] *Brazil–Retreaded Tyres* (n 22) [140], [210].

[176] The present section of this chapter expands upon this author's forthcoming contribution to the *Encyclopedia of Environmental Law, Trade Law*, ed P Delimatsis and L Reins: N Dobson 'Article XX GATT as Guardian of the Environment' (Cheltenham, Edward Elgar, forthcoming 2021).

[177] *Brazil–Retreaded Tyres* (n 22) [151], [178]. See also, *Korea – Measures Affecting Imports of Fresh, Chilled and Frozen Beef*, Appellate Body Report (10 January 2001) WT/DS161/AB/R (*Korea–Beef*) [161]; and *EC–Asbestos (AB)* (n 16) [169]–[175].

[178] *Brazil–Retreaded Tyres* (n 22) [210].

[179] ibid [151].

[180] *Brazil–Retreaded Tyres* (n 22) [151].

[181] RED (n 28) and Delegated Regulation 2019/807 supplementing Directive (EU) 2018/2001 as regards the determination of high indirect land-use change-risk feedstock for which a significant expansion of the production area into land with high carbon stock is observed and the certification of low indirect land-use change-risk biofuels, bioliquids and biomass fuels [2019] OJ L133/1.

[182] *European Union – Certain Measures Concerning Palm Oil And Oil Palm Crop-Based Biofuels, Request for the Establishment of a Panel Indonesia* (24 March 2020) WT/DS593/9 (*EU–Palm Oil and Biofuels*) 5.

and Merriman point out that Indonesia has in fact included reducing emissions associated with land use change under its *own* NDC, raising questions as to the actual contribution of the EU's additional measure.[183]

Another more general debate pertains to the role of carbon leakage for the effectiveness of climate-protection measures. On the one hand, it has been argued that higher climate protection standards may cause carbon leakage because businesses will relocate to other jurisdictions where the price of carbon is lower.[184] On the other hand, the EU points to the threat of carbon leakage as a *justification* for the application of its measures to extraterritorial conduct and circumstances.[185] This assumes that the large EU market will continue to draw suppliers and operators. There is a risk, however, that imposing costs on foreign producers may favour EU actors in a way that allows them to increase their own production of CO_2. This was discussed in relation to border carbon adjustment taxes by Colares and Rode, who allude to the danger that EU lobbying efforts aimed at levelling the playing field may result in the economically suboptimal imposition of tariffs or other trade restrictions.[186] While this could certainly decrease the measures' 'material contribution' to climate-change mitigation, these negative effects could be avoided by careful design of the tariff and scope of the envisioned measures.[187] As such, the risk of carbon leakage need not in itself preclude a measure's necessity.

Importantly, in *Korea-Beef*, the AB found that the 'relative importance' of the common interests or values that the measure serves may be considered.[188] The more vital or important the common interests, the easier it would be to accept the measure as 'necessary'. Applied to the present case, there can be no doubt that the mitigation of climate change is a 'vital' common interest meriting protection.[189] While there must be no less trade-restrictive alternative reasonably available,[190] WTO members cannot reasonably be expected to adopt an alternative measure that would not allow them to achieve their desired level of protection.[191]

[183] Mitchell and Merriman (n 128) 46–47.

[184] See further in relation to aviation emissions J Meltzer, 'Climate Change and Trade – The EU Aviation Directive and the WTO' (2012) 15 *Journal of International Economic Law* 111.

[185] Commission (EU) 'The European Green Deal' (Communication) COM(2019) 640 final, 11 December 2019, 5.

[186] JF Colares and A Rode, 'Climate Change Mitigation and Trade Rules: The Opportunities and Limitations of Neutral Border Tariffs' (Research Paper, Energy Policy Institute at the University of Chicago, 2015).

[187] This would also have to take into account the principle of common but differentiated responsibilities and capabilities discussed below in relation to the chapeau of Art XX and mentioned in the analysis of customary international law in section 4.2.

[188] *Korea–Beef* (n 177) [162].

[189] United Nations Framework Convention on Climate Change (adopted 9 May 1992, entered into force 21 March 1994) 1771 UNTS 107 (UNFCCC) rec 1.

[190] ibid [307].

[191] *EC–Asbestos (AB)* (n 16) [165]. Nor may a proposed alternative be 'merely theoretical in nature' (*Brazil–Retreaded Tyres* (n 22) [156]).

4.1.2. *Article XX(g): Measures 'Related to the Conservation of Exhaustible Natural Resources'*

Carbon-footprint measures may also be exempted under Article XX(g) if they 'relate to', 'the conservation of exhaustible natural resources'. Such measures must be made effective in conjunction with domestic restrictions.[192] Interestingly, there has been some willingness to engage with evolving environmental norms in the interpretation of this provision. Thus, when interpreting 'conservation' the Panel in *China–Rare Earths* drew on the broader interpretative rules in Article 31 of the Vienna Convention of the Law of Treaties (VCLT), considering the recognition of sustainable development in the WTO Agreement preamble, and the international law principle of sovereignty over natural resources as 'relevant' to the 'interpretive exercise.[193] The Panel found that conservation policies need not merely be concerned with 'preservation', but with a 'full range of policy considerations and goals' including the use of resources in a sustainable manner.[194] On appeal, the AB added to this, finding that the precise meaning of 'conservation' will depend on the exhaustible natural resource at issue.[195]

As regards 'the term "exhaustible natural resources"', in *US–Shrimp* the AB held that this 'must be read … in light of *contemporary concerns of the community* of nations about the protection and conservation of the environment'.[196] Considering the sustainable development objective embodied in the WTO Agreement, it went on to find that 'the generic term "natural resources" in Article XX(g) is not "static" in its content or reference but rather "by definition, evolutionary".[197] Acknowledging developments in environmental law, the AB found that 'modern international conventions and declarations make frequent references to natural resources as embracing both living and non-living resources'.[198] It relied upon the principle of 'effectiveness in treaty interpretation' to hold that 'measures to conserve exhaustible natural resources, whether living or non-living, may fall within Article XX(g)'.[199] Here too, Article XX is thus interpreted flexibly to allow states to respond to emerging scientific evidence on

[192] Note that, assuming a maritime ETS would have the same scope as the MRV, it would also meet the requirement of being 'made effective in conjunction with restrictions on domestic production or consumption', as all intra-EU voyages would also be subject to the scheme.

[193] *China – Measures Related to the Exportation of Rare Earths, Tungsten, and Molybdenum*, Panel Report (26 March 2014) WT/DS431/R, WT/DS432/R, WT/DS433/R [7.263].

[194] ibid [7.266].

[195] *China – Measures Related to the Exportation of Rare Earths, Tungsten, and Molybdenum*, Appellate Body Report (7 August 2014) WT/DS431/AB/R, WT/DS432/AB/R, WT/DS433/AB/R [5.89].

[196] *US–Shrimp* (n 33) [129] (emphasis added). The AB continues: 'the preamble attached to the WTO Agreement shows that the signatories to that Agreement were, in 1994, fully aware of the importance and legitimacy of environmental protection as a goal of national and international policy'.

[197] ibid [130].

[198] ibid.

[199] ibid [131]–[132].

common environmental concerns. Whether or not whether multilateral environmental agreements (MEAs) to which not all members are parties may be relied upon as 'relevant' sources of international law under Article 31(3)(c) VCLT is a topic of considerable discussion.[200]

In *US–Gasoline*, the Panel found that renewable resources may also 'exhaustible'.[201] Clean air can be considered an exhaustible natural resource because it can be depleted by means of pollution from fuel combustion.[202] It has been argued that, by analogy, a stable atmosphere is an exhaustible natural resource because the necessary composition of gases is also disrupted by CO_2 emissions from fuel combustion.[203]

Under Article XX(g), a measure must also 'relate to' its objective. This pertains to the 'relationship between the general structure and design of the measure' and 'the policy goal it purports to serve'.[204] What is required is 'a close and genuine relationship of the ends and means', where the rules are not merely 'incidentally or inadvertently' aimed at conservation.[205] The 'related to' threshold is lower than the necessity requirement contained in Article XX(b).[206]

4.2. An Implied Jurisdictional Limitation under the First Tier of Article XX GATT?

Given the interconnected nature of the world's ecosystems, it is perhaps unsurprising that, over time, a number of unilateral environmental policy measures have given rise to trade law disputes on the jurisdictional limitations of Article XX GATT.[207] However, despite recognising its 'systemic importance', to date the AB has avoided ruling on the issue. Engaging with debates in the literature, this following section will consider the key case law, and explain the 'integrated approach' advocated for here.

In briefly sketching the relevant cases, a key starting point is the well-known 1994 *Tuna-Dolphin* dispute.[208] At issue was a US import ban on tuna caught by suppliers in countries listed as failing to require the use of dolphin-friendly fishing nets, as well as 'intermediary' countries in which the tuna was subsequently processed.[209] This led to objections from the EC and the

[200] See *EC–Biotech* (n 132) [7.64]–[7.68].
[201] *US–Gasoline (Panel)* (n 172) [6.37].
[202] ibid.
[203] BJ Condon and T Sinha, 'Unresolved Issues in WTO Law' in B Condon and T Sinha (eds), *The Role of Climate Change in Global Economic Governance* (Oxford Scholarship Online, 2013) 53, 72.
[204] *US–Shrimp* (n 33) [137].
[205] ibid.
[206] See further *Canada – Measures Affecting Exports of Unprocessed Herring and Salmon* (1988) GATT BISD 35S/98, [4.4]–[4.7].
[207] This section partly reproduces the author's work in the related contribution, see Dobson (n 13).
[208] *US–Tuna II* (n 30).
[209] ibid [2.7].

Netherlands, raising the question whether the measure could be defended under Article XX GATT. The GATT Panel confirmed that neither paragraphs (b) nor (g) were clear on the 'nature and precise scope of the policy area' covered.[210] Based on a contextual analysis it concluded that the GATT did not 'proscribe … in an absolute manner' measures 'taken with respect to things located, or actions occurring, outside the territorial jurisdiction of the party taking the measure'.[211] However, the Panel found that 'measures taken so as to force other countries to change their policies, and that were effective only if such changes occurred, could not be considered "necessary" for the protection of animal life or health in the sense of article XX (b)'.[212] Nor could they be considered 'primarily aimed either at the conservation of an exhaustible natural resource, or at rendering effective restrictions on domestic production or consumption, in the meaning of article XX (g)'.[213]

Not long after, however, in the 1998 *US–Shrimp* case, the AB departed from this ruling. The case concerned the permissibility of a similar US measure banning the import of shrimp from countries that did not use turtle-friendly fishing nets.[214] In interpreting the general-exemptions provision, the AB found that 'requiring from exporting countries compliance with … certain policies' does not render a measure 'a priori incapable of justification under article XX', as this would render 'most, if not all, of the specific exceptions of article XX, inutile'.[215] The AB then found that as the 'highly migratory' turtles were known to occur within US territorial waters, there was a 'sufficient nexus' between the endangered population and the United States. This passage is widely interpreted to imply that a 'sufficient nexus' is needed between the regulating state and the objective pursued by the measure, in order for that state to claim jurisdiction. That being said, the AB explicitly restricted its findings to the specific circumstances of the case, declining 'to pass upon the question of whether there is an implied jurisdictional limitation in article XX(g)'.[216]

In *EC–Seals*, the AB did come tantalisingly close to answering this question, this time in the more controversial context of public morals under Article XX(a).[217] As discussed in section 3.2.3, the case concerned an EU ban on seals and seal products, with certain exemptions that appellants claimed violated the GATT.[218] Considering, on its own accord, the issue of jurisdiction, the AB referred to

[210] ibid [5.15] and [5.31].

[211] ibid [5.16] and [5.32]. In doing so it notably disagreed, in [5.26]–[5.27], with the Panel in the earlier case *US–Tuna I* (n 30).

[212] *US–Tuna II* (n 30) [5.39].

[213] ibid [5.27].

[214] *US–Shrimp* (n 33) [98].

[215] ibid [121].

[216] ibid.

[217] *EC–Seals* (n 9).

[218] ibid [1.4], [5.183]. As the EU had defended its measures based on the animal welfare concerns of its citizens, and 'never submitted that the protection of seal welfare as such was an objective of the seal regime', it had failed to establish an additional prima facie case under Art XX(b) GATT.

US–Shrimp, and the 'sufficient nexus' found in the 'specific circumstances' of that case. Without explicitly linking the cases together, it then considered the facts of the case before it, noting that the EU seal regime was 'designed to address seal hunting activities occurring "within and outside the Community" and the seal welfare concerns of "citizens and consumers" in EU Member States'.[219] However, while 'recognizing the systemic importance of the question of whether there is an implied jurisdictional limitation in Article XX(a), and, if so, the nature or extent of that limitation', the AB once again decided not to examine this question.[220] Nevertheless, this appears to imply that the presence of certain activities regulated within the EU, together with the seal welfare concerns of EU citizens in EU Member States, would be enough to constitute a 'sufficient nexus' to support jurisdiction.

Amidst the continuing uncertainty, commentators have explained these cryptic findings in different ways. According to Young, in the case of PPMs, '[i]f there is a requirement for a nexus between the aim of the measure and the importing State … it is implicitly part of the assessment of whether the relevant products are "like" or "directly competitive or substitutable"'.[221] Arguably however, the current test for 'likeness' does not entirely support this view. As discussed in section 3.2.1, physical characteristics and consumer preferences are key for differentiating between goods with different carbon footprints. Yet consumer preferences cannot be equated with state interests in legislating. As compellingly observed by Charnovitz, unincorporated PPM measures may be used to achieve social goals that do not matter to consumers.[222]

Accepting that a sufficient nexus is required, the question remains how the nexus should be interpreted. One way of looking at it is as a requisite *physical* territorial connection between the regulated subject matter and the acting state. This appears to be supported, for example, by Van den Bossche, Schrijver and Faber, who argue that while a nexus 'definitely exists' when the measure concerns unincorporated PPMs affecting a global situation (eg climate change), it 'clearly does not exist' where the measure concerns unincorporated PPMs affecting a 'purely national situation in the country of production', such as local environment and animal welfare.[223] Writing in 2007, before *EC–Seals*, the authors conclude that the 'Appellate Body has still to rule on whether measures of this kind, when otherwise GATT inconsistent, can be justified under article XX of the GATT 1994'.[224]

The subsequent finding in *EC–Seals* may well indicate that the sufficient-nexus requirement is not limited to measures *physically* affecting the territory

[219] ibid [5.173].
[220] ibid.
[221] M Young, 'Trade Measures to Address Environmental Concerns in Faraway Places: Jurisdictional Issues' (2014) 23 *Review of European, Comparative & International Environmental Law* 302, 309.
[222] Charnovitz (n 48) 65.
[223] ibid 95–96.
[224] ibid.

of the legislating state. The AB's vague reference to hunting activities 'occurring within and outside the community' leaves uncertainty here.[225] Nevertheless, its acceptance of measures protecting public morals primarily concerned with situations outside the regulating state raises the possibility of a broader interpretation than that based purely on a physical territorial connection. This finding may then have great implications for the overarching interpretation of the jurisdictional limitations in Article XX GATT as a whole.

Looking beyond the physical connection, other commentators consider the location of a measure's *focus* as of primary relevance to the jurisdictional limitations. A key example is Charnovitz, who distinguishes between 'inwardly-' and 'outwardly-directed' measures protecting public morals under Article XX(a) GATT.[226] 'Outwardly-directed' measures are those 'used to protect the morals of foreigners residing outside one's own country', while 'inwardly-directed' measures are those which 'protect morals of persons in one's own country'.[227] While these terms are 'somewhat arbitrary' given that they are 'two sides of a transaction', the defining factor is *who* the measure is primarily trying to protect.[228] In interpreting Article XX(a), the underlying assumption is that '[i]mport measures to safeguard the morals of a domestic population would probably receive the lightest scrutiny', while 'outwardly-directed' measures might 'receive more intense scrutiny'.[229] According to Charnovitz, the point at which this scrutiny occurs is not, however, in relation to the scope of 'public morals' under Article XX(a), but rather in relation to whether a measure is 'necessary' to achieve the stated objective.[230]

Cooreman builds on this approach, applying a similar reasoning to the physical environmental objectives of Article XX(b) and (g) GATT.[231] In doing so, she proposes a 'decision tree' to assess the acceptability of PPMs regulating extraterritorial conduct more generally.[232] Step one of the decision tree requires an identification of the 'location of the concern', where 'inward-looking' measures focus on environmental issues located within the territory of the regulating state, while 'outward-looking' measures seek to regulate concerns located outside the state.[233] Measures may also look both inward and outward, as is the case for

[225] *EC–Seals* (n 9) [5.173].

[226] S Charnovitz, 'The Moral Exception in Trade Policy' (1997) 38 *Virginia Journal of International Law* 689, 695.

[227] ibid, noting that '[o]ther terms that have been employed to describe laws that seek to promote values in foreign countries are "extrajurisdictional" and "extraterritorial"'.

[228] ibid. Notably, Charnovitz suggests that this may be a point of contention between states in concrete cases (737).

[229] ibid 730.

[230] ibid 730–31. With regard to scope, the only question is whether the subject matter of the measure 'falls within the range of policies covered by article XX(a)'.

[231] B Cooreman, 'Addressing Environmental Concerns through Trade? A Case for Extraterritoriality' (2016) 65 *ICLQ* 229.

[232] ibid 235.

[233] ibid 234–35, arguing that 'distinguishing between measures with an inward- or outward-looking purpose allows for a better assessment of the acceptability of PPMs that address activities occurring outside the territory of the regulating country'.

climate protection which is both a domestic and global concern. Similarly to Charnovitz, Cooreman reasons that '[p]urely inward-looking measures, even when non-product-related, will have a much stronger (territorial) connection or nexus than purely outward-looking measures'.[234] In fact, she argues that for inward-looking measures, 'no problems arise from a jurisdictional perspective as those concerns fall within the territorial jurisdiction and sovereign rights of the regulating State'.[235] Conversely, 'outward-looking' measures without any substantial territorial effects do raise jurisdictional issues. According to Cooreman, 'moral concerns or effects' need to be assessed under Article XX(a) GATT, and in their absence, 'it is very unlikely that a PPM addressing a fully demarcated foreign harm with no, or indirect, environmental impact would be accepted under Article XX GATT'.[236] As a second step in her decision tree, Cooreman then suggests an inquiry into the degree of international support for the measure's objective, which may buttress otherwise weaker claims of jurisdiction over outward-looking concerns.[237]

This book advocates for a different reading of the sufficient-nexus requirement, based neither on a territorial connection nor a measure's focus. To start with, interpreting Article XX GATT as requiring a physical territorial connection appears too narrow an approach. This is because it fails to reflect all of the permissive bases open to states under customary law, which have not, to date, been ruled out by the AB. As discussed in chapter 1, following the objective of 'systemic integration', parties to an agreement are considered to 'refer to customary international law and general principles of law for all questions which the treaty does not itself resolve in express terms'.[238] This finds expression in Article 31(3)c VCLT, according to which treaties may be interpreted in light of '[a]ny relevant rules of international law applicable in the relations between the parties'.[239] Article 3.2 of the WTO Dispute Settlement Understanding (DSU) supports this approach, providing that the covered agreements must be interpreted 'in accordance with customary rules of interpretation of public international law'.[240] In *US–Gasoline*, it was confirmed that this includes the Article 31 VCLT, as Article 3.2 DSU 'reflects a measure of recognition that the [GATT] is not to be read in clinical isolation from public international law'.[241]

[234] ibid.

[235] Cooreman (n 23) 65.

[236] Cooreman (n 231) 238.

[237] ibid 233. For a similar approach, see EU Petersmann, 'International Trade Law and International Environmental Law' (1993) 27 *Journal of World Trade* 34, 71.

[238] ILC, 'Fragmentation of International Law: Difficulties arising from the Diversification and Expansion of International Law – Report of the Study Group of the International Law Commission' (18 July 2006) UN Doc A/CN.4/L.702 [14 (19)], discussed further in the introduction to this book.

[239] Vienna Convention on the Law of Treaties (adopted 23 May 1969; entered into force 27 January 1980) 1155 UNTS 31. See further Conrad (n 48) 250.

[240] Dispute Settlement Rules: Understanding on Rules and Procedures Governing the Settlement of Disputes, Marrakesh Agreement Establishing the World Trade Organization (adopted 15 April 1994, entered into force 1 January 1995), Annex 2, 1869 UNTS 401 (DSU).

[241] *US–Gasoline (AB)* (n 172) 17.

It would then seem consistent that one should turn to the customary rules and general principles of state jurisdiction in full. In this case, even assuming that the connection is based on both territorial presence and effects, states may still wish to rely on elements of the protective or even the universality principles to support their jurisdictional assertions. This is not implausible for climate-protection measures, which aim to mitigate severe domestic harm as well as negative extraterritorial externalities contributing to a common concern of mankind.

Furthermore, while certainly valuable, relying so heavily on a measure's internal or external focus to determine the strength of a jurisdictional nexus is not necessarily the most straightforward approach. Firstly, characterising a measure as inward or outward looking is not always an objective exercise. As noted by Young, the categories of 'domestic, foreign, transboundary or global' for the possible framing of environmental concerns, are 'political and changeable'.[242] Others too have noted that 'a given measure can invariably be recast as "outwardly-directed" or "inwardly-directed," depending on the interests emphasized'.[243] Furthermore, the characterisation is simply not dispositive for common environmental concerns such as climate change, located both inside and outside all states' territories. International support is relevant, but may weigh-in irrespective of a concern's location.

More fundamentally, however, inward-looking measures may well raise jurisdictional questions. As argued in chapter 3, what matters for determining 'relevant extraterritoriality' are the interests of the *affected* states. These are sufficiently engaged when the operation of another state's measure is de facto dependent on conduct inside its territory or of its nationals. Framing the jurisdictional limitation of Article XX GATT in terms of a measure's inward or outward focus thus fails to adequately recognise the sovereign equality of other actors, as is particularly clear for public morals where the object of moral concern is located abroad.

Based on these considerations, it is argued here that one should simply interpret the AB's sufficient-nexus considerations as a reference to the 'substantial connection' requirement under customary international law. This more 'integrated approach' allows customary law to clarify the persistent uncertainties under WTO law, in line with Article 3.2 DSU and Article 31 VCLT. Where WTO law remains silent or unclear on the scope of states' regulatory competence, both compliant and non-compliant measures then ultimately remain subject to the customary international law of state jurisdiction as the relevant *lex generalis*.[244]

Applied to Article XX(b) and (g) GATT, this would mean that a state could regulate matters threatening 'human and animal life and health' or the

[242] Young (n 221) 306.

[243] Ankersmit, Lawrence and Davies (n 48) 28.

[244] L Bartels, 'Article XX of GATT and the Problem of Extraterritorial Jurisdiction – The Case of Trade Measures for the Protection of Human Rights' (2002) 36 *Journal of World Trade* 353, 360.

'conservation of exhaustible resources' when the subject matter it regulates is, for example, physically present in its territory, or causes substantial territorial effects. This approach can also be applied to Article XX(a), although the intangible nature of public morals does not fit as intuitively with most of the classical customary bases. As moral concerns are convictions held by a state's citizens (and consumers), it would seem that a state is inherently connected to its own 'internal' public morals.[245] As discussed above, it is argued that this is not a *territorial* connection but rather an abstract moral interest, recognised within the WTO regime as giving rise to regulatory competence. Clearly there remains a risk that states might attempt to expand their regulatory reach by claiming that a vast array of issues offend public morals. As noted by Cooreman, the primary safeguard for abuse of this competence then lies in maintaining a high threshold for which concerns truly constitute 'morals of a state's public'.[246]

4.3. Further Limitations in Application: The Chapeau of Article XX GATT

Finally, the chapeau of article XX GATT contains additional obstacles for the application of prescriptive measures provisionally justified under the provision's subparagraphs. Such measures must not constitute 'arbitrary or unjustifiable discrimination' or a 'disguised restriction on international trade'. According to the AB in *US–Shrimp*, 'the chapeau of article XX is, in fact, but one expression of the principle of good faith', prohibiting the abuse of rights and requiring states to exercise their rights 'reasonably'.[247] The delicate art of interpreting the chapeau entails the 'locating and marking out a line of equilibrium' between the substantive rights of other members under the GATT and the right to invoke an exception.[248]

The analysis of 'arbitrary or unjustifiable discrimination' 'relates primarily to the cause or the rationale of the discrimination'.[249] As such, the discriminatory effects of the measure must be 'explained by a rationale that bears … [a] relationship to the objective of a measure'.[250] In *EC–Seals*, the AB held that discriminating seal products from commercial hunts compared with the seal products hunted by Inuit or other indigenous communities could not be reconciled with the objective of protecting seal welfare.[251] The EU's desire to simultaneously protect the interests of indigenous communities (IC exception) did not justify this exemption, as 'IC hunts can cause the very pain and suffering

[245] The same does not hold for morals of another state, considered by Charnovitz as 'outwardly-directed' measures, see Charnovitz (n 226) 695.
[246] Cooreman (n 231) 235, referring to the risks of an 'uncontainable' exception.
[247] *US–Shrimp* (n 33) [158].
[248] ibid [159].
[249] *Brazil–Retreaded Tyres* (n 22) [225].
[250] ibid [232].
[251] *EC–Seals* (n 9) [5.338].

for seals that the EU public is concerned about'.[252] Somewhat controversially, through deferring to the EU's desired level of animal welfare protection, the AB reduced the Union's latitude to incorporate other policy objectives within the same measure. Such a restriction is particularly problematic for environmental protection measures which are often designed to include both an environmental and an economic benefit, under the 'green economy' paradigm.[253]

In addition, to avoid 'unjustifiable discrimination', states must make serious best efforts to reach a multilateral solution before resorting to unilateral action.[254] In *US–Shrimp (Article 21.5 Malaysia)*, the AB held that while a multilateral approach would be 'preferred', the actual conclusion of an agreement is not required.[255] Where a state maintains a unilateral approach its measure must be sufficiently flexible so as not to effectively require 'all other exporting Members … to adopt essentially the same policy', allowing for 'comparably effective third country measures', and taking into account 'the specific conditions prevailing in its territory'.[256] It has been suggested that consideration for third-country conditions must also take into account the principle of common but differentiated responsibility and respective capabilities (CBDRRC).[257] This will be considered further in chapter 10 on jurisdictional limitations.

The concept of a 'disguised restriction of international trade' pertains to overtly public policy measures which are in fact applied in bad faith to restrict international trade.[258] In practice, the requirements of the chapeau have proven a serious obstacle for states. To date, the only dispute in which a member was successful in justifying a GATT inconsistent measure has been *US–Shrimp (Article 21.5 – Malaysia)*, and this measure had already been adjusted after being found inconsistent in the 1998 *US–Shrimp* dispute.

5. CONCLUSION

Looking at the trends in WTO case law, we see a gradual increase in receptiveness to unincorporated PPMs seeking to reduce production externalities abroad.

[252] ibid [5.320].

[253] A Cosbey and PC Mavroidis, 'Heavy Fuel: Trade and Environment in the GATT/ WTO Case Law' (2014) 23 *Review of European, Comparative & International Environmental Law* 288, 300.

[254] *United States – Import Prohibition of Certain Shrimp and Shrimp Products (Recourse to Article 21.5 of the DSU by Malaysia)*, Appellate Body Report (21 November 2001) WT/DS58/AB/RW [124].

[255] ibid.

[256] *US–Shrimp* (n 33) [144] [161].

[257] See further P Larbprasertporn, 'The Interaction Between WTO Law and the Principle of Common but Differentiated Responsibilities in the Case of Climate-Related Border Tax Adjustment' (2014) 6 *Göttingen Journal of International Law* 145. See also F Morosini, 'Trade and Climate Change: Unveiling the Principle of Common but Differentiated Responsibilities from the WTO Agreements' (2010) 42 *George Washington Law Review* 713.

[258] *US–Gasoline* (n 172) 25.

Thus, over time it has become clear that carbon-footprint measures may fall within the scope of Article III GATT (and possibly Articles II and XVII GATS), and are therefore permissible as long as they are applied even-handedly. That being said, the AB's 'likeness' threshold sets a high bar for measures regulating non-physical characteristics, making it difficult for states to regulate embodied foreign production externalities. While legitimate regulatory distinctions may preclude a finding of 'less favourable treatment' under Article 2.1 TBT, such measures must still comply with Articles III and I of the GATT, where the AB has excluded the consideration of a measure's regulatory objective. Legitimate regulatory distinctions are also excluded from the NT and MFN provisions of the GATS. This means that it is likely that foreign carbon-footprint measures will need to be defended under the general exemption provisions of Articles XX GATT and XIV GATS.

It is then a welcome development that the AB has moved away from the categoric rejection of unincorporated environmental PPMs in the *Tuna/Dolphin* disputes. Nevertheless, the conditions of the subparagraphs and chapeau of Articles XX GATT and XIV GATS again set strict limitations on states' regulatory competence to regulate lifecycle emissions originating abroad. Importantly, the key question of whether Article XX GATT contains an implied jurisdictional limitation remains unanswered to date by the AB, which continues to avoid the issue. Drawing on the relevant case law and literature, this chapter has argued for a more 'integrated approach' whereby the sufficient-nexus requirement under WTO law is simply read as a reference to the significant-connection requirement in customary international law. This approach is consistent with the interpretative rules of the DSU, and helps to ensure the coherence of the two concurrently applicable regimes. It remains to be seen just how customary jurisdictional principles apply to the emerging issue of climate change. As a central question of the present study, this issue is considered further in part III.

5

Regulating Emissions from International Maritime Transport under the Law of the Sea

1. INTRODUCTION

Within the international climate regime, international aviation and maritime emissions occupy a unique position, remaining excluded from states' mandatory commitments under the Kyoto Protocol and, implicitly, the Paris Agreement.[1] Instead, Article 2(2) of the Kyoto Protocol encourages Annex I parties to seek multilateral solutions 'working through' the IMO and the ICAO. In light of the increasing political tensions and legal complexities, chapters 5 and 6 will explore the legal framework for the regulation of emissions from international maritime and aviation transport, respectively.

At the outset, it must be noted that there remains discussion as to whether the present construction under the Kyoto Protocol and Paris Agreement endows the IMO and ICAO with exclusive competence to regulate international transport emissions.[2] This book follows the widely accepted view that competence is not exclusively transferred under the climate change agreements, with state parties retaining the right to regulate these emissions.[3]

In practice, however, parallel unilateral measures certainly remain contentious. This is an issue growing in relevance as the IMO and ICAO take further strides towards multilateral responses. For its part, the European Union has been

[1] Kyoto Protocol to the United Nations Framework Convention on Climate Change (adopted 11 December 1997, entered into force 16 February 2005) UN Doc FCCC/CP/1997/7/Add.1, 10 December 1997 ('Kyoto Protocol'), Art 2(2). Reference to aviation and maritime emission was dropped late in negotiations. See 'Shipping Dropped from Paris Climate Deal' *World Maritime News* (10 December 2015) worldmaritimenews.com /archives/178438/shipping-dropped-from-paris-climate-deal/.

[2] Arguing in favour of exclusive competence, see eg UM Erling, 'How to Reconcile the European Union Emissions Trading System (EU ETS) for Aviation with the Carbon Offsetting and Reduction Scheme for International Aviation (CORSIA)?' 2018 43 *Air and Space law* 371, 376.

[3] See T Bäuerle, 'Integrating Shipping into the EU Emissions Trading Scheme?' in HJ Koch, D König and J Sanden (eds), *Climate Change and Environmental Hazards Related to Shipping: An International Legal Framework. Proceedings of the Hamburg International Environmental Law Conference 2011* (Leiden, Martinus Nijhoff 2013); H Ringbom, 'Global Problem – Regional Solution? International Law Reflections on an EU CO_2 Emissions Trading Scheme for Ships' (2011) 26 *International Journal of Marine and Coastal Law* 613.

particularly provocative, its unilateral policy in both of these fields giving rise to both political and legal criticisms. In the context of maritime transport, this can be found in the EU's monitoring, reporting and verification scheme for ships ('the EU Maritime MRV'), as its first step towards the inclusion of international maritime emissions into a unilateral market-based measure (MBM).[4] From the outset, the EU was not content to fully align with parallel IMO standards under the latter's Data Collection Scheme.[5] Indeed, at the 2019 Madrid climate summit the Union noted that 'the current global targets and measures envisaged' by the IMO (and ICAO), 'even if implemented in full, would fall short of the necessary emissions reductions' for the EU's goal of decarbonisation by 2050.[6]

This chapter explores the legal framework for unilateral measures seeking to reduce extraterritorial maritime emissions. Section 2 begins by sketching out the jurisdictional power structure within the law of the sea regime, with a particular emphasis placed on the United Nations Law of the Sea Convention (LOSC).[7] This is applicable to both the EU and its Member States, the Union having, ratified the Convention as an international organisation in 1998.[8] Section 3 then focuses on the issue of extraterritoriality, analysing the lively debate on the existence of territorial limitations on unilateral entry conditions under the law of the sea regime. Finally, section 4 turns to the policy developments regarding GHG emissions at the IMO since 2016, considering their relationship with the EU's unilateral measures.

2. 'EXTRATERRITORIALITY' AND THE DIVISION OF STATE POWERS UNDER THE LAW OF THE SEA REGIME

The UN LOSC forms the bedrock of states' rights and obligations in relation to maritime affairs, and is in part a codification of customary international law.[9]

[4] Parliament and Council (EU) Regulation 2015/757 on the monitoring, reporting and verification of carbon dioxide emissions from maritime transport, and amending Directive 2009/16/EC [2015] OJ L123/55 ('EU Maritime MRV').

[5] IMO Data Collections Scheme adopted in IMO Resolution MEPC.278(70), 'Amendments to the Annex of the Protocol of 1997 to amend the International Convention for the Prevention of Pollution from Ships, 1973, as modified by the Protocol of 1978 relating thereto – Data Collection System for Fuel Oil Consumption of Ships' (adopted 28 October 2016), MEPC 70/18/Add.1, Regulation 22A, 'Collection and reporting of ship fuel oil consumption data' (IMO MEPC.278(70)).

[6] European Parliament resolution of 28 November 2019 on the 2019 UN Climate Change Conference in Madrid, Spain (COP 25) (2019/2712(RSP)) ('EP Resolution COP 25') [70].

[7] United Nations Convention on the Law of the Sea (adopted 10 December 1982, entered into force 16 November 1994) 1833 UNTS 3 (LOSC). Also of relevance is the International Convention for the Prevention of Pollution from Ships (signed 2 November 1973, entered into force 2 October 1983) 1340 UNTS 62 (MARPOL).

[8] See 'Chronological lists of ratifications of, accessions and successions to the Convention and the related Agreements' (un.org, 9 March 2020) www.un.org/Depts/los/convention_agreements/convention_declarations.html. See also Competence of the European Communities with regard to matters governed by the Convention on the Law of the Sea (Declaration made pursuant to Article 2 of Annex IX to the Convention) (February 1985) 4 *Law of the Sea Bulletin* 16–19.

[9] See further T Treves, 'Historical Development of the Law of the Sea' in D Rothwell et al (eds), *The Oxford Handbook of the Law of the Sea* (Oxford, Oxford University Press, 2015) 2.

The LOSC is essentially 'a massive structure of powers' which balances different interests according to different maritime zones.[10] The zonal system is therefore fundamental to the scope of states' unilateral jurisdiction, and will now be set out briefly.

To start with, states exercise unlimited sovereignty over their ports and internal waters as part of their territory.[11] As a corollary, in their capacity as a 'port state', states may regulate and enforce conditions in relation to their ports' maritime zones.[12] Port states also qualify as 'coastal states', which, while nowhere defined in the LOSC, have been authoritatively described in the literature as 'the state in one of whose maritime zones a particular vessel lies'.[13] As noted by Marten, however, while 'as a matter of geography, a state exercising port state jurisdiction will also be a coastal state', port state jurisdiction is 'best discussed as a separate jurisdictional concept'.[14] This is because port state jurisdiction is restricted to vessels voluntarily within a state's territory, while coastal state jurisdiction extends to further maritime zones and is subject to far more detailed rules, with a greater emphasis on freedom of movement.[15]

With regard to geographical scope, coastal state sovereignty extends to the territorial waters, as the belt of sea adjacent to their land territories and internal waters.[16] Such sovereignty is conditioned by the obligation to respect the right of innocent passage of foreign ships.[17] In the exclusive economic zone (EEZ), coastal states have even more limited rights, and are only competent to regulate in relation to the exploitation, conservation and management of the natural resources of the waters, seabed and subsoil, as set out in Part V of the LOSC.[18]

Beyond states' territorial waters and EEZ lie the high seas, which 'no state may validly purport to subject to its sovereignty' (Article 89 LOSC). Here the freedom of the high seas plays a central role, though it must be exercised 'under the conditions laid down by this Convention and by other rules of international law' (Article 87 LOSC). This freedom applies to all states 'whether coastal or landlocked', a primary element of which is the freedom of navigation

[10] P Allott, 'Power Sharing in the Law of the Sea' (1983) 77 *American Journal of International Law* 1, 10. On the different interests in the context on pollution, see D Bodansky, 'Protecting the Marine Environment from Vessel-Source Pollution: UNCLOS III and beyond' (1991) 18 *Ecology Law Quarterly* 719, 720.

[11] Art 2 LOSC.

[12] E Molenaar, 'Port State Jurisdiction: Toward Comprehensive, Mandatory and Global Coverage' (2007) 38 *Ocean Development & International Law* 225, 227.

[13] R Churchill and V Lowe, *The Law of the Sea*, 3rd edn (Manchester, Manchester University Press, 1999) 355. See also E J Molenaar, 'Port and Coastal States', in D Rothwell et al (eds), *Oxford Handbook of the Law of the Sea* (2015) 282.

[14] B Marten, 'Port State Jurisdiction, International Conventions, and Extraterritoriality: An Expansive Interpretation' in H Ringbom (ed), *Jurisdiction over Ships: Post UNCLOS Developments in the Law of the Sea* (Leiden, Brill Nijhof, 2015) 112.

[15] ibid.

[16] Art 2(1) LOSC. Art 3 further provides that: 'The territorial sea extends 12 nautical miles from baselines determined in accordance with the Convention.'

[17] See s 3 LOSC on innocent passage in the territorial sea, in particular Art 24.

[18] See in particular Arts 55–56 LOSC.

(Article 87(a) LOSC). For their part, ships have the nationality and sail under the flag of the state in which they are registered ('the flag state') (Article 91 LOSC). Ships sail under the flag of one state only, and save for express exemptions in international treaties or custom, 'are subject to its exclusive jurisdiction on the high seas' (Article 92 LOSC). As will be discussed in section 3, there is much discussion as to whether these freedoms limit the jurisdiction of port states to set entry conditions dependent on prior conduct on the high seas.

Also of relevance to port state jurisdiction over vessel emissions is the MARPOL, as a key multilateral agreement regulating ships' pollution of the marine environment.[19] The setting of global standards for the safety, security and environmental performance of international shipping falls under the auspices of the IMO. In 2011, the IMO adopted two amendments to MARPOL Annex VI on the prevention of air pollution from ships, introducing the Energy Efficiency Design Index (EEDI) for new ships and the Ship Energy Efficiency Management Plan (SEEMP) for all ships.[20] The mandatory global data collection system for CO_2 emissions discussed above was also adopted a further amendment to Annex VI.[21] Notably, Regulation 11(6) of MARPOL Annex VI applies 'the international law concerning the prevention, reduction, and control of pollution of the marine environment from ships' to its own rules on atmospheric pollution.[22] As observed by Bauerle and others, this essentially links the jurisdictional framework of the LOSC to the rules and standards set out in Annex VI, at least between MARPOL Annex VI parties.[23]

The EU is not a formal party to the MARPOL or its Annex VI, and does not consider itself bound by these agreements.[24] Nevertheless, the latter are binding on the vast majority of EU Member States, conditioning their competences under public international law. The resulting tensions will be discussed further in section 4.

Perhaps unsurprisingly, disagreement concerning the correct characterisation of 'true' extraterritoriality is quite prominent in a maritime context. Here, a distinction is generally drawn between construction, design, equipment and manning (CDEM) standards and operational measures. The former are 'static' measures which 'follow the ship wherever it is', and cannot be easily

[19] MARPOL (n 7).

[20] Resolution MEPC.203(62) making mandatory the Energy Efficiency Design Index (EEDI) for new ships; Ship Energy Management Plan (SEEMP) for all ships in Annex VI of the International Convention for the Prevention of Pollution from Ships, 1340 UNTS 184 (1973).

[21] Resolution MEPC.278(70) (n 5).

[22] Regulation 11(6) of MARPOL Annex VI states: 'The international law concerning the prevention, reduction, and control of pollution of the marine environment from ships, including that law relating to enforcement and safeguards, in force at the time of application or interpretation of this Annex, applies, *mutatis mutandis*, to the rules and standards set forth in this Annex.'

[23] See further T Bäuerle et al, 'Integration of Marine Transport into the European Emissions Trading System – Environmental, Economic and Legal Analysis of Different Options' (German Federal Environment Agency (Umweltbundesamt) 2010) Report No (UBA-FB) 001372 88.

[24] Case C-537/11 *Manzi and Compagnia Naviera Orchestra (Manzi)* [2014] EU:C:2014:19 [37].

changed during a voyage.[25] These are contrasted with measures regulating vessel operations such as operational pollution, which pertain to conduct on board of vessels.[26] As regards EU law, both the maritime MRV and envisioned ETS require vessels to be fitted with certain equipment necessary for monitoring CO_2 emissions, and thus contain CDEM standards.[27] The requirements regarding the monitoring itself, as well as the reporting and attainment of verification and compliance documentation, pertain to foreign conduct.[28]

It is quite well-accepted that operational measures regulating behaviour occurring outside a state's territory may raise issues of extraterritoriality.[29] This aligns with the approach advocated by this book, which identifies a jurisdictionally relevant 'extraterritorial element' when a measure's operation is de facto dependent on foreign conduct or circumstances. There is more debate, however, on the extraterritoriality of CDEM standards which, due to their static nature, remain uniform throughout a vessel's voyage.[30] On the one hand, as the New Zealand court found in the *Sellers* case, the 'effect, if not the purpose' of such CDEM standards 'is to place requirements on the exercise of the freedom to navigate on the high seas by reference to the adequacy of the ship, her crew and her equipment for the voyage'.[31] As noted by Ringbom, as ship operators have little choice but to comply with CDEM standards throughout the whole voyage, these requirements are 'often considered to be the most intrusive ones' on ships' navigation rights.[32]

On the other hand, it has been argued that 'paradoxically' CDEM standards are in fact 'easier to justify in jurisdictional terms' because non-compliant vessels entering port would be in 'continuous violation' of the standard in question, at which point they fall under states' legislative and enforcement jurisdiction based entirely on their territorial sovereignty.[33] Indeed, Marten considers that vessel conditions fall 'comfortably within the territorial basis of jurisdiction'

[25] Ringbom (n 3) 621.

[26] See further R Churchill, 'Port State Jurisdiction Relating to the Safety of Shipping and Pollution from Ships – What Degree of Extra-Territoriality?' (2016) 31 *International Journal of Marine & Coastal Law* 442, 443.

[27] See EU Maritime MRV (n 4) Annex I.

[28] Note, however, that questions can be raised as to the nature of information sharing requirements, which are more difficult to 'locate'; see further B Marten, 'Port State Jurisdiction over Vessel Information: Territoriality, Extra-Territoriality and the Future of Shipping Regulation' (2016) 31 *International Journal of Marine & Coastal Law* 470, 484.

[29] See eg Molenaar (n 12) 229; C Ryngaert and H Ringbom, 'Introduction: Port State Jurisdiction: Challenges and Potential' (2016) 31 *International Journal of Marine & Coastal Law* 379, 383: 'However, to the extent that PSJ [port state jurisdiction] pertains to activities occurring entirely outside areas within national jurisdiction (the high seas or other states' coastal waters), territoriality cannot be the basis of jurisdiction and its exercise will need to rely on other potential jurisdictional bases to be lawful'. See also, Churchill 'Port State Jurisdiction Relating Safety and Pollution from Ships' (2016) 454.

[30] See further, Molenaar (n 12) 230.

[31] ibid; *Sellers v Maritime Safety Inspector* [1999] 2 NZLR 44 [5 November 1998] (*Sellers*).

[32] Ringbom (n 3) 621.

[33] ibid 622. See also Molenaar (n 12) 230; S Kopela, 'Making Ships Cleaner: Reducing Air Pollution from International Shipping' (2017) 26 *Review of European, Comparative & International Environmental Law* 231, 240.

as a port state is entitled to prescribe such requirements 'whenever a vessel is in one of its ports'.[34] In this regard, Ringbom distinguishes between CDEM standards and 'truly extraterritorial' measures as those that may raise issues with freedom of navigation.[35] Molenaar, too, supports this approach, arguing that the extraterritorial effects of a CDEM standard are 'incidental rather than its purpose'.[36] Churchill follows a similar reasoning, arguing that it 'is not the port State's *objective* to regulate the construction, design, equipment or manning of a foreign ship when it is outside that State's territory, but only when it is within its ports'.[37] As such, this is 'purely an exercise in territorial jurisdiction'.[38] According to the author, this conclusion is bolstered by the fact that ships have a choice whether to call at a port, knowing that they must then meet the CDEM standards that the port state prescribes.[39]

This book takes the view that a measure's effects, rather than its 'primary' or 'incidental' purpose, serve as a better yardstick for assessing whether issues of extraterritoriality arise under international law.[40] As noted by Kopela, whether a measure's extraterritorial effect is incidental or not 'can be a matter of perception', demonstrating the uncertainty of using territoriality as the (only) jurisdictional basis for CDEM standards.[41] Importantly, the question of a measure's extraterritorial element must be separated from that of its permissibility, both under the specific provisions of the LOSC and customary jurisdictional rules. Indeed, according to Ryngaert and Ringbom, despite the fact that CDEM measures will 'almost as a matter of course produce extra-territorial *effects* … this need not detract from their principled legality'.[42] This question will now be discussed further in section 3, which considers the territorial limitations on unilateral port state measures with an extraterritorial element under the LOSC.

3. TERRITORIAL LIMITATIONS ON PORT STATE JURISDICTION IN THE LAW OF THE SEA CONVENTION?

As we have seen above, the zonal system of the LOSC balances states' sovereign rights to regulate entry to their territories against the right of all states

[34] Marten (n 14) 27, noting that: 'Of course the state in this situation wants the vessel to continue complying with the rule after it has left port, but it does not have to frame it this way as a matter of law.'

[35] Ringbom (n 3) 626.

[36] Molenaar (n 12) 230. See also Churchill (n 26) 454, hinging relevant extraterritoriality on a measure's 'primary purpose'.

[37] Churchill (n 26) 454.

[38] ibid.

[39] ibid.

[40] See further chapter 3, section 4 of this book.

[41] S Kopela, 'Port-State Jurisdiction, Extraterritoriality, and the Protection of Global Commons' (2016) 47 *Ocean Development & International Law* 89, 96.

[42] Ryngaert and Ringbom (n 29) 383: 'Given the static nature of such standards, such assertions of territorial jurisdiction will almost as a matter of course produce extra-territorial *effects*, but this need not detract from their principled legality (although perhaps from their desirability)'.

to freedom of navigation. An essential question which arises in this context is whether the freedom of navigation and the principle of exclusive flag state jurisdiction on the high seas limit the scope of port state jurisdiction to prescribe conditions of entry. Generally speaking, two schools of thought can be identified on this question.[43] According to the first, more restrictive approach, port entry conditions with an extraterritorial element are precluded in the absence of an explicit treaty basis. In contrast, the second school of thought does not consider the LOSC to limit port state jurisdiction, leaving port states with residual jurisdiction to set entry conditions, although these remain limited by the customary international law.[44] As will now be discussed, this 'residual approach' is preferred here. Sections 3.1 and 3.2 will now explore this debate in more detail.

3.1. The Restrictive Approach: An Explicit Jurisdictional Basis Needed for Climate-Protective Measures with an Extraterritorial Element

Freedom of navigation is one of the most defining characteristics of the high seas, constituting part of the broader 'freedom of the high seas' codified in Article 87 LOSC. As mentioned, this is supported by Article 89 LOSC, according to which no state may purport to subject any part of the high seas to its sovereignty. It is further complemented by Article 92 LOSC which provides that ships 'shall be subject to the exclusive jurisdiction' of the flag state on the high seas. On a restrictive view, these provisions, taken together, indicate that port state measures which have effect on the high seas are precluded by the LOSC, unless an explicit basis can be demonstrated.[45] Measures such as the EU maritime MRV and envisioned expanded ETS that require foreign vessels to have complied with certain conduct requirements prior to entry would therefore require such a basis.

As contextual support, commentators point to Article 218 LOSC, which provides that port states may not institute proceedings pertaining to discharges occurring outside of their territorial waters or EEZ other than those 'in violation of applicable international rules and standards'. This, they argue, indicates *a contrario*, that states (and the EU) are not competent to regulate *other* conduct

[43] Note that Molenaar considers a further subcategory, namely 'port State residual jurisdiction under customary international law was brought about by specific treaty provisions', ie 'no-more-favorable-treatment' (NMFT) clauses. E Molenaar, 'Port State Jurisdiction' in R Wolfrum (ed), *Max Planck Encyclopaedia of Public International Law*, online edn (Oxford, Oxford University Press) [8] (revised version 2020 on file with author).

[44] Ringbom (n 3) 624.

[45] See eg Bodansky (n 10) 760; T McDorman, 'Port State Enforcement: A Comment on Article 218 of the 1982 Law of the Sea Convention' (1997) 28 *Journal of Maritime Law & Commerce* 305, 307, 313; D König, 'Flags of Ships' in R Wolfrum (ed), *Max Planck Encyclopaedia of Public International Law*, online edn (Oxford, Oxford University Press, 2009) [25]. For a more comprehensive analysis and overview of the literature, see A Honniball, 'The Exclusive Jurisdiction of Flag States: A Limitation on Pro-active Port States?' (2016) 31 *International Journal of Marine & Coastal Law* 499, 505.

on the high seas, ie conduct not in violation of international standards.[46] Thus Article 218 LOSC is interpreted as an extension of otherwise limited port state jurisdiction, to include enforcement of 'applicable international standards' allegedly violated by foreign vessels on the high seas.[47]

With regard to possible bases for unilateral measures, commentators refer to IMO Conventions, the MARPOL being especially important for vessel source pollution.[48] Of particular relevance is the 2011 amendment to MARPOL Annex VI to include mandatory technical and operational energy efficiency standards to reduce CO_2 emissions from new ships.[49] Nowhere in the relevant international agreements is there a specific provision regarding unilateral port state regulation of CO_2 emitted on the high seas, however. For this reason, the argument goes, states (and the EU) lack jurisdiction to regulate emissions from international maritime transport under the LOSC.[50]

Looking at the underlying assumptions, we see that the restrictive approach implicitly rests on an expansive interpretation of the scope of Articles 87 and 92 LOSC as precluding all measures with extraterritorial 'steering effects' on the high seas.[51] In this regard, Hermeling and others go so far as to argue that the 'freedom of navigation' in Article 87(a) should in fact be read in conjunction with Article 24 LOSC on the right of innocent passage to mean 'not only freedom from legal restrictions but also the effective freedom of navigation by absence of all influences not authorized under the UNCLOS regime'.[52] According to the authors, the rationale of the prohibition in Article 24 of measures with the 'practical effect of "denying or impairing" the freedom of navigation' 'can be transposed by analogy to the freedom on the high seas'. This is because a guarantee of merely 'legal freedom' would, 'aside the flag-state principle … and the prohibition to purport to subject any part of the high seas to national sovereignty … be superfluous'.[53]

An older expression of the restrictive view can be found in the aforementioned *Sellers* case before the New Zealand Court of Appeal.[54] There, Mr Sellers was prosecuted for allowing his Maltese vessel, the *Nimbus*, to leave a New Zealand port without being equipped with a radio, as required by

[46] For support of this view, see C Hermeling et al, 'Sailing Into a Dilemma – An Economic and Legal Analysis of an EU Trading Scheme for Maritime Emissions' (Centre for European Economic Research 2014) Discussion Paper No 14-021 14; Bodansky (n 10) 762: 'The better interpretation, then, [of Art 218] is that port state enforcement authority is limited to discharges in violation of international standards that, by their own terms, apply to the vessel in question.'

[47] For a more detailed analysis of Art 218 LOSC in this regard, see McDorman (n 45).

[48] See eg Bodansky (n 10) 760.

[49] Resolution MEPC.203(62) (n 20).

[50] See eg Kopela (n 41) 93; Hermeling et al (n 46) 11.

[51] Hermeling et al (n 46) 13. See also *Sellers* (n 31) 49, where the court also considered the practical 'effect' of the measure in question on the high seas.

[52] Hermeling et al (n 46) 14.

[53] ibid.

[54] *Sellers* (n 31).

the guidelines of the New Zealand Maritime Safety Authority. As it was of 'religious' importance to Mr Sellers to be 'alone with the sea' without a radio, the defendant had failed to seek – and gain – clearance for departure, in violation of section 21(1) of the Maritime Transport Act 1994.[55]

The question to be answered in that case was whether the requirement of a radio on board a foreign vessel violated the freedom of the high seas, an 'essential feature' of which, according to the Court, was the principle of exclusive flag state jurisdiction (EFSJ). The Court of Appeal stressed the customary nature of Article 92, which it considered 'subject only to "exceptional cases expressly provided for in international treaties"'. According to the Court:

> The exceptions are to be related to the recognition in art 87(2) that the freedoms of the high seas are to be exercised by all states with due regard for the interests of other states in their exercise of the freedoms.[56]

While the world community 'occasionally and cautiously' expressly provides for such exemptions, the Court did not find sufficient support for unilateral measures containing safety obligations for foreign ships on the high seas.[57] The Court also analysed port state jurisdiction under certain international agreements, including MARPOL, noting their emphasis on the role of the flag state, while only 'acknowledging a role for the port state in limited circumstances'.[58]

According to the Court, this view was further supported by Article 21(2) LOSC which provides that permitted coastal state laws and regulations relating to innocent passage 'shall not apply to' CDEM standards for foreign ships 'unless they are giving effect to generally accepted international rules or standards'. Extending this beyond the territorial sea, the court found that 'a port state has no general power to unilaterally impose its own requirements on foreign ships relating to their construction, their safety and other equipment and their crewing if the requirements are to have effect on the high seas'.[59] Taken together, the *Sellers* case thus argues that outside of specific provisions, such as those in MARPOL, port states are not competent to set entry requirements that 'have effect' on the high seas.[60]

This finding has, however, not been without criticism. Ringbom, for example, notes that the argument 'fails to convince' because 'it is not explained why, if the LOSC limitations for prescription in the territorial sea apply, the even more onerous limitations for the EEZ and the high seas would not'.[61] 'Following the

[55] ibid 46.
[56] ibid 47.
[57] ibid 48.
[58] ibid 52.
[59] ibid 57.
[60] ibid 52–4. See also, B Marten, 'Port State Jurisdiction in New Zealand: The Problem with Sellers' (2013) 44 *Victoria University of Wellington Law Review* 559, 565.
[61] Ringbom (n 3) 622. In relation to the EEZ, see Art 211(5) LOSC which limits coastal state jurisdiction to generally accepted international standards, with certain exemptions contained in Art 211(6) LOSC.

Court's logic would mean that the majority of the world's port states are acting unlawfully in applying their domestic shipping standards.'[62] Fundamentally, as will be discussed in the following section, this disregards states' sovereignty over their ports, to which there is no general right of access.[63]

Strikingly, twenty years later, two international disputes also appear to follow the restrictive approach. The first is the majority finding in the 2019 *M/V 'Norstar'* case before the International Tribunal for the Law of the Sea (ITLOS).[64] The case concerned a Decree of Seizure issued by the Italian public prosecutor against the Panamanian oil tanker, the M/V *Norstar*, which had been supplying gasoil to mega yachts 'outside the territorial waters' of France, Italy and Spain (ie 'bunkering'), prohibited under Italian law. Pursuant to the European Agreement on Mutual Assistance in Criminal Matters, Spanish authorities seized the M/V *Norstar* when it was in the Spanish Bay of Palma de Mallorca (internal waters).[65]

According to ITLOS, the bunkering activities on the high seas constituted a 'central element' of the subject matter regulated by the Decree, whereby Article 87 LOSC may be applicable.[66] In interpreting this provision, the Tribunal found that 'any act of interference with navigation of foreign ships or any exercise of jurisdiction over such ships on the high seas constitutes a breach of the freedom of navigation, unless justified by the [LOS] Convention or other international treaties'.[67] This is not limited to enforcement but also includes prescriptive jurisdiction, whereby 'Italy's application of its criminal and customs laws to bunkering activities of the M/V "Norstar" on the high seas could in itself … constitute a breach of the freedom of navigation under article 87 of the Convention'.[68] As an 'inherent component of the freedom of navigation', states violate the EFSJ principle not only by enforcement but 'also the extension of their prescriptive jurisdiction to lawful activities conducted by foreign ships on the high seas'.[69]

Interestingly, the Tribunal explicitly rejected Italy's argument that 'extraterritoriality is not the test to assess a breach of article 87', the latter of which is concerned with 'interference with navigation'.[70] According to ITLOS, 'even when enforcement is carried out in internal waters, article 87 may still be applicable

[62] H Ringbom, *The EU Maritime Safety Policy and International Law* (Leiden, Martinus Nijhoff, 2008) 339.

[63] *Case concerning Military and Paramilitary Activities In and Against Nicaragua (Nicaragua v United States of America)* (Merits) [1986] ICJ Rep 3, 213 (*Nicaragua* case) 213; Molenaar (n 12) 227.

[64] *The M/V 'Norstar' Case (Panama v Italy)* (Judgment of 10 April 2019) ITLOS Reports 2018–19, 10 (*M/V 'Norstar'*)). See also *The M/V 'Norstar' Case (Panama v Italy) (Preliminary Objections)* (Judgment of 4 November 2016) ITLOS Reports 2016, 44 (*M/V 'Norstar'* (Preliminary Objections)).

[65] *M/V 'Norstar'* (Preliminary Objections) (n 64) [41]–[43].

[66] *M/V 'Norstar'* (n 64) [186]–[187].

[67] ibid [222]. See further Molenaar (n 43) [9].

[68] *M/V 'Norstar'* (n 64) [224].

[69] ibid [225].

[70] ibid.

and be breached if a State extends its criminal and customs laws extraterritorially to activities of foreign ships on the high seas and criminalizes them'.[71] This part of the Tribunal's finding was, however, heavily contested in the seven-judge dissenting opinion, which considered that:

> [N]othing in the text of the Convention, in its travaux préparatoires, in other international treaties, in customary international law, or in the practice of States suggests that article 87 and its corollary article 92 altogether excludes the right of non-flag States to exercise their prescriptive criminal jurisdiction with respect to activities on the high seas.[72]

The dissenting opinion further expressed favour for the permissive approach set out in the cornerstone *Lotus* case, whereby the relevant *prescriptive* jurisdiction may be exercised, 'not when it is justified or allowed by international law to do so, but when it is not prohibited by international law to do so'.[73] The *Lotus* case itself notably takes the opposing view as regards enforcement jurisdiction, which must be territorial unless otherwise agreed.[74]

Following hot on the heels of *M/V 'Norstar'*, the *Enrica Lexie* case before the Permanent Court of Arbitration (PCA) also supports a restrictive approach.[75] The case concerned the shooting of two Indian nationals aboard the Indian-flagged vessel, the *St Antony*, by two Italian marines aboard the Italian-flagged oil tanker, the *Enrica Lexie*, while outside of India's territorial waters. Subsequent to the shooting, the *Enrica Lexie* was stopped by Indian officials, and 'guided' towards an Indian port, although it was debated by the parties whether the docking was entirely voluntary.[76] There the Italian marines were arrested for a violation of Indian penal legislation.[77]

According to Italy, India violated Articles 92 and 87(1)(a) LOSC by 'directing and inducing the *Enrica Lexie* to change course and proceed into India's

[71] ibid.

[72] *M/V 'Norstar'* (n 64) Joint Dissenting Opinion of Judges Cot, Pawlak, Yanai, Hoffmann, Kolodkin and Lijnzaad and Judge ad hoc Treves [19].

[73] ibid [36], referring to *The SS Lotus (France v Turkey)* 1927 PCIJ Series A, No 10. See chapter 7 for further discussion of the *Lotus* case.

[74] For critique of the majority judgment, as failing to recognise this distinction, see A Honniball, 'Freedom of Navigation Following the M/V "Norstar" Case ' (worldcourts.com, 4 June 2019) www.site.uit.no/nclos/2019/06/04/freedom-of-navigation-following-the-m-v-norstar-case/.

[75] *The 'Enrica Lexie' Incident (Italy v India) (2016)* (Provisional Measures, Order of 29 April 2016) PCA Case No 2015-28 (*'Enrica Lexie'* (PCA Provisional Measures)). *The 'Enrica Lexie' Incident (Italy v India)* (Award of 21 May 2020) PCA Case No 2015-28 (*'Enrica Lexie'* (PCA Award). Notably, Italy also brought provisional measures proceedings before the ITLOS, demanding release of its nationals based on the same argument, that 'India breached the Convention by its 'exercise of jurisdiction over the Enrica Lexie Incident and the Marines notwithstanding Italy's exclusive jurisdiction over the same by virtue of the undisputed fact that the Incident took place beyond India's territorial sea'. See, *The "Enrica Lexie" Incident (Italy v India)* (Provisional Measures, Order of 24 August 2015) ITLOS Reports 2015 (*Enrica Lexie* (ITLOS, Provisional Measures)), [40], [49].

[76] The Italian authorities allege that the *Enrica Lexie* was brought to anchorage in Kochi 'by ruse or coercion'. *The 'Enrica Lexie' Incident (Italy v India)*, (Notification of the Italian Republic, 26 June 2015) ITLOS Reports 2015, 3 [11].

[77] Indian Penal Code (IPC) 1860, ss 3 and 4; The Code of Criminal Procedure, S188 1973 (CrPc).

territorial sea' and 'by interdicting the *Enrica Lexie* and escorting her to Kochi'.[78] In response, India claimed that Italy had 'violated India's freedom and right of navigation' under Articles 87 and 90 LOSC, when 'firing at the St Antony and killing two Indian fishermen on board'.[79]

Drawing on the customary jurisdictional rules, the Tribunal recognised that 'where an offence was commenced on board one vessel and completed on board another vessel, the flag States of both vessels may have concurrent jurisdiction over the offence'.[80] According to the Tribunal, 'India's exercise of jurisdiction over the "Enrica Lexie" incident is not only compatible with the Convention, but justified by Article 92, paragraph 1', 'pursuant' to which:

> India, as the flag State, has exclusive jurisdiction over the 'St Antony' and may assert its jurisdiction in respect of the offence that was allegedly completed on board its vessel in the exclusive economic zone, in the same way as Italy, as the flag State, has exclusive jurisdiction over the 'Enrica Lexie' and may assert its jurisdiction in respect of the offence that was allegedly commenced on board its vessel.[81]

As regards the more general interpretation of Articles 87 and 92 LOSC, the Tribunal closely followed the *M/V 'Norstar'* majority finding. Thus it found that 'the exercise of jurisdiction over a foreign ship on the high seas, unless justified by the Convention or other international treaties, is generally agreed to constitute a breach of freedom of navigation'.[82] Other than the reference to the *M/V 'Norstar'* case, however, it is not clear where such 'general agreement' is found.

Turning to the EFSJ principle, after stressing its nature as a 'corollary of the open and free status of the high seas', the Tribunal distinguished very generally between the different types of jurisdiction.[83] It then reiterated the widely accepted international legal theory that 'the exercise of jurisdiction by a State entails an element of prescribing laws, rules, or regulations over conduct, or applying or enforcing such laws, rules, or regulations over persons or property'. According to the tribunal:

> It follows from the above analysis that the principle of exclusive flag State jurisdiction under the Convention is violated when a State other than the flag State seeks to prescribe laws, rules, or regulations over a ship of the flag State, or applies or enforces such laws, rules, or regulations in respect of such a ship. The Arbitral Tribunal also recalls in this respect the observation of ITLOS in *M/V 'Norstar'* that the principle of exclusive flag State jurisdiction 'prohibits not only the exercise of enforcement jurisdiction on the high seas by States other than the flag State but also the extension of their prescriptive jurisdiction to lawful activities conducted by foreign ships on the high seas'.[84]

[78] '*Enrica Lexie*' (PCA Award) (n 75) [68].
[79] ibid [76(6)].
[80] ibid [366].
[81] ibid [368].
[82] ibid [473].
[83] *Enrica Lexie* (PCA Award) (n 75) [524], [526].
[84] Ibid [527].

On its face, it is not very clear how this conclusion 'follows' from the above very general analysis – indeed questions have been raised as to whether there was much of an 'analysis' at all.[85] Furthermore, Honniball points out that the Tribunal's first finding that two flag states may have concurrent jurisdiction over the same offence as *supported* by EFSJ appears to contradict the final conclusion. Were EFSJ and the freedom of navigation to preclude extraterritorial *prescriptive* jurisdiction, then concurrent prescriptive jurisdiction would not be possible. It is hard to see how jurisdiction can be both exclusive and concurrent at the same time. There is an unrealistic assumption that a single set of facts can be neatly divided into distinct jurisdictional spheres subject only to the prescriptive jurisdiction of a single flag state.

To conclude, the *M/V 'Norstar'* and *Enrica Lexie* cases certainly reignite discussions on the scope of port state jurisdiction. As noted by Collins, the majority finding in *M/V 'Norstar'* is 'arguably at odds with a substantial body of opinion in the literature that flag state exclusivity extends only to enforcement activity occurring on the high seas'.[86] It can further 'perhaps be criticized for simply asserting the validity of the opposite proposition, without any corresponding precedent cited' aside from the *Lotus* case, which in fact better supports the dissenting opinion.[87] The *Enrica Lexie* case faces a similar critique, Honniball noting that it was advanced 'without reasoning', its interpretation of Article 92 LOSC in fact being inconsistent with its own findings elsewhere in the Award.[88] It remains to be seen to what extent these tightly knit cases will set a precedent for future disputes.

3.2. The Residual Approach: No Explicit Basis Needed for Climate-Protective Measures with an Extraterritorial Element

The alternative approach supported here focuses on states' residual jurisdiction to regulate entry to their ports, for which no explicit basis is required under the law of the sea regime.[89] States exercise sovereignty over their ports as part of their territory (Article 2 LOSC). Under international law ships have no general right of access to foreign ports.[90] As a result, states may exercise wide discretion

[85] A Honniball, 'The 'Enrica Lexie' Incident Award and Exclusive Flag State Jurisdiction' (National University of Singapore Center for International Law Blog, 10 August 2020) www.cil.nus.edu.sg/the-enrica-lexie-incident-award-and-exclusive-flag-state-jurisdiction-by-arron-n-honniball/.

[86] R Collins, 'The M/V "Norstar" Case (Panama v Italy) (ITLOS)' (2019) 58 *International Legal Materials* 673, 674.

[87] ibid.

[88] A Honniball, 'Inconsistencies Abound: The 'Enrica Lexie' Incident Award and Exclusive Flag State Jurisdiction' (National University of Singapore Center for International Law Blog (forthcoming, document on record with author).

[89] See e, Molenaar (n 12) 227; Ringbom (n 3) 625; Marten (n 14) 109; Churchill (n 26) 447; Kopela (n 41) 93.

[90] *Nicaragua* case (n 63) 213. See also J Crawford, *Brownlie's Principles of Public International Law*, 8th edn (Oxford, Oxford University Press, 2012) 458.

in regulating entry to their ports, and merely denying such entry does not contravene the LOSC.[91] In particular, as will now be argued, this discretion is not limited by the freedom of navigation or exclusive flag state jurisdiction. In fact, unilateral environmental protection measures find implicit support in various provisions of international maritime law.

A premise of this approach is that the LOSC *deliberately* says little on the question of prescriptive jurisdiction for port states, leaving them with a wide residual discretion to set port entry conditions.[92] In this vein, Crawford observes that any reference to 'jurisdiction' in the LOSC is therefore of an enforcement nature.[93] While the LOSC does not strictly regulate prescriptive jurisdiction, it does create certain entitlements for its exercise, including in the field of environmental protection. In particular, Article 211(3) LOSC recognises the competence of coastal states to 'establish particular requirements for the prevention, reduction and control of pollution of the marine environment'. According to article 1(4) LOSC:

> 'pollution of the marine environment' means the introduction by man, directly or indirectly, of substances or energy into the marine environment … which results or is likely to result in such deleterious effects as harm to living resources and marine life, hazards to human health, hindrance to marine activities, including fishing and other legitimate uses of the sea, impairment of quality for use of sea water and reduction of amenities.

On an 'effects-based' view, maritime CO_2 emissions can then be considered 'pollution' in the sense of Article 1(4) LOSC because they contribute to climate change and air pollution, which in turn harm marine life and human health.[94] In particular, as noted by Redgwell, anthropogenic climate change destroys the ecosystems that bind stores of so-called 'blue carbon', which is 'carbon stored, sequestered, and released from the oceans' vegetated habitats'.[95] Focusing on more linear effects, CO_2 emissions result in severe acidification of the seas, also causing direct harm to the marine environment.[96]

Further support for prescriptive port state competence can be found in Article 25(2) LOSC, which provides that:

> In the case of ships proceeding to internal waters or a call at a port facility outside internal waters, the coastal State also has the right to take the necessary steps to

[91] Molenaar (n 12) 227.

[92] See Crawford (n 90) 301; Marten (n 14) 111; Marten, 'Port State Jurisdiction in New Zealand' (2013) 561; E Molenaar, *Coastal State Jurisdiction over Vessel-Source Pollution* (The Hague, Kluwer Law International 1998) 94.

[93] See Crawford (n 90) 301, observing that unlike enforcement jurisdiction, prescriptive jurisdiction is not in fact regulated by the LOSC but by general international law.

[94] See Bäuerle et al (n 23) 91.

[95] C Redgwell, 'UNCLOS and Climate Change' (2012) 106 *ASIL Proceedings* 406, 409.

[96] See further on CO_2 and ocean acidification, National Oceanic and Atmospheric Administration, 'What Is Ocean Acidification?' (pmel.noaa.gov, 2017) www.pmel.noaa.gov/co2/story/What+is+Ocean+Acidification%3F.

> prevent any breach of the conditions to which admission of those ships to internal waters or such a call is subject.

According to commentators, this provision implicitly recognises port state competence to prescribe entry conditions, as well as, arguably, to enforce them in cases of breach.[97]

Another provision of relevance here is Article 194 LOSC, which instructs states to take all measures consistent with the LOSC, 'necessary to prevent, reduce and control pollution of the marine environment from any source'. According to Boyle, while anthropogenic GHGs are not specifically listed in the indicative provision of Article 194(3), it is 'entirely plausible' to read CO_2 from maritime pollution as falling with the 'toxic, harmful or noxious substances, especially those which are persistent … from or through the atmosphere'.[98] Furthermore, Article 194(5) stipulates that 'measures taken in accordance with this Part shall include those necessary to protect and preserve rare or fragile ecosystems as well as the habitat of depleted, threatened or endangered species and other forms of marine life'. Given the overwhelming scientific evidence of the harmful effects of climate change on marine ecosystems, it seems consistent that CO_2 reduction measures are supported by this provision.[99]

In addition, there are arguments to be made that Article 21 LOSC on the right of innocent passage supports rather than precludes certain environmental protection measures. Thus, while paragraph 2 does limit jurisdiction to prescribe CDEM standards, this is in fact the exception to the general provision in paragraph 1, that:

> The coastal State may adopt laws and regulations, in conformity with the provisions of this Convention and other rules of international law, relating to innocent passage through the territorial sea, in respect of all or any of the following: …
>
> (d) the conservation of the living resources of the sea;
>
> (e) the prevention of infringement of the fisheries laws and regulations of the coastal State;
>
> (f) the preservation of the environment of the coastal State and the prevention, reduction and control of pollution thereof.

This last subparagraph could be seen as an expression of effects-based jurisdiction, which limits the right of innocent passage where *conduct* has harmful effects on the environment of the coastal state. Contrary to the New Zealand

[97] See eg Molenaar (n 12) 230; Ringbom (n 3) 625.

[98] A Boyle, 'Law of the Sea Perspectives on Climate Change' in D Freestone (ed), *The 1982 Law of the Sea Convention at 30: Successes, Challenges and New Agendas* (Leiden, Brill, 2013) 157, 158.

[99] On the effect of climate change on marine ecosystems, see further NL Bindoff, et al, 'Changing Ocean, Marine Ecosystems, and Dependent Communities' in H-O Pörtner et al (eds), *IPCC Special Report on the Ocean and Cryosphere in a Changing Climate* (2019) 448, www.ipcc.ch/site/assets/uploads/sites/3/2019/11/09_SROCC_Ch05_FINAL-1.pdf.

Court's approach in *Sellers*, this suggests that port state jurisdiction is not limited to the CDEM standards prescribed in international agreements.[100]

According to the residual approach, port state control measures confirm rather than create specific regulatory competences.[101] In fact, Molenaar notes that several IMO instruments clearly recognise port states' residual jurisdiction.[102] For example, Article 1(3) of the International Convention on the Control of Harmful Anti-Fouling Systems on Ships prohibits that Convention from being interpreted as 'preventing a State from taking, individually or jointly, more stringent measures with respect to the reduction or elimination of adverse effects of anti-fouling systems on the environment, consistent with international law'.[103] While several IMO Conventions, in particular MARPOL, set CDEM standards for pollution prevention,[104] Article 211(3) LOSC does not specify whether port state pollution measures are limited to those international standards.[105]

Of course, it is possible that international agreements themselves *limit* port state jurisdiction to set CDEM standards. However, as noted by Churchill, in the context of MARPOL, such provisions 'appear few and far between', one example being Regulation 15(1) of Annex VI, prohibiting states from imposing unilateral standards regulating emissions of volatile organic compounds from vessels.[106] More generally, MARPOL implicitly recognises port state jurisdiction to set CDEM standards, Article 4(2) requiring states to prohibit and sanction violations of that Convention 'within their jurisdiction' which, according to Article 9(3) 'shall be construed in the light of international law in force at the time'.[107]

Turning to the freedom of the high seas and the EFSJ principle, it is argued that these norms only apply to vessels when on the high seas, excluding enforcement jurisdiction by non-flag states.[108] Port state measures are not problematic in this regard as they leave vessels free to navigate the high seas, only imposing

[100] See eg Churchill (n 26) 450; Ringbom (n 3) 622; EJ Molenaar, 'Residual Jurisdiction under IMO Regulatory Conventions' in H Ringbom (ed), *Competing Norms in the Law of Marine Environmental Protection: Focus on Ship Safety and Pollution Prevention* (Alphen aan de Rijn, Kluwer Law International, 1997) 201; Marten (n 60) 565.

[101] Marten (n 60) 563; Molenaar (n 12) 231.

[102] Molenaar (n 18) 213, see footnote 39 of that contribution for the complete list of examples.

[103] International Convention on the Control of Harmful Anti-Fouling Systems on Ships (adopted 5 October 2001, entered into force 17 September 2008) IMO Doc AFS/CONF/26.

[104] MARPOL (n 7).

[105] Churchill (n 26) 450. An example of such a unilateral CDEM standard is Parliament and Council (EC) Regulation 417/2002 on the accelerated phasing-in of double-hull or equivalent design requirements for single hull oil tankers (as amended) [2002] OJ L64/1. See also Molenaar (n 100) 201.

[106] Churchill (n 26) 450.

[107] ibid 448–49, also pointing to Art 5(4) LOSC (n 7) which requires states to apply the LOSC requirements to ensure no more favourable treatment is given to vessels of non-parties.

[108] See eg Crawford (n 90) 530; Marten (n 14) 113; D Guilfoyle, 'The High Seas' in D Rothwell et al (eds), *The Oxford Handbook of the Law of the Sea* (Oxford, Oxford University Press 2015) 209.

conditions when vessels choose to come within a state's territory.[109] Guilfoyle notes that the phrase 'exclusive jurisdiction' in Article 92 LOSC 'may be misleading': 'Certainly, the most important aspect of so-called "exclusive" flag State jurisdiction is that it confers immunity upon a ship from interference by foreign government vessels.'[110] However, he notes that the 'high seas are a commons into which all States can, theoretically, project their authority to varying extents. There may then well be concurrent prescriptive jurisdiction over activities on the high seas.'[111]

Consistently with this view, Honniball points out that the 'express Convention exemptions' to EFSJ referred to in Article 92 all relate to enforcement matters, for example piracy (Article 105), and hot pursuit (Article 111).[112] Additional contextual support can be found in the 'exception which proves the rule' in Article 97 LOSC.[113] Paragraph 1, which limits penal jurisdiction in matters of collision or other incidents of navigation, provides that:

> In the event of a collision or any other incident of navigation concerning a ship on the high seas' involving penal responsibility, 'no penal or disciplinary proceedings may be instituted … except before the judicial or administrative authorities either of the flag State or of the State of which such person is a national.

This provision would be quite redundant if it were not implicit that port states could otherwise in theory also assert jurisdictional over the high seas conduct.

In terms of EU case law, the *Paulsen Diva Navigation* case before the CJEU also deserves a mention.[114] The case concerned the applicability to a Panamanian vessel of an EU regulation prohibiting the transport and storage on board of salmon caught outside areas under the sovereignty of EU Member States.[115] There the CJEU found that the regulation in question 'may not be applied to a vessel on the high seas registered in a non-member country, since in principle such a vessel is there governed only by the law of its flag'.[116] The same was found for vessels registered to a non-Member State sailing through

[109] Ringbom (n 3) 625. Crawford (n 90) 530; Marten (n 14) 113; AV Lowe, 'The Right of Entry into Maritime Ports in International Law' (1977) 14 *San Diego Law Review* 597.

[110] Guilfoyle (n 108) 209.

[111] ibid (emphasis added). In this regard, Rayfuse draws a distinction between port state enforcement in relation to matters on the high seas, and non-flag state enforcement on the high seas. R Rayfuse, *Non-Flag State Enforcement in High Seas Fisheries* (Leiden, Martinus Nijhoff, 2004) 52.

[112] Honniball (n 45) 522, referring further inter alia to Arts 109(4) (unauthorized broadcasting), 110 LOSC (right of visit, in respect of defined activities), 221 (maritime casualties or 'related' acts, reasonably expected to result in major harmful consequences), and 220(3)–(6) LOSC (various degrees of EEZ pollution).

[113] Honniball (n 45) 525.

[114] Case C-286/90 *Anklagemyndigheden v Poulsen and Diva Navigation Corporation* [1992] ECR I-6019 (*Paulsen Diva Navigation*), concerning Council Regulation (EEC) No 3094/86 7 of October 1986 laying down certain technical measures for the conservation of fishery resources [1986] OJ L288/ 1, Art 6(1) b.

[115] ibid [7].

[116] ibid [22].

the EEZ and territorial waters, exercising their freedom of navigation and innocent passage rights.[117] However, the Court then held that 'conversely, Community legislation may be applied to [the vessel] when it sails in the inland waters or, more especially, is in a port of a Member State, where it is generally subject to the unlimited jurisdiction of that State'.[118] An analogous reasoning was also used by the CJEU in the *ATAA* case concerning the scope of the EU ETS which included high seas overflight.[119]

As discussed in chapter 3, a problematic issue when interpreting these cases is where the Court draws the line between prescriptive and enforcement jurisdiction. A measure may be 'applied' to subject matter both through its formulation and through enforcement. Generally formulated measures, for example prohibiting salmon transport, would on a broad interpretation like that in *M/V 'Norstar'* and *Enrica Lexie* violate the EFSJ principle, even when only enforced in port. In this sense, the CJEU's distinction between legal 'application' inside ports and internal waters and illegal 'application' beyond these areas logically seems to support a restrictive interpretation of EFSJ as pertaining only to enforcement.

On balance, it is argued that the context and *travaux préparatoires* of the LOSC as well as a considerable body of literature weigh in favour of the residual approach. Importantly, this does not mean that port states are not subject to any limitations to their regulatory autonomy. Indeed, the LOSC itself contains more general conditions on state acts, requiring them to respect the principles of good faith, non-abuse of rights and non-discrimination.[120] As noted by Marten, states must also respect the principle of proportionality, 'ensuring that the measures they dictate in relation to visiting vessels are commensurate with the outcome they seek'.[121] While not a general principle in the LOSC, it is reflected in specific provisions, a key example being Article 221(1) which provides that:

> Nothing in this Part shall prejudice the right of States, pursuant to international law, both customary and conventional, to take and enforce measures beyond the territorial sea proportionate to the actual or threatened damage to protect their coastline or related interests, including fishing, from pollution or threat of pollution following upon a maritime casualty or acts relating to such a casualty, which may reasonably be expected to result in major harmful consequences.[122]

The role of these 'reasonableness' principles in limiting unilateral prescriptive jurisdiction more generally is discussed further in part IV.

[117] ibid [26]–[17].

[118] ibid [28].

[119] C-366/10 *Air Transport Association of America and Others* [2011] ECR I-13755 (*ATAA* case) [124].

[120] See further Marten (n 14) 114, listing as examples, Arts 24(1)(b), 25(3), 26(2), 42(2), 52(2), 119(3), 227, 234 and 300 LOSC. See also Ringbom (n 3) 621.

[121] Marten (n 14) 114.

[122] ibid. Other examples cited by the author include Arts 60(4), 66(2) and 232 LOSC.

4. COMPETING RESPONSES TO INTERNATIONAL MARITIME EMISSIONS: IMO AND EU MEASURES

As discussed, the present construction under Article 2(2) of the Kyoto Protocol and the Paris Agreement leaves the IMO as an important forum for the reduction of GHG emissions from international maritime transport. On an institutional level, the EU is not a member of the IMO, having observer status as an international organisation.[123] Section 4.1 will first set out the competing climate change responses as they evolved around the turn of the decade in 2020. Section 4.2 then considers the relationship between the IMO and EU schemes.

4.1. The EU 'Ultimatum Strategy' in the Field of International Maritime Emissions

At its 70th meeting in 2016, the IMO Marine Environmental Protection Committee (MEPC) adopted the mandatory global data collection system (IMO DCS) as an amendment to Annex VI to the MARPOL Convention.[124] As of 1 January 2019, the IMO DCS obliges ships above 5,000 gross tonnes to monitor and report fuel consumption to their Administration (flag state).[125] In addition, the Committee also agreed to a broader Roadmap for 2017–2023 on developing a Comprehensive IMO strategy on reduction of GHG emissions from ships ('the Roadmap'). In 2018 an Initial Strategy on the Reduction of GHG Emissions from Ships was reached as the Roadmap's first 'milestone'.[126] According to the IMO Initial Reduction Strategy, the 'level of ambition' is to

> peak GHG emissions from international shipping as soon as possible and to reduce the total annual GHG emissions by at least 50% by 2050 compared to 2008 whilst pursuing efforts towards phasing them out … as a point on a pathway of CO_2 emissions reduction consistent with the Paris Agreement temperature goals.[127]

Data collection forms the first phase of the Roadmap, which will be followed by 'data analysis' and then by 'policy decisions' in phases 2 and 3. Importantly, though, the reduction strategy is not definitive, and is to be revised in 2023.

The EU is not a not a party to the MARPOL and its Annex VI containing the IMO DCS. Rather, it had long been pursuing its own unilateral policy, having determined in 2013 that the 'deadline has passed without sufficient

[123] 'Intergovernmental Organizations which have concluded agreements of cooperation with IMO' (imo.org, 2019) www.imo.org/en/About/Membership/Pages/IGOsWithObserverStatus.aspx.

[124] IMO MEPC.278(70) (n 5), adding a new 'Regulation 22A, Collection and reporting of ship fuel oil consumption data' to MARPOL Annex VI.

[125] ibid Regulation 22A [3].

[126] See IMO Resolution MEPC.304(72), 'Initial IMO Strategy on Reduction of GHG Emissions from Ships' (adopted 13 April 2018), MEPC 72/17/Add.1, (IMO Initial Reduction Strategy) [1.4].

[127] ibid [3.1.3].

international action' on maritime emission reductions.[128] Indeed, it was the EU Regulation 2015/757 on the monitoring, reporting and verification of maritime emissions ('the EU maritime MRV') that prompted the IMO to develop a multilateral reduction strategy. Even in the initial stages, the EU and the IMO measures did not mirror each other.[129] Article 22(3) of the EU Maritime MRV is said to have 'anticipated' this situation, instructing the Commission to 'review this Regulation' and, 'if appropriate, propose amendments … in order to ensure alignment with that international agreement'.[130] However, the Commission's Proposal for a Regulation amending the Maritime MRV to 'take appropriate account of global data collection system', already rejects complete alignment.[131] According to this proposal, 'the objective is *not to replace* the EU MRV Regulation by the IMO DCS'.[132] Rather, the 'main challenge' is 'to find appropriate ways *to help market actors implement both schemes* while streamlining and reducing administrative burden as possible, and while preserving the objectives of the EU MRV Regulation'.[133]

Interestingly, these objectives appear to be framed largely in terms of the contentious differences between the data-collection measures.[134] Thus, according to the IMO DCS, vessels must include a description and methodology of their recording method in their Ship Energy Efficiency Management Plan (SEEMP) in order to obtain a 'statement of compliance' from the Administration.[135] Contrary to the EU Maritime MRV, the IMO data-collection system does not require data on the actual load carried or CO_2 emitted, focusing only on the fuel consumed during a ship's voyage.[136] The EU 2019 Impact Assessment accompanying the proposed regulation does not support further alignment, considering that this would undercut the required data for the design of 'coherent and cost-effective climate, energy and environmental policies'.[137]

[128] Commission (EU), 'Integrating maritime transport emissions in the EU's greenhouse gas reduction policies' (Communication) COM(2013) 479 final, 4.

[129] For a comprehensive tabulated overview, see Commission Staff Working Document, Impact Assessment Accompanying the document 'Proposal for a regulation of the European Parliament and of the Council amending Regulation (EU) 2015/757 in order to take appropriate account of the global data collection system for ship fuel oil consumption data' SWD (2019) 10 final, 4 February 2019 ('Impact Assessment MRV Amendment') 15: 'Table 2.1. Comparison of EU MRV Regulation and IMO DCS features'.

[130] ibid 5.

[131] Commission (EU), 'Proposal for a Regulation of the European Parliament and of the Council amending Regulation (EU) 2015/757 in order to take appropriate account of the global data collection system for ship fuel oil consumption data' (Communication) COM(2019) 38 final.

[132] ibid Explanatory Memorandum 2 (emphasis added).

[133] ibid (emphasis added).

[134] ibid 2.

[135] ibid Annex 3, Regulation 22A [1]. See Appendix X for the 'Statement of Compliance' template.

[136] See EU Maritime MRV (n 4), Annexes I, II for the data required by the EU Maritime MRV. See Resolution MEPC.278(70) (n 5) Annex 3, Appendix IX for the 'Information to be Submitted to the IMO Fuel Oil Consumption Database'. For further analysis, see J Dufour, 'EU MRV vs IMO Fuel Consumption Data Collection System' (green4sea.com, 2 December 2016) www.green4sea.com/eu-mrv-vs-imo-fuel-consumption-data-collection-system/.

[137] Impact Assessment MRV Amendment (n 129) 26.

Verification of the IMO monitoring and reporting activities is to be carried out by a ship's Administration according to national procedures, which differs from the approach taken in the EU Maritime MRV of appointing independent accredited verifiers.[138] A 'departure' from third-party accreditation was considered unacceptable for the EU, potentially harming the 'reliability' and 'accuracy' of the system.[139]

As regards transparency, under the IMO scheme, the Administration must transfer the collected data to the IMO Ship Fuel Oil Consumption Database.[140] The Secretary General of the IMO will produce an annual summary of the aggregated anonymised data to be presented to the MEPC.[141] This differs from the EU Maritime MRV which plans to publish information 'with the aim of informing the public and allowing for an assessment of the CO_2 emissions and the energy efficiency of maritime transport per size, type of ships, activity, or any other category deemed relevant'.[142] This has a potential naming and shaming effect, and is intended to 'incentivise the uptake' of energy efficiency measures by operators.[143] The EU 2019 Impact Assessment considered that following the IMO's lower transparency standards would reduce the capacity for the EU maritime MRV to address market failures and achieve 'positive environmental impacts'.[144]

Perhaps most ominously, the EU has been clear that concrete reduction measures must follow to ensure that the sector 'contributes its fair share' to the objective of the Paris Agreement on keeping climate change 'well below 2°C'.[145] To this end, Directive 2018/410 instructs the Commission to keep IMO progress 'under regular review'.[146] In the second half of 2020, the European Parliament voted in favour of the inclusion of shipping emissions in the EU ETS by 2022.[147]

4.2. The Relationship between the IMO DCS and the EU Unilateral Measures

The aforementioned developments illustrate that the EU clearly does not feel bound to strictly follow IMO policy. For its part, the CJEU has repeatedly

[138] Resolution MEPC.278(70) (n 8) Annex 3, Regulation 22A.7. For the EU approach, see EU Maritime MRV (n 6) Art 16.

[139] Impact Assessment MRV Amendment (n 129) 30.

[140] MEPC.278(70) (n 8) Annex 3, Regulation 22A [10].

[141] ibid Annex 3, Regulation 22A.11.

[142] EU Maritime MRV (n 6) Art 21(4).

[143] Impact Assessment MRV Amendment (n 129) 12.

[144] ibid 30.

[145] Parliament and Council (EU) Directive 2018/410 of 14 March 2018 amending Directive 2003/87/EC to enhance cost-effective emission reductions and low-carbon investments, and Decision (EU) 2015/1814 [2018] OJ L76/3, rec. 4.

[146] ibid.

[147] 'Parliament says shipping industry must contribute to climate neutrality' (Europa website, 16 September 2020) www.europarl.europa.eu/news/en/press-room/20200910IPR86825/parliament-says-shipping-industry-must-contribute-to-climate-neutrality.

stressed that the EU 'is not a contracting party to the Marpol 73/78 Convention, including Annex VI, and is not bound by it'.[148] One could theoretically consider whether the EU, when acquiring competence from its Member States, had succeeded to their relevant prior obligations under the doctrine of functional succession. According to this doctrine, when an organisation acquires competence from its Member States, it succeeds to the relevant obligations already incumbent upon all of its Member States.[149] This doctrine will be discussed further in chapter 6 in relation to aviation emissions. It would not, however, seem applicable here. Firstly, both the MARPOL and Annex VI are younger agreements, the latter having been added by the 1997 Protocol.[150] Fundamentally, the IMO DCS is itself an amendment to Annex VI made by another international organisation, the IMO, *subsequent* to the EU's acquisition and exercise of its own competence. Logically, such a later amendment would not fall within the scope of functional succession, the rationale of which relies on the obligations existing prior to conferral of power. In addition, two EU Member States, namely Austria and Hungary, were not party to Annex VI upon its amendment.[151] This presents a further doctrinal problem, as accepting functional succession would effectively impose obligations on non-contracting states without their consent, contrary to the principle expressed in Article 34 VCLT. Accepting this, clear-cut rules of priority are difficult to establish.[152]

In the absence of a formal hierarchy, there are arguments to be made that the EU must respect the obligations of its Member States when exercising its competences. As such exercise is an extension of its Member States' sovereignty, it seems logical that the EU must not place them in a stranglehold with their other obligations. There is notably some recognition for this in the duty of sincere cooperation enshrined in Article 4(3) TEU. In the case of *Manzi and Compagnia Naviera Orchestra*, the question was raised whether the EU had violated Article 4(3)TEU and the *pacta sunt servanda* principle, 'on the ground that that provision of the [relevant] Directive may lead to an infringement of [MARPOL] Annex VI and thereby require Member States party to the 1997

[148] *Manzi* (n 24) [37].

[149] See further eg J Klabbers, 'The Sources of International Organizations Law' in J d'Aspremont and S Besson (eds) *The Oxford Handbook of the Sources of International Law* (Oxford, Oxford University Press, 2017) 987, 988.

[150] The Protocol of 1997 amending the International Convention of 1973 for the Prevention of Pollution from Ships, as amended by the Protocol of 1978 (26 September 1997), adding Annex VI – 'Regulations for the Prevention of Air Pollution from Ships'.

[151] The current status of the conventions can be found at: www.imo.org/en/About/Conventions/Pages/StatusOfConventions.aspx.

[152] This has notably been discussed considerably in the context of the United Nations and the EU, but there the UN has a clear claim to primacy based on Art 103 of the UN Charter. According to H Schermers and N Blokker, *International Institutional Law: Unity within Diversity* (Leiden, Brill, 2011) 1005 '[s]ome decisions of international organizations may apply to other organizations because they bind the member states of those other organizations'. There does not appear to be a clear institutional instruction to this effect in the case of the EU and the IMO, however.

Protocol to infringe their obligations with regard to the other Contracting Parties thereto'.[153] The CJEU however, declined to answer this question, finding that as the Union is not a party it had no competence to review compatibility with MARPOL Annex VI.[154] According to the Court, this 'may not be circumvented by relying on the alleged infringement of the principle of cooperation in good faith laid down in the first subparagraph of Article 4(3) TEU'.[155]

Notably, it was recognised that 'although the European Union is not bound by an international agreement, the fact that all its member states are contracting parties to it is liable to have consequences for the interpretation of European Union law', in particular relevant secondary law.[156] From an international law perspective, it is questionable whether this construction gives sufficient respect to Member States' other obligations. Such respect arguably extends beyond consistently interpreting concurrent rules to the creation of these rules themselves.

What results in the meantime is a 'conflict' of norms in the broader sense, defined here as 'a situation where two rules or principles suggest different ways of dealing with a problem'.[157] There is a considerable group affected by the competing regulatory frameworks, as the EU measures seek to regulate conduct and circumstances beyond its territory. From a jurisdictional perspective, important questions arise as to the delineation of the crowded regulatory space. This is a question of jurisdictional limitations or 'reasonableness' on which – at the time of writing – there are no clear-cut answers. This book engages with this essential and contentious issue further in part V.

5. CONCLUSION

The law of the sea is no stranger to the complexities of interest balancing in the face of competing claims. The zonal system of the LOSC provides an important foundation, with exclusive coastal state competences in territorial waters, and greater freedoms for ships on the high seas. However, precisely at the point of contact where foreign vessels enter territorial waters, the Convention says little, leaving open the question of the territorial limits of port state prescriptive jurisdiction.

In this regard, some consider that the freedom of the high seas and the principle of exclusive flag state jurisdiction preclude measures that have effect on the high seas. Indeed, this view finds reflection – though not much

[153] *Manzi* (n 24) [36].
[154] ibid [41].
[155] ibid [40].
[156] ibid [45].
[157] International Law Commission, 'Fragmentation of International Law: Difficulties Arising from the Diversification and Expansion of International Law', Report of the Study Group of the International Law Commission (13 April 2006), A/CN.4/L.682 [25].

explanation – in the *M/V 'Norstar'* and *Enrcia Lexie* cases, before the ITLOS and PCA. This study, however, supports the opposing view that Articles 87 and 92 LOSC only restrain enforcement jurisdiction, and that port states retain residual prescriptive jurisdiction to legislate entry conditions on prevention reduction and control of polluting activities, including activities contributing to climate change outside of their territories. Neither the LOSC nor MARPOL appear to contain territorial limitations for such measures, which in fact find support in several provisions, such as Articles 211(3) and 25(2) LOSC.

The more recent IMO policies on emission reduction from maritime transport put pressure on the EU's maritime plans. While dual monitoring and reporting requirements already raise an administrative burden for ships, more acute legal tensions will arise should there be competing market-based measures for maritime emissions. This is not without relevance, given the EU's moves towards the inclusion of the maritime sector in its ETS. The complex legal relationship between the IMO, the EU and the EU Member States gives rise to increasing tensions between competing rules. In the absence of a clear hierarchical relationship between the applicable norms, an important role remains for the general international law of jurisdiction, explored further in parts III and IV of this book. First, however, chapter 6 will consider the equally contentious issue of emissions from international civil aviation.

6

Regulating Emissions from International Aviation Transport under International Civil Aviation Law

1. INTRODUCTION

THIS CHAPTER CONSIDERS the legal framework for the unilateral regulation of extraterritorial emissions from international aviation transport. Alongside maritime transport, emissions from international aviation transport occupy a special position under the climate change regime. As discussed in the previous chapter, Article 2(2) of the Kyoto Protocol instructs parties to pursue reduction of these emissions 'working through' the ICAO, a matter left untouched under the Paris Agreement.[1]

As is well known, the EU has not been content to wait on multilateral developments. One of its most controversial moves has been the EU Aviation Directive, which extended the ETS to include international aviation emissions from flights arriving at and departing from EU airports.[2] This resulted in the *ATAA* dispute before the CJEU.[3] Following political push-back, the full application of the Directive was 'paused' and reduced to flights within the European Economic Area.[4] In 2016, responding to EU pressure, the ICAO adopted CORSIA.[5] Despite

[1] See for further analysis: B Martinez Romera, 'The Paris Agreement and the Regulation of International Bunker Fuels' (2016) 25 *Review of European, Comparative & International Environmental Law* 215.

[2] Parliament and Council (EC) Directive 2008/10 of 19 November 2008 amending Directive 2003/87/EC of 13 October 2003 so as to include aviation activities in the scheme for greenhouse gas emission allowance trading within the Community [2008] OJ L8/3 (Aviation Directive).

[3] Case C-366/10 *Air Transport Association of America and Others (ATAA)* [2011] ECR I-13755 [124].

[4] Parliament and Council (EU) Decision 377/2013 of 24 April 2013 derogating temporarily from Directive 2003/87/EC of 13 October 2013 establishing a scheme for greenhouse gas emission allowance trading within the Community [2013] OJ L113/1; Parliament and Council Regulation (EU) 421/2014 of 16 April 2014 establishing a scheme for greenhouse gas emission allowance trading within the Community, in view of the implementation by 2020 of an international agreement applying a single global market-based measure to international aviation emissions [2014] OJ L129/1–4, regulates the interim period.

[5] ICAO Resolution A39-3, 'Consolidated statement of continuing ICAO policies and practices related to environmental protection – Global Market-based Measure (MBM) scheme' (adopted at the 39th Session of the ICAO Assembly, 27 September–6 October 2016), (CORSIA).

its nominal support for this agreement, the EU has refused to align its unilateral measures, maintaining an 'ultimatum strategy' contingent on the level of ambition in ICAO policy.[6] In a resolution of late 2019, a frustrated ICAO adopted an 'exclusivity clause', 'determining' CORSIA to be 'the *only* global market-based measure applying to CO_2 emissions from international aviation'.[7] This has not deterred the EU, which at the time of writing appears equally reluctant to recognise international offsets 'deemed to be eligible' under CORSIA under the EU ETS as of January 2021.[8]

In light of these developments, this chapter will now consider the place of unilateral extraterritorial climate protection measures in the field of international aviation transport. Section 2 first sets out the core division of state powers under international civil aviation law, with a focus on the Convention on International Civil Aviation ('the Chicago Convention'). Notably, in the *ATAA* case, the CJEU found that, as a matter of EU law, the EU was not bound by the latter instrument because it had not entirely assumed the 'powers previously exercised by the Member States in the field of application of the Chicago Convention'.[9] Nevertheless, as will be discussed, as a matter of international law, all EU Member States are bound as signatories of the Chicago Convention.[10] It is therefore necessary to analyse whether they have the original competence under the Chicago Convention to legislate such a measure, as only then can this be validly attributed to the EU. Section 3 analyses the limitations posed by the Chicago Convention on unilateral environmental entry conditions, exploring both issues of extraterritoriality and the contentious provisions on airport service charges and excise duty exemptions.[11] Finally, section 4 turns to CORSIA, considering its relationship with the EU's competing unilateral policy on aviation emissions.

[6] NL Dobson, 'Competing Climate Responses: Reflections on EU Unilateral Regulation of International Transport Emissions in Light of Multilateral Developments' (2020) 67 *Netherlands International Law Review* 183. The aforementioned article by this author is partly reproduced and built upon in this chapter.

[7] ICAO Resolution A40-19, 'Consolidated statement of continuing ICAO policies and practices related to environmental protection – Carbon Offsetting and Reduction Scheme for International Aviation (CORSIA)' (adopted 40th Session of the ICAO Assembly, 24 September–4 October 2019) [18] (emphasis added). See also S Morgan, 'EU Emissions Scheme Excluded from UN Aviation Offsets' *Climate Change News* (7 October 2019) www.climatechangenews.com/2019/10/07/eu-emissions-scheme-excluded-aviation-carbon-offsets/.

[8] See further EASA, EEA, EUROCONTROL, 'European Aviation Environmental Report' (Europa website 2019) ec.europa.eu/transport/sites/transport/files/2019-aviation-environmental-report.pdf.

[9] *ATAA* (n 3) [71]. See also Case C-21–24/72 *International Fruit Company et al* [1972] ECR 1219.

[10] Under the international law doctrine of *pacta sunt servanda*, states are bound by the treaty obligations they consent to, see Art 26 of the Vienna Convention on the Law of Treaties (adopted 23 May 1969, entered into force 27 January 1980) 1155 UNTS 331 (VCLT).

[11] These are Articles 15 and 24 of the Chicago Convention on International Civil Aviation (adopted 7 December 1944, entered into force 4 April 1947) 15 UNTS 295 ('Chicago Convention').

2. ROLES AND AGREEMENTS UNDER INTERNATIONAL CIVIL AVIATION LAW

Since the rapid growth of the civil aviation industry after the Second World War, international civil aviation law has emerged as a comparatively new regime. A central agreement is the 1944 Chicago Convention, the aim of which is to develop civil aviation 'in a safe and orderly manner' and to establish international air transport services 'on the basis of equality of opportunity' ensuring that they are 'operated soundly and economically'.[12] With a near universal membership of 193 parties, the Chicago Convention forms the foundation of today's international civil aviation regime, setting the parameters for aviation-related measures aimed at protecting the global climate.[13]

At the time of its conclusion, the drafters of the Chicago Convention had high aspirations, the United States leading the way in an attempt to open up the global market for the aviation industry.[14] However, this clashed ideologically with the agenda of other less competitive states, in particular the United Kingdom, which was more focused on coordinating transport, frequencies and tariffs and appropriating air routes. As a result, the Chicago Convention was something of a minimalistic compromise, and did not end up creating an overarching structure for the distribution of economic rights and privileges. Rather, the latter were 'relegated' to the International Air Services Transit (Two Freedoms) Agreement, and the more expansive International Air Transport (Five Freedoms) Agreement which contains an additional three freedoms.[15]

The freedoms of the air granted by states are listed in Article 1 section 1 of the Five Freedoms Agreement as:

1. The privilege to fly across its territory without landing;
2. The privilege to land for non-traffic purposes;
3. The privilege to put down passengers, mail and cargo taken on in the territory of the State whose nationality the aircraft possesses;
4. The privilege to take on passengers, mail and cargo destined for the territory of the State whose nationality the aircraft possesses;
5. The privilege to take on passengers, mail and cargo destined for the territory of any other contracting State and the privilege to put down passengers, mail and cargo coming from any such territory.

[12] Recital 3 of the Chicago Convention.

[13] 'List of Parties to the International Air Services Transit Agreement Signed at Chicago on 7 December 1944', www.icao.int/secretariat/legal/List%20of%20Parties/Chicago_EN.pdf.

[14] E Giemulla and L Weber, *International and EU Aviation Law – Selected Issues* (Alphen aan den Rijn, Kluwer Law International, 2011) 130.

[15] B Havel and G Sanchez, *The Principles and Practice of International Aviation Law* (New York, Cambridge University Press, 2014) 36–37. International Air Services Transit [Two Freedoms] Agreement, (adopted 7 December 1944) 84 UNTS 389; International Air Transport [Five Freedoms] Agreement, (adopted 7 December 1944) 171 UNTS 387.

Over time, other privileges have developed, recognised by the ICAO as 'so-called' freedoms because they have not been officially recognised in an international agreement.[16] These are:

6. The right to carry passengers between two foreign countries via the home state;
7. The right to base aircraft in a foreign country for use on international flights without this being connected to the home state;
8. The right to transport traffic between two domestic points in the granting state on a service which originates or terminates in either the home country or another country ('consecutive' cabotage);
9. The right to transport traffic of the granting state on a service performed entirely within its territory ('stand-alone' cabotage).[17]

Today, most states grant each other the first two freedoms through the Two Freedoms Agreement, which now has a wide membership.[18] However, the remaining freedoms are generally granted by states on a reciprocal basis through multilateral and bilateral Air Service Agreements, which distribute market access privileges through air traffic rights.[19] While this complex web of Air Service Agreements will not be discussed here, the applicable rules will of course be relevant for the permissibility of individual aviation-related measures. Importantly, according to this mechanism of 'concessionary' market access, there is no right of innocent passage analogous to that through states' territorial waters under the LOSC.[20] Like ships, however, aircraft have the nationality of the state in which they are registered, and may only be registered to one state at a time.[21]

An important achievement of the Chicago Convention was the establishment of the ICAO, created to 'develop the principles and techniques of international air navigation and foster the planning and development of international air transport'.[22] The ICAO aims to 'reach a consensus' between its 193 Member States and industry groups on 'international civil aviation Standards and Recommended Practices (SARPs) and policies in support of a safe, efficient, secure, economically sustainable and environmentally responsible civil aviation sector'.[23] Notably, the ICAO's interpretations of the Chicago Convention are not considered legally binding.[24] Indeed, some go so far as to argue that the

[16] See further ICAO, 'Freedoms of the Air' (icao.int, 2017) www.icao.int/Pages/freedomsAir.aspx.

[17] ibid.

[18] See the 'List of Parties to the International Air Services Transit Agreement' (n 13).

[19] See eg the extensive list of air services agreements of the EU: Directorate General for International Policies, 'An Overview of the Air Service Agreements Concluded by the EU', Report of the Committee on Transport and Tourism' (Europa website 2013) www.europarl.europa.eu/RegData/etudes/note/join/2013/495849/IPOL-TRAN_NT(2013)495849_EN.pdf.

[20] See Art 6 of the Chicago Convention.

[21] ibid Arts 17, 18.

[22] ibid Art 44.

[23] See further ICAO, 'About ICAO' (icao.int, 2020) www.icao.int/about-icao/Pages/default.aspx.

[24] See further S Oberthür, 'Climate Change Regime, Interactions with ICAO, IMO and the EU Burden Sharing Agreement' in S Oberthür and T Gehring (eds), *Global Environmental Governance: Synergy and Conflict among International and EU Policies* (Cambridge, MA, MIT Press, 2006) 65.

ICAO's industry-oriented views *should* not influence the interpretation of the Chicago Convention.[25] Nevertheless, ICAO policy at least provides a valuable starting point because the organisation's wide membership indicates considerable international support for the policy it develops.

The ICAO has potential for an important role in dispute settlement. Article 84 provides that disagreements as to the interpretation of the Chicago Convention and its Annexes that cannot be settled by negotiation, 'shall, on the application of any State concerned in the disagreement, be decided by the Council'. Council decisions may be appealed to the ICJ. In practice, however, the ICAO has been critiqued as 'ineffective' and 'impotent' in its quasi-judicial functions.[26] Intrinsically, the ICAO Council is a political creature, composed of state representatives.[27] To date, very few disputes have arisen under this provision, although in the 2020 *Appeal Relating to the Jurisdiction of the ICAO Council under Article 84 of the Convention on International Civil Aviation (Bahrain, Egypt, Saudi Arabia and United Arab Emirates v Qatar)*, the ICJ recognised quite broad jurisdiction of the ICAO to examine 'issues outside matters of civil aviation for the exclusive purpose of deciding a dispute which falls within its jurisdiction'.[28]

Turning to the conceptualisation of extraterritoriality in an aviation context, here legal discourse has focused largely on the EU's Aviation Directive.[29] As this has already been discussed extensively in chapter 3, it will not be repeated here.[30] Where a measure's operation is de facto dependent on conduct or circumstances abroad it is considered here to have an 'extraterritorial element' of jurisdictional relevance. Such measures interfere with the regulatory freedom of affected states, requiring the acting state (or the EU) to be able to demonstrate a sufficient jurisdictional basis for regulating a particular subject matter. Section 3 will

[25] This was reason for the Advocate General in the *Ticket-tax* case of the Dutch High Court disregarding some of the ICAO's policy guidance altogether. See *BARIN v The State of the Netherlands* HR 10-07-2009 ECLI:NL:HR:2009:BI3450 (*Ticket-tax* case), Opinion of the Advocate General (ECLI:NL:PHR:2009:BI3450) [7.2].

[26] J Bae, 'Review of the Dispute Settlement Mechanism Under the International Civil Aviation Organization: Contradiction of Political Body Adjudication' (2013) 4 *Journal of International Dispute Settlement* 65, 66; GS Sanchez, 'The Impotence of the Chicago Convention's Dispute Settlement Provisions' (2010) 10 *Issues in Aviation Law and Policy* 27.

[27] See further A de Mestral 'Settlement of Disputes at the ICAO and Sustainable Development' in A de Mestral, P Paul Fitzgerald and Md. Tanveer Ahmad (eds), *Sustainable Development, International Aviation, and Treaty Implementation* (Cambridge, Cambridge University Press, 2018) 199.

[28] *Appeal Relating to the Jurisdiction of the ICAO Council under Article 84 of the Convention on International Civil Aviation (Bahrain, Egypt, Saudi Arabia and United Arab Emirates v Qatar)* (Merits) [2020] General List No 173. For analysis, see A Ventouratou 'Defences and Indispensable Incidental Issues: The Limits of Subject-matter Jurisdiction in View of the Recent ICJ ICAO Council Judgments' (Blog of the European Journal of International Law 2020) www.ejiltalk.org/defences-and-indispensable-incidental-issues-the-limits-of-subject-matter-jurisdiction-in-view-of-the-recent-icj-icao-council-judgments/.

[29] Aviation Directive (n 2).

[30] See further chapter 3, section 4.

now consider the extent to which the Chicago Convention may limit the territorial scope of unilateral environmental entry conditions with an extraterritorial element.

3. LIMITATIONS ON UNILATERAL ENVIRONMENTAL ENTRY CONDITIONS UNDER THE CHICAGO CONVENTION

As a hard-fought compromise, the Chicago Convention provides only a basic framework for state competence to regulate aviation-related activities. Perhaps unsurprisingly, there is then considerable debate on whether the Chicago Convention limits the territorial scope of unilateral measures. Given that this debate follows similar lines to the discussion under the LOSC considered in chapter 5, it will be discussed here more briefly in section 3.1. In relation more specifically to the Chicago Convention, there are two further provisions which some argue preclude unilateral measures imposing costs on aircraft to cover environmental externalities of the aviation industry.[31] These are Article 15 on 'airport and similar charges' and Article 24 on 'customs duty' for fuels on board aircraft. The interpretation of these provisions will be considered in more detail in sections 3.2 and 3.3, respectively.

3.1. Territorial Limitations on Home State Entry Conditions?

In analysing the legal parameters of the Chicago Convention, an important starting point is Article 1, which recognises 'that every State has complete and exclusive sovereignty over the airspace above its territory'. Article 1 codifies the customary principle of air sovereignty which, as noted in the *Nicaragua* case, is an application of the 'basic legal concept of State sovereignty in customary international law'.[32] According to Article 2, the territory of a state is deemed to be 'the land areas and territorial waters adjacent thereto under the sovereignty, suzerainty, protection or mandate of such State'.

On one view, Article 1 of the Chicago Convention 'constrains the regulatory reach of States seeking to control the emissions released by foreign carriers into the common planetary atmosphere'.[33] It is argued here that this interpretation is not supported by the text or context of Article 1. The plain meaning of this provision is to establish in a positive manner states' sovereign competence within their territory, rather than to limit in a negative manner their legislative competence beyond their territory. The common planetary atmosphere is not

[31] See in particular Havel and Sanchez (n 15) 45.

[32] *Case concerning Military and Paramilitary Activities In and Against Nicaragua (Nicaragua v United States of America)* (Merits) [1986] ICJ Rep 3, 213 (*Nicaragua* case) [212].

[33] See eg Havel and Sanchez (n 15) 235.

mentioned. For its part, the ICAO position at its 2013 Worldwide Air Transport Conference appears to support a more flexible reading of territorial sovereignty. Thus it notes that while 'sovereignty' refers to 'the exclusive competence of a State to exercise its legislative, administrative and judicial powers … air navigation services require a global, seamless, and performance-based approach to management of airspace, rather than one based on national borders'. A 'fully developed understanding of the meaning of national sovereignty' is 'consistent with present and future political, economic and social realities' and 'does not require any amendment to the Convention on International Civil Aviation'.[34]

It is argued that the treaty context in fact suggests that – as with the LOSC – a distinction should be drawn between prescriptive and enforcement jurisdiction. There are several provisions which confirm state competence to set conditions of entry without territorial limitations. For example, article 6 provides that:

> No scheduled international air service may be operated over or into the territory of a contracting State, except with the special permission or other authorization of that State, and in accordance with the terms of such permission or authorization.

This concessionary principle of market access precludes a right of innocent passage such as that under the LOSC,[35] expressly endowing states with competence to set conditions of 'permission or authorisation'. Article 11 provides an important condition, requiring that entry or exit rules 'shall be applied to the aircraft of all contracting States without distinction as to nationality, and shall be complied with by such aircraft upon entering or departing from or while within the territory of that State'. This is complemented by Article 12(1) which requires states to ensure that 'every aircraft carrying its nationality mark, wherever such aircraft may be, shall comply with the rules and regulations relating to the flight and maneuver of aircraft there in force'.

As a matter of practical necessity, static entry conditions such as aircraft design standards will have effect before an aircraft enters a state's territory. They may, however, only be enforced when the aircraft is within that state's territory. This is, of course, not as self-obvious for non-static requirements such as GHGs emitted en route. Indeed, in the *ATAA* case, the Air Transport Association of America argued that Article 11 precludes measures that take into account the 'extraterritorial' duration of flights.[36] This interpretation does not, however, appear supported by the provision itself. As noted by Advocate General Kokott, 'the only substantive requirement' in the text of Article 11 is that 'the laws and regulations of a contracting State' relating to admission or departure

[34] Working Paper, 'Airspace Sovereignty' (Worldwide Air Transport Conference, 6th Meeting, Montreal, 18–22 March 2011) ATConf/6-WP/80. P.1.

[35] See further Havel and Sanchez (n 15) 42.

[36] *ATAA* case (n 3) [45]. See also the Opinion of AG Kokott, noting 'no inference can be drawn from Article 11 of the Chicago Convention as to whether an emissions trading scheme applied by one Contracting State is to be permitted to take account of parts of flights that take place outside the territory of that State' [166].

are 'applied to the aircraft of all contracting States without distinction as to nationality'.[37] In the case of an Aviation ETS-based neutrally on CO_2 emitted throughout a particular flight, no such distinction is applied to aircraft on the basis of their nationality. Article 12, which pertains to the 'rules of the air' more specifically, also contains no clear territorial limitations applicable to an ETS such as the EU Aviation Directive.[38]

As proponents of the restrictive approach, Havel and Sanchez present a further argument that Article 12 of the Chicago Convention should be read in conjunction with Article 87 LOSC as precluding unilateral measures that have effect over the high seas.[39] In doing so they rely on Article 87 LOSC, which codifies the freedom of the high seas, including the 'freedom of overflight'.[40] Article 87 LOSC provides that this freedom must be exercised 'under the conditions laid down by other rules of international law'.[41] According to the authors, such a rule can be found in Article 12 of the Chicago Convention, which provides that '[o]ver the high seas, the rules in force shall be those established under this Convention'.[42] That provision is argued to implicitly endow the ICAO with exclusive competence to regulate matters over the high seas.[43]

In the view of this author, while Article 12 may imply that the ICAO, through the powers attributed to it under the Chicago Convention, is competent to regulate civil aviation matters over the high seas, nowhere does it appear that this competence is exclusive. Indeed, under Article 38, parties maintain the right to depart from international standards and procedures set by ICAO found to be 'impracticable'. Later ICAO policy also stresses the 'importance of ICAO continuing to demonstrate its leadership role on all international civil aviation matters related to the environment'.[44] The ICAO's desire to take the lead implies, however, that states, in principle, retain competence themselves. The extent to which this may be altered by the conclusion of CORSIA will be discussion further in section 4.

[37] ibid [167]; Art 11 Chicago Convention.

[38] Opinion of AG Kokott in the *ATAA* case (n 3) [169], noting that 'no such rules of the air are to be found in Directive 2003/87 as amended by Directive 2008/101, whether for the territory of the European Union, for the airspace above third countries, or over the high seas, which are specifically mentioned in the third sentence of Article 12 of the Convention. In particular, as already mentioned, the EU emissions trading scheme does not require airlines and the aircraft operated by them to adhere to any particular flight path, specific speed limits, or limits on fuel consumption and exhaust gases.'

[39] Havel and Sanchez (n 15) 235.

[40] Article 87(1)(b) United Nations Convention on the Law of the Sea (adopted 10 December 1982, entered into force 16 November 1994) 1833 UNTS 3 (LOSC). Notably, overflight above the EEZ is governed by the same regime as that of the high seas (Art 58 LOSC). See further S Hobbe, 'Airspace' in R Wolfrum (ed), *Max Planck Encyclopaedia of Public International Law*, online edn (Oxford, Oxford University Press, 2008) [7].

[41] Art 81(1) LOSC.

[42] ibid.

[43] Havel and Sanchez (n 15) 235.

[44] ICAO Resolution A37-18, 'Consolidated statement of continuing ICAO policies and practices related to environmental protection – General provisions, noise and local air quality' (adopted at the 37th Session of the ICAO Assembly, 28 September–8 October 2010) Appendix A, [2].

With regard more generally to the question of whether the freedom of high seas overflight limits the territorial scope of prescriptive jurisdiction, it is argued once again that the answer should be negative. As discussed in chapter 5, the freedom of the high seas pertains to uninhibited travel over the high seas and does not in itself limit the subject matter of entry conditions to which aircraft subject themselves when entering another state. This is supported by the treaty context discussed above, in which there is ample recognition for state competence to set entry conditions. Should no distinction be drawn between prescriptive and enforcement jurisdiction, it would be impossible for states to set a vast number conditions which are widely accepted today. Examples of such measures will now be considered below in the context of Articles 15 and 24 of the Chicago Convention.

3.2. A Limitation on Environmental Levies under Article 15 of the Chicago Convention?

For unilateral measures pursuing environmental protection through levies, Article 15 of the Chicago Convention presents another front of debate. The relevant parts of Article 15 on 'airports and related charges', read as follows:

> Article 15: Airport and Similar Charges
>
> Any charges that may be imposed or permitted to be imposed by a contracting State for the use of such airports and air navigation facilities by the aircraft of any other contracting State shall not be higher, …
>
> (b) As to aircraft engaged in scheduled international air services, than those that would be paid by its national aircraft engaged in similar international air services. …
>
> No fees, dues or other charges shall be imposed by any Contracting State in respect solely of the right of transit over or entry into or exit from its territory of any aircraft of a Contracting State or persons or property thereon.

Lacking the more robust dispute-settlement options of the LOSC, the Chicago Convention has been subject to somewhat more fragmented interpretation by domestic courts. Notably, in the *ATAA* case, the CJEU did not interpret Article 15 as it did not consider the EU to be bound by the Chicago Convention.[45] Some guidance on the interpretation of Article 15 is provided by the ICAO Council interpretation of the Chicago Convention in its 2012 'Policies on Charges for Airports and Air Navigation Services' ('the ICAO Policies on Airport and Navigation Service Charges').[46] These too, however, have been interpreted differently in legal discourse.

[45] *ATAA* case (n 3) [71].

[46] 'ICAO Policies on Charges for Airports and Air Navigation Services' (2012) ICAO Doc 9082/7 ('ICAO Policies on Airport and Navigation Service Charges').

Distilling this discourse, three layers of argumentation can be identified whereby Article 15 would constitute a potential obstacle for environmental levies: (1) That article 15 is more than purely a non-discrimination provision because its last sentence includes a more general prohibition of certain charges; (2) that the reference to 'charges' in the final sentence should be read as including 'taxes' (which an Aviation ETS would qualify as); and (3) that *environmental* taxes fall within the scope of the final sentence. These three issues will now be considered in turn.

3.2.1. *Is Article 15 more than Purely a Non-Discrimination Provision?*

The first argument to be addressed is that Article 15 of the Chicago Convention is more than purely a non-discrimination requirement; rather it is a 'wider prohibition of certain fees and charges'.[47] This view can for example be found in the 2005 case *BAR Belgium v Belgian State* ('the *Zaventem Passenger Tax* case'), concerning a Belgian passenger tax.[48] There the Court held that the last paragraph 'prohibits altogether the establishment of tariffs, dues or other costs, which are just imposed for flying over, into or out and which have nothing to do with the use of the airport and airport facilities'.[49] It is then

> essentially to be read and understood, not in the first place as a measure to ensure that international air transport services can be established on the basis of equal opportunities, but as a measure to ensure that the air transport services ... 'can operate in a sound and economic way'.

The alternative approach support here considers that the last sentence 'should not be read in isolation' from the provision's overall context. This was expressed by Advocate General Kokott in her Opinion on the *ATAA* case.[50] According to the Advocate General:

> [I]t is apparent from the first paragraph of Article 15 that the overall aim of that provision is to afford all aircraft access to airports in Contracting States which are open to public use 'under uniform conditions' irrespective of their nationality.[51]

Further support for this conclusion can be found in the case *R (on the application of the Federation of Tour Operators and others) v Her Majesty's Treasury* ('the *Air Passenger Duty* case') of the English High Court. This case concerned the permissibility of the Air Passenger Duty (APD) charged to aircraft operators for each passenger on board flights departing from the UK. The 2007 judgment

[47] Opinion of AG Kokott in the *ATAA* case (n 3) [213].

[48] *BAR Belgium v the Belgian State*, Belgian Council of State, Decision 144.081 (3 May 2005) (*Zaventem Passenger Tax* case).

[49] ibid [3.10].

[50] Opinion of AG Kokott in the *ATAA* case (n 3) [211].

[51] ibid. AG Kokott further notes that 'the third paragraph of Article 15 follows on seamlessly from this with the use of the words '[a]ll such charges'.

explicitly did not follow the *Zaventem Passenger Tax* case.[52] Rather, Judge Burnton found that is '*essentially an anti-discrimination provision* (or most favoured State provision), precluding a State from favouring its national airline or airlines when imposing charges'.[53]

Considering further the *travaux préparatoires* of article 15, it was found that:

> None of the precursors to the final Article 15 went beyond prohibiting discrimination. It would be surprising if the final text did so, at least without some indication in the open proceedings of the Convention that an extension of the prohibition was intended. It would be similarly surprising if an absolute prohibition were included as the last sentence of what is otherwise a non-discrimination provision.[54]

This reading was also reflected in the 2009 Dutch Supreme Court in the case *BARIN v the State of the Netherlands* ('the *Ticket-tax* case') concerning the compatibility of a Dutch environmental ticket tax with Article 15 of the Chicago Convention.[55] According to the Dutch Court, the final sentence of Article 15 aims to prevent situations where the use of airspace above a state party's territory by flying above, in or out, is subject to a levy that would undermine the requirement of equal treatment contained in the preceding text of Article 15.[56]

Nonetheless, light of the remaining uncertainties, the following sections will now focus on the interpretation of the final sentence of Article 15, if it *were* to constitute an independent regulatory limitation.

3.2.2. Does Article 15 of the Chicago Convention Include Taxes?

Were Article 15 to include an independent limitation on levies, it would then be important to determine the limitation's scope. A first question in this regard is whether the reference to 'fees, dues or other charges' in the provision's final sentence also includes taxes. According to the ICAO Policies on Airport and Navigation Charges:

> *Charges* are levies to defray the costs of providing facilities and services for civil aviation while *taxes* are levies to raise general national and local governments' revenues that are applied for non-aviation purposes.[57]

Whether or not Article 15 also includes taxes is then relevant because a narrower reading of 'charges' according to the above definition would be likely to exclude a wide range of environmental levies.

[52] *R (on the application of the Federation of Tour Operators and others) v Her Majesty's Treasury* [2007] EWHC 2062 (Admin), (*Air Passenger Duty* case) [13].

[53] ibid [56] (emphasis added).

[54] ibid [75], see [82]: 'While according its decision [of the Belgian Council of State in *BAR Belgium v the Belgian State*] all due respect, I regret that it does not lead me to alter my above conclusion.'

[55] *Ticket-Tax case* (n 25). See further M Bisset, 'Taxes and Charges under the Chicago Convention' in P Mendes de Leon (ed), *From Lowlands to High Skies: A Multilevel Jurisdictional Approach Towards Air Law* (Leiden, Brill, 2013) 67.

[56] *Ticket-Tax case* (n 25) [3.7].

[57] ICAO Policies on Airport and Navigation Service Charges (n 46) [3] (emphasis added).

According to Havel and Sanchez, a 'sensible reading' of Article 15 necessarily understands taxes to fall under the provision, as the contrary view would deprive Article 15 of substantive force, allowing states to levy 'all kinds of treasury taxes' without the need for justification.[58] The authors also point to the other authentic language versions of Russian, French and Spanish, which they argue 'use their languages' respective terms for taxation instead of "dues"'.[59] The same view was advanced by the claimants in the *Air Passenger Duty* case, where it was found that, while there may be some discussion about the French translation, the Spanish and Russian texts 'unequivocally translate as taxes'.[60]

On the opposing view, Pache argues that these other language versions do not sufficiently corroborate the inclusion of taxation in the English version because the terms used there do not correspond accurately with the characterisation of a 'tax' in English.[61] He further argues that, as the ICAO itself consistently distinguishes between 'charges' and 'taxes', the provision would have expressly referred to taxes if the drafters had intended them to be covered. Indeed, analysing subsequent ICAO policy documents, Pache notes that 'there is a consensus of ICAO members that the term "charges" applies only when there is connection with a service provided in return', while '"taxes" are levied to cover general financing needs'.[62] It is further worth noting that the regulation of taxes was not central to the agenda of the Chicago Convention parties at the time of negotiation. Indeed, the 2000 ICAO Policies on Taxation in the Field of International Air Transport ('the ICAO Policies on Taxation for Air Transport'), explicitly state that the Chicago Convention 'did not attempt to deal comprehensively with tax matters'.[63]

Another argument against the inclusion of taxes under Article 15 has to do with the context and phrasing of the provision. In the *Air Passenger Duty* case, Judge Burnton considered that while, '[b]y itself, the word "dues" is apt to include taxes ... it does not stand alone'. The heading of the provision 'airport and similar charges' 'indicates that it does not deal with taxes'. Furthermore, the phrase '"fees, dues or other charges" indicates that "dues" are charges; and if so, taxes are not "dues"'.[64]

[58] Havel and Sanchez (n 15) 237.

[59] ibid 236. The authors do refer to the Protocol on the Authentic Trilingual Text of the Convention on International Civil Aviation (adopted 24 September 1968, entered into force 24 October 1968).

[60] The appellants had argued that if the French text had intended to refer to 'tax' in the English sense, the word, '*impôt*' would have been used rather than 'taxe'. *Air Passenger Duty* case (n 52) [52].

[61] E Pache, 'On the Compatibility with International Legal Provisions of Including Greenhouse Gas Emissions from International Aviation in the EU Emission Allowance Trading Scheme as a Result of the Proposed Changes to the EU Emission Allowance Trading Directive' (Legal opinion commissioned by the Federal Ministry for the Environment, Nature Conservation and Nuclear Safety, 2018) 20.

[62] ibid 18.

[63] 'ICAO's Policies on Taxation on the Field of International Air Transport' (2000) ICAO Doc 8362, (ICAO Policies on Taxation for Air Transport). See also Pache (n 61) 19; *Air Passenger Duty case* (n 52) [65].

[64] *Air Passenger Duty case* (n 52) [55]. For further analysis, see R Lawson, 'UK Air Passenger Duty Held to be Consistent with the Chicago Convention' (2008) 33 *Air & Space Law* 3.

Finally, the argument that excluding taxation would deprive Article 15 of substantive meaning may not do justice to the provision's function on a narrower reading. The provision would namely still serve to ensure the non-discriminatory application of service charges, and, reading the final part of the provision separately, to preclude 'gatekeeper' charges levied purely for entry, exit or transit over a state's territory.

Despite these arguments, whether or not Article 15 of the Chicago Convention also refers to taxes remains a tenuous linguistic question which, in the absence of a definitive interpretation, is difficult to answer here. For its part, through its analysis of the compatibility of the Dutch environmental ticket-tax with Article 15, the Dutch Supreme Court in the *Ticket-tax* case also appears to support the view that the provision may apply to 'taxes', as does the Belgian Court in the *Zaventem Passenger Tax* case.[65] The same can be said of the Opinion of Advocate General Kokott, which implicitly considers that both taxes and charges may, in principle, fall within the scope of Article 15.[66] As such, it is necessary to proceed with the analysis and consider whether Article 15 then includes environmental levies, and whether an Aviation ETS would fall within the scope of this provision.

3.2.3. Does Article 15 of the Chicago Convention Preclude Environmental Levies?

The final issue for the interpretation of Article 15 is the substantive scope of the 'fees, dues or other charges' precluded by the final sentence. These may not be imposed 'in respect solely of the right of transit over or entry into or exit from its territory of any aircraft of a Contracting State or persons or property thereon'.[67]

Taking, once again, a restrictive view, Havel and Sanchez argue that the ICAO Policies on Airport and Navigation Charges have 'glossed Article 15 to mean that the Convention permits the imposition of charges *specifically (and only) to recover the costs of providing facilities and services* to airlines engaged in international air transport'.[68] According to the authors, as MBMs aimed at offsetting emissions are 'unrelated to the provision of airport and navigation services', they would thus constitute a levy 'in respect solely of the right of transit or entry into or exit', contravening the provision.

It is questionable, however, whether this approach reflects the intention of the drafters and subsequent state practice. To start with, it does not appear that the drafters of the 1944 Chicago Convention intended to prohibit environmental

[65] *Ticket-tax case* (n 25) [3.8]; *Zaventem Passenger Tax* case (n 48) [3.12].

[66] Opinion of AG Kokott in the *ATAA* case (n 3) [213]–[216].

[67] Art 15 Chicago Convention, final sentence.

[68] Havel and Sanchez (n 15) 236, referring to ICAO Policies on Airport and Navigation Service Charges (n 46) [1] (emphasis added).

taxation measures. Based on the *travaux préparatoires*, Advocate General Wattel in the *Ticket-tax* case noted that, at the time, there was very little societal consciousness of environmental issues, and that the drafters furthermore did not envision the great expansion of the aviation industry which followed in the next half century.[69] Rather, the preamble of the Chicago Convention points to the aim of establishing transport services 'on the basis of equality of opportunity' to be operated 'soundly and economically'.[70] In addition to their lack of focus on environment, it has also been argued that the drafters did not intend to impose such a great restriction on taxation measures. As we have seen, this appears to be supported by the ICAO Policies on Taxation for Air Transport which confirm that the drafters of the 1944 Chicago Convention were not focused on comprehensively regulating taxes.[71]

Fundamentally, however, environmental taxes are simply not levied 'solely' in respect of the right of transit over, entry into or exit from the territory of a contracting state. An interesting case in this regard is the 2015 German *Air Transport Tax* (*Luftverkehrsteuer*) case before the Fiscal Court of Hesse.[72] The case concerned the legality of the German Air Transport Tax Act (ATTA) containing tax incentives for environmentally friendly conduct, in particular inclusion of air transport in the EU ETS.[73] According to the German Court, the ATTA was not precluded by Article 15 of the Chicago Convention because it was not payable specifically for the right of exit.[74] Erling notes, however, that as the 'right of departure is *linked* to the payment of taxes', aircraft under the German ATTA are effectively denied an independent right of exit.[75]

Despite the de facto limitation in the case of non-compliance, Article 15 points to the objective of a tax as the determining factor. The finding of the Court in the *Zaventem Passenger Tax* case provides some guidance for determining this objective. According to the Belgian Court, 'the reason why a tax becomes payable' 'must correspond to the basis for its calculation'.[76] In the case of the EU Aviation Directive, the calculations are based on the quantity of CO_2 emitted. This quantity corresponds to a certain contribution to environmental harm. As held in the Dutch *Ticket-tax* case, this is the 'reason' for environmental taxes, which are intended to compensate for, or recover, the costs of pollution

[69] *Ticket-tax* case (n 25), Opinion of AG Wattel [7.2].

[70] ibid. See for further analysis, B Havel and N van Antwerpen, 'Dutch Ticket Tax and Article 15 of the Chicago Convention on International Civil Aviation (Continued)' (2009) 34 *Air & Space Law* 447.

[71] ICAO Policies on Taxation for Air Transport (n 63) [2].

[72] Hessisches Finanzgericht, 3 June 2015, 7 K 631/12 (*German Air Transport Tax* case).

[73] For a critical analysis, see UM Erling, A Treaty Override of International Law' (2015) 10 *Florida International University Law Review* 467. See further J Faber and T Huigen, 'A Study on Aviation Ticket Taxes' (November 2018, CE Delft Report 18.7L14.149) 19.

[74] *German Air Transport Tax* case (n 72) 21.

[75] Erling (n 73) 474.

[76] *Zaventem Passenger Tax* case (n 48) [3.12]. According to the Court, the final sentences refer to the 'establishment of tariffs, dues or other costs which are just imposed for flying over, in or out and which have nothing do with the use of airport or airport facilities'.

not otherwise reflected in the price of airline tickets.[77] Indeed, in the words of Advocate General Kokott in the *ATAA* case, the 'various take-offs and landings' are not being 'paid for as such', rather, 'account is being taken of the greenhouse gas emissions generated by the relevant flights'.[78]

Turning to state practice, there appears considerable evidence that unilateral (environmental) taxes are not prohibited by Article 15 of the Chicago Convention.[79] The *Air Passenger Duty* case, for example, refers to the widespread support by ICAO states in 2005 for the proposed 'Chirac-tax', which would be levied on air travel to provide funds for developing countries.[80] In 2010, an emissions charge was also implemented at Copenhagen Airport, inspired by the models already in place in Sweden and Switzerland, while Germany and England also have emission charges.[81] Although these developments have been criticised by the ICAO as imposing undesirable costs on the provision of air services, it was not implied that such measures were illegal.[82]

Finally, and importantly, the view that climate-protective MBMs are in principle permitted by the Chicago Convention also finds support in ICAO policy itself. ICAO Resolution 33-7 in Appendix I on 'Market-based measures regarding aircraft emissions' recognises parties right to regulate for environmental protection.[83] According to the preamble, the funds collected from 'emission-related charges and taxes … should be applied in the first instance to mitigating the environmental impact of aircraft engine emissions'.[84] '[S]uch charges should be based on the costs of mitigating the environmental impact of aircraft engine emissions to the extent that such costs can be properly identified and directly attributed to air transport.'[85]

Past ICAO policy, for example Resolution A 39-2, has incorporated 'guiding principles for the design and implementation of market-based measures (MBMs) for international aviation'.[86] Principle (a) provides that 'MBMs should support

[77] *Ticket-tax* case (n 25) [3.6]. On the objective, see further B Havel and N van Antwerpen (n 70) 450.

[78] Opinion of AG Kokott in the *ATAA* case (n 3) [217].

[79] For an overview of aviation taxes at the time of writing, see European Commission Directorate-General for Mobility and Transport, 'Taxes in the Field of Aviation and their impact: Final Report' (June 2019, CE Delft) 24, www.cedelft.eu/en/publications/download/2768.

[80] *Air Passenger Duty* case (n 52) [68], referring to 'The Declaration on Innovative Sources of Financing for Development' (signed 14 September 2005, New York).

[81] For emission charges at the time of writing, see 'Charges Regulations applying to Copenhagen Airport' (Københavns Lufthavne A/S, 9 November 2019) www.cph.dk/48dd4b/globalassets/9.-cph-business/5.-aviation/charges-and-slot/takster/charges-regulations-cph-uk-1-january-2020-final.pdf.

[82] Working Paper, 'ICAO Standards and Policies Related to Environmental Protection', ICAO Doc A39-WP/1521 (Presented at the 39th Meeting of the ICAO Assembly, August 2016) www.icao.int/Meetings/a39/Documents/WP/wp_152_en.pdf.

[83] ICAO Resolution A33-7 'Consolidated statement of continuing ICAO policies and practices related to environmental protection' (adopted at the 33rd Session of the ICAO Assembly, 25 September–5 October 2001) Appendix I, rec 9.

[84] ibid.

[85] ibid Appendix I, rec 10.

[86] See the Appendix to Assembly Resolution A 37-19, 'Consolidated statement of continuing ICAO policies and practices related to environmental protection – Climate change' (adopted at the 37th Session of the ICAO Assembly, 28 September–8 October 2010).

sustainable development of the international aviation sector', while principle (b) continues that 'MBMs should support the mitigation of GHG emissions from international aviation'. Of particular relevance is principle (f), which states that 'MBMs should not be duplicative and international aviation CO_2 emissions should be accounted for only once'. This implies that unilateral MBMs were not a priori precluded by the Chicago Convention. Care must be taken in designing the measures to avoid situations where multiple schemes seek to regulate the same GHG emissions.[87] This issue has become particularly contentious since the adoption of CORSIA, which will be discussed further below.

3.2.4. Does Article 15 of the Chicago Convention Preclude the EU Aviation ETS?

The above sections have focused on the interpretation of Article 15 of the Chicago Convention more generally. Yet, important questions also arise as to the specific characterisation of an ETS, and whether it can be considered a 'tax' or a 'charge' in the sense of this provision.

To start with, as noted by Pache, an Aviation ETS is not a 'charge' in the sense of Article 15 of the Chicago Convention, as it is not levied to 'defray the costs of providing facilities and services for civil aviation'.[88] Advocate General Kokott shared this view, considering 'charges' to be 'levied as consideration for a public service used', where '[t]he amount is set unilaterally by a public body and can be determined in advance'.[89] As a market-based measure, an ETS makes no provision for fees or charges in order to obtain emission allowances.[90] In fact, at the time, 85 per cent of the allowances were allocated free of charge, and the remaining 15 per cent were auctioned, the price being set by supply and demand rather than being fixed in advance by the authorities.[91] Furthermore, the ICAO bodies have recognised a distinction between environmental charges and emission trading schemes, as can be seen, for example, in the 2007 ICAO Resolution A36-22.[92]

[87] On double counting in the context of the UN Framework Convention on Climate Change, see further L Schneider, A Kollmuss and M Lazarus, 'Addressing the Risk of Double Counting Emission Reductions under the UNFCCC' (2014, Stockholm Environmental Institute 2014 Working Paper 2014/02) www.sei-international.org/mediamanager/documents/Publications/Climate/SEI-WP-2014-02-Double-counting-risks-UNFCCC.pdf; United Nations Framework Convention on Climate Change (adopted 9 May 1992, entered into force 21 March 1994) 1771 UNTS 107 (UNFCCC).

[88] See in particular Aviation Directive (n 2) rec 5: 'The European Council emphasised that the EU is committed to a global and comprehensive agreement for reductions in greenhouse gas emissions beyond 2012, providing an effective, efficient and equitable response on the scale required to face climate change challenges.'

[89] Opinion of AG Kokott in the *ATAA* case (n 3) [214].

[90] ibid [215].

[91] ibid.

[92] ibid [218], referring to Assembly Resolution A36-22 (adopted at the 36th Session of the ICAO Assembly, September 2007) Appendix L, [1], where mention is made in subpara (a) of 'Emissions-related charges and taxes' and in subpara (b) of 'Emissions trading'.

The next issue is whether an ETS can be characterised as a 'tax' within the meaning of the Chicago Convention. Looking again at the purpose of an ETS, Pache argues that this too does not match that in the definition of 'tax' in the ICAO Policies on Airport and Navigation Service Charges. As we have seen, there taxes are defined as 'levies to raise general national and local governments' revenues that are applied for non-aviation purposes'.[93] However, according to Pache, an ETS such as that of the EU is not 'primarily' aimed at raising government revenue, but rather at creating market incentives for airlines to reduce their GHG emissions.[94] For this reason, despite 'certain similarities', Pache argues that the EU ETS cannot be characterised as a 'tax' according to the ICAO's definition.

Importantly, though, the above approach emphasizes the measure's *primary* aim, rather than the de facto functioning. The EU ETS does in fact raise government revenue, designating the funds to be invested in climate change responses.[95] The brings us to the second, perhaps more persuasive, argument against the characterisation of an ETS as a 'tax', namely the fact that it functions as an MBM rather than a fixed charge imposed in exchange for a government service. In the words of Advocate General Kokott:

> It would be unusual, to put it mildly, to describe as a charge or tax the purchase price paid for an emission allowance, which is based on supply and demand according to free market forces, notwithstanding the fact that the Member States do have a certain discretion regarding the use to be made of revenues generated.[96]

As such, even accepting that Article 15 may preclude environmental taxes and changes, it remains questionable whether an Aviation ETS, as an MBM, falls within the scope of this provision.

3.3. A Limitation on Unilateral Emissions Trading Schemes in Article 24 of the Chicago Convention?

A final provision put forward as precluding a unilateral ETS more specifically is Article 24(a) of the Chicago Convention on excise duties. The relevant part of the provision reads as follows:

> Aircraft on a flight to, from, or across the territory of another contracting State shall be admitted temporarily free of duty, subject to the customs regulations of the State.

[93] ICAO Policies on Airport and Navigation Service Charges (n 46) [3].

[94] Pache (n 61) 14. According to Pache, this holds true despite the fact that the EU's use of revenue bears a 'certain similarity' to that of a tax.

[95] ibid, referring to G Schwarze, 'Including Aviation into the European Union's Emissions Trading Scheme' (2007) 16 *European Energy and Environmental Law Review* 10, 13.

[96] Opinion of AG Kokott *ATAA* case (n 3) [216].

> *Fuel*, lubricating oils, spare parts, regular equipment and aircraft stores on board an aircraft of a contracting State, on arrival in the territory of another contracting State and *retained on board on leaving the territory of that State shall be exempt from customs duty, inspection fees or similar national or local duties and charges.* (emphasis added).

On one view, put forward by Havel and Sanchez, Article 24 is 'merely a specific example of the general provision on airport and air navigation charges in Article 15'. This can be deduced from the provision's 'respective placement' in a subsequent chapter on 'Measures to Facilitate Air Navigation', where it is the only other provision in the Chicago Convention in which the term 'charge' is used.[97] According to Havel and Sanchez, Article 24 defines as 'impermissible' charges 'including "customs duties, inspection fees, or similar national or local duties or charges"'.[98] In their view, this interpretation finds support in the ICAO Council Resolution on Taxation of International Air Transport, paragraph 1(b)(e), which precludes the imposition of customs duties on fuel, lubricants or aircraft stores other than those calculated and spent to recover the actual costs of airport and air navigational facilities and services.[99]

However, even accepting that an ETS is a 'charge' or 'duty' within the scope of the provision, it is not directed at the fuel stored on board aircraft. As noted by Advocate General Kokott, Article 24 is designed to protect airlines 'from having their aircraft and stores treated as "imported" when they merely land in other Contracting States', while an ETS has the 'entirely different objective' of environmental protection.[100] Rather than being linked to fuel *stocks*, as the quantity of fuel on board an aircraft while stationary, an ETS is related to the quantity of fuel 'actually used' during a flight.[101] For this reason, an ETS is also not a customs duty on goods, as customs duties are 'charges to which goods are subject by virtue of the fact that they cross a border'.[102] This interpretation finds support in the German *Air Transport Tax* case, where the ATTA was not found to violate Article 24 of the Chicago Convention because it was not linked to the fuel aboard the aircraft when entering or leaving the territory.[103] In the case of an ETS, allowances are surrendered due to the emission of GHGs and not due to the fact that fuel is taken across a border.

[97] Havel and Sanchez (n 15) 237.
[98] ibid.
[99] ibid 238.
[100] Opinion of AG Kokott in the *ATAA* case (n 3) [230].
[101] ibid [234]. AG Kokott also notes that there is no direct 'inseverable link' between fuel consumption and GHG emissions, as the emissions factor must also be included in the calculation. This will depend on the type of fuel, where some fuels have very low emission factors [233].
[102] ibid [239].
[103] *German Air Transport* Tax (n 72) 21. See further UM Erling (n 73) 474.

4. COMPETING RESPONSES TO INTERNATIONAL AVIATION EMISSIONS: ICAO AND EU MEASURES

In late 2016, the ICAO reached an agreement on an offsetting scheme in the form of CORSIA.[104] While at the time of writing the finer details are still being agreed, the core design of CORSIA is set out in ICAO Resolution A39-3, with more detailed provision adopted as ICAO SARPs in Annex 16 of the Chicago Convention.[105] Section 4.1 first sets out the basic architecture of CORSIA, and the emerging divergencies with the EU's unilateral policy. Section 4.2 then considers the legal relationship between these competing climate change responses.[106]

4.1. The EU 'Ultimatum Strategy' in the Field of International Aviation Emissions

Seeking to take into account parties' 'special circumstances and respective capabilities', CORSIA has a 'phased' and 'routes-based' approach, which originally had a base year of 2019–20.[107] In response to the dramatic drop in air travel as a result of COVID-19, the ICAO Council decided not to include 2020 when determining the baseline.[108] This was supported by the EU.[109] Participation in the 'pilot phase' from 2021 to 2023, and the 'first phase' from 2024 to 2026, is voluntary.[110] It is only during the second phase from 2027 to 2035 that states whose share in the total international revenue tonnes per kilometre (RTK) is above a certain threshold are obliged to participate.[111] As noted by Erling, the 'most distinct feature' of such an offset scheme is that overall emissions can grow *without limits*, as long as emissions are compensated by 'offset units' coming from different emission-reduction projects in other industries.[112]

[104] CORSIA (n 5) [5].

[105] First Edition of Annex 16, Environmental Protection, vol IV 'Carbon Offsetting and Reduction Scheme for International Aviation (CORSIA)' (adopted by the ICAO Council on 27 June 2018) ('CORSIA SARPs').

[106] Section 4 partly reproduces the work of this author in Dobson (n 6).

[107] ibid Art 10(a). Under the 'routes-based' approach, aircraft operators are only subject to the scheme when the states of both landing and departure participate.

[108] ICAO, 'Impact of COVID-19 on CORSIA implementation in 2020' (2020) www.icao.int/environmental-protection/CORSIA/Pages/CORSIA-and-Covid-19.aspx.

[109] Council Decision (EU) 2020/768 of 9 June 2020 amending Decision (EU) 2016/915 of 30 May 2016 as regards the reference period intended to be used for measuring the growth of CO_2 emissions, to take account of the consequences of the COVID-19 pandemic in the context of CORSIA [2020] OJ L187.

[110] ibid Art 9(a), (b).

[111] ibid Art 9(e). This applies to countries with an individual share of at least 0.5% of the total international revenue tonne kilometre (RTK) in 2018, and to states whose cumulative share in the list of states from the highest to the lowest amount of RTKs reaches 90% of the total RTKs.

[112] UM Erling 'International Aviation Emissions under International Civil Aviation Organization's Global Market Based Measure: Ready for Offsetting?' (2017) 42 *Air Space Law* 1, 5 (emphasis added). See also UM Erling 'How to Reconcile the European Union Emissions Trading System (EU ETS)

This differs fundamentally from the EU ETS, which sets a quantitative cap on emissions, allotting a set amount of credits to be traded on the market.

Responding to international developments, the EU adopted Regulation 2017/2392, 'amending Directive 2003/87/EC to continue current limitations of scope for aviation activities and to prepare to implement a global market-based measure from 2021'.[113] While the title suggests an intention to align EU and ICAO measures, this has not proven to be entirely the case. Rather, the Commission is instructed to present a report considering ways to implement the 'relevant ICAO instruments' through a revision of the ETS.[114] This report 'shall also examine the ambition and overall environmental integrity of the global market-based measure, including its general ambition in relation to targets under the Paris Agreement, the level of participation, its enforceability, transparency, [and] the penalties for non-compliance'.[115] Based on its assessment of these criteria, the Commission must provide a proposal to, 'where appropriate', 'amend, delete, extend or replace' the current derogations (Article 28b(3) Aviation Directive). Importantly, this proposal shall be 'consistent with the Union economy-wide greenhouse gas emission reduction commitment for 2030 with the aim of preserving the environmental integrity and effectiveness of Union climate action'.[116] EU policy expressly states that 'in the absence of a new amendment, the EU ETS would revert back to its original full scope from 2024'.[117]

In the meantime, some alignment is sought through amendments to the EU's existing Regulation on monitoring and reporting (MRR) and Regulation on verification and accreditation of verifiers (AVR).[118] A further, more contentious measure is the Delegated Regulation 'supplementing' the Aviation Directive as regards the adopted ICAO MRV measures ('the Delegated Regulation regarding

for Aviation with the Carbon Offsetting and Reduction Scheme for International Aviation (CORSIA)?' (2018) 43 *Air Space Law* 371.

[113] Parliament and Council (EU) Regulation 2017/2392 of 13 December 2017 amending Directive 2003/87/EC to continue current limitations of scope for aviation activities and to prepare to implement a global market-based measure from 2021 [2017] OJ L350/7 ('Regulation 2017/2392').

[114] ibid Art 7 (emphasis added).

[115] ibid, inserting 28b(2) into the Parliament and Council (EU) Directive 2003/87/EC establishing a scheme for greenhouse gas emission allowance trading within the Community and amending Council Directive 96/61/EC [2003] OJ L275 ('ETS Directive').

[116] ibid, inserting 28b(3) to the ETS Directive (n 115). Comparing ICAO and EU targets, see further A van Velzen, 'CORSIA, EU ETS and the EU2030 Aviation Emissions Target. Report Prepared for Transport and Environment' (September 2018, report no 18-13) 5.

[117] Statement on the Commission website, 'Reducing emissions from aviation' (Europa website, 2019) ec.europa.eu/clima/policies/transport/aviation_en.

[118] Commission Implementing Regulation (EU) 2018/2066 of 19 December 2018 on the monitoring and reporting of greenhouse gas emissions pursuant to Directive 2003/87/EC of 13 October 2003 of the European Parliament and of the Council and amending Commission Regulation (EU) No 601/2012 [2018] OJ L334/1 ('EU MRR'); Commission Implementing Regulation (EU) 2018/2067 of 19 December 2018 on the verification of data and on the accreditation of verifiers pursuant to Directive 2003/87/EC of 13 October 2003 of the European Parliament and of the Council [2018] OJ L334/94 ('Commission AVR Implementing Regulation').

ICAO MRV measures').[119] This delegated act 'complements' the existing EU measures in respect of flights and operations that are *not currently covered* by the EU ETS Directive'.[120] The new Article 28c of the Aviation Directive requires that these measures be 'based on the relevant instruments adopted in the ICAO' and 'avoid any distortion of competition'.[121] However, they must also be consistent with the EU's own monitoring and reporting principles and its verification requirements.[122]

Embedded in EU policy is thus a tension between alignment with ICAO standards and maintaining its desired level of environmental protection. At the time of writing, this is already leading to several divergencies between EU and ICAO measures. For example, the Implementing Regulation for the MRR only recognises two methods for the monitoring of fuel consumption, whereas the CORSIA SARPs recognise five.[123] This poses a restriction on the newly included group of operators based in EEA outermost regions or dependencies and territories of EU Member States.[124] Furthermore, the EU MRV requirements do not foresee in an accommodation for small-scale operators equivalent to the simplified CORSIA 'CO_2 Estimation and Reporting Tool' (CERT).[125] The EU does have its own Small Emitters Tool (SET); however, this is only open to a more restricted group.[126] As regards verification, the EU measures require verifier accreditation by a 'national accreditation body', of which each EU Member State has one.[127] Under CORSIA, 'verification bodies' are defined more broadly as an 'accredited independent third party'.[128] This could be accredited by any CORSIA member, not just an EU Member State.[129]

[119] Commission Delegated Regulation (EU) Supplementing Directive 2003/87/EC of the European Parliament and of the Council as regards measures adopted by the International Civil Aviation Organisation for the monitoring, reporting and verification of aviation emissions for the purpose of implementing a global market-based measure', COM(2019) 1644 final, 6 March 2019 ('Delegated Regulation regarding ICAO MRV measures').

[120] Explanatory Memorandum to the Delegated Regulation regarding ICAO MRV measures (n 119) 2 (emphasis added).

[121] Regulation 2017/2392 (n 113) Art 7.

[122] ibid.

[123] The EU recognises 'Method A' or 'Method B' only. Compare the EU MRR (n 118) art 53, referring to the methods laid down in s 1 of Annex III, with the CORSIA SARPs (n 105), Appendix 2.

[124] Regulation (EU) 421/2014 (n 4). Operators must also report emissions from flights between the EU and 'outermost regions, dependencies or territories of other Member States' (Delegated Regulation regarding ICAO MRV measures (n 119) art 2(2)).

[125] The CERT may be used by operators with annual emissions below 500,000 tonnes in the year 2019–20; see CORSIA SARPs (n 105) ch 2.2.2.

[126] The Eurocontrol SET may be used by emitters of less than 25,000 tonnes of CO_2 per year (or annually flying less than 243 flights per consecutive four-month period). See EU MRR (n 118) art 55.

[127] Commission AVR Implementing Regulation (n 118) art 44. Art 55(1) reads: 'The tasks related to accreditation pursuant to this Regulation shall be carried out by the national accreditation bodies appointed pursuant to Article 4(1) of Regulation (EC) No 765/2008.'

[128] CORSIA SARPs (n 105) ch 2.4.1.1 referring to definitions in ch 1 of the SARPs.

[129] Commission AVR Implementing Regulation, (n 118). Art 56 does foresee in the possibility 'cross-border accreditation', where an EU Member State considers it 'economically not meaningful or sustainable' to establish its own accreditation body. Nevertheless, this is limited to EU Member States.

In addition, in terms of scope, the categories exempted from MRV requirements under the EU and ICAO measures do not match entirely. For example 'scientific research and testing' is exempt under the EU measures but not the CORSIA. Interestingly, under the EU Delegated Regulation, covered aircraft operators are only 'recommended' but not obliged to verify and report emissions from flights between two third countries (Article 2(3)). This contrasts with the CORSIA SARPs, which for operators from participating countries are applicable to 'all international flights' on or after January 2019.[130] The EU's rationale, however, is largely based on doubts as to the jurisdiction of the Commission to regulate these 'extraterritorial' flights.[131]

The above comparison illustrates that the EU is already maintaining a stricter standard at the stage of MRV requirements. Responding to the emerging divergencies, in late 2019 ICAO Resolution 40-19 was adopted, providing that 'the CORSIA is the only global market-based measure applying to CO_2 emissions from international aviation'.[132] The aim of this move is 'to avoid a possible patchwork of duplicative State or regional MBMs'.[133] Intriguingly, despite calls from both the European Parliament and the Commission, none of the EU Member States made a formal reservation to the exclusivity clause.[134] Taken together, interesting questions thus arise for the legal relationship between these overlapping measures.

4.2. The Relationship between the CORSIA and EU Unilateral Measures

As mentioned, unlike its Member States, the EU is a formal party to the Chicago Convention, and does not consider itself bound by this agreement. In addition, the EU is not a member of the ICAO. In order to explore the dynamics between these actors, it is necessary to distinguish between the different legal sources at issue.

To start with, as noted by Martinez Romera in her comprehensive study, neither the Convention's Annexes nor ICAO resolutions are strictly binding on ICAO members, as these were not originally an 'integral part' of the Convention.[135] The ICAO's adoption of the 'exclusivity clause' in Resolution

[130] CORSIA SARPs (n 105) ch 2.1.1, applicable to 'international flights' as defined in ch 1.1.2 as 'the operation of an aircraft from take-off at the aerodrome of State or its territories, and landing at an aerodrome of another State or its territories'.

[131] See further the Explanatory Memorandum to the Delegated Regulation regarding ICAO MRV measures (n 119) 4, explaining Art 2(3).

[132] ICAO Resolution A40-19 (n 7) [18].

[133] ibid.

[134] For consideration of future options, see F Rothenberg, 'CORSIA Exclusivity Clause – Potential EU ETS Implication' (Independent Commodity Intelligence Services, 8 October 2019) www.icis.com/explore/resources/news/2019/10/11/10427666/corsia-exclusivity-clause-potential-eu-ets-implications.

[135] B Martinez Romera, *Regime Interaction and Climate Change: The Case of International Aviation and Maritime Transport* (Abingdon, Routledge, 2017).

A40-19 would then seem to have more of a political than a legal weight, particularly for the EU. Nonetheless, the European Parliament was 'deeply concerned', 'urging' Member States to file reservations, 'so as to *preserve the Union's legislative autonomy* with regard to measures intended to reduce GHG emissions from the aviation sector'.[136] From this statement, it is unclear whether the Parliament considers its legislative *competence* actually limited, or whether the use of the word 'autonomy' is intended to refer to the de facto pressures that will arise if its Member States face conflicting ICAO standards. The latter seems more likely, given the EU's position on its relationship with the Chicago Convention.

Turning to the Chicago Convention, one element that does bind the parties is the procedure in situations of non-compliance with SARPs. This can be found in Article 38, which provides that:

> [A]ny State which finds it impracticable to comply in all respects with any such international standard or procedure [as adopted by the ICAO according to Article 37], or to bring its own regulations or practices into full accord with any international standard or procedure after amendment of the latter, or which *deems it necessary* to adopt regulations or practices *differing* in any particular respect from those established by an international standard, shall give immediate notification to the International Civil Aviation Organization of the differences. (emphasis added)

The question then arises whether the EU, while not a formal party, would be subject to Article 38 of the Chicago Convention, and on what basis this would occur. One option is through functional succession, according to which an organisation, when acquiring competence from its Member States, succeeds to the relevant obligations already incumbent upon all of its Member States. There is, however, much debate on the meaning and validity of this doctrine, with differing views in both EU and public international law. From an EU law perspective, in *International Fruit Company*, the CJEU in principle recognised the possibility for functional succession, accepting that the EU had succeeded to its Member States' obligations under the 1947 GATT.[137] However, it set the bar for functional succession very high, and in the *ATAA* case, explicitly rejected such succession in relation to the Chicago Convention.[138] According to the CJEU, 'in order for the European Union to be capable of being bound, it must have assumed, and thus had transferred to it, all the powers previously exercised by the Member States that fall within the convention in question'.[139] Here, EU Member States were found to have retained rights falling within the scope of the Chicago Convention.[140]

[136] European Parliament resolution of 28 November 2019 on the 2019 UN Climate Change Conference in Madrid, Spain (COP 25) (2019/2712(RSP)) (2019) P9_TA(2019)0079, [72] (emphasis added).

[137] *International Fruit* (n 9) [18].

[138] *ATAA* case (n 3), [63] and [69], referring to Case C-308/06 *Intertanko and Others* [2008] ECR I-4057 [50].

[139] ibid [63].

[140] ibid [70], referring to air traffic rights and charges.

This strict approach to the functional succession doctrine has been criticised in the literature as being 'too simplistic',[141] and one which 'makes little sense'.[142] According to Eeckhout, the doctrine itself rests on the notion that 'a transfer of powers from the Member States to the EU also entails a transfer of the Member States' international obligations'.[143] The CJEU's narrow interpretation undermines the EU's likeliness to adhere to important international treaties,[144] and generally exacerbates legal fragmentation.

This critique is related to a debate, also avid under public international law, on the validity of the functional succession doctrine as such. The discussion is not only relevant for succession to treaties as a whole, but in relation to discrete international obligations. On one approach, international organisations, having a 'separate legal identity', are not bound by their members' obligations, as this 'would make a mockery of their independent legal existence'.[145] Accepting this, the CJEU could then be seen to have created its own sui generis approach, allowing the applicability of international agreements in its legal order for its own functional reasons, rather than as a matter of international law. An opposing view supported here, focuses on the functional nature of international organisations' competence.[146] This competence is derived from the sovereignty of its Member States, who cannot transfer more power than they have.[147] As noted by Schermers and Blokker, 'an organization formed by states will be bound by the obligations to which the individual states were committed when they transferred powers to the organization'.[148] Contrary to the view of the CJEU, this should not be made dependent on whether there are other competences in a broader international agreement that have not been conferred to the international organisation.

As the 1944 Chicago Convention predates the 1958 EC Treaties, it could then well be argued that the EU must exercise said competence under the same conditions as those originally in place upon its Member States. This is notably different to the existing EU law provision in Article 351 TFEU, that rights and obligations

[141] K Ziegler, 'The Relationship between EU Law and International Law' (University of Leicester School of Law Research Paper no 15-04, 2015) 9.

[142] P Eeckhout, *EU External Relations Law*, 2nd edn (Oxford University Press, Oxford, 2011) 400.

[143] ibid 397.

[144] ibid 400.

[145] Discussed by J Klabbers, 'The Sources of International Organizations Law' in J d'Aspremont and S Besson (eds), *The Oxford Handbook of the Sources of International Law* (Oxford, Oxford University Press, 2017) 988.

[146] See *Reparation for injuries suffered in the service of the United Nations* (Advisory Opinion) [1949] ICJ Rep 174, 180. In the context of international human rights law, see further T Ahmed and I Butler 'The European Union and Human Rights: An International Law Perspective' (2006) 17 *European Journal of International Law* 771, 791.

[147] K Daugirdas, 'How and Why International Law Binds International Organizations' (2016) 57 *Harvard International Law Journal* 325, 336, referring to this phenomenon as being 'transitively bound'. See also Ahmed and Butler (n 146) 791.

[148] H Schermers and N Blokker *International Institutional Law: Unity within Diversity* (Leiden, Brill, 2011) 996.

with third countries made before 1 January 1958 or before the date of acceding states' accession 'shall not be affected by the provisions of the Treaties'. This has namely been interpreted as an obligation to allow Member States to adhere to their agreements, not to bind the EU itself to these obligations.[149]

Taken together, while the EU may arguably be obliged to notify the ICAO of differences, it appears free to consider it 'necessary' to pursue – through its Member States – higher environmental integrity standards. This latter point was indeed relied upon by the EU in establishing its position within the ICAO in respect of the first edition of the CORSIA SARPs.[150] In practice, however, this is politically tenuous, and was criticised by industry as being 'extremely damaging' as 'it creates the perception that it is acceptable for ICAO Member States to depart at their discretion' from ICAO agreements.[151] For their part, EU Member States are left facing dual and sometimes conflicting regulatory burdens. In such a situation, the customary law of jurisdiction may have more to offer, as it deals more generally with the issue of delineating regulatory competence. The customary jurisdictional rules will be discussed further in the following chapters of this book.

5. CONCLUSION

From an area of relative inaction, the field of international aviation transport emissions has swiftly become quite crowded. This chapter has sought to analyse the place of unilateral 'extraterritorial' climate protective measures, both under the Chicago Convention and since the adoption of CORSIA.

Turning first to the Chicago Convention, Article 1 on the principle of aircraft sovereignty, codifies a specific application of the principle of territorial sovereignty in relation to airspace. This, together with the principle of concessionary market access contained in Article 6 of the Chicago Convention, underscores the right of states to set and enforce market access conditions for aircraft above or within their territory. It does not, however, indicate precise territorial limits on the subject matter of the entry and exit requirements that they may set. The same can be said for the last part of Article 12 which, although it endows the ICAO with competence to regulate high seas overflight, does not preclude states from doing so as well. In the same vein as regards port state jurisdiction, it is argued that the principle of high seas overflight does not preclude states from

[149] *ATAA* case (n 3) [61].

[150] Council Decision (EU) 2018/2027 of 29 November 2018 on the position to be taken on behalf of the European Union within the International Civil Aviation Organization in respect of the First Edition of the International Standards and Recommended Practices on Environmental Protection – Carbon Offsetting and Reduction Scheme for International Aviation (CORSIA) [2018] OJ L325/25.

[151] 'Comments on the Commission's draft Delegated Regulation on reporting measures to implement CORSIA' (International Air Transport Association, 13 December 2018) 2.

setting entry conditions for foreign aircraft choosing to enter its territory. Such a conclusion is supported by the growing practice of states imposing emission levies upon entry or exit from their territories.

More complex is the prohibition in Article 15 of the Chicago Convention on charges or other duties imposed solely in respect of entry, exit or transit over a territory. While some argue that this provision precludes environmental levies, including taxes, the present study does not consider such measures to fall within the scope of the provision. In relation more specifically to an Aviation ETS, it is submitted that, given its aim to incorporate the environmental costs of aviation emissions, such a measure, when applied equally, is not precluded by the provision. In fact one could question whether it can correctly be characterised as a 'tax' or a 'charge' in the sense of Article 15 at all. An ETS also does not impose a levy on fuel stocks stored and maintained on board foreign aircraft in violation of Article 24 of the Convention. This conclusion appears supported by the ICAO's own principles on the design of MBMs for international civil aviation.

The adoption of CORSIA has raised political tensions between the ICAO and the EU, which at the time of writing, are yet to come to head. Much debate remains on the precise relationship between the EU and ICAO measures, with divergencies in perspectives both under international and EU law. As the EU is not a member of the ICAO, and the ICAO resolutions are not strictly binding on members, formally speaking, the EU would appear free to take a unilateral approach. Problematically, however, in the event that the EU maintains its own unilateral standards, aircraft operators will be faced with dual regulatory burdens. In the absence of clear hierarchical rules, it is argued that, here too, an important role remains for the customary law of jurisdiction. The customary jurisdictional rules function as more general rules governing the scope of states' regulatory competence, and will now be considered further in part III of this book.

Part III

Lex Generalis: The Crystallisation of 'Climate Change Jurisdiction' under Customary International Law

7

The Classical Principles of State Jurisdiction under Customary International Law

1. INTRODUCTION

THE PREVIOUS CHAPTERS have explored the conditions on state competence to regulate the foreign carbon footprint under WTO law, the law of the sea and international civil aviation law. While debates continue, it has been argued that these regimes alone do not exhaustively determine the scope of states' prescriptive jurisdiction for market-entry conditions. In order to complete the analysis, it is necessary to turn to the customary international law of state jurisdiction as a *lex generalis* supplementing these regimes. As discussed, the covered agreements of the WTO recognise the complementary role of customary law through Article 3.2 of the DSU, and the Appellate Body has stressed that trade law should not be read in 'clinical isolation' from other rules of international law.[1] It is also well recognised that customary law may supplement international aviation law and the law of the sea.[2]

The present analysis of the customary law of jurisdictional is divided into two distinct enquiries. The first enquiry, undertaken in this chapter and chapter and 8, investigates the existence of a permissive basis to legislate. As will now

[1] WTO, *United States – Standards for Reformulated and Conventional Gasoline – Panel Report* (29 April 1996) WT/DS2/R (*US – Gasoline (Panel)*)17, For further discussion on the interaction between these regimes, see J Pauwelyn, *Conflict of Norms in Public International Law: How WTO Law Relates to Other Rules of International Law* (Cambridge, Cambridge University Press, 2003). This is discussed further in chapter 4.

[2] With regard to international aviation law, see B Havel and G Sanchez, *The Principles and Practice of International Aviation Law* (New York, Cambridge University Press, 2014) 16: 'traditional public international law sources such as custom and treaties are overwhelmingly dominant in creating what this book regards as the modern body of international aviation law'. With regard to the law of the sea, see H Ringbom, 'Global Problem – Regional Solution? International Law Reflections on an EU CO_2 Emissions Trading Scheme for Ships' (2011) 26 *International Journal of Marine and Coastal Law* 613, 629 and 637, describing the Law of the Sea Convention as a 'clarification' and 'manifestation' of customary international law of the sea, including the law of jurisdiction (United Nations Convention on the Law of the Sea (adopted 10 December 1982, entered into force 16 November 1994) 1833 UNTS 3 (LOSC)).

be seen, the existence of a basis to legislate depends on the acting state's link with the regulated subject matter. The second enquiry, undertaken in chapters 9 and 10, concerns the existence of limitations on the exercise of jurisdiction in a particular case. This pertains to questions of 'reasonableness', and the protection of *other*, affected states' regulatory autonomy. In concrete terms, such autonomy is protected through conditions on whether, and in particular, *how* unilateral jurisdiction is exercised. It is argued that distinguishing the consideration of the acting and affected states' interests supports a clearer and more constructive legal analysis.

This chapter starts by setting out the recognised bases of prescriptive jurisdiction under customary law more generally. To this end, section 2 briefly considers the key principles of 'extraterritorial' jurisdiction, widely recognised in legal theory. While not seeking to present and exhaustive overview, its aim is to sketch out the contours of these principles, examining their roots in criminal and economic law.[3] Section 3 then examines the overarching 'substantial connection' requirement and its relationship with the traditional principles.

2. A LEGAL BASIS TO LEGISLATE UNDER THE CLASSICAL JURISDICTIONAL PRINCIPLES

All jurisdictional assertions require a valid basis in international law. As we have seen, however, there is no overarching or 'universal' treaty clearly defining such a basis, and relevant case law is scarce.[4] As one of the cornerstone cases before an international court explicitly dealing with jurisdiction, the 1927 *Lotus* case remains an important starting point for the present analysis.[5] In the *Lotus* case, the Permanent Court of International Justice (PCIJ) considered the threshold question of if and when, according to customary international law, a state may exercise jurisdiction over conduct or circumstances outside of its territory. The case concerned the arrest by Turkey of a French officer, after the collision of the Turkish vessel *Boz-Kourt* with the French mail steamer *Lotus* on the high seas.[6] Following the collision, the *Lotus* docked at a Turkish port where the local authorities investigated the incident, and arrested and sentenced the French officer on watch.[7] After much protest from France, the parties submitted

[3] For more thorough analyses, see eg C Ryngaert, *Jurisdiction in International Law*, 2nd edn (Oxford, Oxford University Press, 2015); *Restatement (Fourth) of the Foreign Relations Law of the United States* (St Paul, MN, American Law Institute Publishers, 2018) ('US Fourth Restatement').

[4] International Bar Association, 'Report of the Taskforce on Extraterritorial Jurisdiction' (2009) tinyurl.com/taskforce-etj-pdf ('IBA Report on Extraterritorial Jurisdiction') 88; M Kamminga 'Extraterritoriality', in R Wolfrum (ed), *Max Planck Encyclopaedia of Public International Law*, online edn (Oxford, Oxford University Press, 2011).

[5] *The SS Lotus (France v Turkey)* 1927 PCIJ Series A, No 10 (*Lotus* case) 18–19.

[6] ibid 12.

[7] ibid.

a dispute by special agreement to the PCIJ regarding whether Turkey had jurisdiction under international law to instigate the criminal proceedings.[8]

In deciding the issue, the PCIJ started by stressing the importance of state independence as fundamental to 'the very nature and existing conditions of international law'. In doing so it famously held that:

> The rules of law binding upon States therefore emanate from their own free will as expressed in conventions or by usages generally accepted as expressing principles of law and established in order to regulate the relations between these co-existing independent communities or with a view to the achievement of common aims. Restrictions upon the independence of States cannot therefore be presumed.[9]

The PCIJ then went on to set out a restrictive approach to enforcement jurisdiction, holding that:

> [T]he first and foremost restriction imposed by international law upon a State is that – failing the existence of a permissive rule to the contrary – it may not exercise its power in any form in the territory of another State. In this sense jurisdiction is certainly territorial; it cannot be exercised by a State outside its territory except by virtue of a permissive rule derived from international custom or from a convention.[10]

That the above reference to the 'exercise of state power' refers to *enforcement* is clarified by the subsequent finding of the Court that:

> It does not, however, follow that international law prohibits a State from exercising jurisdiction in its own territory, in respect of any case which relates to acts which have taken place abroad, and in which it cannot rely on some permissive rule of international law.[11]

This indicates that the Court distinguishes between enforcement and prescription, taking a permissive approach to the latter. Thus, the PCIJ found that acts of prescriptive jurisdiction are in principle permitted, unless there is a restrictive rule of international law prohibiting its exercise.

Subsequent state practice, however, is now widely recognised to have turned the *Lotus* principle 'upside down'.[12] States seeking to regulate conduct or events outside their territory are considered to bear the burden of demonstrating a *permissive* jurisdictional basis in international law. It is widely accepted that in order to demonstrate such a permissive basis, a state must be able to show a

[8] ibid 5.
[9] ibid 18.
[10] ibid.
[11] ibid 19.
[12] For further discussion, see Ryngaert (n 3) 35. Although note B Oxman, 'Jurisdiction of States' in R Wolfrum (ed), *Max Planck Encyclopaedia of Public International Law*, online edn (Oxford, Oxford University Press, 2007), who argues that it is 'unclear' what the current state of affairs is in relation to the *Lotus* case finding [10].

'sufficient nexus' or 'substantial connection' to the regulated subject matter.[13] To substantiate this connection, states may draw on one or more of the five classical bases or 'principles' of prescriptive jurisdiction, namely:

(1) the territoriality principle (subjective or objective);
(2) the 'effects-doctrine';
(3) the nationality principle (active or passive);
(4) the protective principle; and
(5) the universality principle.

Sometimes seen as an extension of the territoriality principle, the 'effects-doctrine' provides a basis for jurisdiction relating to conduct that has actual or foreseeable substantial effects on a state's territory.[14] According to the nationality or personality principle, states may regulate foreign conduct or circumstances relating to their nationals. The protective principle provides a basis to regulate foreign conduct posing a threat to vital state interests. With regard to the universality principle, the recognised common interest in regulating the subject matter – traditionally grave crimes – provides a basis for *all* states to legislate.

The customary bases mentioned above represent situations in which states can claim a 'substantial' or legitimate interest or connection in the regulation of certain subject matter. Such regulation typically aims to achieve certain public policy objectives.[15] Although a measure's public policy objective and a state's interest or connection with the regulated subject matter may overlap, they are not entirely the same. A state may, for example, have an objective of preventing impunity, and therefore extend its jurisdiction to the illegal conduct of its citizens abroad. In such cases, the state's connection with the subject matter is the nationality of its citizens. In an environmental context, a state may have the objective of mitigating climate change, while its link with the subject matter is the harmful effects on its territory.

As will now be seen, the contours of the permissive prescriptive principles are determined by fragmented and diverse state practice, not all of which has been equally well accepted. They also differ in scope and applicability to matters of civil and criminal law. For this reason, as argued by Kamminga, it is 'far too simplistic' to suggest that any regulation of foreign conduct or events based on one of these principles is 'automatically lawful'.[16] Still, the traditional bases do

[13] See eg Oxman (n 12) [10]; Kamminga, 'Extraterritoriality' (2011) [9]; Report of the International Law Commission on the Work of its 58th Session (1 May–9 June and 3 July–11 August 2006) UN Doc A/61/10, Annex E ('ILC Report on Extraterritorial Jurisdiction') 521.

[14] See further section 2.2 of this chapter.

[15] Note, however, C Ryngaert, *Selfless Intervention: The Exercise of Jurisdiction in the Common Interest* (Oxford, Oxford University Press, 2020) 93, cautioning that: 'If one accepts unilateralism in principle, one should make sure, however, that one takes seriously concerns over self-serving behaviour, undue interference in other nations' internal affairs, normative competency conflicts, and "false universalism"' (references omitted).

[16] Kamminga (n 4) [10].

provide important indications of the elements which *may*, individually or cumulatively, constitute a 'substantial connection', and will now be explored further.

2.1. The Territoriality Principle

The centrality of territory was aptly captured by Mann, who in 1984 noted that, '[s]ince in the present world sovereignty is undoubtedly territorial in character, in assessing the extent of jurisdiction the starting point must necessarily be its territoriality'.[17] Indeed, state practice since the *Lotus* case has confirmed that, as a general rule, states may only legally exercise certain competences within their defined territory.[18] This is known as the territoriality principle, which is a corollary of sovereign equality, and the primary principle of jurisdiction. A state's territory includes not only its land, but also the air space above its territory, its internal waters, the territorial sea adjacent to its coast, and, for archipelagic states, also the archipelagic waters.[19]

The primacy of this principle finds support in the 'presumption against extraterritoriality', a rule of construction applied by courts, particularly in common law jurisdictions.[20] In the United States, for example, this is construed as the assumption that the 'legislation of Congress, unless a contrary intent appears, is meant to apply only within the territorial jurisdiction of the United States'.[21] Notably, however, according to the 2018 Fourth Restatement of Foreign Relations Law of the United States ('the US Fourth Restatement'), while its rationale 'rested initially on the presumed desire of Congress to avoid violations of international law', the 'modern' presumption is focused on preventing conflicting claims and 'reflects the assumption that Congress is primarily concerned with domestic conditions'.[22] A further example is England, where courts also depart from the 'presumption that in the absence of clear and specific words to the contrary, an offence-creating section is not intended to make conduct outside the territorial jurisdiction of the Crown an offence triable in an English court'.[23]

Predictably, the application of the territoriality principle becomes more complicated when an event does not occur entirely within a state's territory.

[17] FA Mann, 'The Doctrine of International Jurisdiction Revisited After Twenty Years' (1984) 186 *Recueil des Cours* 9, 20.

[18] See Oxman (n 13) [13]; Ryngaert (n 3) 36.

[19] Oxman (n 13) [13].

[20] Ryngaert (n 3) 54, citing also as a civil law example, Reichsgerichtshof, 18 April 1921, Fontes Juris Gentium, series A, s II, vol I, 69.

[21] *EEOC v Arabian American Oil Co*, 499 US 244, 248 (1991) (*Aramco*).

[22] US 4th, §404, Reporters' Notes 2. See further, WS Dodge, 'Jurisdiction in the Fourth Restatement' (2016/17) 18 *Yearbook of Private International Law* 143, 150 explaining the evolution of the two-step test for the presumption against extraterritoriality in *RJR Nabisco, Inc v European Community*, 136 SCt 2090 (2016).

[23] See eg *Liangsiriprasert v Government of the United States of America* [1991] 1 AC 225 (PC) (UK) (*Liangsiriprasert*). See also *Air-India v Wiggins* [1980] 1 WLR 815; *Stanley v The Queen* [1985] LRC (Crim) 52; and *Public Prosecutor v Rajappan* [1986] 1 MLJ 152.

At what point does a state have a sufficient 'territorial link' to the regulated subject matter so that it can still rely on this jurisdictional basis? In the field of criminal law, a widely accepted approach is to distinguish between 'objective' and 'subjective' territoriality. According to the subjective territoriality principle, a state may exercise jurisdiction where an act has been initiated in its territory, but completed abroad.[24] According to the objective territoriality principle, a state may exercise jurisdiction over 'persons, property or acts outside its territory when a *constitutive element* of the conduct sought to be regulated occurred in the territory of the State'.[25]

The application of the 'constituent elements' approach is complicated by the fact that the constituent elements of crimes or offences are determined by national law. Indeed, some acts may fall under criminal jurisdiction in certain states whereas they are considered civil offences in others (eg cartel forming).[26] In order to remedy this, it has been argued that international law may support a jurisdictional claim when part of a crime or offence or its effects take place within the territory of the legislating state, irrespective of how the constituent elements are construed under national law.[27]

The latter issue of territorial *effects* remains somewhat contested and is discussed further in section 2.2. Formally speaking, the distinction between the effects-doctrine and the objective territoriality principle is that the effects-doctrine does not require an element of conduct to occur in its territory.[28] In practice it is, however, difficult to identify a 'bright-line' distinction between the completion of an act and its effects, particularly where the effects of an act can qualify the regulated conduct (eg involuntary manslaughter).

An interesting example of the diffuse scope of the territoriality principle concerns the right to be forgotten (de-referenced) on the internet. This is another field in which the EU has been extending the reach of its desired level of protection.[29] In the landmark *Google Spain* case, Google contested the legality of an order of the Spanish Data Protection Agency to de-reference personal data relating to a Spanish national.[30] The domestic measure was based on

[24] IBA Report on Extraterritorial Jurisdiction (n 4) 143, citing *US v Pasquantino*, 544 US 349 (2005).

[25] ILC Report on Extraterritorial Jurisdiction (n 13) 521 (emphasis added).

[26] In the United States companies and individuals can be criminally prosecuted for cartel forming, whereas in the EU this has traditionally been considered a civil matter, though individual Member States are changing their approach. See further IBA Report on Extraterritorial Jurisdiction (n 4) 52–53.

[27] Ryngaert (n 3) 78.

[28] See eg ILC Report on Extraterritorial Jurisdiction (n 13) 522; US Fourth Restatement (n 3) §408, comment c and Reporters' Note 4.

[29] In more depth, see M Taylor, 'The EU's Human Rights Obligations in Relation to its Data Protection Laws with Extraterritorial Effect' (2015) 5 *International Data Privacy Law* 426.

[30] Case C-131/12 *Google Spain SL, Google Inc v Agencia Espanola de Protección de Datos (AEPD), and Mario Costeja González* [2014] ECLI:EU:C:2014:317 (*Google Spain*) [2].

Directive 95/46 on the protection of individuals with regard to the processing of personal data. According to article 4(1)(a), an EU Member State must

> apply the national provisions it adopts pursuant to this Directive to the processing of personal data where … the processing is carried out in the context of the activities of an establishment of the controller on the territory of the Member State.

Google argued that the processing in question was not 'carried out in the context of the activities' of Google Spain, but rather 'exclusively by Google Inc'.[31] The former was tasked with 'providing support to the Google group's advertising activity which is separate from its search engine service'.

The CJEU rejected this perspective, finding that in light of the directive's objective of 'ensuring effective and complete protection' of the right to privacy, Article 4 should not be 'interpreted restrictively'. The perambulatory provisions and wording of Article 4 indicate the intention of the EU legislature to prevent circumvention of this protection 'by prescribing a particularly broad territorial scope'.[32] In the view of the Court, the processing of personal data outside the EU will be carried out 'in the context of the activities' of an establishment in a Member State, 'if the latter is intended to promote and sell, in that Member State, advertising space offered by the search engine which serves to make the service offered by that engine profitable'.[33]

Applied to the facts, the activities of Google Spain and Google Inc were found to be 'inextricably linked'. Advertising activities oriented towards Spanish nationals are both enabled by the search engine and render the search engine economically profitable.[34] This case has been extensively analysed in the literature, Van Alsenoy and Koekkoek arguing that, in fact, the judgment does not rest only on a rather 'virtual' interpretation of the territoriality principle, but on the effects doctrine as well.[35] Section 2.2 will now consider this doctrine, reflecting further on its relationship with the territoriality principle.

2.2. The Effects-Doctrine

The effects-doctrine was traditionally a controversial jurisdictional basis, and has strong roots in US practice. Interestingly, however, in the US Fourth Restatement, 'effects' was 'upgraded' to its own separate §409, which 'reflects the evolution of the effects principle into a distinct basis for jurisdiction to prescribe

[31] ibid [51].
[32] ibid [54].
[33] ibid [55].
[34] ibid [56].
[35] B van Alsenoy and M Koekkoek, 'Internet and Jurisdiction after Google Spain: The Extraterritorial Reach of the 'Right to Be Delisted'' (2015) 5 *International Data Privacy Law* 105, 108.

under customary international law'.[36] According to §409, 'international law recognizes a state's jurisdiction to prescribe law with respect to conduct that has [or is intended to have] a substantial effect within its territory'.[37] The rationale of the effects-doctrine is essentially that states, having sovereign power over their territory, may regulate conduct that interferes with their domestic affairs.[38] In fact, Hertogen goes so far as to propose that in the absence of the 'locality of effects', territorial presence alone may be insufficient to justify jurisdictional assertions.[39]

One example of effects-based jurisdiction can be found in Article 21(1)(h) LOSC, according to which:

> [The] coastal State may adopt laws and regulations, in conformity with the provisions of this Convention and other rules of international law, relating to innocent passage through the territorial sea, in respect of … the prevention of infringement of the customs, fiscal, immigration or sanitary laws and regulations of the coastal State.

This is complemented by Article 27 LOSC which provides for criminal enforcement jurisdiction on board a foreign ship passing through its territorial sea '(a) if the consequences of the crime extend to the coastal state' and '(b) if the crime is of a kind to disturb the peace of the country or the good order of the territorial sea'.

Use of the effects-doctrine is particularly prominent in the field of antitrust, where economic effects may constitute a sufficient basis to legislate.[40] In the well-known 1945 *United States v Aluminum Co of America (Alcoa)* case, the US Federal Court held that 'it is settled law … that any state may impose liabilities, even upon persons not within its allegiance, for conduct outside its borders that has consequences within its borders which the state reprehends'.[41] As such, the legislation in question (the Sherman Act) was held to apply to foreign anti-competitive conduct where this was 'intended to affect imports and did affect them'.[42]

Notably, this 'intended effects test' did not originally consider the interests of other states, and has been criticised as 'a wholesale exportation of US competition policy' ignoring 'the policies and concerns of foreign governments'.[43] In response to international objections, the *Timberlane* and *Mannington Mills* cases

[36] US Fourth Restatement (n 3) §409, Reporters' Notes 5.

[37] ibid §409.

[38] A Hertogen, 'Letting Lotus Bloom' (2016) 26 *European Journal of International Law* 901, 921.

[39] ibid 921–22. This is the core of the 'locality principle' proposed by Hertogen, according to which territorial effects are necessary but not determinative for the exercise of jurisdiction.

[40] For a more detailed analysis, see C Ryngaert, *Jurisdiction over Antitrust Violations in International Law* (Antwerp, Intersentia 2008).

[41] *United States v Aluminum Corp of America*, 148 F 2d 416, 443 (2nd Cir 1945) (*Alcoa*).

[42] ibid 444.

[43] P Zagalis, 'Hartford Fire Insurance Company v California: Reassessing the Application of the McCarran–Ferguson Act to Foreign Reinsurers' (1994) 27 *Cornell International Law Journal* 241, 250.

developed additional conditions for the exercise of effects-based jurisdiction.[44] The outcome of these cases was the finding that, even where the United States can claim jurisdiction based on effects, it should abstain from exercising it in certain cases, based on a jurisdictional 'rule of reason', consisting of a considerable list of interest-balancing factors.[45] The key case law developments were incorporated into the Foreign Trade Antitrust Improvements Act (FTAIA).[46] The FTAIA amended the Sherman Act and the Federal Trade Commission Act, exempting from their scope international commerce and trade except such conduct that has a 'direct, substantial, and reasonably foreseeable effect' on commerce with the United States.[47] The trajectory of the 'rule of reason' developed in *Timberlane* will be discussed further in chapter 9 on jurisdictional limitations.

While traditionally adverse to the effects-doctrine, the EU has become more receptive in the field of antitrust. In the 1999 *Gencor* case, the European Court of First Instance (CFI) considered the compatibility of a merger between two companies incorporated in South Africa with the EC Merger Regulation.[48] In doing so it held that the application of the Merger Regulation to the companies incorporated abroad 'is justified under public international law when it is foreseeable that a proposed concentration will have an immediate and substantial effect in the Community'.[49] The CFI found that 'the concentration would have the direct and immediate effect of creating the conditions in which the abuses were not only possible but economically rational'.[50] This implicitly indicated some acceptance of a so-called 'qualified' effects test under EU law.[51]

In parallel, however, the CJEU has also maintained its own 'implementation doctrine'. A leading case in this regard is *A Ahlström Osakeyhtiö v Commission (Wood Pulp)*,[52] which concerned an alleged violation of the former Articles 85

[44] *Timberlane Lumber Co v Bank of America* 549 F.2d 597 (9th Cir 1976) (*Timberlane*); *Mannington Mills, Inc v Congoleum Corp*, 595 F.2d 1287 (3d Cir 1979) (*Manning Mills*).

[45] Zagalis (n 43) 251, discussing amongst other cases, *Manning Mills* (n 44) 1297–98.

[46] Foreign Trade Antitrust Improvements Act of 1982, 15 USC § 6a (FTAIA). For later affirmation of the effects-doctrine, see *Hartford Fire Insurance Co v California*, 509 US 764, 113 SCt 2891 (1993) (*Hartford Fire*); *F Hoffman-LaRoche, Ltd v Empagran*, 542 US 155, 124 SCt 2359 (2004) (*Empagran*); and *Morrison v National Australia Bank*, 561 US 247 (2010) (*Morrison*). See also US Fourth Restatement §402, Reporters' Notes 6.

[47] FTAIA (n 46) § 6a.

[48] Case T-102/96 *Gencor Ltd v Commission* [1999] ECR II-753 (*Gencor*). Council Regulation (EEC) 4064/89 of 21 December 1989 on the control of concentrations between undertakings [1989] OJ L395/1 ('Merger Regulation').

[49] *Gencor* (n 48) [90].

[50] ibid [94].

[51] See eg European Commission Roundtable on Cartel Jurisdiction Issues Including the Effects Doctrine, Working Party No 3 on Cooperation and Enforcement (21 October 2008) DAF/COMP/WP3/WD(2008)93 ('Commission Roundtable on Cartel Jurisdiction') 4. The Competition Committee notes: 'Although the Court did not expressly adopt the effects doctrine, but rather considered that the thresholds were an application of the implementation principle, the wording which was used can be considered as the acknowledgement of the effects doctrine.'

[52] Joined Cases C-89, 104, 114, 116, 117 and 125–129/85 *A Ahlström Osakeyhtiö v Commission* [1988] ECR 5193 (*Wood Pulp*).

and 81 of the EC Treaty (now Articles 105 and 101 TFEU) prohibiting 'all agreements between undertakings and concerted practices which may affect trade between Member States and which have as their object or effect the restriction of competition within the common market'.[53] While these provisions base their prescriptive scope on economic effects, the CJEU held that an infringement of Article 85 TEC 'consists of conduct made up of two elements, the *formation* of the agreement, decision or concerted practice and the *implementation* thereof'.[54] According to the CJEU:

> If the applicability of prohibitions laid down under competition law were made to depend on the place where the agreement, decision or concerted practice was formed, the result would obviously be to give undertakings an easy means of evading those prohibitions. The decisive factor is therefore the place where it is *implemented*.[55]

In the view of the CJEU, jurisdiction based on the implementation doctrine 'is covered by the territoriality principle as universally recognized in public international law'.[56]

Discussion remains in legal discourse on whether the implementation test is appropriately based on territoriality or the effects-doctrine.[57] Indeed, the CJEU's reasoning is once again illustrative of the fluidity of the territoriality principle, and one can certainly question the material distinction between the 'implementation' and 'effects' doctrines in a case such as this.[58] According to the Competition Committee, the effects-doctrine does differ from the implementation doctrine in that it is 'more precise and cover[s] more areas of competition restrictive conduct'.[59] In particular, it may cover situations in which corporations based abroad make the negative decision not to sell into the EU market in a situation similar to the *Alcoa* case.[60]

In the 2017 *Intel v Commission* case, the CJEU directly addressed the validity of both the qualified effects and implementation tests.[61] The case concerned the conduct of the US-based company Intel, which attempted to exclude a competitor, Advanced Micro Devices Inc (AMD) from the market for 68x central

[53] Treaty establishing the European Community [2002] OJ C325/33 (TEC) Arts 81 and 85; *Wood Pulp* (n 52) [11].

[54] *Wood Pulp* (n 52) [16].

[55] ibid.

[56] ibid [18] (emphasis added).

[57] See further eg L Prete, 'On Implementation and Effects: The Recent Case-law on the Territorial (or Extraterritorial?) Application of EU Competition Rules' (2018) 8 *Journal of European Competition Law & Practice* 487.

[58] See further P Capps, MD Evans and S Konstadinidis (eds), *Asserting Jurisdiction* (Oxford, Hart Publishing, 2003) 111; C Smitherman, *Transatlantic Merger Cases: United States–European Community Merger Review Cooperation* (London, Cameron May, 2007) 40, who argues that '[i]n practice the implementation or "quasi-effects" doctrine *of Wood Pulp* has been seemingly co-existent with the US formulation'.

[59] Commission Roundtable on Cartel Jurisdiction (n 51) 3.

[60] ibid.

[61] Case C-413/14 P *Intel v Commission* [2017] EU:C:2017:632 (*Intel v Commission*).

processing units (CPUs).[62] This was found by the Commission to be an abuse of its dominant position.[63] Intel argued that the Commission lacked territorial jurisdiction to apply the relevant Articles 101 and 102 TFEU, particularly to agreements it made with manufacturers Acer and Lenovo in Asia, as 'their manufacturing facilities were outside the EEA, and that they did not purchase CPUs in the EEA from Intel or AMD'.[64] In first instance, the General Court found that 'in order to justify the Commission's jurisdiction under public international law, it was sufficient to establish either the qualified effects of the practice in the European Union or that it was implemented in the European Union'.[65] The General Court found that Intel's conduct was capable of meeting both tests. On appeal, Intel argued that the General Court 'misapplied' the implementation test, in relation to the so-called 'Lenovo Agreements', 'since the conduct at issue was not implemented in the EEA and Intel did not sell products to Lenovo in the EEA'.[66] It further argued that the implementation test was the 'only test allowed by the case-law'.

In its judgment, the CJEU first reiterated its standpoint 'that the fact that an undertaking participating in an agreement is situated in a third country does not prevent the application of that provision if that agreement is operative on the territory of the internal market'.[67] It further confirmed its acceptance of the implementation test in the *Wood Pulp* case. According to the Court, the 'qualified effects test pursues the same objective, namely preventing conduct which, while not adopted within the EU, has anticompetitive effects liable to have an impact on the EU market'.[68] As such, '[t]he argument put forward by Intel … that the qualified effects test cannot serve as a basis for the Commission's jurisdiction is therefore incorrect'.

Providing further clarification, the Court noted that 'the qualified effects test allows the application of EU competition law to be justified under public international law when it is foreseeable that the conduct in question will have an immediate and substantial effect in the European Union'.[69] To assesses this, 'it is necessary to examine the conduct of the undertaking or undertakings in question, viewed as a whole', where the foreseeability requirement may be satisfied based on the 'probable effects of conduct on competition'.[70] Applied in this case, the Court found that 'Intel's conduct vis-à-vis Lenovo formed part

[62] ibid [6]–[12]. Two types of problematic conduct were identified, conditional rebates and 'naked restrictions', in the form of payments to four original equipment manufacturers 'so that they would delay, cancel or restrict the marketing of certain products equipped with AMD CPUs'.

[63] ibid [12].

[64] General Court Case T-286/09 *Intel v Commission* [2014] ECLI:EU:T:2014:547 [227].

[65] ibid 244.

[66] *Intel v Commission* (n 61) [31].

[67] ibid [43], referring to C-22/71 *Béguelin Import v GL Import Export* [1971] ECR 949 [11].

[68] ibid [44]–[45].

[69] ibid [49].

[70] ibid [50]–[51].

of an overall strategy intended to ensure that no Lenovo notebook equipped with an AMD CPU would be available on the market, including in the EEA'. This was correctly found by the General Court to be 'capable of producing an immediate effect in the EEA'.[71] The *Intel* case has been hailed in the literature as a 'major development', 'finally, embracing a qualified effect test the purposes of Articles 101 and 102 TFEU' in a 'clear and unambiguous' judgment.[72] In doing do, the CJEU also aligns the EU approach with that of the United States discussed above.

Notably, in the 2019 case *Google v Commission Nationale de l'Informatique et des Libertés (CNIL)*, the CJEU appeared to embrace the effects-doctrine in the field of data protection as well.[73] Building on its finding in *Google Spain*, the CJEU again interpreted the territorial scope of both Directive 95/46 and its successor, the GDPR.[74] There the question arose whether the relevant provisions in these agreements

> are to be interpreted as meaning that, where a search engine operator grants a request for de-referencing … that operator is required to carry out that de-referencing on all versions of its search engine, or whether, on the contrary, it is required to do so only on the versions of that search engine corresponding to all the Member States.[75]

In answer, the Court found that:

> In a globalised world, internet users' access – including those outside the Union – to the referencing of a link referring to information regarding a person whose centre of interests is situated in the Union is thus *likely* to have *immediate and substantial effects* on that *person within the Union itself.*
>
> Such considerations are such as to *justify the existence of a competence on the part of the EU legislature to lay down the obligation*, for a search engine operator, to carry out, when granting a request for de-referencing made by such a person, a de-referencing on *all* the versions of its search engine.[76]

Here the Court finds that it has, in principle, prescriptive jurisdiction to require de-refencing beyond EU territory based on 'immediate and substantial effects'. Its reliance on the effects-doctrine in the newer field of data protection appears to imply acceptance of effects as a general basis applicable across different areas of law.

At the same time, however, the court 'emphasized' the lack of broader consensus on the recognition and definition of a right to de-referencing. It also

[71] ibid [52].

[72] Prete (n 57) 492.

[73] Case C-507/17 *Google v CNIL* [2019] ECLI:EU:C:2019:772.

[74] Parliament and Council Regulation (EU) 2016/679 of 27 April 2016 on the protection of individuals with regard to the processing of personal data and on the free movement of such data and repealing Directive 95/46 [2016] OJ L119 ('General Data Protection Regulation').

[75] *Google v CNIL* (n 73) [43].

[76] ibid [57], [58] (emphasis added).

acknowledged that the personal right to data protection is not absolute, and that the EU legislature has struck its own balance between protection of this right and the freedom of information of internet users within the Union.[77] However, 'it has not, to date, struck such a balance as regards the scope of a de-referencing outside the Union'.[78] In particular, according to the Court, from the wording of the relevant provisions, it was not apparent that the legislature had '*chosen*' to confer such extraterritorial scope on the enshrined rights.[79] For this reason, operators are not required to ensure de-refencing is carried out on all search engines. The Court thus placed great emphasis on the intention of the EU legislator when interpreting the territorial scope of operators' obligations. This appears more an application of the presumption against extraterritoriality than a restrictive view of the Union's competence as such.[80] The consideration of other states' regulatory autonomy in *Google v CNIL* will be discussed further in chapter 9 on jurisdictional limitations.

Today, according to the Report of the IBA Taskforce, 'virtually all jurisdictions apply some form of the effects test', although the meaning and application vary considerably.[81] The growth in acceptance of the effects-doctrine illustrates the capacity of the law of jurisdiction to adapt to the changing realities of increased economic interdependence. It is quite plausible that this same interdependence may drive an extension of this doctrine beyond the field of economic regulation to that of environmental concerns. How the effects-doctrine may then be applied will be discussed further in chapter 8.

2.3. The Nationality Principle

Although the territoriality principle serves as the general rule, it remains 'subject to exceptions or refinements required by the character or, more particularly, the limits of the State's sovereignty'.[82] These refinements are intrinsically linked to the components of the sovereign state which, in addition to territory, include its

[77] ibid [59]–[60].

[78] ibid [61].

[79] ibid [62] (emphasis added).

[80] For support of this view, see C Ryngaert and M Taylor, 'Implementing the Right to Erasure: The Judgment of the EU Court of Justice in Google v CNIL' (Renforce Blog, 2019) blog.renforce.eu/index.php/en/2019/10/08/implementing-the-right-to-erasure-the-judgment-of-the-eu-court-of-justice-in-google-v-cnil-2/. See also J Globocnik, 'The Right to Be Forgotten Is Taking Shape: CJEU Judgments in GC and Others (C-136/17) and Google v CNIL (C-507/17)' (2020) 69 *GRUR International* 380.

[81] IBA Report on Extraterritorial Jurisdiction (n 4) 13. The US Fourth Restatement (n 3) §409, Reporters' Notes 1, lists a considerable number of examples, including: Código Penal, Art 1 (Argentina); Código Penal 33 Federal, Art 2, Diario Oficial de la Federación 14-08-1931, últimas reformas DOF 34 14-07-2014 (Mexico); Straffeloven (Act of 22 May 1902 No 10) § 12 35 (Norway); Criminal Code, 22 September 1994, Art 11 (Uzbekistan).

[82] Mann (n 17) 20.

own permanent population and form of government.[83] Intuitively, therefore, one of the most well-accepted 'exceptions' or rather, 'additional' grounds for jurisdiction is the nationality (or personality) principle, according to which a state may exercise jurisdiction in respect of its citizens.[84] This constitutes the basis for the 'active' nationality principle, as well as the somewhat more disputed 'passive' nationality principle, which will now be examined briefly.

The active nationality principle refers to the legal basis for a state to exercise jurisdiction in relation to activities of its own nationals, even when they are abroad.[85] This includes activities of both natural persons and corporations, and can also be applied to an individual who is no longer a national or who becomes a national after committing the activity in question.[86] Dating back to pre-Westphalian times, the active nationality principle is widely accepted because it is seen as an exercise of the sovereign authority of a state over its citizens.[87] A key rationale is the prevention of impunity, which can be particularly valuable should a state not wish to extradite its citizens to another state where the conduct took place.[88] Resources are also saved for the territorial state which would otherwise prosecute the offence. In addition, domestic enforcement of an extraterritorial rule may bridge an enforcement gap, should the territorial state not have the resources to enforce effectively.

The active nationality principle can be used to make punishable all acts which violate the law of the country in which the national is present (*lex loci delicti*); however, particularly in Europe, it is often conditional upon the requirement of dual criminality.[89] Some (typically common law) states such as the UK and Australia restrict their jurisdictional reach to certain crimes, in particular sexual offences committed by nationals abroad.[90] It has been argued, however,

[83] Montevideo Convention on the Rights and Duties of States (adopted 26 December 1933, entered into force 26 December 1934) 165 LNTS 19, Art 1; Oxman (n 13) [11].

[84] IBA Report on Extraterritorial Jurisdiction (n 4) 142.

[85] ILC Report on Extraterritorial Jurisdiction (n 13) 522; Harvard Draft Convention on Jurisdiction with Respect to Crime, 'Article 5. Jurisdiction Over Nationals' (1935) 29 *American Journal of International Law* Supplement: Research in International Law 519.

[86] Note also the principle of flag state jurisdiction with regard to ships, contained in Art 91 LOSC: 'Ships have the nationality of the State whose flag they are entitled to fly. There must exist a genuine link between the State and the ship'. With regard to aircraft jurisdiction, Art 17 of the Chicago Convention provides that: 'Aircraft have the nationality of the State in which they are registered.' Dual registration is prohibited (Art 18).

[87] Kamminga (n 4) [11]; ILC Report on Extraterritorial Jurisdiction (n 13) 522.

[88] See Ryngaert (n 3) 106, who notes that this can also protect a state's reputation.

[89] See IBA Report on Extraterritorial Jurisdiction (n 4) 145. With regards to the older practice, the Harvard Draft Convention on Jurisdiction with Respect to Crime (n 64) 524, also refers to the examples of the German Project of Penal Code (1927) Art 7; and the Dutch Penal Code (1881) Art 5, which cover actions committed by nationals which constitute crimes both at home and in the state where they are committed.

[90] See eg the Australian Criminal Legislation Amendment (Sexual Offences against Children) Act 201 (Cth), which criminalises child sex offences outside Australia. For the UK, see the Offences Against the Person Act 1861 c 100, ss 9 and 57(1) (UK); Perjury Act 1911 c 6, s 8 (UK). See also the US criminalisation of '[a]ny United States citizen or alien admitted for permanent residence who travels in foreign commerce or resides, either temporarily or permanently, in a foreign country, and engages in any illicit sexual conduct with another person' (18 US Code §2423(c)).

that such a restriction is not required by international law, with common law states not objecting to the broader approach taken by civil law countries.[91]

Examples of the active personality principle can also be found in the United Nations Convention against Corruption (UNCAC),[92] the 1999 International Convention for the Suppression of the Financing of Terrorism[93] and the 1984 Convention against Torture and Other Cruel, Inhuman or Degrading Treatment or Punishment.[94]

Based on the 'domicile' or 'residence' principle, states sometimes claim jurisdiction over actors who are domiciled in their territory and commit crimes abroad, even when they are not nationals.[95] Domicile can be used in foreign liability cases to prosecute legal persons (ie multinational corporations) domiciled in one state for human rights violations committed in another state.[96] In addition, states sometimes subject corporations to economic sanctions when they are 'controlled' by their nationals but engage in business abroad.[97] The active nationality principle has also been used in family law and tax law, with several bilateral tax treaties having used the principle to avoid double taxation.[98]

The passive nationality principle addresses the inverse situation, providing a basis for jurisdiction where a state's national is injured by conduct committed by an actor abroad.[99] This principle is more controversial than the active nationality principle, although it has gained acceptance over time, particularly in the field of criminal law.[100] Some states assert jurisdiction based on the passive nationality

[91] Ryngaert (n 3) 106.

[92] See United Nations Convention against Corruption (signed 31 October 2003, entered into force 14 December 2005) A/58/422, Art 42.

[93] See International Convention for the Suppression of the Financing of Terrorism (signed 9 December 1999, entered into force 10 April 2002) 2178 UNTS 197, Art 7 (1)(a).

[94] See Convention against Torture and Other Cruel, Inhuman or Degrading Treatment or Punishment of 1984 (adopted 10 December 1984, entered into force 26 June 1987) 1465 UNTS 112 ('CAT') Art 5 (1)(b).

[95] According to the IBA Report on Extraterritorial Jurisdiction (n 4) 145, the following countries engage in this practice: Denmark, Finland, Malaysia, Netherlands, Norway, Russia, Sweden and UAE.

[96] See eg the US Alien Tort Statute (ATS), which provides a mechanism to hold foreign investors *indirectly* liable for human rights violations committed by governments of the state in which they conduct business. The reach of the ATS was restricted by the 2013 case *Kiobel v Royal Dutch Petroleum Co*, 133 SCt 1659 (2013). For further analysis, see N Jägers, K Jesse, and J Verschuuren, 'The Future of Corporate Liability for Extraterritorial Human Rights Abuses: The Dutch Case Against Shell' (2014) *American Journal of International Law* unbound 36.

[97] Ryngaert (n 3) 108 notes, however, that the control theory is not generally in line with international law, in particular the *Barcelona Traction* case: ICJ, *Barcelona Traction, Light and Power Co Ltd (Belgium v Spain)* (Judgment Preliminary Objections) [1970] ICJ Rep 3 [41].

[98] On double taxation conventions of EU Member States, see further 'Double Taxation Conventions' (ec.europa.eu, 29 August 2017) https://ec.europa.eu/taxation_customs/individuals/personal-taxation/double-taxation-conventions_en.

[99] IBA Report on Extraterritorial Jurisdiction (n 4) 146; ILC Report on Extraterritorial Jurisdiction (n 13) 522–23.

[100] ILC Report on Extraterritorial Jurisdiction (n 13) 523. See eg the US Fourth Restatement (n 3) §402, Reporters' Notes 2, 'The United States once strenuously objected to passive-personality jurisdiction, but today exercises passive-personality jurisdiction in a number of statutes.'

principle for all crimes with a certain minimum punishment.[101] One example is the Netherlands, which applies its Criminal Code to all persons outside of the Netherlands who are guilty of a crime against a Dutch national punishable by at least eight years' imprisonment, where the act is also criminalised in the state where it was committed.[102] Other states are more hesitant in their application, only recognising the principle for certain grave crimes such as terrorism.[103] In a multilateral setting, the passive nationality principle can be found in several international conventions, including the Convention on Offences and Certain Other Acts Committed on Board Aircraft,[104] the International Convention against the Taking of Hostages[105] and the Convention against Torture.[106]

As noted in the separate opinion to the *Arrest Warrant* case, the principle 'today meets with relatively little opposition, as least so far as a particular category of offences is concerned'.[107] While it remains debated whether there is a permissive rule for the exercise of the passive nationality principle in the absence of an international convention, it has been argued that the 'lack of international protest may surely boost its legality'.[108] Nevertheless, such a norm remains difficult to discern as states do not often make such jurisdictional assertions, and when they do they are subject to restrictive conditions which help to avoid international conflict (eg dual criminality, serious crimes, the presence requirement and the executive consent requirement).[109] This perhaps reflects the critique that the principle lacks legitimacy, doing little to close any enforcement gap or support public order in the state in which the act is committed.[110] In the absence of a dual-criminality requirement, the passive personality principle also risks violating the rights of the accused, as foreigners acting abroad may be subjected to the rules of another state which they cannot be expected to know, merely by virtue of the individual they encounter.[111]

[101] See ILC Report on Extraterritorial Jurisdiction (n 13) 524, noting that China, Italy and Denmark recognise but limit jurisdiction to 'certain classes of crimes or to crimes with a certain minimum degree of punishment'. Greece, Finland, Norway, and Sweden require dual criminality for exercises of the passive nationality principle.

[102] Art 5(1) of the 1881 Netherlands Criminal Code (Wetboek van Strafrecht).

[103] Although see the US Fourth Restatement (n 3) §402, Reporters' Notes 8, noting that the US has used passive-personality to create a civil liability, eg in the Antiterrorism Act 18 U.C §2333, which provides US victims with treble damages.

[104] Convention on Offences and Certain Other Acts Committed on Board Aircraft (signed 14 September 1963, entered into force 4 December 1969) 704 UNTS 219, Art 4.

[105] International Convention against the Taking of Hostages (signed 17 December 1979, entered into force 3 June 1983) UNTS 1316 Art 5.

[106] CAT (n 94) Art 5(1)b.

[107] See further Kamminga (n 3) [12], referring to the Joint separate opinion of Judges Higgins, Koojimans and Buergenthal in the *Case Concerning the Arrest Warrant of 11 April 2000 (Democratic Republic of the Congo v Belgium)* ICJ Reports (2002) [47].

[108] Ryngaert (n 3) 112.

[109] ibid; IBA Report on Extraterritorial Jurisdiction (n 4) 149.

[110] Ryngaert (n 3) 110.

[111] FA Mann, 'The Doctrine of Jurisdiction in International Law' (1964) 111 *Recueil des Cours* 1, 39–41, 92–93; ILC Report on Extraterritorial Jurisdiction (n 13) 147.

2.4. The Protective Principle

The protective principle provides a basis for states to exercise jurisdiction over persons, property or acts outside of their territory that threaten vital national interests, in particular security.[112] Due to the narrower focus on matters concerning vital or fundamental national interests, some argue that the principle acts as a specific application of the effects-doctrine or the objective territoriality principle.[113] Unlike these bases, however, concrete harm need not yet have occurred in order for states to claim jurisdiction.[114] The protective principle classically serves as a basis to prosecute foreigners acting abroad for crimes such as counterfeiting, espionage and immigration violations.[115]

The broad scope and anticipatory nature of this principle is considered necessary to effectively respond to certain activities. A clear illustration can be found in the case *United States v Bowman*, where Chief Justice Taft noted that 'criminal statutes ... are, as a class, not logically dependent on their locality for the Government's jurisdiction, but are enacted because of the right of the Government to defend itself against obstruction, or fraud wherever perpetrated'.[116] Limiting the *locus* of certain crimes to 'strictly territorial jurisdiction' would greatly 'curtail the scope and usefulness of the statute'.[117] A similar rationale can also be found in *Liangsiriprasert*, concerning the offence of conspiracy to defraud. According to English law, such conspiracy can be committed where an agreement is formed outside England to commit an offence within its territory, even where no overt act has been taken in its jurisdiction.[118] The Privy Council reasoned that the 'nature of the common law crime of conspiracy ... is analogous to attempt, is preventative in character, and its utility lies in forestalling crime'.[119] According to Lord Griffiths:

> Their lordships can find nothing in precedent, comity or good sense that should inhibit the common law from regarding as justiciable in England inchoate crimes committed abroad which are intended to result in the commission of criminal offences in England.[120]

[112] IBA Report on Extraterritorial Jurisdiction (n 4) 14; ILC Report on Extraterritorial Jurisdiction (n 13) 522.
[113] ILC Report on Extraterritorial Jurisdiction (n 13) 522.
[114] US Fourth Restatement (n 4) §412, Reporters' Notes 1.
[115] IBA Report on Extraterritorial Jurisdiction (n 4) 14. With regard to immigration fraud, see eg *United States ex rel Majka v Palmer* 67 F (2d) 146 (1933); Min Pub c Glass (Trib Corr de Boulogne sur Mer, 25 February 1858) DP 1858.3.39. See also the Harvard Draft Convention on Jurisdiction with Respect to Crime, 'Article 7. Protection – Security of the State' (1935) 29 *American Journal of International Law Supplement: Research in International Law* 543, containing a requirement of double criminality.
[116] *United States v Bowman*, 260 US 94 (1922) [94].
[117] ibid [97].
[118] *Liangsiriprasert* (n 23) 16. The case concerned a violation of the common law crime of conspiracy and s 39 of the Dangerous Drugs Ordinance.
[119] ibid.
[120] ibid.

States may base their jurisdiction on the protection of national interests without explicitly referring to the protective principle.[121] In this regard, Crawford refers to *Naim Molovan v Attorney General of Palestine*, which concerned the UK's seizure of a stateless ship on the high seas, as it transported migrants to Palestine.[122] Another high seas example is the US claim of jurisdiction over foreigners engaging in the trade of illegal narcotics in the 1986 Maritime Law Drug Enforcement Act.[123] In *United States v Davis*, the US Court of Appeals dealt with the question of whether this measure applied to the acts of an individual sailing on a ship of British registry on the high seas.[124] The Court found that '[w]here an attempted transaction is aimed at causing criminal acts within the United States, there is a sufficient basis for the United States to exercise its jurisdiction'.[125]

In the interest of international comity, the threshold for what constitutes a national interest is relatively high, Article 7 of the Harvard Draft Convention referring to matters of 'security, territorial integrity or political independence' of the state.[126] For its part, the US Fourth Restatement refers to security, and a 'limited class of other fundamental state interests *such as* espionage, certain acts of terrorism, murder of government officials', counterfeiting currency, official document falsification, 'perjury before consular officials and conspiracy to violate immigration or customs laws'.[127] There is, however, no limited list or set of criteria to determine what constitutes a 'vital national interest'.[128] Thus it has been noted that, although the principle itself is relatively uncontested, it is a 'rather uncertain' jurisdictional basis because the 'conditions under which it may be relied upon are ill-defined'.[129] Nevertheless, these ill-defined boundaries allow for the protective principle to adapt to present-day concerns relating to national security including in the field of environment.

An interesting, albeit 'treaty-based', example is the inclusion of the protective principle in Article 42(2)d UNCAC. According to this provision, a state

[121] A more extensive historical overview of national penal codes' incriminating acts which threaten state security can be found in the Harvard Draft Convention on Jurisdiction with Respect to Crime (n 115) 546 et seq. See also the IBA Report on Extraterritorial Jurisdiction (n 4) 149–50.

[122] J Crawford, *Brownlie's Principles of Public International Law,* 8th edn (Oxford, Oxford University Press, 2012) 462, referring to *Naim Molvan v Attorney General for Palestine* 81 *Lloyd's List Law Reports* 277.

[123] Maritime Drug Law Enforcement Act, 46 USC app Secs 1903(a), 1903(j) (Supp IV 1986).

[124] *United States v Davis*, 905 F.2d 245 (1990).

[125] ibid [20]. This finding was not based on international law, in particular the limited exemptions to exclusive flag state jurisdiction under Part VII of the LOSC (n 2). Rather, the reasoning focused on the US's own canon of the 'presumption against extraterritoriality', which relied on Congressional intent ([17]–[19]).

[126] Harvard Draft Convention on Jurisdiction with Respect to (n 115) 543. In analysing US practice, the Draft considers 'offences which interfere with the functioning of its public agencies and instrumentalities, irrespective of the place of the offence or the nationality of the offender'.

[127] US Fourth Restatement (n 3) §412 (emphasis added).

[128] Crawford (n 122) 462.

[129] Kamminga (n 4) [13].

may establish jurisdiction over corruption offences contained in the UNCAC, when they are 'committed against the State party'. The rationale for this appears in the foreword, where the then UN Secretary-General Kofi Annan noted the harm caused by corruption, which 'undermines democracy and the rule of law, leads to violations of human rights, distorts markets, erodes the quality of life and allows organized crime, terrorism and other threats to human security to flourish'. Implicitly then, these offences against economic security are sufficient threats to vital state interests on which to base the protective principle, at least in the treaty sense. There are many conceptual overlaps between the damage caused by corruption and that caused by environmental harm including climate change, and it is not unthinkable that such harm could also merit protective jurisdiction. This will be examined further in chapter 8.

2.5. Universality

The universality principle provides a basis for states to exercise jurisdiction with respect to certain grave crimes under international law, irrespective of the location of the crime or the nationality of the perpetrator or victim.[130] The principle can be defined negatively as a basis for jurisdiction not requiring any link or nexus with the legislating state.[131] In such cases, jurisdiction is exercised in the interest of the international community, rather than the narrower interest of the state.[132] Crimes recognised as giving rise to universal jurisdiction include piracy, crimes against humanity, genocide, torture, slavery and war crimes.[133] Examples of state practice include the 2003 Dutch International Crimes Act (Article 2(1)a), the 1988 UK Criminal Justice Act (section 134), and the older 1930 Italian Penal Code (Article 10).[134]

[130] ILC Report on Extraterritorial Jurisdiction (n 13) 522; Kamminga (n 4) [14]; L Reydams, 'The Rise and Fall of Universal Jurisdiction', (KU Leuven Working Paper no 36, 2010) 7; 'Princeton Principles on Universal Jurisdiction' (Princeton University, 2001) Principle 1 lapa.princeton.edu/hosteddocs/unive_jur.pdf.

[131] R O'Keefe, 'Universal Jurisdiction Clarifying the Basic Concept' (2004) 2 *Journal of International Criminal Justice* 735, 745. O'Keefe writes: '[i]t would seem sufficiently well agreed that universal jurisdiction amounts to the assertion of jurisdiction to prescribe in the absence of any other accepted jurisdictional nexus at the time of the relevant conduct'. See also US Fourth Restatement §413, defining universal jurisdiction as valid 'even where no specific connection exists between the state and the persons or conduct being regulated'.

[132] O'Keefe (n 131) 745.

[133] Kamminga (n 4) [14]; Reydams (n 130) 8. See also the Separate Opinion of Judges Higgins, Kooijmans and Buergenthal in the *Arrest Warrant* case (n 107) [61]–[65]. Under the LOSC, jurisdiction in relation to piracy is quite far-reaching (see in particular Art 105 LOSC). For a critical analysis of the analogous force of this jurisdiction, note, however E Kontorovich, 'The Piracy Analogy: Modern Universal Jurisdiction's Hollow Foundation' (2004) 45 *Harvard International Law Journal* 183.

[134] For a further overview of older practice, see Harvard Draft Convention on Jurisdiction with Respect to Crime, 'Article 10. Universality – Other Crimes' (1935) 29 *American Journal of International Law* Supplement: Research in International Law 573, 575. Some acts cover crimes

In addition to crimes which have been recognised under customary international law as giving rise to universal jurisdiction, there is also a growing number of treaties providing a form of 'universal' jurisdiction for certain crimes through the *aut dedere aut judicare* ('extradite or prosecute') principle. According to this principle, where the perpetrator of such a crime is present in the territory of a state which chooses not to extradite, then that state must establish jurisdiction.[135] This principle serves to avoid impunity by providing for the 'residual jurisdiction' of the custodial state.[136] Well-known examples of treaties containing such provisions include the Convention on the Prevention and Punishment of the Crime of Genocide and the 1949 Geneva Conventions.[137] More recent examples can be found in the Convention against Transnational Organized Crime.[138] It is generally accepted that such provisions in fact give rise to 'quasi' or conditional universal jurisdiction rather than 'pure' universal jurisdiction.[139] This is because, in contrast to universal jurisdiction 'proper', jurisdiction is only granted for specific crimes to treaty parties who 'pool their sovereignty', reciprocally granting each other authority to exercise jurisdiction over crimes committed in their territory or by their nationals.[140]

In their Separate Opinions to the *Arrest Warrant* case, several judges also drew a distinction between universal jurisdiction exercised when the accused is in the territory of the prescribing state (also described as the 'co-operative universality principle'),[141] and jurisdiction in absentia.[142] The latter is exercised

committed by aliens abroad during World War II, but only provide jurisdiction when the accused has later acquired that state's nationality or residency, see eg the 1991 United Kingdom War Crimes Act (s 1), and the 1945 Australian War Crimes Act (as amended) s3, which reads: 'This Act extends to all external Territories and has extra-territorial operation according to its tenor.'

[135] See ICJ, *Questions Concerning the Obligation to Prosecute or Extradite (Belgium v Senegal)* [2012] ICJ Rep 422; O'Keefe (n 131) 752.

[136] ILC Draft Code of Crimes against the Peace and Security of Mankind with commentaries (adopted by the ILC at its 48th Session, 1996), Yearbook of the International Law Commission, 1996, vol II, part two ('ILC Draft Code of Crimes against the Peace and Security of Mankind') 29.

[137] Convention on the Prevention and Punishment of the Crime of Genocide (adopted 9 December 1948, entered into force 12 August 1949) 78 UNTS 277, Art IV; Convention (I) for the Amelioration of the Condition of the Wounded and Sick in Armed Forces in the Field (adopted 12 August 1949, entered into force 21 October 1950) 75 UNTS 31, Art 49; Convention (II) for the Amelioration of the Condition of Wounded, Sick and Shipwrecked Members of Armed Forces at Sea (adopted 12 August 1949, entered into force 21 October 2950) 75 UNTS 85, Art 50; Convention (III) relative to the Treatment of Prisoners of War, Geneva (adopted 12 August 1949, entered into force 21 October 1950) 75 UNTS 135, Art 129; and Convention (IV) relative to the Protection of Civilian Persons in Time of War (adopted 12 August 1949, entered into force 21 October 1951) 75 UNTS 287, Art 146.

[138] United Nations Convention against Transnational Organized Crime (adopted 8 January 2001) UNGA Res 55/25 ('Convention Against Transnational Organized Crime'), see eg Art 3.

[139] M Shaw, *International Law,* 7th edn (Cambridge, Cambridge University Press, 2014) 489; *Arrest Warrant* case (n 107), Separate Opinion of Judges Higgins, Kooijmans and Buergenthal, 74–75.

[140] Ryngaert (n 3) 124.

[141] L Reydams, *Universal Jurisdiction – International and Municipal Legal Perspectives* (Cambridge, Cambridge University Press, 2003) 38.

[142] *Arrest Warrant* case (n 107), Separate Opinion of Judge Guillaume [9], and Dissenting Opinion of Judge Van den Wyngaert, [54]–[55] and [58].

in relation to a foreigner who was not present in the state exercising jurisdiction either at the time of the crime or at the time the state sought to prosecute or 'exercise' its jurisdiction in relation to that crime.[143] The legality of such jurisdiction remains a topic of discussion, and was deliberately left undecided in the *Arrest Warrant* case.[144] It has been argued that while there is no definitive legal evidence in favour of such jurisdiction, there is also no definitive prohibition, with the four Geneva Conventions seeming to hint that it is not ruled out.[145]

On a cautionary note, O'Keefe persuasively argues that the discussion on jurisdiction in absentia risks conflating the concepts of prescriptive and enforcement jurisdiction.[146] This is because when a state takes action to exercise its jurisdiction in relation to a crime (eg issuing an arrest warrant), it is in fact taking enforcement action. The legality of such enforcement action is a separate question to the legality of prescriptive jurisdiction, and can be either in absentia or in personam.[147] Universal prescriptive jurisdiction provides a legal basis to create a rule in the absence of a territorial nexus with the legislating state at the time when the crime is *committed*.[148] The legality of such a rule is not qualified by subsequent enforcement, even though enforcement in absentia may indeed not be very practical or desirable.

Universal jurisdiction also has some recognition in a civil law context, although this is more controversial.[149] For example, courts may rely on acts of universal civil jurisdiction to award compensation to victims of serious international human rights violations. In this vein, the US Alien Tort Statute grans universal tort jurisdiction to district courts over 'any civil action by an alien for a tort only, committed in violation of the law of nations'.[150] In the 2013 *Kiobel* case, however, the US Supreme Court restricted the scope of this statute, requiring that 'claims touch and concern the territory of the United States ... with sufficient force' in order to displace the presumption against extraterritorial application.[151] With regards to EU practice, Regulation 1215/2012 does not seem

[143] For example, through issuing an arrest warrant for a suspect who is not present in that state's territory.

[144] See further the Commentary to the 'Princeton Principles on Universal Jurisdiction' (n 130), where the matter was deliberately left open 'to avoid stifling the evolution of universal jurisdiction' [43].

[145] A Zimmerman, 'Violations of Fundamental Norms of International Law and the Exercise of Universal Jurisdiction in Criminal Matters' in J M Thouvenin and C Tomuschat (eds), *The Fundamental Rules of the International Legal Order – Jus Cogens and Erga Omnes Violations* (Leiden, Brill, 2006) 335, 352.

[146] O'Keefe (n 131) 750.

[147] ibid.

[148] ibid 755. A similar reasoning is also applicable to the distinction sometimes drawn between 'true' or 'pure' universal jurisdiction and 'territorial jurisdiction over persons, albeit in relation to acts committed elsewhere'. See Separate Opinion of Judges Higgins, Kooijmans and Buerg in the *Arrest Warrant* case (n 107) [41].

[149] See US Fourth Restatement §413, comment d, noting that 'in general customary international law does not make a clear distinction between civil and criminal jurisdiction'.

[150] Alien Tort Statute 28 USC §1350.

[151] *Kiobel* case (n 96).

to favour universal tort jurisdiction, though some Member States do provide a *forum necessitatis* provision establishing jurisdiction where no alternative forum is available.[152]

In the field of environmental protection, one treaty-based example bearing a considerable resemblance to an application of universality is Article 218(1) LOSC, which provides that:

> When a vessel is voluntarily within a port or at an off-shore terminal of a State, that State may undertake investigations and … institute proceedings in respect of any discharge from that vessel outside the internal waters, territorial sea or exclusive economic zone of that State in violation of applicable international rules and standards established through the competent international organization or general diplomatic conference.

A further example is Article 65 together with Article 120 LOSC, the former of which relates to states' more limited competence in the exclusive economic zone (EEZ). According to Article 65 LOSC, 'nothing in this Part [on the EEZ] restricts the right of a coastal State …, as appropriate, to prohibit, limit or regulate the exploitation of marine mammals more strictly than provided for in this Part'. The scope of this provision is extended by Article 120 LOSC to the 'conservation and management of marine mammals *in the high seas*' (emphasis added).[153] Notably, this example is directed at coastal states only, which makes sense given that it also contains enforcement competences. However, it assumes that states can prescribe unilateral environmental protection standards for marine mammals in the high seas beyond their territorial jurisdiction.

Universal jurisdiction arguably provides the clearest example of where matters of common concern to the international community (ie the punishment or compensation for damages of grave crimes) create jurisdictional rights and, arguably, obligations for states. In the famous words of the Israeli Supreme Court in the *Eichmann* case, 'it is the universal character of the crimes in question which vests in every State the authority to try and punish those who participated in their commission'.[154] As noted in the 1996 commentary to the ILC Draft Code, 'the world remains plagued by the all too frequent occurrence of the most serious crimes that are of *concern to the international community*

[152] Ryngaert (n 3) 139, discussing Parliament and Council (EU) Regulation 1215/2012 of 12 December 2012 on jurisdiction and the recognition and enforcement of judgments in civil and commercial matters [2012] OJ L351/1.

[153] For further analysis, see L Paul, 'Using the Protective Principle to Unilaterally Enforce Transnational Marine Pollution Standards' (Proceedings of the Second International Conference on Marine Debris, 1989) NOM Tech Hemo NHFS, NOM-Tn-NMFS-SUFSC-154.

[154] See *Attorney-General of the Government of Israel v Adolf Eichmann* 36 ILR 298 (Isrl SCt, 29 May 1962). See also *Prosecutor v Anto Furundzija* (Judgment) IT-95-17/1-T (10 December 1998) [156], where the International Criminal Tribunal for the former Yugoslavia (ICTY) held that the 'inherently universal character of the crime' of torture constituted the 'foundation' of universal jurisdiction.

as a whole'.[155] This wording echoes the formulation of the common concern concept discussed in chapter 2, as well as its intrinsic logic. Certain matters are, by their nature, of common concern to the international community, and have been recognised as giving rise to rights and obligations for all states. In the case of certain crimes, these rights and obligations are directly translated into the law of jurisdiction through the universality principle. The extent to which this may be applied to environmental issues of common concern, such as climate change, is a topic of focus in chapter 9.

3. THE 'SUBSTANTIAL CONNECTION' REQUIREMENT

From the discussion above it is clear that the classical jurisdictional principles, while well recognised in legal theory, are far from clear-cut or consistently applied in practice. As already reflected by Mann half a century ago, '[i]t should, indeed, be obvious that the principle of territorial jurisdiction has to be reconsidered for practical rather than doctrinal reasons' as the 'complications of modern life are responsible for the steadily increasing reluctance to "localize" facts, events or relationships'.[156] As such, the traditional bases do not form a 'coherent and straightforward model' to authoritatively determine the legality of an exercise of prescriptive jurisdiction.[157] Rather, it is now generally accepted that what is required for a valid assertion of prescriptive jurisdiction is a 'sufficient nexus' or 'significant connection' between the legislating state and the regulated subject matter at issue.[158] As mentioned above, the classical principles can provide, either together or individually, evidence of such a link.[159] It is useful to stress once again that the link in question need not be coextensive with a measure's (public policy) objective.

[155] ILC Draft Code of Crimes against the Peace and Security of Mankind (n 136), Commentary to Art 8, 28 (emphasis added).

[156] Mann (n 111) 36–37.

[157] Kamminga (n 4) [16].

[158] See eg Crawford (n 2122) 447; Mann (n 17) 28; Kamminga (n 4) [9]. A Bianchi, 'Reply to Professor Maier' in KM Meessen (ed), *Extraterritorial Jurisdiction in Theory and Practice* (The Hague, Kluwer Law International, 1996) 64, 83–84. This approach has also been explicitly accepted by some states, including Australia, the UK and Canada; see Brief of the Government of the Commonwealth of Australia as Amicus Curiae in Support of the Defendants-Appellees in *Morrison* (n 46) 24; Brief of the United Kingdom of Great Britain and Northern Ireland, Ireland and the Kingdom of the Netherlands as Amici Curiae in Support of Petitioners, *Empagran* (n 46) 18; and *Tolofson v Jensen* [1994] SCR 1022, 1049 (Can).

[159] See also DJB Svantesson, 'A New Jurisprudential Framework for Jurisdiction: Beyond the Harvard Draft' (2015) 109 *American Journal of International Law* Unbound 69, 70–71, who goes so far as to argue that these bases are 'merely proxy principles for, and simplified expressions of underlying core principles', which constructed through compromises, reflect a 'convenient summary of what courts did and what legislators thought'. The 'essence of the jurisdictional principles' is that there be a 'substantial connection' and that a state must have a legitimate interest in legislating.

While certainly more flexible than the classical bases, the 'significant connection' requirement also remains diffuse, to a certain extent merely reshuffling the underlying legal uncertainties. A particular issue is whether the genuine connection requirement should be framed to incorporate other states' interests. Crawford, for example, describes the requirement as 'a cardinal principle' of a 'genuine connection between the subject-matter of jurisdiction and the territorial base and reasonable interest of the state in question'.[160] *Oppenheim's International Law* focuses rather on the hierarchy of jurisdictional claims, framing the requirement as a 'sufficiently close connection to justify that state in regulating the matter and perhaps also to override any competing rights of other states'.[161] In proving this, the use of the traditional jurisdictional bases could be seen as more of a 'matter of convenience than of substance'.[162] As mentioned above, this book takes a different approach, preferring to define the 'substantial connection' based purely on the connection between the acting state and the circumstances regulated. Considerations of 'reasonableness' and a hierarchy of competing claims deserve independent attention in a subsequent enquiry.

Another issue is how to discern the threshold of a 'substantial connection'. In his seminal 1964 contribution, *The Doctrine of Jurisdiction in International Law*, Mann formulated the following definition:

> [A] State has [legislative] jurisdiction, if its contact with a given set of facts is so close … that legislation in respect of them is in harmony with international law and its various aspects (including the practice of States, the principles of non-interference and reciprocity and the demands of inter-dependence). A merely *political, economic, commercial or social interest does not in itself constitute a sufficient connection.*[163]

Later, in 1996, Andrea Bianchi proposed an alternative approach, suggesting that rather than using 'factual links or similar criteria', one should seek an 'effective and significant connection between the regulating state and the activity or fact to be regulated'.[164] This would be evidenced by state practice in a given area. Essentially, the measure of a sufficient connection then comes down to the perception of the majority of states, rather than principles of the classical doctrine of jurisdiction.

While disagreeing with Bianchi's interpretation of Mann's 'factual connection' requirement, Bartels takes a similar methodological approach, arguing that there is 'nothing wrong, in principle, with attempting to derive legal principles

[160] Crawford (n 122) 456–57 (emphasis added). See also Mann (n 17) 29.

[161] R Jennings and A Watts, *Oppenheim's International Law*, 9th edn (Oxford, Oxford University Press, 1992) 456–58. See also V Lowe and C Staker, 'Jurisdiction' in MD Evans (ed), *International Law*, 3rd edn (Oxford, Oxford University Press, 2010) 230, 313, who refer to a 'clear connecting factor, of a kind whose use is approved by international law, between the legislating state and the conduct that it seeks to regulate'.

[162] Jennings and Watts, (n 161) 458.

[163] Mann (n 17) 49 (emphasis added).

[164] Bianchi (n 158) 90.

from mere "factual" interests', and that Mann's emphasis on the legal nature of the connection is 'somewhat unfair'.[165] Where state practice and *opinio juris* demonstrate that certain interests merit the exercise of jurisdiction, this may support the development of a customary rule.[166] This indeed seems a more logical approach, as the categoric rejection of economic and social interests leaves little room for the development of customary law.

The Harvard Draft Convention raises an important evidentiary caution with regard to the development of customary legal support for a substantial connection.[167] The fact that states exercise jurisdiction in certain cases does not necessarily mean that these are the *only* cases where assertions are considered to be legitimate.[168] As such, it is not always possible to infer from individual jurisdictional assertions the theory upon which they are based. To remedy this, one could also use a negative approach, whereby 'the lawfulness of a jurisdictional assertion is … a measure of the amount of foreign protest levelled at it'.[169] However, as noted by Ryngaert, this too has weaknesses from a doctrinal perspective because the argumentative strength of a jurisdictional assertion is a function of relative power.[170]

To complicate matters further, in the emerging area of climate change jurisdiction, state practice has yet to crystallise, with provocative unilateral action such as that of the EU breaking new ground. Furthermore, climate change, as a new type of regulatory challenge, does not align with the often more delineated factual matrixes upon which the traditional (largely criminal) doctrines are premised. This will be explored further in the following chapter.

4. CONCLUSION

Classic jurisdictional principles demonstrate various interests recognised as providing a basis for a state to regulate a certain subject matter. Indeed, state practice appears to demonstrate that customary international law has 'become less territorial'.[171] This is particularly evident in relation to the objective territoriality and effects bases, which have gained wider acceptance in the fields of criminal and competition law, even being applied to the right to privacy

[165] L Bartels, 'Article XX of GATT and the Problem of Extraterritorial Jurisdiction – The Case of Trade Measures for the Protection of Human Rights' (2002) 36 *Journal of World Trade* 353, 372. Bartels notes that Mann was not focused on a 'factual' connection as construed by Bianchi, but rather a *legal* connection based on international law.

[166] ibid.

[167] Harvard Draft Convention on Jurisdiction with Respect to Crime (n 115) 546.

[168] ibid.

[169] Ryngaert (n 3) 42. See also M Akehurst, 'Jurisdiction in International Law' (1973) 46 *British Yearbook of International Law* 145, 176.

[170] Ryngaert (n 3) 42.

[171] US Fourth Restatement (n 3) §404 Reporters' Note 1.

by the CJEU. This trend is perhaps unsurprising in light of the increasing independencies of globalisation. Promisingly, the evolving interpretations of the various principles and the overarching 'substantial connection' test illustrate the ability of customary rules to adapt to the needs of further integration. This offers possibilities for other emerging issues such as the mitigation of harm caused by climate change, which will be considered further in chapter 9.

8

Exploring the Basis of 'Climate Change Jurisdiction' under Customary International Law

1. INTRODUCTION

IF STATES MAY assert jurisdiction over the firing of a gun because the bullet lands in their territory, may they also regulate foreign carbon emissions that contribute to their sinking coastlines? As we have seen in previous chapters, the origins of the classical jurisdictional principles in criminal and economic law have determined the legal mechanisms used to delineate regulatory competences. It is clear, however, that these are not immediately fit for purpose in the context of climate change. Given the growing frictions caused by states' competing regulatory claims, clarity is needed as to the jurisdictional rules applicable in this field. This chapter will now turn to the challenging question of how the classical jurisdictional principles could be applied to unilateral climate protective measures.

The first section of this chapter considers the general, non-hierarchical relationship between the classic principles in the context of climate change. The following sections then delve into an exploration of the principles' possible operationalisation in relation to climate-protective measures with an extraterritorial element. A key issue here is how to deal with the non-linear, cumulative causation that characterises climate change as a complex system. It is suggested that precaution should have a role to play, as this norm concerns the relationship between states' regulatory action and the prevention of grave environmental harm in the face of scientific uncertainty. While precaution is by no means a mirror of prescriptive jurisdiction, this chapter seeks to demonstrate that the international consensus and debates on the foreseeability and causation requirements in the context of precaution are both relevant and helpful in a jurisdictional context.

Tying together these explorative strands, the final section constructs the overarching 'substantial connection' requirement as it might typically apply to climate-protective trade measures. As will be seen, there is no one-size-fits-all solution here. Nevertheless, reasoning by analogy from its criminal and economic roots, it seems plausible that customary law envisages quite a broad basis for 'climate change jurisdiction'.

2. RELATIONSHIPS BETWEEN THE CLASSICAL PRINCIPLES IN THE CONTEXT OF CLIMATE CHANGE

At the outset, it is important to stress once again that there is no hierarchy between the classical principles of jurisdiction. Rather, the extent to which a jurisdictional assertion may rely on a particular basis will depend on the circumstances of the case. In some instances, one basis may itself be enough to substantiate a link between the state and the regulated subject matter. Most of the time, however, claims will be based on a combination of different 'connecting factors' drawn from the traditional principles.

As a starting point, Figure 8.1 illustrates the generalised relationships between the classic bases as they apply to climate-protection measures with an extraterritorial element. Logically, the effects-doctrine overlaps with the principle of territoriality as one cannot draw a bright-line distinction between the completion of an act and its effects. For example, measures regulating the carbon footprint of goods produced abroad may target emissions from manufacturing and transportation, which have territorial effects. Through importation, the goods are ultimately brought into the territory of the regulating state, consumption and eventual disposal forming a territorial facet of their carbon footprint.

Figure 8.1 Connecting factors evidencing the 'substantial connection' requirement for unilateral measures regulating the foreign carbon footprint under customary international law

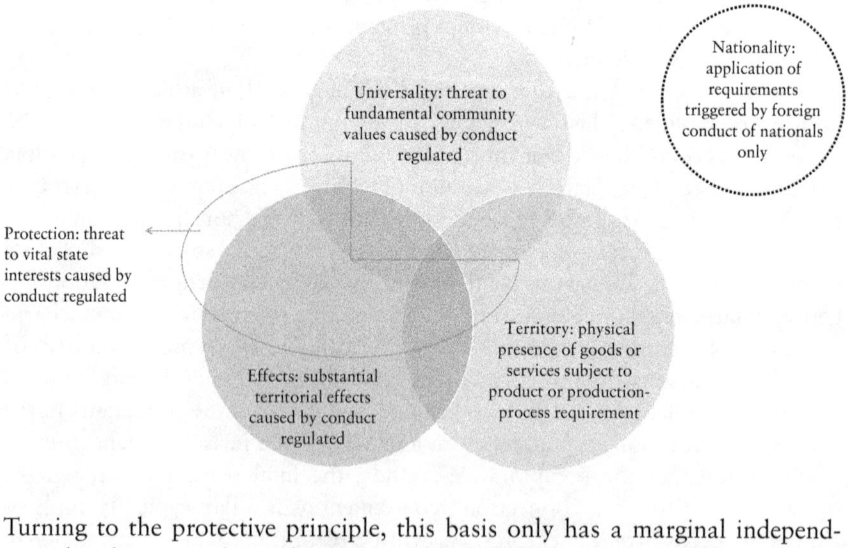

Turning to the protective principle, this basis only has a marginal independent value due to its close relationship with the effects-doctrine. Protection does not require actual effects to have occurred yet; however, it applies to a more

limited category of 'vital national interests'.[1] Universality underpins all three of the aforementioned principles, as global environmental harm is a matter of vital interest to the international community. Contrastingly, the nationality principle will not be analysed further here, as none of the measures in question are dependent for their application upon the foreign conduct of EU nationals *only*.[2] This is perhaps unsurprising, as the prescription of such measures would almost certainly raise tensions with non-discrimination requirements in the more specific regimes discussed in Part II.[3]

In order to better understand these relationships, the following sections will now examine each principle in turn. The primary aim is to consider how, and to what extent, the classic principles may support jurisdictional assertions with an extraterritorial element that aim to protect the global climate.

3. THE TERRITORIAL PRESENCE OF GOODS AND SERVICES CREATING THE CARBON FOOTPRINT

The application of entry-conditions to goods and services is triggered by virtue of the physical presence of that good or service within, or at the border of, the territory of the regulating state. As we have seen, however, where the way in which a measure applies is de facto dependent on conduct or circumstances prior to the entry of those goods or services, physical presence alone is not enough to justify the extraterritorial element. Essentially then, unlike enforcement measures, prescriptive measures that seek to regulate foreign production processes cannot rely solely on subsequent territorial presence. This has been discussed extensively in chapter 3, where it was argued that the extraterritorial impacts of measures designed to influence foreign conduct require further jurisdictional justification, as they may substantially interference with the independence of other equal sovereign states and their citizens.

The territoriality principle notably has greater weight when the consumption of goods or services has direct territorial externalities, ie immediate effects resulting from domestic conduct. One can think, for example, of fuel consumption, which causes immediate atmospheric pollution as well as long-term effects on the global climate. In such cases, the effects-doctrine also has an important role to play, as the domestic consumption externalities are a result of both

[1] This is discussed further in section 5 of this chapter.

[2] See further chapter 3 on the discussion of what constitutes a relevant 'extraterritorial element'. What matters is not only the conduct or circumstances that are formally addressed in the measure, but also any prior conduct upon which the actual application of a measure is de facto dependent.

[3] In particular the 'national treatment' and 'most-favoured-nation' requirements in WTO law, discussed further in chapter 4, as well as well as the non-discrimination requirements under the law of the law of the sea and international civil aviation law discussed in chapters 5 and 6, respectively.

foreign production processes and the related product characteristics (eg fuel composition).

In terms of policy strategy, regulators often seek to kill two birds with one stone by regulating matters that are detrimental to both the short-term health of persons and the environment, as well as to long-term climate stability. For example, the EU Fuel Quality Directive 98/70/EC clearly embraces both objectives, the preamble noting that

> primary air pollutants … which contribute to the formation of secondary pollutants such as ozone are emitted in significant amounts through the exhaust and evaporative fumes of motor vehicles thereby posing *directly and indirectly* a *considerable risk* to *human health and the environment*.[4]

From a jurisdictional perspective, immediate environmental and health impacts provide a great evidentiary advantage, as states may sidestep the obstacle of proving a link between environmental harm and the conduct in question. As will be seen, this is one of the greatest obstacles to the crystallisation of 'climate change jurisdiction'.

4. THE EFFECTS-DOCTRINE AND ENVIRONMENTAL HARM

The effects-doctrine appears to offer one of the most plausible avenues for demonstrating a substantial connection to extraterritorial conduct contributing to climate change. The rationale is simple: a state, as sovereign over its territory, may exercise jurisdiction over conduct or circumstances abroad resulting in substantial effects at home. While the doctrine has strong roots in the field of economic regulation, it has also been applied in other fields such as tort and criminal law, and more recently, the protection of privacy as a fundamental right.[5]

An interesting example of the doctrine's application in an environmental context is the US case *PMSA v Goldstene*, where the Pacific Merchant Shipping Association (PMSA) challenged the constitutionality of a Californian regulation on clean fuel requirements, applicable beyond its territorial waters.[6] The Court of Appeal found that California had jurisdiction to 'regulate and control extraterritorial conduct substantially affecting its territory'.[7] Such an assertion

[4] Parliament and Council Directive 98/70/EC relating to the quality of petrol and diesel fuels and amending Council Directive 93/12/EEC [1998] OJ L350/58 ('Fuel Quality Directive') rec 3 (emphasis added).

[5] For state practice in the field of economic law, see *Restatement (Fourth) of the Foreign Relations Law of the United States* (St Paul, MN, American Law Institute Publishers, 2018) ('US Fourth Restatement') §409 Reporters' Notes 2–3; International Bar Association, 'Report of the Task Force on Extraterritorial Jurisdiction' (2009) ('IBA Report on Extraterritorial Jurisdiction') 12.

[6] *PMSA v Goldstene*, 639 F.3d 1154, 1172–73 (9th Cir 2011). For further analysis, see S Kopela, 'Port-State Jurisdiction, Extraterritoriality, and the Protection of Global Commons' (2016) 47 *Ocean Development and International Law* 89, 122.

[7] *PMSA v Goldstene* (n 6) 1170.

was reasonable given the 'specific environmental impacts' of the activities, the 'harmful effects' of which could be 'significantly reduced' by the regulation in question.[8] Notably, this case concerned more direct, specific environmental harm caused by conduct on the high seas 'immediately adjacent' to the state's territorial waters. The application of the effects-doctrine to more indirect environmental effects, particularly in the context of climate change, presents some unique complexities, and it remains to be seen just how the doctrine may crystallise in this emerging field.[9]

Drawing on the core elements of the effects-doctrine discussed in chapter 7, this section will first consider the requirement of 'substantial effects', followed by the testy issues of foreseeability and causation. It is argued that precaution should have a role to play here, as this norm governs issues of state competence to take anticipatory action in the face of scientific uncertainty. As will be demonstrated below, the international support for precaution is also relevant in the context of state jurisdiction, and should shape the legality assessment in the context of climate change.[10]

4.1. Substantial Territorial Effects

To rely on the effects-doctrine, a first key requirement is that there are identifiable effects in the territory of the legislating state. While it has been argued that requiring a de minimis 'quantity' of effects conflicts with sovereign regulatory autonomy, state practice appears to support a minimum threshold of 'substantial' effects.[11] These effects may be economically measurable, as is the case in antitrust law, but may also be more abstract 'detrimental' effects, as is the case in criminal law.

Climate change has a plethora of interlinked detrimental effects, the large-scale physical phenomena resulting in economic losses, and threatening human rights.[12] A wealth of scientific studies have investigated the past and potential

[8] ibid 1175–76.

[9] See further eg H Ringbom, 'Global Problem – Regional Solution? International Law Reflections on an EU CO_2 Emissions Trading Scheme for Ships' (2011) 26 *International Journal of Maritime & Coastal Law* 613630; Kopela, 'Port-State Jurisdiction' (2016) 107; B Cooreman, 'Addressing Environmental Concerns through Trade? A Case for Extraterritoriality' (2015) 65 *ICLQ* 229, 236–38.

[10] This argument partly reproduces and builds upon the present author's contribution, NL Dobson, 'Exploring the Crystallization of "Climate Change Jurisdiction": A Role for Precaution?' (2018) 8 *Climate Law* 207, 207.

[11] On the former view, see A Hertogen, 'Letting Lotus Bloom' (2016) 26 *European Journal of International Law* 901, 921. For an analysis of the 'direct' or 'immediate and substantial' effects threshold in antitrust law, see C Ryngaert, *Jurisdiction over Antitrust Violations in International Law* (Antwerp, Intersentia, 2008) 59.

[12] On human rights, see further M Wewerinke-Singh, *Climate Change and Human Rights under International Law* (Oxford, Hart Publishing, 2019). For an analysis of the economic and social costs of climate change, see N Irwin, 'How to Think About the Costs of Climate Change', *New York Times* (17 January 2019) www.nytimes.com/2019/01/17/upshot/how-to-think-about-the-costs-of-climate-change.html.

future environmental effects of climate change, an important example being the Fifth Assessment Report (AR 5) of the Intergovernmental Panel on Climate Change (IPCC) and the 2018 Special Report on Global Warming of 1.5 °C.[13] While there remains uncertainty as to the precise degree of environmental detriment, there is great international consensus that damage will occur.

Domestic courts are increasingly playing a catalytic role attaching a role for states to the substantial effects of climate change. A somewhat older example is the 2007 case *Massachusetts v EPA*, concerning the question of whether the Commonwealth of Massachusetts had standing to challenge a decision of the Environmental Protection Agency (EPA) not to regulate GHG emissions from motor vehicles.[14] In analysing this question, the US Supreme Court noted that 'the harms associated with climate change are serious and well recognized'.[15] A 'strong consensus among qualified experts' indicated, amongst other threats, 'a precipitate rise in sea levels, severe and irreversible changes to natural ecosystems'.[16] Importantly, the Court also held that the fact 'that these changes are widely shared does not minimize Massachusetts' interest in the outcome of this litigation'.[17] In the context of the effects-doctrine, this could mean that the global nature of the overall effects does not preclude jurisdictional assertions as long as a state can demonstrate effects on its own territory. This is a matter of 'specific causation', discussed further below.

Ten years later, in the 2017 New Zealand case *Thomson v Minister for Climate Change Issues*, it was similarly noted that '[g]lobal warming will have many severe impacts [… which …] will accelerate as the world gets warmer'.[18] There the petitioner had claimed that New Zealand's national reduction commitments were insufficient to meet its obligations under the UNFCCC.[19] New Zealand's

[13] RK Pachauri and LA Meyer (eds), 'Climate Change 2014: Synthesis Report. Contribution of Working Groups I, II and III to the Fifth Assessment Report of the Intergovernmental Panel on Climate Change to the Intergovernmental Panel on Climate Change (Geneva, 2014). See also V Masson-Delmotte et al (eds), 'Summary for Policymakers', in *Global Warming of 1.5°C. An IPCC Special Report on the impacts of global warming of 1.5°C above pre-industrial levels and related global greenhouse gas emission pathways, in the context of strengthening the global response to the threat of climate change, sustainable development, and efforts to eradicate poverty* (2018) (IPCC Summary for Policymakers).

[14] *Massachusetts v EPA*, 549 US 497 (2007) (*Massachusetts v EPA*) 503. For further analysis and context, see M Gerrard and B Wannier, 'United States of America' in R Lord et al (eds), *Climate Change Liability: Transnational Law and Practice* (Cambridge, Cambridge University Press, 2011) 574.

[15] For further analysis of the intersection between science and law, see HM Osofsky, 'The Intersection of Scale, Science, and Law in Massachusetts v EPA' in WCG Burns and HM Osofsky (eds), *Adjudicating Climate Change* (Cambridge, Cambridge University Press, 2009) 129.

[16] *Massachusetts v EPA* (n 14) 521.

[17] ibid.

[18] *Thomson v Minister for Climate Change Issues* (2017) NZHC 733 (2 November 2017) 8; United Nations Framework Convention on Climate Change (adopted 9 May 1992, entered into force 21 March 1994) 1771 UNTS 107 (UNFCCC).

[19] *Thomson v Minister for Climate Change Issues*, Statement of Claim, NZHC (filed 10 November 2015) [85], [90].

reduction effort would, if also adopted by other developed countries in combination with the appropriate targets for less-developed countries, be insufficient to prevent 'dangerous anthropogenic interference with the climate system'.[20] In that case, however, as the newly elected government had since announced plans to adjust its 2050 target, the cause of action was found to have been 'overtaken by subsequent events'.[21]

The gravity of environmental effects was also a key element in the *Urgenda* litigation, which concerned the obligations of the Dutch state to meet its duty of care to respond to the 'genuine threat of dangerous climate change'. Large parts of the Appeal Court judgment were devoted to an analysis of scientific evidence, taking 'as a starting point' the fact that if the earth 'warms by a temperature of substantially more than 2°C, this will cause more flooding due to rising sea levels, heat stress' and, among many other things, 'disruption in the food production and potable water supply'.[22] These facts were not disputed in cassation, and in 2019 accepted by the Supreme Court as a material basis for its findings on the Netherlands' duty of care.[23]

These are but some of the domestic cases starting to recognise and attach legal consequences to the harmful effects of climate change. Based on the overwhelming scientific evidence as well as its acceptance by states in both environmental treaties and domestic practice, it is safe to conclude that climate change causes 'substantial' effects on states' territories.

4.2. Foreseeable Harm caused by the Regulated Conduct or Circumstances

In addition to the existence of substantial effects, two requirements must be met, namely foreseeability and causation. Here, foreseeability is defined as pertaining to the *nature* of the harm, which must be foreseeably substantial. It also concerns and overlaps with the causation requirement, as the harm must be the foreseeable *consequence* of a particular situation. Climate change poses a dilemma here, as it is simply impossible to attribute specific effects directly to specific conduct. To start with, there is a complex combination of contributing factors, both from natural and anthropogenic sources, as well as an antecedent situation which renders the current environment more vulnerable.[24] This is compounded

[20] ibid, referring to the UNFCCC.

[21] *Thomson v Minister for Climate Change Issues* (n 18) 178–80.

[22] *Urgenda Foundation v Kingdom of the Netherlands*, The Hague Court of Appeal (9 October 2018) ECLI:NL:GHDHA:2018:2591, (*Urgenda* case (Appeal Judgment)) 44.

[23] See in particular *Urgenda Foundation v Kingdom of the Netherlands*, Supreme Court (20 December 2019) ECLI:NL:HR:2019:2006, (*Urgenda* case (Supreme Court)) [2] 'Assumptions and facts'.

[24] See further C Voigt, 'State Responsibility for Climate Change Damages' (2008) 77 *Nordic Journal of International Law* 1, 15; R Verheyen, *Climate Change Damage and International Law: Prevention, Duties and State Responsibility* (Leiden, Brill, 2005) 263.

by the fact that the actual greenhouse effect occurs through an accumulation of GHGs in the atmosphere, where global mixing roughly equalises concentrations around the world.[25] As such, there is a spatial redistribution of cause and effect. This contributes to the nature of climate change as a complex system, where 'the whole has properties that cannot be deduced from the behaviour of its components'.[26]

The cumulative, non-linear causation intrinsic to climate change does not match the traditional conception of causation under the effects-doctrine. The latter is namely premised on a direct link between the subject matter regulated and the territorial effects. On one view, this is reason enough not to apply the doctrine, which should be interpreted strictly, focusing, like the traditional principle of harm prevention, on delineated damage with a direct causal link to another actor.[27] According to this restrictive view, a state (or the EU) must be able to identify 'a specific environmental outcome' in its territory caused by GHG emissions from the subject matter it regulates.[28] This essentially entails a 'but for' or *conditio sine qua non* test, which would present near insurmountable evidentiary hurdles.[29]

It is argued here, however, that such a strict approach to the effects-doctrine is not suitable in the present context. The effects-doctrine is functional in nature, allowing states to respond to situations affecting their sovereignty that would otherwise be outside their reach. It seems inconsistent that cumulative causation should render regulatory responses impossible. The fact that cause (emissions) and effects (climate change) cannot be *isolated* to one specific environmental outcome does not mean that the two are not linked.[30] States should be competent to regulate this relationship where it results in substantial harm on their territory. Indeed, this is the very rationale of the mitigation and adaptation

[25] J Peel, 'Climate Change' in A Nollkaemper and I Plakokefalos (eds), *The Practice of Shared Responsibility in International Law* (Cambridge, Cambridge University Press, 2016) 1009. For a theoretical approach in the field of state responsibility, see I Plakokefalos, 'Causation in the Law of State Responsibility and the Problem of Overdetermination: In Search of Clarity' (2015) 26 *European Journal of International Law* 471.

[26] J Quiggin, 'Complexity, Climate Change and the Precautionary Principle' (Risk and Sustainable Management Group – Climate Change Working Paper C07:3, Australian Research Council Federation Fellow, University of Queensland 2007) 8.

[27] See eg C Hermeling et al, 'Sailing Into a Dilemma – An Economic and Legal Analysis of an EU Trading Scheme for Maritime Emissions' (Discussion Paper No 14-021, Centre for European Economic Research 2014) 15, who argue that '[d]ue to the high complexity of the climate change process, a chain of causes and effects that would clearly link GHG emissions from vessels anywhere in the world with specific environmental outcome, can scarcely be identified'.

[28] ibid. Along similar lines, others have argued that climate change damages should not be subject to the law of state *responsibility*, because proof of causation is impossible; for a literature overview, see Verheyen (n 24) 252.

[29] See ibid 254.

[30] T Bäuerle et al, 'Integration of Marine Transport into the European Emissions Trading System – Environmental, Economic and Legal Analysis of Different Options' (Report No (UBA-FB) 001372, German Federal Environment Agency (Umweltbundesamt) 2010). 3.

measures agreed to in the international climate regime. Such a view finds support in the 2019 *Urgenda* Supreme Court case, where it was found that:

> There is a direct, linear connection between the greenhouse gas emissions caused by humans, which are partly caused by the burning of fossil fuels, and the warming of the planet. …
>
> The rise in the planet's temperature can be prevented or reduced by ensuring that fewer greenhouse gases are emitted into the atmosphere. This is referred to as 'mitigation'. Measures can also be taken to anticipate the effects of climate change, such as raising dikes in low-lying areas. The taking of such measures is referred to as 'adaptation'.[31]

A broader approach to causation was also accepted by the Supreme Court in the 2020 case *Friends of the Irish Environment CLG*, where it held that:

> Studies have indicated that there is a consistent and almost linear relationship between carbon dioxide emissions and projected global temperature increases over the next 80 years. Climate change is already having a profound environmental and societal impact in Ireland and is predicted to pose further risks to the environment, both in Ireland and globally, in the future.[32]

That being said, in a jurisdictional context, *some* foreseeability and causation threshold is necessary in order to facilitate the delineation of regulatory competence. It is argued that here, precaution comes into play. While precaution has been considered in the literature in the context of climate change and state responsibility, there the focus is largely on its implications for the burden of proof.[33] Yet precaution is also relevant for jurisdiction, as it focuses on the competence of states to take preventative action when there is uncertainty as to the link between the regulated conduct and the expected grave environmental harm.

To further explore the potential role of precaution, section 4.2.1 first briefly considers the continuing legal debates on precaution in the context of climate change. Section 4.2.2 then suggests how this should inform the operationalisation of the foreseeability and causation requirements under the effects-doctrine, and with it, the overarching 'substantial connection' requirement.

4.2.1. *Precaution in the Context of Climate Change*

At the outset it must be noted that there is no single agreed definition of precaution, and while some argue that it is a principle, others consider it better

[31] *Urgenda* case (Supreme Court) (n 23) [2.1].

[32] *Friends of the Irish Environment CLG v Government of Ireland*, Appeal No 205/19 [2020] IESC 49 (*Friends of the Irish Environment*) [3.3].

[33] See eg Quiggin (n 26); Verheyen (n 24); Voigt (n 24) 12; LA Omuko, 'Applying the Precautionary Principle to Address the "Proof Problem" in Climate Change Litigation' (2016) 21 *Tilburg Law Review* 51.

characterised as an 'approach' or 'general posture for policy-making'.[34] An authoritative formulation can be found in Principle 15 of the Rio Declaration, which provides that:

> Where there are threats of serious irreversible damage, lack of full scientific certainty shall not be used as a reason for postponing cost-effective measures to prevent environmental degradation.

As noted by Wiener, this formulation takes a permissive approach, and is helpful 'as a rebuttal to the mistaken claim that uncertainty warrants inaction'.[35] An alternative formulation goes a step further, providing that uncertainty not only removes a defence for inaction, but positively mandates action.[36] This rests its legitimacy on the risk of grave and 'irreversible' harm.[37]

Notably, some consider precaution as an integral part of the prevention principle.[38] A well-accepted version of the latter can be found in Principle 21 of the 1972 Stockholm Declaration, which provides that states, while maintaining the sovereign right to exploit their own resources, have a 'responsibility to ensure that activities within their jurisdiction or control do not cause damage to the environment of other States or of areas beyond the limits of national jurisdiction'. In *Responsibilities in the Area*, ITLOS used due diligence to 'build a bridge' between prevention and precaution,[39] considering the precautionary approach in the regulations at issue to be

> an integral part of the general obligation of due diligence of sponsoring States, which is applicable even outside the scope of the [relevant] Regulations. The due diligence obligation of the sponsoring States requires them to take all appropriate measures to prevent damage that might result from the activities of contractors that they sponsor. This obligation applies in situations where scientific evidence concerning the scope and potential negative impact of the activity in question is insufficient but where there are plausible indications of potential risks.[40]

As noted by Wiener, while 'sharply controversial', 'if there is any sensible form of precaution to apply to any problem, then climate change seems an especially apt and urgent case'.[41] Article 3(3) of the UNFCCC lends support for the norm's

[34] On the debates surrounding the substance and legal status of precaution, see JB Wiener, 'Precaution' and U Beyerlin, 'Policies, Principles and Rules' in D Bodansky, J Brunnée, and E Hey (eds), *The Oxford Handbook of International Environmental Law* (Oxford, Oxford University Press, 2007) 597 and 425, respectively. See also JB Wiener, 'Precaution and Climate Change', in KR Gray, R Tarasofsky, and C Carlarne, *The Oxford Handbook of International Climate Change Law* (Oxford, Oxford Univeristy Press, 2016) 168.

[35] Wiener (n 34) 610.

[36] ibid 604.

[37] Ibid, referring among others to Art 5 of the 2004 French Environment Charter.

[38] ibid 603.

[39] D Bodansky et al, *International Climate Change Law* (Oxford, Oxford University Press, 2017) 44.

[40] *Responsibilities and obligations of States sponsoring persons and entities with respect to activities in the Area* (Advisory Opinion, Order of 1 February 2011) ITLOS Reports 2011, 131.

[41] Wiener (n 34) 164.

applicability in general terms, providing that the 'Parties should take precautionary measures to anticipate, prevent or minimize the causes of climate change and mitigate its adverse effects'. De Sadeleer points out that this language is 'less forceful' than in other multilateral environmental agreements, using the term 'should' rather than 'shall', and 'encapsulating a right to take preventative measures and not an obligation to act'.[42] For its part, the Dutch Supreme Court in the *Urgenda* case took a more forceful approach, finding that:

> The fact that this risk [of harm caused by dangerous climate change] will only be able to materialise a few decades from now and that it will not impact specific persons or a specific group of persons but large parts of the population does not mean – contrary to the State's assertions – that Articles 2 and 8 ECHR [European Convention on Human Rights] offer no protection from this threat. ... This is consistent with the precautionary principle. ... The mere existence of a sufficiently genuine possibility that this risk will materialise means that suitable measures *must* be taken.[43]

Having established that precaution may legitimise or even mandate climate protection measures in the face of scientific uncertainty, the following section will now consider the implications for prescriptive jurisdiction.

4.2.2. *The Role of Precaution for the Effects-Doctrine*

Despite the different approaches to precaution, an important 'core' element is that the lack of full scientific certainty does not prevent states from taking measures to anticipate and prevent grave environmental harm.[44] The scientific uncertainty may pertain to both the extent of the future damage and the causal relationship between the activity and the damage.[45] It is argued that the widespread legal recognition that full scientific certainty is not needed for states to take regulatory action is equally relevant in a jurisdictional context. Precaution is a functional norm, enabling anticipatory action before it is too late to act. It seems logical that this very practical legal answer to scientific uncertainty should enable states to protect their own territories and respond to common concerns in a jurisdictional context.

Notably, the jurisdictional lens is somewhat different, as the focus is on *balancing* the rights of equal sovereigns. Encroachments on the regulatory freedom of other states must also be laid in the scales. As such, the law of jurisdiction may also *constrain* precaution, setting a higher threshold for when states

[42] N de Sadeleer, 'Climate Change, Uncertainties and the Precautionary Principle' (Jean Monnet Working Paper Series – Environment and Internal Market 2016) 1, 5.

[43] *Urgenda* case (Supreme Court) (n 23) [5.6.2].

[44] Wiener (n 34) 168, noting the second 'core' element of the precautionary approach '(ii) a stance on knowledge, providing that scientific uncertainty about such risks does not preclude policy measures'.

[45] See UNESCO, 'The Precautionary Principle' (Report of the World Commission on the Ethics of Scientific Knowledge and Technology, 2005) 14; de Sadeleer (n 42) 8.

may regulate extraterritorial GHG-emitting activities.[46] In addition, one could argue that the harm need not be environmental in nature, as the basis for states' regulatory competence is their sovereign right to protect their territories and respond to threats to 'fundamental values of the international community' more broadly.[47]

Integrating these arguments into the operationalisation of the effects-doctrine, it is suggested that the analytical approach to determining the jurisdictional link between the state and the regulated subject matter should distinguish the same two elements to which uncertainty may pertain under the precautionary approach: the scope of the predicted harm and the causal link between the regulated activity and the harm. These may correspond with the jurisdictional requirements of 'foreseeability' and 'causation'.

Both foreseeability and causation hinge on how much uncertainty is permitted. In this regard, legal discourse on precaution provides support for an element of 'reasonableness'. For example, De Sadeleer considers that the 'lack of full scientific certainty' element 'allows public authorities to reckon their action upon reasonable scientific uncertainty', where 'the application of the precautionary measures depends on minimal evidence of the probability of a risk … that is to say, to scientific grounds with a demonstrated degree of consistency'.[48] Quiggin too argues for a reformulation of precaution, whereby those acting are required to demonstrate the 'reasonable belief" that their course of action will not be harmful.[49] Article 7B of the ILA Legal Principles Relating to Climate Change also incorporates reasonableness, referring to the 'reasonably foreseeable threat of serious or irreversible damage'.[50] In light of the complexity of the policy choices demanded of regulators, the flexible yardstick of 'reasonably foreseeable' grave harm would also appear valuable in a jurisdictional context.

It is further argued that the causal link between the conduct regulated and the territorial harm should be construed in terms of 'contribution to an increase in risk', rather than a direct and specific relationship. The international consensus that the risk of grave environmental harm does not preclude states from acting supports a lower causation threshold in a jurisdictional context. This differentiates environmental effects from economic effects under the traditional effects-doctrine. Neither a risk- nor a contribution-oriented approach to causation is new – an example of the former being the *Risikoerhöhungslehre*

[46] This also holds in the context of WTO law; see further I Cheyne, 'Gateways to the Precautionary Principle in WTO Law' (2007) 19 *Journal of Economic Literature* 155, 165: 'The only apparent restriction on the use of the precautionary principle is the unknown quantity of the 'sufficient nexus' test that may potentially restrict the extrajurisdictional reach of precautionary actions.'

[47] I am most indebted to Benoit Mayer for this argument, provided in the context of J Brunnée, B Mayer and A Zahar, 'Special Issue on Climate Law as a New Discipline' (2018) 8 *Climate Law* 135.

[48] de Sadeleer (n 42) 7.

[49] Quiggin (n 26) 11.

[50] ILA Resolution 2/2014, 'Declaration of Legal Principles Relating to Climate Change' (International Law Association, 2014) Art 7B(1).

in German criminal law, which holds an individual liable for an increase in risk that results in harm.[51] As noted by Verheyen, both the ILC and the ILA have also recognised that causation may in principle be based on contribution rather than a sine qua non test.[52]

In the present context, causation may require the consideration of two additional factors, namely consistent scientific evidence that the *type* of activity actually contributes to climate change, and a threshold for the *extent* of the contribution to climate change. This latter element is particularly important in order to set a limit on the regulatory reach of powerful states. Here, legal discourse in the field of climate change liability offers valuable considerations. It must be borne in mind, however, that the function of causation is different in the law of jurisdiction, as it is not concerned with apportioning responsibility but rather legitimising 'extraterritorial' regulatory action. For this reason, the legal analysis should focus on 'causation in fact', which bears upon the factual causal chain, and not so much on 'normative causation', which bears upon the fact that the actor 'ought to have known' and therefore should incur responsibility.[53]

Analysing climate change in US tort law, Duffy proposes a probabilistic 'market share' approach, 'which requires plaintiffs only to show that human influences were a *measurable factor* in creating the risk of harm to the plaintiff'.[54] Another approach is to require that the conduct regulated makes a *meaningful contribution* to the risk of harm. As noted by Peel, the 'meaningful contribution' requirement finds acceptance in several national systems as an approach to causation in the case of cumulative harm.[55] In a jurisdictional context, the establishment of a de minimis contribution will be necessary to afford protection for the regulatory space of other states. This constraining function differentiates the analysis of states' jurisdiction from that of states' obligations.[56] Although undeniably legally challenging, this could be based on recognised data and calculation methods.[57] Qualitative factors such as the activity's duration or divergence from international environmental standards may also be considered.

[51] Verheyen (n 24) 255, referring to *Woodyear v Schaeffer* 57 MD 1 (MD 1881) 9–10, though noting that this case did not apply to cumulative causation.

[52] ibid 256.

[53] On this distinction, see further ibid 250.

[54] See M Duffy, 'Climate Change Causation: Harmonizing Tort Law and Scientific Probability' (2009) 28 *Temple Journal of Science, Technology & Environmental Law* 185, 242 (emphasis added). According to Duffy's theory: 'Liability is apportioned among tort defendants based on the percentage by which anthropogenic influences contributes to the risk of harm, and further divided based on each individual plaintiff's share of the GHG "market"' (189).

[55] For further analysis, see Peel (n 25) 28.

[56] Such a de minimis was, for example, not found necessary to establish a causal link for the duty of care under Dutch law in the *Urgenda Foundation v Kingdom of the Netherlands*, The Hague District Court (24 June 2015) ECLI:NL:RBDHA:2015:7145 (*Urgenda* case (District Court)) [4.90].

[57] The national GHG inventories required under UNFCCC may be useful here. See Verheyen (n 24) 254; and B Mayer, 'The Applicability of the Principle of Prevention to Climate Change: A Response to Zahar' (2015) 5 *Climate Law* 1, 13, noting that, although challenging, the difficulties in determining such a threshold can be overcome.

The precise de minimis threshold would need to be determined by subsequent practice, as it comes down to a complex balancing of interests appropriately calibrated according to widespread international consensus.

Drawing together these considerations, a substantial connection based on the effects-doctrine may exist, when, relying on consistent scientific evidence, a state can demonstrate that the conduct measurably contributes to an increase in the risk of reasonably foreseeable grave harm. The contribution must exceed an agreed de minimis threshold, itself based on accepted science and state practice. It is not necessary to prove the precise scope of the future harm or its linear link with specific GHG-emitting activities. This incorporates the more recent international consensus on the role of states in responding to complex environmental threats, and is consistent with the functional rationale of both precaution and the permissive principles of state jurisdiction.

5. THE PROTECTIVE PRINCIPLE AND CLIMATE CHANGE AS A THREAT TO VITAL STATE INTERESTS

Sometimes considered an extension of the effects-doctrine, the protective principle provides a basis for jurisdiction over conduct threatening vital national interests.[58] As discussed in chapter 7, the notion of 'threat' encompasses a causal relationship between the regulated source and the expected consequences. As such, there is considerable conceptual overlap between effects and protection, where the latter is defined by the gravity of the effects which must threaten 'vital state interests'. This in turn legitimises a greater degree of pre-emption, in that the anticipated consequences need not have started yet. In terms of causation it seems logical that the same considerations discussed under the effects-doctrine would apply here, where based on consistent scientific evidence, a state must be able to demonstrate that the regulated conduct measurably contributes to an increase in the threat to vital state interests.

Like most of the classical bases, the protective principle has evolved primarily in relation to certain crimes, or conduct attempting to result in a crime. GHG-emitting activities are an integral part of the production and use of goods and services in industrialised economies, and are not typically crimes. Nevertheless, it has been argued that the protection principle's rationale, together with the openness of the 'vital interest' threshold, may well support its future application to environmental concerns. Indeed, according to the Harvard Draft Convention on Jurisdiction with Respect to Crime, the core 'basis' of

[58] As noted by Paul, this is derived from the ancient right of self-defence. See L Paul, 'Using the Protective Principle to Unilaterally Enforce Transnational Marine Pollution Standards' (Proceedings of the Second International Conference on Marine Debris, 1989) NOM Tech Hemo NHFS, NOM-Tn-NMFS-SUFSC-154, 1048.

the protective principle is 'the 'nature of the interest injured' as being vital to the state.[59] These are matters of state 'security, territorial integrity or political independence'.

The following section will briefly consider recent recognition in both scientific and legal fields of the relationship between climate change and these vital state interests. Specifically, it will explore the current and future threats posed to the territorial integrity of states at the 'frontline' of climate change, particularly Small Island Developing States (SIDS). It will then consider the growing recognition for climate change as a threat to national security and political independence.

5.1. Climate Change as a Threat to Territorial Integrity

Territorial integrity 'refers to the territorial "oneness" or "wholeness" of the State'.[60] As an 'essential foundation' of state sovereignty, it extends beyond land territory to the territorial sea, and its seabed and subsoil. Territorial integrity is linked to political independence, as it is a prerequisite for state autonomy in its internal affairs. As noted by Blay, together these elements provide the basis for the right of states to make decisions affecting their territory,[61] and logically, therefore, also for protection-based jurisdiction.

According to the World Economic Forum and the 2019 UNEP Emissions Gap Report, the current trajectory set out in countries' commitments under the Paris Agreement will lead to a rise in temperature above 3°C by the end of the century.[62] This is over double the 'safer' 1.5°C limit indicated in the 2018 Special Report of the IPCC, and in Article 2(1)(a) of the Paris Agreement.[63] It is of particular concern for coastline cities, which are currently underprepared for the anticipated water rise. Alterations to baselines due to receding coastlines will affect the corresponding maritime zones, and as such, the areas over which a state may 'legitimately claim jurisdiction'.[64]

[59] Harvard Draft Convention on Jurisdiction with Respect to Crime, 'Article 7. Protection – Security of the State' (1935) 29 *American Journal of International Law Supplement: Research in International Law* 543: 'The basis of such jurisdiction is the nature of the interest injured rather than the place of the act or the nationality of the offender.'

[60] S Blay, 'Territorial Integrity' in R Wolfrum (ed), *Max Planck Encyclopaedia of Public International Law*, online edn (Oxford, Oxford University Press, 2010) [1].

[61] ibid.

[62] World Economic Forum, 'The Global Risks Report 2020' (Insight Report, 15th edn 2020) 30; United Nations, 'Emissions Gap Report' (Nairobi, United Nations Environmental Programme, 2019) www.wedocs.unep.org/bitstream/handle/20.500.11822/30797/EGR2019.pdf?sequence=1&isAllowed=y.

[63] IPCC Summary for Policymakers (n 13).

[64] H Stallard, 'Turning up the Heat on Tuvalu: An Assessment of Compensation for Climate Change Damage in Accordance with State Responsibility under International Law' (2009) 15 *Canterbury Law Review* 163, 169.

It is in countries at the 'frontline of climate change' that threats to territorial integrity are becoming immediately apparent.[65] Rising sea levels have begun to submerge low-lying coastlines, and entire parts of SIDS.[66] A key example is Tuvalu, where the highest elevation is less than four metres above sea level.[67] Before it even submerges the islands, the rising sea level threatens to contaminate fresh water resources with serious knock-on effects for agriculture and the availability of other natural resources.[68] In 2002 the Prime Minister of Tuvalu threatened to sue the United States and Australia for their failure to take sufficient climate action, as the two had both refused to sign the Kyoto Protocol.[69] While this move was subsequently retracted by the new leadership, it only marked the beginning of attempts address the territorial threats of climate change through legal channels.[70]

The *Kivalina* litigation in the United States illustrates another climate-related threat to territorial integrity that has spilled into the legal arena. There, a native Alaskan village was forced to relocate due to a reduction in protective sea ice and increase in flooding and storms caused by climate change.[71] To recover the costs, the village brought a suit against large US energy companies, arguing that the latter's emissions substantially interfered with their right to property.[72] On appeal it was found that the plaintiffs lacked standing because, after the finding in the parallel case *American Electric Power v Connecticut*, it was established that claims of nuisance against GHG emitters were displaced by the Clean Air Act.[73] While this was clearly unsatisfactory from a material perspective, the instigation of the suit illustrates the very real threats to the territorial integrity of vulnerable communities, which continue to be translated into legal claims.

As a later example, in 2019 the Human Rights Committee considered a claim of Ioane Teitiota regarding an infringement of the International Covenant on

[65] F von Paepcke, *Statehood in Times of Climate Change: Impacts of Sea Level Rise on the Concept of States* (Bern, Peter Lang, 2014); 'On the Frontlines of Climate Change' (UNESCO Project, September 2017) www.climatefrontlines.org/.

[66] See further J Crawford and R Rayfuse, 'Climate Change and Statehood' in R Rayfuse and S van Scott, *International Law in the Era of Climate Change* (Cheltenham, Edward Elgar, 2012) 234. Unsurprisingly, therefore, in 1992 Fiji, Kiribati, Nauru and Tuvalu entered a declaration at the signing of the UNFCCC, reserving the right to bring a claim against other states.

[67] H Ralston, B Horstmann and C Holl, 'Climate Change: Challenges Tuvalu' (German Watch, 2004) 14, www.germanwatch.org/sites/germanwatch.org/files/publication/3632.pdf.

[68] 'Tuvalu and Climate Change – Rising Sea Levels Threatening Pacific Islands' (September 2017) www. worldatlas.com.

[69] 'Tiny Tuvalu Sues United States Over Rising Sea Level' (29 August 2002) www.tuvaluislands.com.

[70] Stallard (n 64) 169.

[71] See further Gerrard and Wannier (n 14) 582.

[72] *Native Village of Kivalina v Exxon Mobil Corp*, 663 f Supp 2d 863 (ND Cal. 2009) (*Kivalina* case) 879–80. See further Gerrard and Wannier (n 14) 582; QM Sorenson, 'Native Village of Kivalina v ExxonMobil Corp: The End of "Climate Change" Tort Litigation?' (2013) 44(3) *American Bar Association, Section of Environment, Energy, and Resources Newsletter Trends* 1.

[73] *Kivalina* case (n 72) 858; *American Electric Power v Connecticut* 564 US 410 (2011).

Civil and Political Rights (ICCPR).[74] According to Mr Teitiota, '[t]he situation in Tarawa [in the Republic of Kiribati] has become increasingly unstable and precarious due to sea level rise caused by global warming'.[75] Interpreting the ICCPR, the Committee 'accepts the author's claim that sea level rise is likely to render the Republic of Kiribati uninhabitable'.[76] This case will be considered further in section 5.2, as it pertains to the issue of climate refugees.

Of course, more developed countries and regions must also deal with increasing risks to their vulnerable coastlines, a key example being California in the United States.[77] Large cities such as Hamburg, Amsterdam and Lisbon will feel the impacts before the end of this century.[78] This was recognised by the Dutch Supreme Court in the *Urgenda* case, where it was found that the 'real and immediate risk' of dangerous climate change, including 'the possible sharp rise in the sea level, which could render part of the Netherlands uninhabitable', could 'seriously jeopardise' the welfare of Dutch residents.[79] In seeking to mitigate this harm, it is not implausible that these more economically powerful actors will engage in 'extraterritorial' climate protection relying on the protective principle. Ultimately, it may well be more developed states that further the crystallisation of this principle's application.

5.2. Climate Change as a Threat to National Security and Political Independence

In addition to the physical disappearance of territory, there is now increasing evidence that climate change poses a serious threat to state security in general. The 2020 Global Risks Report of the World Economic Forum identifies 'climate action failure' as the number one of its top ten long-term risks in terms of predicted impact.[80] According to the report, '[t]he near-term consequences of climate change add up to a "planetary emergency"', with implications that are 'catastrophic, wide-ranging and intersecting'.[81]

[74] *Ioane Teitiota v New Zealand* (advance unedited version) United Nations Human Rights Committee (7 January 2020) CCPR/C/127/D/2728/2016.

[75] ibid [2.1].

[76] ibid [9.12].

[77] See further AC Mulkern, 'Rising Sea Levels Will Hit California Harder than Other Places' (September 2017) www.scientificamerican.com/article/rising-sea-levels-will-hit-california-harder-than-other-places/.

[78] ibid. See also D Grossman, 'A Tale of Two Northern European Cities: Meeting the Challenges of Sea Level Rise' (Yale Environment 360, 3 November 2015) www.360.yale.edu/features/a_tale_of_two_northern_european_cities_meeting_the_challenges_of_sea _level_rise.

[79] *Urgenda* case (Supreme Court) (n 23) [5.6.2].

[80] Global Risks Report 2020 (n 62) 12.

[81] ibid 30.

A first intersecting issue is that of environmental refugees. It is predicted that at least half a billion people will be displaced by climate change within the next century.[82] Despite the present realities, parties to the 2015 COP (Conference of the Parties) 21 failed to expand the definition of 'refugee' to include climate-based migration, the 1951 UN Refugee Convention only recognising those fleeing war and persecution.[83] This gap in legal protection is therefore being grappled with in different fora. An interesting example is the New Zealand case *Ioane Teitiota v The Chief Executive of the Ministry of Business, Innovation and Employment*, where the Supreme Court of New Zealand refused to expand the definition in the UN Refugee Convention to grant refugee status based on climate change displacement to a Kiribati national.[84] It did, however, note that its decision 'did not mean that environmental degradation resulting from climate change or other natural disasters could never create a pathway into the Refugee Convention or protected person jurisdiction'.[85]

As mentioned above, in 2019, the Human Rights Committee assessed whether the denial of refugee status to Mr Teitiota constituted a violation of the right to life under the ICCPR.[86] There the Committee found that:

> Both sudden-onset events (such as intense storms and flooding) and slow-onset processes (such as sea level rise, salinization, and land degradation) can propel cross-border movement of individuals seeking protection from climate change-related harm. The Committee is of the view that without robust national and international efforts, the effects of climate change in receiving states may expose individuals to a violation of their rights under articles 6 or 7 of the Covenant. … Furthermore, given that the risk of an entire country becoming submerged under water is such an extreme risk, the conditions of life in such a country may become incompatible with the right to life with dignity before the risk is realized.[87]

The Committee accepted Mr Teitiota's claim that Kirbati would likely become uninhabitable due to sea-level rise. However, in light of 'the time left for the Kiribati authorities and the international community to intervene and the efforts already underway to address the very serious situation of the islands', the assessment of the New Zealand authorities was not found to violate the right to life. In the view of this author, relying on time left for change seems a very short-term solution given current predictions that there is only 'a decade left' to 'confront the runaway climate threat'.[88]

[82] J Knefel, 'Paris COP 21 Agreement Fails Millions of Potential Climate Refugees' (December 2015) www.inverse.com/article/9370-paris-cop21-agreement-failed-millions-of-potential-climate-change-refugees.

[83] Convention Relating to the Status of Refugees (adopted 28 July 1951, entered into force 22 April 1954) 189 UNTS 137, Art 1.

[84] *Ioane Teitiota v The Chief Executive of the Ministry of Business, Innovation and Employment* (2015) NZSC 107.

[85] ibid [13].

[86] *Ioane Teitiota v New Zealand* (n 74).

[87] ibid [9.11] (references omitted).

[88] Global Risks Report 2020 (n 62) 28.

Notably, alternative possibilities do exist for the protection of internally and internationally displaced persons due to climate change under various human rights agreements, such as the European Convention on Human Rights and the ICCPR.[89] These have been a topic of considerable debate within the United Nations Human Rights Council (UNHCR) and the International Organization for Migration (IOM).[90]

Extreme weather is also causing severe security threats around the world.[91] A key example is the 2017 Hurricane Irma, which cost dozens of lives, causing enormous destruction to the Caribbean islands in its path, particularly St Martin and Cuba, and leaving Florida under water for days.[92] Another famous example is the 2005 Hurricane Katrina disaster which killed almost 2,000 people, with many more subsequently moving away as they were unable to afford the costs of rebuilding.[93] The EU is also not immune to national security concerns, and it has been suggested that this is in fact a key motive behind its continued climate leadership ambitions.[94]

The third 'vital' interest – political independence – is in many ways dependent on a government being able to ensure territorial sovereignty, national security and basic resources.[95] A leadership without effective control over its territory is likely to be vulnerable to interference from other actors, both public and private. Where authorities are unable to provide basic resources to their citizens, the risk also arises that other groups will destabilise the political system.[96] Climate change may contribute to this process, as changing weather patterns lead to crop

[89] J McAdam, 'Climate Change Displacement and International Law: Complementary Protection Standards', UNHCR Legal Protection and Policy Research Series (PPLA/2011/03, United Nations High Commissioner for Refugees, 2011). See further also J McAdam (ed), *Climate Change and Displacement: Multidisciplinary Perspectives* (Oxford, Hart Publishing, 2010).

[90] See eg McAdam, 'Climate Change Displacement and International Law' (n 89); 'International Dialogue on Migration 2017: Strengthening International Cooperation on and Governance of Migration towards the Adoption of a Global Compact on Migration in 2018' (IOM, 19 April 2017) www.iom.int/international-dialogue-migration-2017-strengthening-international-cooperation-and-governance.

[91] 'Climate Change Poses Increasing Risks to Global Stability: Commitment to Building Resilience is Required' (UNFCC, 23 February 2017) unfccc.int/news/climate-change-poses-increasing-risks-to-global-stability.

[92] E Mackintosh and K Fox, 'A Week after Irma – Caribbean Devastation s Laid Bare', *CNN* (14 September 2017) www.edition.cnn.com/2017/09/13/americas/hurricane-irma-caribbean-one-week-on/index.html.

[93] D Haynes, 'Effects of Hurricane Katrina Still Visible 10 Years Later', *United Press International* (29 August 2015) www.upi.com/Top_News/US/2015/08/29/Effects-of-Hurricane-Katrina-still-visible-10-years-later/5581440167964/.

[94] S Bogojević, 'Climate Change Law and Policy in the European Union' in *The Oxford Handbook of International Climate Change Law* (2016) 674, 682–83.

[95] For an interesting visual of these connections, see The Risks–Trends Interconnections Map 2020 in 'The Global Risks Report 2020' (n 62) 5.

[96] See JO Adeyeri, 'Nationalism and Political Independence in Africa' in S Oloruntoba and T Falola (eds), *The Palgrave Handbook of African Politics, Governance and Development* (New York, Palgrave Macmillan, 2018) 203, referring to the militant nationalism of Boko Haram in Nigeria, which has spillover effects in the neighbouring countries of Cameroon, Niger and Chad.

failure and spikes in food prices.[97] Indeed, it has been argued that the uprisings of the Arab Spring can be linked to droughts and dust storms in the 2010–11 period, exacerbated by the La Niña weather event in the southern hemisphere, all of which can be traced to climate change.[98] In this way, global warming acts as a clear 'threats multiplier' with lasting knock-on effects on states' political independence.[99] An interesting initiative in this regard is the 2019 climate security governance framework on a 'Responsibility to Prepare and Prevent' (R2P2).[100] Drawing on the 'combination of unprecedented risks and unprecedented foresight', the R2P2 aims to fill an acute governance gap. The proposed responsibility to prepare has been presented to the UN Security Council, the latter being increasingly receptive to climate security issues.[101]

These examples illustrate increasing global recognition for climate change as a threat, not only to the environmental commons but also to individual states' territorial integrity and security. Although it would be a novel claim, it is then not unthinkable that the protective principle may be relied upon in support of a substantial connection to activities contributing to global warming. This principle may serve to buttress effects-based claims, as its anticipatory nature can overcome the fact that certain foreseeable effects may not have occurred, or even started yet.

6. THE UNIVERSALITY PRINCIPLE AND CLIMATE CHANGE AS A COMMON CONCERN OF HUMANKIND

With its focus on the interests of the international community, it seems intuitive that the universality principle may also lend support to jurisdictional assertions responding to climate change as a common concern of mankind. However, 'pure' universality also remains one of the most contested and vaguely defined bases of classical jurisdictional doctrine, with very little concrete state practice,

[97] M Cimons, 'Crop Failure and Fading Food Supplies: Climate Change's Lasting Impact (Op-Ed)' (16 January 2016) www.livescience.com/53400-crop-failure-draining-food-supplies-as-planet-warms.html.

[98] CE Werrell and F Femia (eds), 'The Arab Spring and Climate Change: A Climate and Security Correlations Series' (Center for American Progress, 28 February 2013) www.americanprogress.org/issues/security/reports/2013/02/28/54579/the-arab-spring-and-climate-change/.

[99] ibid.

[100] C Werrell and F Femia, 'The Responsibility to Prepare and Prevent a Climate Security Governance Framework for the 21st Century' (The Centre for Climate and Security, October 2019) www.climateandsecurity.org/wp-content/uploads/2019/10/the-responsibility-to-prepare-and-prevent_a-climate-security-governance-framework-for-the-21st-century_2019_10.pdf.

[101] C Werrel and F Femia, 'Vide and Summary: UN Security Council Meeting on Climate and Security' (The Center for Climate & Security, 9 December 2017) www.climateandsecurity.org/2017/12/video-and-summary-un-security-council-meeting-onclimate-and-security/. See further United Nations, 'Climate Emergency "A Danger to Peace", UN Security Council Hears' (UN News, 24 July 2020) www.news.un.org/en/story/2020/07/1068991.

particularly outside of criminal law.[102] This raises the question whether, and how, the universality principle may be applied to prescriptive measures seeking to protect common environmental interests.

As we have seen in chapter 7, several different conceptualisations of universal jurisdiction exist in legal discourse. Here the focus is on what some commentators have termed 'pure universal concern' jurisdiction, assertions of which are 'based solely on the universal concern character of the crime'.[103] As noted by Yee, this is the rationale underlying the principle's negative definition as jurisdiction in the 'absence of a link' between the subject matter and the regulating state.[104] To employ Reydams's terminology, this book is furthermore primarily interested in 'unilateral universality', that is, jurisdiction which does not rest on treaty provisions but rather on customary international law.[105]

In a criminal context, it is generally accepted that the key factor justifying jurisdictional assertions is the gravity or morally abhorrent nature of the crimes in question. Such crimes threaten fundamental community values such as individuals' physical integrity, right to life and even right to property, and are considered to constitute an attack on the international community as a whole.[106] Breaching 'values in which every state has an equal concern',[107] core crimes are also considered to violate obligations erga omnes owed to all states, creating a basis for states' jurisdictional rights.[108]

The rationale of the universality principle thus lies in the notion that states, as 'agents of the international community', must have the jurisdictional competence to protect certain recognised shared values.[109] This was clearly formulated

[102] For a comprehensive study of practice in criminal law, see eg L Reydams, *Universal Jurisdiction – International and Municipal Legal Perspectives* (Cambridge, Cambridge University Press, 2003) 81. Yee even questions whether it finds application to any conduct other than piracy: see S Yee, 'Universal Jurisdiction: Concept, Logic, and Reality' (2011) 10 *Chicago Journal of International Law* 503.

[103] See eg Yee (n 102) 508; KC Randall, 'Universal Jurisdiction under International Law' (1987) 66 *Texas Law Review* 785, 788.

[104] Yee (n 102) 505, noting: 'Behind the "absence" façade however, rests the basis for such an assertion of jurisdiction, normally formulated this way: The alleged crime is an attack on the fundamental values of the international community as a whole.'

[105] Reydams (n 102) 38. This Reydams contrasts with 'cooperative universality', which is treaty-based.

[106] ibid 73, citing Rapporteur de Grailly of the Consultative Assembly of the Council of Europe, Commentary to the 1965 Draft European Convention on Jurisdiction in Criminal Matters (AS/Jur X (16) 9), [34]: 'the principle arose from the need to ensure the safety of certain basic values in which every state has an equal concern'.

[107] C Ryngaert, *Jurisdiction in International Law*, 2nd edn (Oxford, Oxford University Press, 2015) 126–27; Yee (n 102) 505.

[108] Ryngaert (n 107) 126.

[109] As noted by Judge ad hoc van den Wyngaert in his Dissenting Opinion to the *Case Concerning the Arrest Warrant of 11 April 2000 (Democratic Republic of the Congo v Belgium)* [2002] ICJ Rep 141, the fundamental question was 'about what international law requires or allows States to do as "agents" of the international community when they are confronted with complaints of victims of" heinous crimes.

in the Israeli Supreme Court's judgment in the *Eichmann* case, where it held that:

> Not only do all the crimes attributed to the appellant bear an international character, but their harmful and murderous effects were so embracing and widespread as to shake the international community to its very foundations. The State of Israel therefore was entitled, pursuant to the principle of universal jurisdiction and in the *capacity of a guardian of international law* and an agent for its enforcement, to try the appellant.[110]

Although this rationale may support extension of the universality principle to the field of environment, doubts have been raised as to the principle's propensity for expansion. According to Yee, there has in fact been a 'trending down' of the doctrine, whereby universality is now a 'moving train without a locomotive'.[111] On its face, this appears consistent with the continuing lack of state practice in support of universal jurisdiction over jus cogens violations, despite their peremptory nature and considerable substantive overlap with crimes subject to universal jurisdiction.

The idea of a link between jus cogens norms and universal jurisdiction gained popularity in the 1990s, with human rights activists promoting a proactive approach to the prosecution of core crimes.[112] In the 1998 *Furundzija* case, the International Criminal Tribunal for the former Yugoslavia (ICTY) also appeared to support such a link, holding that:

> [O]ne of the consequences of the *jus cogens* character bestowed by the international community upon the prohibition of torture is that every state is entitled to investigate, prosecute and punish or extradite individuals accused of torture, who are present in a territory under its jurisdiction. ... This legal basis for states' universal jurisdiction over torture bears out and strengthens the legal foundation for such jurisdiction found by other courts in the inherently universal character of the crime.[113]

Bassiouni went a step further, arguing that jus cogens violations give rise to an *obligation* to exercise universal jurisdiction.[114] In his view, 'the implications of *jus cogens* are those of a duty and not of optional rights; otherwise *jus cogens* would not constitute a peremptory norm of international law'.[115]

110 *Attorney-General of the Government of Israel v Adolf Eichmann* (Israel Supreme Court 1962) 36 ILR 277, 304 (emphasis added).

111 Yee (n 102) 503, 505; L Reydams, 'The Rise and Fall of Universal Jurisdiction' (Working Paper no 36, KU Leuven 2010) 1.

112 See further on the *Zeitgeist* of the 1990s, Reydams (n 111) 3.

113 See *Prosecutor v Anto Furundzija* (Judgment) IT-95-17/1-T (10 December 1998) (*Furundzija* case) 156.

114 C Bassiouni, 'International Crimes: Jus Cogens and Obligations Erga Omnes' (1996) 59 *Law & Contemorary Problems* 63.

115 ibid. See also A Mills, 'Rethinking Jurisdiction in International Law' (2014) 84 *British Yearbook of International Law* 187, 212, arguing that the growth of treaties including the *aut dedere aut judicare* principle, evidences a shift in the very conception of jurisdiction as not only a right but also, sometimes, an obligation.

Yet despite these doctrinal arguments, studies from a number of commentators have concluded that state practice does not appear to support these claims.[116] A key explanation for states' reluctance to recognise universal jurisdiction for jus cogens violations is the highly political nature of the enquiry. These violations are often carried out by state organs themselves, and prosecution very much depends on the power of the actor and forum in which it is investigated.[117] As such, there is a perceived risk that the principle will be relied upon, or indeed ignored, for ulterior political purposes.[118] In practice, when universal jurisdiction is nominally exercised it is often done on the basis of a treaty. As discussed in chapter 7, this provides more of a 'quasi' universalism based on a codified agreement to pool the sovereignty of parties, rather than a customary rule granting all states jurisdiction. Commentators therefore persuasively argue that the politicised nature of the crimes together with the somewhat contradictory state practice indicates that the jus cogens characterisation is, in itself, insufficient to justify the lawfulness of universal jurisdiction.[119] Rather, jurisdictional assertions regarding specific crimes must also be supported by state practice and opinio juris, which is lacking at the moment.[120]

It is argued, however, that the situation regarding universal jurisdiction in the context of jus cogens norms is not necessarily analogous to that in the context of climate change. Universal jurisdiction for climate protection measures fundamentally differs from that for core crimes because it does not focus on a violation of obligations, but rather on the competence to fulfil them. As a result, such 'climate universality' does not face quite the same political sensitivities as

[116] Yee (n 102) 511: 'Reasonable as the idea of universal jurisdiction sounds, persuasive as its logic appears, one must not forget the teaching that "The life of the law has not been logic: it has been experience". The experience and reality of international relations are such that universal jurisdiction over crimes other than piracy has not been established as a matter of international law' (references omitted). See also Reydams (n 102) 223; N Nedeski, 'Shared Obligations in International Law' (doctoral thesis, University of Amsterdam, 2017) 74, noting that 'the VCLT does not address the potential implications of the peremptory nature of certain norms'. For further analysis of the practice of states and international organisations and tribunals, see A Zimmerman, 'Violations of Fundamental Norms of International Law and the Exercise of Universal Jurisdiction in Criminal Matters' in JM Thouvenin and C Tomuschat (eds), *The Fundamental Rules of the International Legal Order – Jus Cogens and Erga Omnes Violations* (Leiden, Martinus Nijhoff, 2006) 340.

[117] See Ryngaert (n 107) 129, noting that as, in practice, such crimes are often committed using the 'state's machinery' their prosecution is highly politicised and subject to foreign protest.

[118] See in particular the request by certain African states for the inclusion on the UN agenda of the item: 'Abuse of the principle of universal jurisdiction', in the Agenda of the 63rd Session of the United Nations General Assembly (3 February 2009) UN Doc A/63/237.

[119] See eg Zimmerman (n 116) 339; Ryngaert (n 107) 129. In the *Armed Activities* case, the ICJ confirmed that the *erga omnes* or *jus cogens* nature of a norm could also not in itself provide the *court* with jurisdiction, which under its statute is always based on the consent of both parties. *Armed Activities on the Territory of the Congo (New Application: 2002), (Democratic Republic of the Congo v Rwanda)* [2006] ICJ Rep 6, 31–32.

[120] In fact, some commentators see universality as a receding trend, see eg Reydams (n 102); Yee (n 102) 503: 'The movement for "pure universal jurisdiction" has been "trending down" since the conspicuous silence on the legitimacy of universal jurisdiction in the Arrest Warrant case.'

those tied to establishing a violation of jus cogens. Furthermore, in terms of the feasibility of state practice, states arguably have a greater incentive to assert jurisdiction in relation to their own 'positive' fulfilment of climate obligations, than to another actor's 'negative' violation of a jus cogens norm. In fact, one could see the EU's continued development of its climate policy as evidence of this.

Taken more broadly, the increasing recognition of the link between serious global climate harm and state obligations to respond could arguably indicate a 'trending up' rather than a 'trending down' of legal receptiveness to extensive competences. Indeed, in a 2016 decision the International Criminal Court (ICC) extended its jurisdiction to cover conduct causing serious destruction of the environment.[121]

From a conceptual perspective, there is a clear window for the application of the universality principle to climate change as a common concern of mankind. As mentioned, in the *Furundzija* case, the ICTY found that the 'the legal foundation for such [universal] jurisdiction' lies in the 'inherently universal character' of the subject matter – there the crime of torture.[122] Intrinsic to the notion of the *common* concern is namely recognition of its universality, both as an interest of all individual states and a value of the 'higher' international community. Furthermore, the reasons why climate change has been recognised as a common concern display important similarities with the prevention and prosecution of grave crimes. In particular, climate change poses a foreseeable and substantial threat to the same or equally fundamental human rights as those infringed by core crimes. This relationship has been extensively analysed in the 2014 OHCHR Report on Human Rights and Climate Change, and also appears in the preamble to the Paris Agreement.[123]

Confirming the observed link, the past decade seen a sharp increase in climate change litigation in the field of human rights.[124] For example, in the 2015 case *Leghari v Federation of Pakistan*, the Lahore High Court found that the government's failure to implement the national climate change policy 'offends the fundamental rights of the citizens which need to be safeguarded'.[125]

[121] 'Policy Paper on Case Selection and Prioritisation' (Office of the Prosecutor, International Criminal Court 2016) www.icc-cpi.int/itemsDocuments/20160915_OTP-Policy_Case-Selection_Eng.pdf. See in particular [7] and [41]: 'The impact of the crimes may be assessed in light of, *inter alia*, the increased vulnerability of victims, the terror subsequently instilled, or the social, economic and environmental damage inflicted on the affected communities.'

[122] *Furundzija* case (n 113) [156].

[123] HRC, 'Report of the Independent Expert on the issue of Human Rights Obligations Relating to the Enjoyment of a Safe, Clean, Healthy and Sustainable Environment – Mapping Report (Office of the United Nations High Commissioner for Human Rights 2014) A/HRC/25/53. See also The Paris Agreement (adopted 15 December 2015, entered into force 4 November 2016) (2016) 55 ILM 740 (in particular rec 9 on food security, and rec 11 on the right to health and the rights of local and indigenous peoples).

[124] See more extensively Wewerinke-Singh (n 12).

[125] *Leghari v Federation of Pakistan* (2015) WP No 25501/2015 [8]. There is also debate about climate security as an independent human right, see further eg A Sinden, 'An Emerging Human

In the aforementioned 2017 advisory opinion, the IACHR 'recognized the existence of an undeniable relationship between the protection of the environment and the realization of other human rights, in that environmental degradation and the adverse effects of climate change affect the real enjoyment of human rights'.[126] According to the IACHR, 'the right to a healthy environment constitutes a *universal value* that is owed to both present and future generations'.[127] Combating climate change is therefore, albeit more indirectly, equally as necessary to protect fundamental community values as preventing and prosecuting the core crimes of universal jurisdiction. This could then plausibly fall within states' rights and obligations as agents of the international community.

On the whole, despite the lack of conclusive state practice, there are certainly doctrinal openings for the universality principle to be applied in the context of common environmental concerns. Given the increasing recognition for the gravity of environmental harm, together with the prospective rather than retrospective focus of environmental protection measures, the possibility should certainly not be excluded. It seems both logically and ethically sound that the protection of fundamental community values at the core of the universality principle's rationale should also encompass threats to those values outside of the criminal field. As will be argued below, taken together with the other bases, the principle may then lend, at the very least, a modest degree of support to jurisdictional assertions responding to climate change as a common concern of mankind.

7. CONCLUSIONS: CONSTRUCTING THE SUBSTANTIAL CONNECTION REQUIREMENT IN THE CONTEXT OF CLIMATE CHANGE

The above analysis has explored the possible application of the classic prescriptive principles to 'extraterritorial' climate change measures. Drawing together these findings, the present section will now consider how the different 'connecting factors' of each basis may interact in evidencing an overarching 'substantial connection' between a state and the regulated subject matter.

To start with, all measures genuinely seeking to mitigate climate change harms may find some support in the universality principle, under which the extraterritorial element of a measure is justified by the fundamental nature of

Right to Security from Climate Change: The Case Against Gas Flaring in Nigeria' in W Burns and H Osofsky (eds), *Adjudicating Climate Change: Sub-National, National, And Supra-National Approaches* (Cambridge, Cambridge University Press, 2008).

[126] *The Environment and Human Rights*, Advisory Opinion OC-23/17, Inter-American Court of Human Rights (15 November 2017) [47].

[127] ibid [59] (emphasis added). See further NA Robinson, 'Environmental Law: Is an Obligation *Erga Omnes* Emerging?' (International Council of Environmental Law, 2018) www.iucn.org/sites/dev/files/content/documents/2018/environmental_law_is_an_obligation_erga_omnes_emerging_interamcthradvisoryopinionjune2018.pdf.

the community value protected. However, given the lack of consistent acceptance of 'pure' universal jurisdiction, particularly outside of the criminal field, this common interest rationale is not in itself sufficient to support the existence of a 'substantial connection'. Systemically, reliance solely on the universality principle would also be problematic because it would effectively remove the need to demonstrate any specific connection between a state and the broad range of non-criminal conduct contributing to climate change. This would seriously undermine the competence delineation function of the law of state jurisdiction, and therefore cannot be accepted here. For these reasons, as illustrated by the first (lowest) level of Figure 8.2, universality provides only a baseline for state interests in climate protection.

Figure 8.2 Constructing the substantial connection requirement for 'extraterritorial' climate-related trade measures

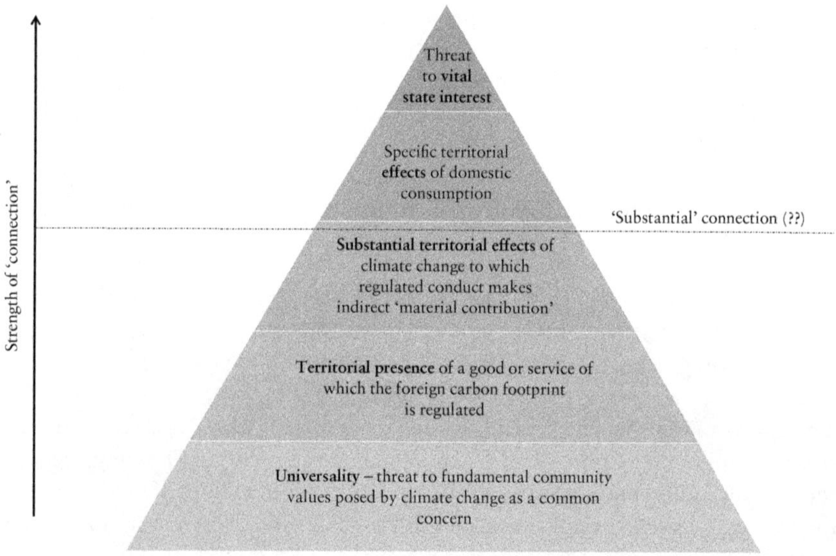

Unilateral climate protection measures with an extraterritorial element typically seek to regulate the foreign carbon footprint of goods or services eventually present on the territory of the regulating state. This territorial presence is then a second connecting factor, providing an indirect link between the state and the production process regulated, even where the process leaves no physical trace in the end product.[128] At a macro level it is domestic demand that triggers the production process, and thus the GHG emissions, in the first place. However, while this may explain a regulator's motive in exercising jurisdiction, the physical presence of the end product or service is primarily a matter of enforcement

[128] See chapter 4 for further discussion on production and process under world trade law.

rather than prescriptive jurisdiction, and this alone cannot justify the intended incentivising effects on the prior conduct of foreign producers. The economic link formed by domestic demand is therefore relevant, but insufficient to independently justify a 'substantial connection' between the state and the production process.

Where production processes *do* leave a physical trace in the end product (causing effects upon consumption), the jurisdictional link is further strengthened by related domestic consumption externalities. As discussed in section 3, this is likely to occur for measures targeting several GHGs with more than one objective, such as air quality, public health and climate protection under the EU Fuel Quality Directive. The direct territorial effects caused by domestic consumption are supported by a combination of the territoriality and the effects principles. This embedding of climate protection amongst other regulatory concerns will tip the scale for most jurisdictional claims (see the fourth level of Figure 8.2).

One of the most important connecting factors for climate protection measures is the existence of substantial territorial effects of climate change more generally (see the third level of Figure 8.2). To rely on this element, a state must be able to demonstrate that the conduct regulated has some causal relationship with the effects in question. As discussed in section 4.2, a possible application of this requirement incorporates a precautionary approach whereby, based on consistent scientific evidence, a state must demonstrate that the conduct measurably contributes to an increase in the risk of reasonably foreseeable grave harm. While this threshold is admittedly difficult to define, it is suggested that both quantitative and qualitative factors may be considered, where the role of others in overriding the marginal benefits of the regulation is not relevant.

Given the non-linear causation between GHG-emitting activities and climate change, it is debatable whether effects alone may be sufficient to justify jurisdictional assertions. From a systemic perspective, this approach poses the same 'floodgates' risk as the universality principle, with the global effects then serving to justify a great many climate-related measures over a broad range of industrial activities in other states. On the other hand, the effects are substantial and foreseeable, and states have a legitimate interest in prescribing mitigation far-reaching measures. Rejecting effects-based jurisdiction fundamentally undermines states' sovereign right to protect their territory. Rather, to remedy the risk of regulatory overcrowding, jurisdictional *limitations* become very important. As will be seen in the following chapter, these pertain to the conditions on whether and how states actually exercise their jurisdictional rights.

Where states can demonstrate that climate change poses an immediate threat to vital national interests such as territorial integrity and national security, the protective principle may provide valuable evidence of a substantial connection. As with the effects-doctrine, it seems logical that states must also be able to demonstrate that the regulated GHG-emitting activities make a 'measurable contribution' to climate change. Unlike the effects-doctrine, however, the protective principle does not require that concrete effects have already occurred (or started).

While this may provide for a somewhat broader prescriptive scope, in practice it is likely that states will be able to demonstrate the territorial effects of climate change already. The sea level is measurably rising, the seasons are measurably more extreme in temperature and there is a visible increase in extreme weather conditions.[129] The added value of the protective principle would then lie in the weight it adds to the strength of a state's substantial connection in that case (see the fifth level of Figure 8.2). As it refers to (an aspect of) the severity of specific effects, successful protection-based arguments may buttress effects-based claims, possibly even lowering the threshold for causation.

What, then, does all this mean for the EU's unilateral climate-related trade measures? Generally speaking, the EU can draw some 'baseline' support from the universality principle, as well as the territorial presence of goods and services regulated by its trade measures. However, this alone is not enough. What would arguably tip the scale is the presence of substantial territorial effects caused by climate change, to which the regulated subject matter makes a measurable contribution. With extreme weather conditions, rising sea levels and increased rainfall causing problems throughout the EU,[130] a plausible case can be made for regulating serious GHG-emitting activities such as international aviation and maritime transport, biofuel sourcing, and the production and consumption of energy-related products. These measures should, of course, be capable of achieving the desired GHG reductions. Although the final determination will always be dependent on the circumstances of the case, it is argued here that the EU can typically claim a 'substantial connection' to the conduct it seeks to regulate.

Clearly, this approach creates quite a broad 'basis' for unilateral 'extra-territorial' climate change jurisdiction. That being said, it does not create a carte blanche for all climate-related *measures*. The *design* of such measures remains conditioned by the specific regimes such as those discussed in part III. Furthermore, and importantly, general international law also has a role to play in conditioning how (and possibly whether) such jurisdiction is actually exercised. This essential next step will now be explored further in part V of this book.

[129] For further analysis, see eg Global Risks Report 2020 (n 62) 30.

[130] This has been signalled for some time now, see eg European Environment Agency, 'Climate Change Evident across Europe, Confirming Urgent Need for Adaptation' (Europa website, 19 November 2012) www.eea.europa.eu/subscription/eea_main_subscription/climate-change-evident-across-europe/view.

Part IV

Jurisdictional Limitations and ‘Considerate Design’

9

Jurisdictional Limitations: The 'Considerate Design' Approach

Comity is an amorphous never-never land whose borders are marked by fuzzy lines of politics, courtesy and good faith. (H Maier*)

1. INTRODUCTION

THE PREVIOUS CHAPTER has considered the application of the classic jurisdictional principles to unilateral climate protection measures. In light of the global effects of climate change and interconnected markets in goods and services it is very plausible that more than one state will be able to demonstrate a 'substantial connection' to particular conduct or circumstances. Situations of concurrent jurisdiction then arise. This may be problematic, as even when jurisdictional assertions are not in direct conflict, they may result in overregulation of specific fields.[1] In addition, unilateral measures with an extraterritorial element have a tendency to infringe on the sovereignty of other equal states.[2] Although there is a general consensus that states must respect the rights of other states likely to be affected by their actions, there is very little clarity on how this fundamental premise translates more concretely in a jurisdictional context. Such consideration of foreign interests is essentially a form of interest-balancing which, in the literature, is often referred to as a question of 'reasonableness'.[3] Once again, however, this term is a debated one and, for

* H Maier, 'Extraterritorial Jurisdiction at a Crossroads: The Intersection Between Public and Private International Law' (1982) 76 *American Journal of International Law* 280, 281.

[1] For the economics-oriented perspective on the optimal level of regulation, see JP Trachtman, 'Externalities and Extraterritoriality, the Law and Economics of Prescriptive Jurisdiction' in J Bhandari and A Sykes (eds), *Economic Dimensions in International Law: Comparative and Empirical Perspectives* (Cambridge, Cambridge University Press, 1997) 642; C Ryngaert, *Jurisdiction in International Law*, 2nd edn (Oxford, Oxford University Press, 2015) 185.

[2] On externalities in the horizontal jurisdictional relationship between states, see further JP Trachtman, 'Trade and … Problems, Cost-Benefit Analysis and Subsidiarity' (1998) 9 *European Journal of International Law* 32, 43.

[3] See eg AF Lowenfeld, 'Sovereignty, Jurisdiction, and Reasonableness: A Reply to A. V. Lowe' (1981) 75 *American Journal of International Law* 629; BJ Gans, 'Reasonableness as a Limit to Extraterritorial Jurisdiction' (1985) 62 *Washington University Law Quarterly* 681; HG Maier, 'Interest Balancing and Extraterritorial Jurisdiction' (1983) 31 *American Journal of Comparative Law*, 579.

reasons of clarity, this chapter will focus on jurisdictional limitations or conditions more generally.

At the core of the discussion on jurisdictional limitations is the question of whether states have an obligation to exercise self-restraint as a matter of binding international law, and if so, what the sources of this obligation may be. Whereas most would accept that state jurisdiction is limited by conditions on sovereignty more generally, there is very little agreement on how principles such as sovereign equality and non-intervention may then be operationalised in relation to prescriptive acts. Going a step further, others have suggested that justice-oriented norms, in particular good faith, non-abuse of rights and equity may have a limiting role as they regulate the way in which states exercise their rights more broadly.[4] Here too, however, questions of application arise, although the case law of international tribunals in related fields may offer valuable inspiration.

This chapter seeks to explore these issues in more detail in order to formulate a framework for the analysis of jurisdictional limitations in custom and general principles of international law. In doing so, section 2 first explains the need for a limitations analysis as a second-order inquiry, subsequent to the establishment of a substantial connection. Section 3 then turns to the Third and Fourth Restatements of the Foreign Relations Law of the United States ('the US Third and Fourth Restatements'), which contain valuable discussion on the extent to which states must consider the interests of other states when exercising jurisdiction.[5] As a source of legal discourse, these Restatements of the American Law Institute offer a perspective on international law 'as it applies to the United States', although the Fourth Restatement stresses that it 'seeks to distinguish clearly between rules of US domestic law and rules of international law'.[6]

Section 4 considers the sources of jurisdictional conditions under international law, and explores their possible operationalisation. In doing so, it distinguishes between 'negative' conditions which restrain prescriptive jurisdiction, and positive conditions which require states to facilitate or ensure certain 'justice' considerations. Based on these findings, section 5 then proposes a regulatory tool for the analysis of jurisdictional limitations, both in general and in relation to climate change measures more specifically. It is argued that, in a prescriptive context, these principles have more value in relation to the *design*

[4] See further eg Ryngaert (n 1) 157; M Akehurst, 'Jurisdiction in International Law' (1973) 46 *British Yearbook of International Law* 145, 189.

[5] *Restatement (Third) of the Foreign Relations Law of the United States* (St Paul, MN, American Law Institute Publishers, 1987) ('US Third Restatement'); *Restatement (Fourth) of the Foreign Relations Law of the United States* (St Paul, MN, American Law Institute Publishers, 2018) ('US Fourth Restatement'). This discussion partly reproduces and builds upon the author's contribution in NL Dobson, 'Reflections on 'Reasonableness' in the Restatement (Fourth) of US Foreign Relations Law' (2019) 62 *Questions of International Law Zoom-In* 19.

[6] See W Dodge, 'Jurisdiction in the Fourth Restatement of Foreign Relations Law' (2016/2017) 18 *Yearbook of Private International Law* 143, 145.

of a measure, rather than as a means of determining whether or not jurisdiction should be exercised in cases of conflict. Drawing together the explorative conclusions, a rule of 'considerate design' is then proposed, which may assist legislatures in avoiding or reducing conflict at the outset when drafting legislation.

2. JURISDICTIONAL LIMITATIONS AS A SECOND-ORDER INQUIRY

As alluded to in chapter 7, there are different schools of thought regarding the stage of the jurisdictional analysis in which the interests of other states should be considered as a possible limitation of state competence.[7] On one view, issues of 'reasonableness' or interest-balancing primarily come into play when establishing a 'substantial connection', and thus in relation to the existence of jurisdiction itself. Crawford, for example, constructs the requirement as a 'genuine connection between the subject-matter of jurisdiction and the territorial base and *reasonable interest* of the state in question'.[8] Similarly, Jennings and Watts formulate the substantial connection threshold as a 'sufficiently close connection to justify that state in regulating the matter and perhaps also to override any competing rights of other states'.[9] While this latter definition does not mention reasonableness explicitly, it integrates a hierarchy of interests into the question of whether a state can demonstrate a substantial connection to the subject matter.

This chapter takes a different approach, considering jurisdictional limitations as a second-order inquiry, after it has been established that a state can demonstrate a prima facie valid basis for its jurisdictional assertion. It is argued here that these two questions speak to different regulatory issues which should be addressed separately. The substantial connection requirement bears upon the competence to act, and is concerned with the substance and strength of the nexus between the *acting* state and the regulated subject matter. Where a state can demonstrate such a connection, it has, in principle, a jurisdictional right. The exercise of this right is subsequently conditioned by the interests of *other* equal states and the international community. In practical terms, this comes down to the *means* with which a state regulates the subject matter, and its choice of whether and how to exercise its right. After all, particularly in cases of common concerns such as climate change, tensions do not so much arise out of disagreements as to the ends, but rather from the fact that one state seeks to impose the design of its 'solution' on foreign actors which also have an interest in the situation. In practice, it is often this issue that determines whether

[7] See further chapter 7, section 3.

[8] J Crawford, *Brownlie's Principles of Public International Law*, 8th edn (Oxford, Oxford University Press, 2012) 456–57 (emphasis added). See also FA Mann, 'The Doctrine of International Jurisdiction Revisited After Twenty Years' (1984) 186 *Recueil des Cours* 9, 29.

[9] R Jennings and A Watts, *Oppenheim's International Law*, 9th edn (Oxford, Oxford University Press, 1992) 456–58.

one state infringes the sovereignty of another. It is furthermore of particular relevance in cases of concurrent jurisdiction, where states may overburden individuals subjected to multiple regulations.[10]

Devoting an independent assessment to the appropriateness of the means further increases the legal clarity on how states can best achieve their desired regulatory objectives. Depending on the circumstances of the case, it may well be possible to fine-tune the design of a measure so as to ensure respect for affected interests. A wholesale rejection of the measure as lacking a jurisdictional basis detracts from states' and law's flexibility in this regard.

Proceeding from this premise, section 3 will now consider the ongoing debate regarding the sources of jurisdictional restraint as 'second-order' jurisdictional limitations.

3. THE SOURCES OF JURISDICTIONAL RESTRAINT: CUSTOM, COMITY AND GENERAL PRINCIPLES

In his Separate Opinion to the *Barcelona Traction* case, Judge Fitzmaurice noted that:

> [U]nder present conditions, international law does not impose hard and fast rules on States delimiting spheres of national jurisdiction. … It does however … involve for every State an obligation to exercise *moderation and restraint* as to the extent of the jurisdiction assumed by its courts in cases having a foreign element, and to avoid *undue encroachment* on a jurisdiction *more properly appertaining to*, or *more appropriately exercisable by another State*'.[11]

To date, this is one of the only cases where a judge on an international tribunal has clearly addressed the question of whether the consideration of other states' interests constitutes an international obligation. While in 1970, Justice Fitzmaurice may have answered this in the affirmative, over the past decades there has been much discussion on whether states have a *legal* obligation to respect other states' interests, or whether this is in fact adhered to out of discretion as a matter of comity.

The evolution of this discussion is particularly clear when comparing the US Third and Fourth Restatements of Foreign Relations Law.[12] Not only do these documents offer a uniquely comprehensive analysis of this topic, they also illustrate a striking transition in perspective on the legal nature and operationalisation of jurisdictional interest-balancing. Where the 1987 Third Restatement contained an extensive second-order 'rule-of-reason' which it asserted to be

[10] See further Ryngaert (n 1) 185; Trachtman (n 1) 643.

[11] *Barcelona Traction, Light and Power Co Ltd* (Belgium v Spain) [1970] ICJ Rep 3, 105 (*Barcelona Traction* case), Separate Opinion, Judge Fitzmaurice (emphasis added).

[12] US Third Restatement (n 5) §403; US Fourth Restatement (n 5), see in particular Reporters' Note 13 to §402, discussed further below.

customary law, the 2018 Fourth Restatement considers second-order interest-balancing primarily a question of comity.[13]

As will now be discussed, however, neither approach is preferred here. In practice, there is a complex interaction between law and comity, where comity is informed by general principles of international law. Not only does this find support in both state practice and the literature, it is also intrinsic to the very rationale of the comity principles, well accepted in domestic legal orders. In order to identify the role of international law in limiting jurisdictional competence, section 3.1 will first examine the short-lived trajectory of the rule-of-reason as a purported norm of customary international law. Section 3.2 will then consider the remaining drivers of jurisdictional restraint, analysing the comity-oriented formulation of reasonableness in the US Fourth Restatement, and the underlying role for general principles of international law.

3.1. A Change of Course for 'Reasonableness' under the Fourth Restatement of US Foreign Relations Law

There is a good reason why the US Restatements contain some of the most comprehensive discussions on the notion of jurisdictional reasonableness. It was namely there that the rise of the controversial effects-based jurisdiction sparked much international criticism for failing to take into account foreign interests.[14] As discussed in chapter 7, the original *Alcoa* 'effects' doctrine did not specify a threshold for the degree of effects on US commerce legitimising jurisdiction; it was applied inconsistently by US courts and received much international criticism for a perceived failure to take into account foreign interests.[15] Responding to international protest, in 1958 commentator Kingman Brewster proposed an adapted approach to antitrust jurisdiction in which foreign interests were considered through a 'jurisdictional rule of reason'.[16]

National case law initially appeared receptive to this approach. Thus in the 1976 *Timberlane I* case, the US Court of Appeals for the Ninth Circuit

[13] Third Restatement (n 5) §403, comment a; Fourth Restatement (n 5) §407, Reporters' Note 6.

[14] On the controversial development of the effects-doctrine, see further DL Hacking, 'The Increasing Extraterritorial Impact of US Laws: A Cause for Concern Amongst Friends of America' (1979) 1 *Northwestern Journal of International Law & Business* 1.

[15] *United States v Aluminum Corp of America*, 148 F 2d 416 443 (2nd Cir 1945) (*Alcoa*). On the controversial development of the effects-doctrine, see further DL Hacking, 'The Increasing Extraterritorial Impact of US Laws: A Cause for Concern Amongst Friends of America' (1979) 1 *Northwestern Journal of International Law & Business* (1979) 1. See further eg P Zagalis, 'Hartford Fire Insurance Company v California: Reassessing the Application of the McCarran–Ferguson Act to Foreign Reinsurers' (1994) 27 *Cornell International Law Journal* 241, 250; C Ryngaert, *Jurisdiction over Antitrust Violations in International Law* (Antwerp, Intersentia, 2008).

[16] JR Atwood and K Brewster, *Antitrust and American Business Abroad* (Colorado Springs, Shepard's/McGraw-Hill, 1958) 301–08. See also EL Gilioli, 'Defining Jurisdictional Limits in International Antitrust: Should the EEC Adopt the Timberlane Approach?' (1981) 5 *Fordham International Law Journal* 469, 483.

sought to remedy the 'incomplete' nature of the effects-doctrine, by introducing the consideration of foreign interests.[17] The case concerned the alleged conspiracy by the Bank of America and its Honduran subsidiaries to prevent the American lumber company, Timberlane, from successfully exporting its lumber from Honduras to the United States.[18] Here the Court inquired into 'whether the interests of, and links to, the United States – including the magnitude of the effect on American foreign commerce – are sufficiently strong, vis-à-vis those of other nations, to justify an assertion of extraterritorial authority'.[19] According to the Court, this depended on a number of factors including the 'degree of conflict with foreign law or policy', 'the relative significance of the effects on the United States as compared with those elsewhere' and 'the relative importance to the violations charged of conduct within the United States as compared with conduct abroad'.[20] Based on these criteria, the District Court found on remand in *Timberlane II* that the United States should abstain from exercising jurisdiction.[21] Shortly after, in 1979, the Third Circuit in *Mannington Mills* developed the interest-balancing considerations even further.[22] Rather than applying the *Timberlane* test to the question of whether subject-matter jurisdiction existed, the Court applied the criteria as a second-level inquiry into whether the state should abstain from exercising jurisdiction.[23]

These cases clearly influenced the drafting of the US Third Restatement, §403 of which incorporated these factors into an extensive interest-balancing test to determine '[w]hether an exercise of jurisdiction over a person or activity is unreasonable'.[24] Importantly, while inspired by antitrust law, the provision claims to represent a requirement of customary international law applicable fields.[25] As noted by commentators, however, the basis for this claim was already

[17] *Timberlane Lumber Co v Bank of America (Timberlane I* case), 549 F.2d 597 (9th Cir 1976) *remanded*, 574 F Supp 1453 (ND Cal 1983). Judge Choy noted that the 'effects test' was 'by itself … incomplete because it fails to consider other nations' interests' (611–12).

[18] ibid 603–05.

[19] ibid.

[20] ibid 614.

[21] For further analysis, see SA Kadish, 'Comity and the International Application of the Sherman Act: Encouraging the Courts to Enter the Political Arena' (1982) 4 *Northwestern Journal of International Law & Business* 130, 154.

[22] *Mannington Mills, Inc v Congoleum Corp* (*Mannington Mills*) 595 F.2d 1287 (3d Cir 1979).

[23] For further discussion on these different approaches, see Kadish (n 21) 171; JW Ongman, 'Be No Longer a Chaos: Constructing a Normative Theory of the Sherman Act's Extraterritorial Jurisdictional Scope' (1976) 71 *Northwestern University Law Review* 733, 742.

[24] US Third Restatement (n 5) §403; Professor Lowenfeld's support for the 'Timberlane test' in his 1979 Hague Lecture suggests that the case clearly influenced his drafting of the Restatement, published in 1987. AF Lowenfeld, 'Public Law in the International Arena: Conflict of Laws, International Law, and Some Suggestions for Their Interaction' (1979) 163 *Recueil des Cours de l'Académie de Droit International de la Haye* 311, 411.

[25] See US 3rd Restatement (n 5) §403, comment a: 'The principle … has emerged as a principle of international law as well. … Some United States courts have applied the principle of reasonableness as a requirement of comity … This section states the principle of reasonableness as a rule of international law.'

quite thin.[26] Matters got worse when subsequent practice of US courts did not embrace the enthusiasm of the drafters. This was particularly clear in the 1984 *Laker Airways* case, which went head-on against the *Timberlane* reasonableness analysis, stating that 'there is no evidence that interest-balancing represents a rule of international law'.[27]

The findings in *Laker Airways* laid the foundation for a definitive change of course by the US Supreme Court in *Hartford Fire Insurance v California*.[28] The US Supreme Court did consider §403(3) of the US Third Restatement to determine whether it had jurisdiction over a UK reinsurance cartel allegedly violating the Sherman Act. However, it found that 'the only substantial question here is whether "there is in fact a true conflict between domestic and foreign law"'.[29] This would not be the case 'where a person subject to regulation by two states can comply with the laws of both'. The Court then referred to the Comment to §415 of the US Third Restatement, which provides that 'the fact that conduct is lawful in the state in which it took place will not, of itself, bar application of the United States antitrust laws, even where the foreign state has a strong policy to permit or encourage such conduct'.[30] This narrow focus on the existence of a 'true conflict' overtly disregards the policy considerations of foreign states and seems to directly contradict the comity considerations envisaged by *Timberlane*.

Writing what was to become an important dissenting view, Justice Scalia disagreed with the majority's focus on the conflict-of-law issue. In doing so he drew a distinction between 'adjudicative comity', which he defined as the possibility for judges to abstain from exercising jurisdiction, and 'prescriptive comity', which is 'the respect sovereign nations afford each other by limiting the reach of their laws'.[31] Justice Scalia noted that 'the Court's comity analysis, which proceeds as though the issue is whether the courts should "decline to exercise ... jurisdiction," ... rather than whether the Sherman Act covers this conduct, is simply misdirected'.[32] This distinction between prescriptive and adjudicative comity greatly informed the US Fourth Restatement, and will be discussed further below.

Notably in *Hoffman-La Roche v Empagran*, the US Supreme Court appeared somewhat to revive §403's reasonableness requirement, holding that it 'ordinarily construes ambiguous statutes to avoid unreasonable interference with the

[26] See eg Ryngaert (n 1) 154, noting that the only source referred to for this statement is the German *Kammergericht* decision *Philip Morris/Rothmans*, Decision of 1 July, 1983, Kart 16/82. See also Dodge (n 6) 152.

[27] *Laker Airways* 731 F.2d 909, 950 (DC Cir 1984). See also *In re Uranium Antitrust Litigation*, 480 F Supp 1138, 1148 (ND Ill 1979) and *In re Uranium Antitrust Litigation* (*Re Uranium*), 617 F.2d 1248, 1255, §63,183 (7th Cir 1980).

[28] *Hartford Fire Insurance Co v California* (*Hartford Fire*) 509 US 764 (1993).

[29] ibid 799.

[30] ibid 799; US Third Restatement (n 5) §415, Comment J.

[31] ibid 817. For further analysis, see Zagalis (n 15) 260.

[32] *Hartford Fire* case (n 28) 820.

sovereign authority of other nations'.[33] Explicitly referring to §403, it went on to state that 'this rule of construction reflects principles of customary international law – law that (we must assume) Congress ordinarily seeks to follow'. As such, legislators are 'cautioned' to 'take account of the legitimate sovereign interests of other nations when they write American laws'. The constriction 'thereby helps the potentially conflicting laws of different nations work together in harmony – a harmony particularly needed in today's highly interdependent commercial world'.[34] However, while acknowledging that 'America's antitrust laws, when applied to foreign conduct, can interfere with a foreign nation's ability independently to regulate its own commercial affairs', the Court considered that 'application of our antitrust laws to foreign anticompetitive conduct is nonetheless reasonable, and hence consistent with principles of prescriptive comity, insofar as they reflect a legislative effort to redress domestic antitrust injury that foreign anticompetitive conduct has caused'.[35] This last passage arguably does away with interest-balancing altogether.[36]

As authoritatively observed by William Dodge, co-reporter for the US Fourth Restatement, these judgments illustrate a moving away from the 'rule-of-reason' in US case law, which now favours a revived presumption against extraterritoriality 'as a framework for analysing extraterritoriality issues'.[37] Indeed, responding to these developments, the US Fourth Restatement then adopts a very different approach to reasonableness compared to its predecessor. To start with, the Restatement 'gives effect to the principle of reasonableness by requiring a genuine connection between the subject of the regulation and the state seeking to regulate'.[38] At the same time it notes that 'states often seek to reduce conflicts of prescriptive jurisdiction through various rules of domestic law that are often motivated by international comity but not required by international law'.[39]

This new approach is based on the view that on the one hand, 'reasonableness in the sense of showing a genuine connection' constitutes 'an important touchstone' of international law.[40] On the other hand, there is insufficient state practice to support a legal requirement of 'case-by-case balancing to establish reasonableness'.[41] Compositely, comment c to §407 notes that international

[33] *F Hoffmann-La Roche Ltd et al v Empagran SA et al* (*Empagran*) 542 US 155, 162 (2004).

[34] ibid. This was later construed by the Draft Fourth Restatement as an application of reasonableness as a form of prescriptive comity.

[35] ibid 165, referring to *Alcoa* (n 15) 444.

[36] See further S Burr, 'The Application of US Antitrust Law to Foreign Conduct: Has Hartford Fire Extinguished Considerations of Comity?' (1994) 70 *University of Pennsylvania Journal of International Law* 221, 233.

[37] See further Dodge (n 6) 150 referring in particular to *RJR Nabisco v European Community* (*RJR Nabisco*) 136 S Ct 2090 (2016).

[38] US Fourth Restatement (n 5) 407, Reporters' Note 6.

[39] ibid.

[40] ibid §407, Reporters' Note 3.

[41] Professor Dodge thus notes that the United States' approach to reasonableness is 'unilateral', seeking only to 'limit the reach of US law without regard to whether another State's law might

law poses no 'rules for assigning priority to competing jurisdictional claims'. Establishing reasonableness as a matter of international law is then not a second-order inquiry but a first-order question of identifying a jurisdictional basis. Further exercises of jurisdictional restraint reflect reasonableness as a matter of prescriptive comity.

An important 'reflection' of reasonableness in a US context is §402(2), which provides that '[i]n exercising jurisdiction to prescribe, the United States takes account of the legitimate interests of other nations as a matter of prescriptive comity'. Legislatures demonstrate prescriptive comity when they 'confine the scope of statutes to a greater extent than international law requires'.[42] Courts may notably do so too when they 'limit the geographical scope of a federal-common-law cause of action' and excuse legal compliance in line with the foreign state compulsion doctrine.[43] Of particular interest here is also that courts follow prescriptive comity when interpreting the law's geographical scope under the principles of interpretation in §404 (presumption against extraterritoriality) and §405 (reasonableness in interpretation).[44]

Throughout the Fourth Restatement, considerable emphasis is placed on the relationship between state practice and the formation of customary international law. Thus it is noted that 'state practice may contribute to the development and interpretation of customary international law if it is done out of a sense of legal right or obligation'.[45] Such practice must be contrasted with that done on the basis of 'international comity', which is defined as 'deference to foreign states that is *not* required by international law'.[46] As such, 'US practice restricting the geographical scope of US law as a matter of international comity is not evidence of what customary international law requires, because it is not followed from a sense of international legal obligation'.[47] It is questionable, however, whether this does not go too far in the opposite direction, largely denying a limiting role for international law. This will now be discussed further in section 3.2.

also apply'. See W Dodge, 'Jurisdictional Reasonableness under Customary International Law: The Approach of the Restatement (Fourth) of US Foreign Relations Law' (2019) 62 *Questions of International Law* 5, 16.

[42] ibid §402, Reporters' Note 3.

[43] ibid.

[44] ibid. The return of the presumption against extraterritoriality, which had been omitted from the Third Restatement in lieu of §403, was confirmed in the 2016 case *RJR Nabisco*, where the US Supreme Court unanimously approved a two-step approach to interpreting the geographical scope of federal legislation. *RJR Nabisco* (n 37) 2101. See further, US Fourth Restatement (n 5) §404, Reporters' Note 1 & 2.

[45] ibid §401, Reporters' Note 2.

[46] ibid Chapter 1: Prescription, Introduction, 147.

[47] ibid §402, Reporters' Note 3. On the nature and role of international comity, see further W Dodge, 'International Comity in a Comparative Perspective' in C Bradley (ed), *The Oxford Handbook of Comparative Foreign Relations Law* (Oxford, Oxford University Press, 2019) 701.

3.2. The Role of International Law in Conditioning Unilateral Jurisdiction

Given the tenuous basis of the US Third Restatement's 'rule of reason', it is understandable that the Fourth Restatement places considerable emphasis on the formation of customary rules of jurisdictional restraint under international law.[48] As suggested by Dodge, §403 of the Third Restatement perhaps offered an opportunity for international acceptance rather than a confirmation of it.[49] It is argued here, however, that more attention is needed for the opposite dynamic, namely the role of customary rules in (in)forming comity. In light of the interaction between international law and comity, it is questionable whether one can establish such a defined boundary between acts committed out of a sense of obligation and acts committed voluntarily.

That international law has a limiting role to play comes down to the nature of jurisdiction as an exercise of sovereignty. As noted by Oxman, while the 'power to take action derives from sovereign independence', its 'scope and exercise' is 'circumscribed' by sovereign equality.[50] By logical implication, where a jurisdictional assertion may interfere with the legitimate sovereign interests of other states, this principle requires that consideration be given to these interests as a matter of international law. Also of relevance here are the principles of non-intervention and non-interference, which are derived from the *Grundnorm* of sovereign equality and serve to realise its protection.[51] Accepting this argument, there appears to be more to these sovereignty-conditioning principles than is reflected in the 'genuine connection' requirement alone, at least as the latter is defined in the US Fourth Restatement. Indeed §407 focuses only on the acting state, noting that '[t]he genuine connection usually rests on a specific connection between the state and the subject being regulated'.[52] Where, then, does this leave the binding sovereignty-conditioning principles, which undoubtedly remain applicable to jurisdictional acts?

It is argued here that, rather than mandating hard-and-fast customary rules of priority, these principles play an important role in informing the development of national comity rules. The interaction between law and comity is aptly described in the Canadian case *R v Hape*, concerning the extraterritorial application of section 8 of the Canadian Charter of Rights and Freedoms on protection against 'unreasonable search and seizure'.[53] While the extraterritorial application of human rights laws differs from the general rules of prescriptive

[48] Fourth Restatement (n 5) §401, Reporters' Note 1.

[49] See Dodge (n 41) 5–6.

[50] B Oxman, 'Jurisdiction of States' in R Wolfrum (ed), *Max Planck Encyclopaedia of Public International Law*, online edn (Oxford, Oxford University Press, 2007) [1].

[51] See further eg J Kokott, 'States, Sovereign Equality' in R Wolfrum (ed), *Max Planck Encyclopaedia of Public International Law*, online edn (Oxford, Oxford University Press, 2007) [1].

[52] US Fourth Restatement (n 5) §407, comment b.

[53] *R v Hape* 2007 SCC 26.

jurisdiction, the finding on the relationship between comity and binding legal principles is relevant in both contexts. In determining whether the Charter applied to searches and seizures carried out by Canadian authorities outside of Canada,[54] the majority judgment, given by Justice LeBel, held that as sovereign equality and its 'foundational principles' of non-intervention and respect for territorial sovereignty are binding upon all states, they 'must also be drawn upon in determining the scope of extraterritorial application of the Charter'.[55] Considering the 'nature and limitations of comity', Justice LeBel held that:

> [M]any rules of international law promote mutual respect and, conversely, courtesy among states requires that certain legal rules be followed. In this way, 'courtesy and international law lend reciprocal support to one another'. … The principle of comity reinforces sovereign equality and contributes to the functioning of the international legal system.[56]

As this case concerned enforcement jurisdiction, the interaction was quite clear. Based on comity, the Canadian officers could voluntarily participate in investigations abroad, but, based on the principles of sovereign equality and non-intervention, 'they must do so under the laws of the foreign state'.[57] Notably, Justice LeBel did consider prescriptive jurisdiction in the abstract, defining the 'real and substantial link' requirement as relative to competing claims.[58] According to the judgment, 'what constitutes a "real and substantial link" justifying jurisdiction may be "coterminous with the requirements of international comity"'.[59]

Much then comes down to how one defines international comity, and some would argue that it cannot be meaningfully separated from international law.[60] However, even if one were to sharply distinguish between these two categories, international law, as a separate body of norms, continues to apply. One could in fact consider *further* legal principles beyond those related to sovereign equality. Indeed, Ryngaert has noted that 'despite a dearth of State practice as to the application of the rule of reason' other 'general principles of international law' such as proportionality and abuse of rights 'may subsume more specific principles of jurisdiction that could inform a practice of jurisdictional restraint or reasonableness on the part of States'.[61]

An interesting case in this regard is *Glawischnig-Piesczek v Facebook Ireland Limited*, where the CJEU considered the permissibility of injunctions from EU

[54] ibid [24].

[55] ibid [46].

[56] ibid [48], [50] (references omitted).

[57] Although there may be exceptions when a state consents to the Charter's extraterritorial application. See ibid [99], [106], [112].

[58] ibid [62], referring to La Forest J noted in *Libman v The Queen*, [1985] 2 SCR 178, 213.

[59] ibid.

[60] For discussion, see Ryngaert (n 1) 147, noting that: 'Comity is widely believed to occupy a place between custom and customary international law.'

[61] Ryngaert (n 1) 181, 231.

Member State courts ordering data removal by host providers.[62] An aspect of this analysis was whether the Electronic Commerce Directive precluded injunction measures 'from producing effects worldwide'.[63] Given the absence of a territorial limitation in the relevant provision, 'with reference' also to the discretion left to EU Member States, the court found that the Directive did not.[64] 'However … in view of the global dimension of electronic commerce, the EU legislature considered it necessary to ensure that EU rules in that area are consistent with the rules applicable at an international level.'[65] Presumably by extension, it was left 'up to Member States to ensure that the measures which they adopt and which produce effects worldwide take due account of those rules'.[66] While the Court did not make specific reference to sovereignty-conditioning principles, it arguably left room for this, finding that the Directive permitted such injunctions 'within the framework of the relevant international law'.[67]

This then, however, leaves an evidentiary dilemma. It is very difficult to determine which part of an act of jurisdictional self-restraint is done on a voluntary basis and which is adhered to as a matter of law.[68] Consequently, acts of self-restraint are likely to reflect both. An important catalyst when considering the influence of binding norms on state practice is the doctrine of consistent interpretation with international law. As noted by the International Law Association, this is a well-accepted principle in a 'significant number' of other national and supranational legal orders, including, for example, Germany (*Völkerrechtsfreundlichkeit*), Switzerland (*Schubert–Praxis*), Australia (principle of consistent interpretation) and the EU (principle of consistent interpretation of EU law with international obligations).[69] The principle can also be found in §406 of the Fourth Restatement on 'Interpretation Consistent with International Law'.

The effect of this interpretative rule and other comity principles is to blur the distinction between voluntary acts and those done out of a sense of obligation. This inevitably affects state practice over time. It then cannot be said with certainty that when states restrict the geographic scope of their laws, despite having a genuine connection to the regulated subject matter, this is done purely on a voluntary basis. As such, it is argued that there remains a 'core' of international law that may be effectuated and built upon by international comity.

[62] Case C-18/18 *Eva Glawischnig-Piesczek v Facebook Ireland Limited* [2019] ECLI:EU:C:2019:821.
[63] ibid [21].
[64] ibid [49], [29].
[65] ibid [51].
[66] ibid [49], [52].
[67] ibid [53].
[68] See further on the hurdles of identifying opinio juris for legitimate jurisdictional assertions, Harvard Draft Convention on Jurisdiction with Respect to Crime (1935) 29 *American Journal of International Law Supplement, Research in International Law Parts I & II* 439; Ryngaert (n 1) 42.
[69] For further detail, see A Tzanakopoulos, 'Principles on the Engagement of Domestic Courts with International Law' (International Law Association Preliminary Report, 2012) 8. The principle of 'conformity with international law' was also discussed extensively in *R v Hape* (n 53) 53.

Admittedly, however, there remains very little clarity on how this core should be defined. This question will now be elaborated upon further in section 4.

4. EXPLORING THE CONDITIONS ON JURISDICTIONAL DESIGN UNDER INTERNATIONAL LAW

In setting out the analytic framework, the present study advocates for a clear division between conditions on prescriptive and adjudicative jurisdiction. This builds on the conceptual distinction found in the US Fourth Restatement between prescriptive and adjudicative comity. As discussed in section 3, the US Fourth Restatement defines prescriptive comity as pertaining to the geographic scope of a measure, while adjudicative comity pertains to the choice of whether or not to apply a state's law in a certain case. Notably, the latter will largely be a matter of domestic or international private law, where comity both informs and complements conflict-of-laws rules.[70] Due to the interplay between comity and binding international law, it is argued here that the 'prescriptive/adjudicative' distinction can and should be applied to limitations stemming both from both law and comity. Furthermore, as the legal principles at issue concern more than merely a measure's geographic scope, it is submitted that the category of 'prescriptive limitations' should be seen as bearing upon a measure's design as a whole.

In line with this book's focus on prescriptive jurisdiction, the remainder of this chapter will focus on 'prescriptive' limitations. Here a distinction is drawn between positive and negative conditions. Negative conditions serve as limitations to the design of a unilateral measure, requiring *deference* to other states' interests. These are discussed further in section 4.1. Positive conditions set requirements on how a measure should be designed in order to better realise just outcomes, and are explored in section 4.2.

4.1. Limitations on Sovereignty as Negative Jurisdictional Conditions

This section explores the possible operationalisation of 'negative' conditions on prescriptive jurisdiction, requiring deference to other states' interests. In doing so, section 4.1.1 first considers the principles of non-intervention and non-interference, which it is argued pose outer limits on states' prescriptive

[70] KM Meessen, 'Conflicts of Jurisdiction under the New Restatement' (1987) 50 *Law and Contemporary Problems* 47, 59: 'the international law of jurisdiction establishes a mere minimum standard that sets outer limits within which national conflicts law may provide for optimum solutions from a domestic perspective'. See eg in an EU context, Parliament and Council (EC) Regulation No 593/2008 on the Law Applicable to Contractual Obligations (Rome I) [2008] OJ L177, and Parliament and Council (EC) Regulation (EC) No 864/2007 on the Law Applicable to Non-Contractual Obligations (Rome II) [2007] OJ L199.

competence, counselling against measures that severely encroach on the regulatory freedom of other states. Section 4.1.2 then turns to the principle of sovereign equality, arguably informing a more general requirement of self-restraint.

4.1.1. Non-intervention and Non-interference

On the outer end of the spectrum of jurisdictional restraint, the principles of non-intervention or non-interference have been raised as possible grounds for a state to refrain from taking measures out of respect for other states. These two concepts are not always consistently distinguished in the literature, with some considering interference to constitute a type of intervention, while others do not.[71] As one of the first to apply the former in a jurisdictional context, in his 1984 contribution in the field of antitrust, Meessen argued that relevant case law evidenced an 'obligation to pay respect to prevailing interests of foreign states'.[72] This he formulated as the balancing rule of 'noninterference', whereby 'a state is prohibited from taking measures of antitrust law if the regulatory interests it is pursuing are outweighed by the interests of one or more foreign states likely to be seriously injured by those measures'.[73] The aim of this rule is to 'prohibit interference with the sovereignty of foreign states, ie, exercising influence short of intervention'.[74]

Building on Meessen's contribution, Ryngaert applies the same threshold to the principle of non-intervention.[75] This well-established principle was defined by the ICJ in the *Nicaragua* case as prohibiting intervention

> bearing on matters in which each State is permitted, by the principle of State sovereignty, to decide freely. One of these is the choice of a political, economic, social and cultural system, and the formulation of foreign policy. Intervention is wrongful when it uses methods of coercion in regard to such choices, which must remain free ones.[76]

As noted by Kunig, however, as violations are frequently alleged and 'proclaimed under completely different circumstances', the 'exact meaning of the principle remains unclear'.[77] Ryngaert notes that the principle of non-intervention cannot have been intended to prohibit 'any jurisdictional assertion that reaches beyond

[71] See eg P Kunig, 'Intervention, Prohibition of', *Max Planck Encyclopaedia of Public International Law*, online edn (Oxford, Oxford University Press, 2008) [25]. See also 'Declaration on the Inadmissibility of Intervention and Interference in the Internal Affairs of States' (9 December 1981) A/RES/36/103, Art 2.

[72] KM Meessen, 'Antitrust Jurisdiction under Customary International Law' (1984) 78 *American Journal of International Law* 783, 784.

[73] ibid.

[74] ibid 804.

[75] Ryngaert (n 1) 155, referring to KM Meessen, *Völkerrechtliche Grundsätze des internationalen Kartellrechts* (1975) 191.

[76] *Case concerning Military and Paramilitary Activities In and Against Nicaragua (Nicaragua v United States of America)* (Merits) [1986] ICJ Rep 3 (*Nicaragua* case) [205].

[77] Kunig(n 71) [1].

a state's borders'. Both the permissive principles and the *Lotus* case make clear that states can, under certain conditions, prescribe laws with an extraterritorial reach. Rather, the principle may serve as a threshold which will only be met when 'the asserting State's interests in having its laws applied to a foreign situation outweigh the interests of another involved State'.[78] Nevertheless, it is questionable whether such an 'inherently vague interest-balancing test' confers 'sufficient legal certainty on international acts … regarding the permissibility of jurisdictional assertions'.[79] It thus 'remains to be seen whether there is sufficient evidence of interest-balancing being the internationally accepted method of ascertaining whether the principle of non-intervention is upheld'.[80]

Interestingly, in an EU context, the principle of non-intervention has been raised in the context of 'extraterritorial' jurisdiction on a number of occasions. In the older *Wood Pulp* and *Gencor* cases, non-interference was defined in terms of true conflict.[81] Turning first to *Wood Pulp*, the case concerned the territorial scope of Article 85 of the (old) EEC Treaty, which prohibited agreements and concerted practices with the object or effect of restricting competition within the Common Market.[82] According to the wood pulp producers, the application of Article 85 EEC to conduct outside the European Community violated international law.[83] In answer, the (then) European Court of Justice (ECJ) set out its 'implementation doctrine' discussed in Chapter 7.[84] The ECJ did note the argument that exercising jurisdiction conflicted with the principle of non-interference. This it defined narrowly,

> according to which where two States have jurisdiction to lay down and enforce rules and the effect of those rules is that a person finds himself subject to contradictory orders as to the conduct he must adopt, each State is obliged to exercise its jurisdiction with moderation.[85]

The Court then held that it did not need to 'enquire into the existence in international law of such a rule', as there was 'not, in this case, any contradiction between the conduct required by the United States and that required by the Community'.[86] Also of relevance was the absence of any objections regarding

[78] Ryngaert (n 1) 155.

[79] ibid.

[80] ibid 156.

[81] Case C-89/85 *A Ahlström Osakeyhtiö v Commission* (*Wood Pulp*) [1988] ECR 5193 [10], [15]; Case T-102/96 *Gencor Ltd v Commission of the European Communities* [1999] ECR II-753 [102]. See also the earlier case *Eastern Aluminium* (1985) OJ L92/37, 48, where the European Commission appeared to take a more accepting stance on comity, arguing that the European Community was precluded from exercising jurisdiction both in cases of true conflict, and when important interests of a third state, which outweighed those of the Community, would be affected.

[82] *Wood Pulp* (n 81) [11].

[83] ibid [15].

[84] ibid [16].

[85] ibid [19].

[86] ibid [20].

conflict of jurisdiction raised by US authorities when consulted by the European Commission.[87]

In addition, the ECJ rejected the argument of Canadian applicants that the principle of international comity been breached as result of the fines' infringement of Canada's sovereignty.[88] According to the ECJ, the argument 'amounts to calling in question the Community's jurisdiction to apply its competition rules to conduct such as that found to exist in this case'.[89] As such, the Court did not appear to distinguish between the basis for jurisdiction (implementation doctrine) and potential limitations arising from international comity. It did, however, leave open the possibility that non-interference may serve as a legal limitation to jurisdiction, should it be found applicable.

Just over a decade later, in the *Gencor* case, the (then) Court of First Instance (CFI) considered the territorial scope of the Merger Control Regulation (EEC) 4064/89.[90] The conflict arose pursuant to a European Commission finding of incompatibility with the Common Market of a concentration between Gencor and Lonrho, two South African platinum-mining companies. The CFI found the application of the Regulation justified according to public international law 'when it is foreseeable that a proposed concentration will have an immediate and substantial effect in the Community'. As discussed in chapter 7, this appears to be an earlier acceptance of the effects-doctrine, at least in the field of mergers.[91] Having established that the effects threshold had in fact been met, the CFI then turned to the question of 'whether the Community violated a principle of non-interference or the principle of proportionality in exercising that jurisdiction'.[92] Echoing the ECJ in *Wood Pulp*, the CFI refused to rule on the existence of a non-interference principle under international law, finding once again that this was unnecessary given the absence of a 'conflict between the course of action required by the South African Government and that required by the Community'.

Notably, in determining the threshold for 'conflict', the CFI was not convinced by an openly formulated letter from the South African competition authorities permitting the undertaking. Far from questioning the EC's jurisdiction, the letter

> *simply expressed a general preference*, having regard to the strategic importance of mineral exploitation in South Africa, for intervention in specific cases of collusion

[87] ibid [22].

[88] ibid [8], [22].

[89] ibid [22].

[90] *Gencor* case (n 81) [18]. See Council Regulation (EC) No 139/2004 of 20 January 2004 on the control of concentrations between undertakings [2004] OJ L24, Arts 2 and 3. The 2004 regulation repealed the Merger Regulation at issue in *Gencor*. See Council Regulation (EEC) No 4064/89 of 21 December 1989 on the control of concentrations between undertakings [1989] OJ L395.

[91] See further Ryngaert (n 15) 160.

[92] *Gencor* case (n 81) [102].

> when they arose and ... *merely expressed the view* that the proposed concentration might not impede competition.[93]

Having found no true conflict between the European Commission's exercise of jurisdiction and South African regulations, the CFI did, however, go on to note that

> neither the applicant nor, indeed, the South African Government in its letter of 19 April 1996 have shown, beyond making mere statements of principle, in what way the proposed concentration would affect the *vital economic and/or commercial interests of the Republic of South Africa*.[94]

This arguably leaves open the possibility that measures which do affect 'vital economic or commercial interests' may limit jurisdiction, either as a violation of the non-interference principle or otherwise. That being said, the interpretation of the 'true conflict' threshold remains very strict, where 'mere preferences' and exemptions which do not align with EU acts are considered insufficient, particularly in the absence of official objections. As noted in section 3.1, this strict approach to the 'true conflict' threshold also finds reflection in US case law, particularly *Hartford Fire*, where it was found that when 'a person subject to regulation by two states can comply with the laws of both', this threshold would not be met.[95]

In the more recent 2019 case *Google v Commission Nationale de l'Informatique et des Libertés (CNIL)*, the CJEU took a somewhat different course. As discussed in chapter 7, the case concerned the question of whether CNIL was correct in requiring Google, when granting a request from a national person for removal of information, to 'apply that removal to all its search engine's domain name extensions'.[96] Google argued that by interpreting its dereferencing obligation without a geographical limitation, 'CNIL disregarded the principles of courtesy and non-interference recognised by public international law'.[97] According to Google, this also 'disproportionately infringed the freedoms of expression, information, communication and the press guaranteed, in particular, by Article 11 of the Charter'.[98]

The CJEU found that in principle, the Union had jurisdiction based on the 'immediate and substantial effects' on persons within its territory.[99] However, it then went on to consider the regulatory choices of other states, 'emphasising' that 'numerous third States do not recognise the right to dereferencing or have a

[93] ibid [104] (emphasis added).
[94] ibid [105] (emphasis added).
[95] *Hartford Fire* (n 28) 799. Commentators have observed, however, that the approach in *Hartford Fire* is in fact an application, or even confusion, of the foreign state compulsion doctrine. See further eg Burr (n 63) 247; Ryngaert (n 15) 85.
[96] Case C-507/17 *Google v Commission Nationale de L'informatique et des Libertés* (*Google v CNIL)* [2019] ECR 772 [30].
[97] ibid [38].
[98] ibid.
[99] ibid [57], [59].

different approach to that right'.[100] It further noted that 'the right to the protection of personal data is not an absolute right', and must be balanced against other fundamental rights'.[101] According to the Court, 'the balance between the right to privacy and the protection of personal data, on the one hand, and the freedom of information of internet users, on the other, is likely to vary significantly around the world'.[102] Ryngaert and Taylor note that here

> the Court appears to apply the notion of jurisdictional reasonableness, pursuant to which, even if a state, or the EU, in principle has jurisdictional authority, it ought to exercise this authority reasonably and balance its own interests against the interests of other states.[103]

Importantly, however, interest-balancing alone was not determinative. Rather, the CJEU turned to the intent of the legislature, finding that it was 'in no way apparent' that for the purposes of ensuring a high level of personal data protection throughout the EU, 'the EU legislature would … have chosen to confer a scope on the rights enshrined in those provisions which would go beyond the territory of the Member States'.[104] This appears to be an application of the presumption against extraterritoriality, stepping away from 'reasonableness' *pur sang*.[105] While the CJEU does not explicitly mention non-interference, it appears to adopt a combined approach of both interest-balancing and legislative intent to implicitly engage with Google's argument.

As a final related observation, it is argued that the principles of non-interference and non-intervention may also counsel against measures which directly conflict with multilateral agreements. Like national legislation, multilateral agreements reflect the interests of other states, albeit through compromised decision-making. Indeed, one could even argue that multilateral agreements carry more weight, as they are the expression of the shared interest of multiple states. Individual actors subject to both unilateral and multilateral regulations will equally be unable to comply with both, raising the same concerns as strict conflict with individual states' measures. This will be discussed further in relation to the EU in chapter 10.

4.1.2. *Sovereign Equality*

Under international law, the fundamental principle balancing sovereign powers is that of sovereign equality. Enshrined in Article 2(1) of the UN Charter, this

[100] ibid [59].
[101] ibid [60].
[102] ibid.
[103] C Ryngaert and M Taylor, 'Implementing the Right to Erasure: The Judgment of the EU Court of Justice in Google v CNIL' (Renforce Blog, 8 October 2019) blog.renforce.eu/index.php/en/2019/10/08/implementing-the-right-to-erasure-the-judgment-of-the-eu-court-of-justice-in-google-v-cnil-2/.
[104] *Google v CNIL* [62].
[105] See further Ryngaert and Taylor (n 103).

principle seeks to guarantee independence between sovereign states, providing that all states have an equal legal voice, and that no state can claim jurisdiction over another.[106] Sovereign equality is an uncontested cornerstone of the law of state jurisdiction, where sovereignty acts as both a source and limitation of jurisdictional power. The inherently limited nature of individual sovereignty was clearly expressed by Judge Shahabuddeeen in his Dissenting Opinion to the *Nuclear Weapons* case Advisory Opinion, where he noted that:

> The existence of a number of sovereignties side by side places limits on the freedom of each State to act as if the others did not exist. ... It is difficult for the Court to uphold a proposition that, absent a prohibition, a State has a right in law to act in ways which could deprive the sovereignty of all other States of meaning.[107]

In a jurisdictional context, as noted by Meessen, sovereign equality entails the equal opportunity of states to pursue their desired regulatory objectives.[108] States' regulatory freedom is not only affected in dramatic circumstances of strict conflict, it can also be unduly restricted by broad jurisdictional assertions of other actors occupying the same regulatory space.[109] It is therefore submitted that sovereign equality requires of states a broader reciprocal respect for each other's regulatory spheres.

Accepting this conclusion, the question is then how the principle may manifest in a jurisdictional context. In her contribution on the seminal *Lotus* case, Hertogen provided one approach to this question.[110] According to the author, while territory has traditionally been a key indicator of the scope of a state's domestic affairs, this is 'too crude an instrument' to allocate prescriptive jurisdiction today.[111] To remedy this weakness, the author proposes a principle of 'locality', supplementing the traditional bases of jurisdiction in order to determine which state is 'better placed' to exercise jurisdiction in a particular case.[112] According to the locality principle, territorial effects are a prerequisite for prescriptive jurisdiction, while territorial presence alone may not be enough.[113] As such, territorial presence in the absence of effects will be insufficient to justify jurisdictional assertions.

[106] Charter of the United Nations (adopted 26 June 1945; entered into force 24 October 1945) UNTS XVI (UN Charter); Kokott (n 51) [2].

[107] Legality of the Threat or Use of Nuclear Weapons (Advisory Opinion) [1996] ICJ Rep 226 (*Nuclear Weapons* case) 393–94 (emphasis added, citations omitted), Dissenting Opinion of Judge Shahabuddeen.

[108] Meessen (n 72) 804.

[109] As noted by Justice Scalia in his Dissenting Opinion to *Hartford Fire*, the predominant conclusion that no 'true conflict' exists unless compliance with one state's law would violate another state's law is a 'breathtakingly broad proposition', which may result in 'sharp and unnecessary conflict with the legitimate interests of other countries – particularly our closest trading partners'. *Hartford Fire* case (n 28) 820.

[110] A Hertogen, 'Letting Lotus Bloom' (2016) 26 *European Journal of International Law* 901, 902.

[111] ibid 920.

[112] ibid.

[113] ibid 921.

Furthermore, only certain 'types' of effects 'on the domestic affairs of the state' may qualify under the locality principle.[114] Thus, while 'physical' and 'pecuniary' externalities may be considered, 'physiological' externalities should not. According to the author, this distinguishes the locality principle from the effects-doctrine, 'under which the presence of effects is enough for a state to exercise jurisdiction'.[115] Notably, however, there should be no de minimis threshold for the required effects, as this would limit states' sovereign right to decide 'whether the effects they are exposed to, however small, warrant a response'.[116]

Although certainly a valuable analysis of when a state may legitimately claim jurisdiction, it is questionable whether such a locality principle would always be capable of managing competing jurisdictional claims. It is submitted that the realisation of sovereign equality in a jurisdictional context does not necessarily require an additional principle that ranks elements of the traditional bases in order to allot a hierarchy of claims. This would come very close to implying that there is a hierarchy between the traditional bases which formally there is not. Furthermore, as the classical bases are only initial 'indicators' of a substantial connection,[117] it is likely that there will often be a combination of factors legitimising action, whereby the compartmentalisation of effects and territorial presence into two separate categories has limited value in practice.

It is argued here that the principle of sovereign equality should rather be read as informing states in the way they exercise their prescriptive competence more generally, serving to avoid rather than to resolve conflicting jurisdictional claims. This draws on Meessen's 1984 contribution that:

> Normally, *reducing the foreign-related impact of regulatory action* is sufficient to maintain sovereign equality. If such accommodation is not possible, equality may eventually suggest to one state that it *refrain from regulation altogether* if the other state's interests may be deemed to be prevailing.[118]

Essential here is the argument that where one state's pursuance of its regulatory goals encroaches upon the regulatory space of other states, it must seek to reduce the 'foreign-related impact' of its measure. Phrased as a general rule, this would mean that, in pursuing their regulatory goals, states have an obligation to minimise the limiting effects of their measures on the regulatory freedom of other states. Notably, the foreign interests considered should not be limited to those expressed by foreign statutory regulation, as this encourages states to enact blocking legislation to protect a 'strong policy'.[119] In addition, respect

[114] ibid 922.
[115] ibid.
[116] ibid 923.
[117] M Kamminga, 'Extraterritoriality' in R Wolfrum (ed), *Max Planck Encyclopaedia of Public International Law*, online edn (Oxford, Oxford University Press, 2011) [10].
[118] Meessen (n 72) 804 (emphasis added).
[119] Meessen (n 70) 64.

for the regulatory space of other states must also extend to the choice *not* to act. The absence of regulation may well indicate an affirmative decision not to burden producers or suppliers of goods and services with certain production costs. Measures of an acting state which effectively burden foreign producers with such costs can then be seen to encroach on the interest of other states. In this way, private interests are considered in the jurisdictional analysis as an extension of the interests of their home state.

Importantly, from a jurisdictional perspective states retain policy discretion over their desired regulatory objectives, as long as they can demonstrate a substantial connection. Nevertheless, while 'practically free' in choosing these goals, Meessen argues that states are 'bound to observe requirements of necessity and of consistency when they delimit the international scope of application of the laws designed to fulfil the goals they have selected'.[120] In practice, the line between the necessity of the foreign-related impacts and the ambition of the goal itself will be a fine one. It remains possible, of course, that 'considerate' design is not enough to prevent severe encroachment on the regulatory freedom of other states, particularly where a policy goal inherently conflicts with those of another state. This is an issue well-recognised under WTO law, and is discussed further in chapter 10.

Accepting these arguments, the role of sovereign equality could be seen as one of proportionality, whereby states must ensure that a measure's 'foreign-related impact' is no greater than necessary to achieve the objective in question. Proportionality is used as an interest-balancing or 'trade-off' tool in many different international legal regimes, including EU law, international human rights law and WTO law.[121] In each context it has its own unique definition and application, rendering the principle somewhat elusive despite its ubiquitous nature. From its widespread use it can be concluded, however, that the principle is a well-accepted means of balancing competing interests and checking states' regulatory discretion. Contrary to the rule-of-reason in the US Third Restatement, such a principle would not entail an extensive balancing of all regulatory interests, in particular as states remain competent to choose their own desired level of protection. Rather, the test is focused on the 'considerate' design of measure, in order to reduce the likelihood of conflict or tensions in the first place. In this way, 'considerate' design arguably offers a flexible and effective means of maintaining the broadest possible simultaneous regulatory freedom.

[120] Meessen (n 72) 800.

[121] For a detailed analysis of proportionality in various regimes, see T Cottier et al, 'The Principle of Proportionality in International Law' (NCCR Trade Regulation Working Paper No 2012/38, 2012). See further Adenas and Zleptnig, who identify three core roles of proportionality in international law: controlling and limiting discretion, balancing competing rights and interests, and acting as a standard of judicial review proportionality and interest balancing. M Adenas and S Zleptnig, 'Proportionality and Balancing in WTO Law: A Comparative Perspective' (2007) 20 *Cambridge Review of International Affairs* 71, 73.

4.1.3. *Interests of the International Community*

The above analysis has considered the limitations on jurisdiction stemming from the equal sovereignty of other states. Today, however, it is well recognised that the role of international law has shifted from 'a law of co-existence' to 'a law of co-operation'.[122] As noted by Judge Bedjaoui in his Declaration to the *Nuclear Weapons* case Advisory Opinion, this development is illustrated by 'the place which international law now accords to concepts such as obligations *erga omnes, rules of jus cogens*, or the common heritage of mankind'.[123] Compositely, there is also increasing recognition that state sovereignty, in the sense of 'independence', is conditioned by community interests.[124] This entails both shared state interests and interests of the 'higher' international community which transcend state boundaries, belonging to all individuals irrespective of their nationality.[125]

The field of environment is particularly illustrative of this point. Thus in his Separate Opinion to the *Gabcikovo Nagyramos* case, Judge Weeramantry famously noted that:

> International environmental law will need to proceed beyond weighing the rights and obligations of parties within a closed compartment of individual State self-interest, unrelated to the global concerns of humanity as a whole.[126]

As such, international law subserves 'not only the interests of individual States' but also the 'greater interests of humanity and planetary welfare'.[127]

In a jurisdictional context, Ryngaert explores the avenues for so-called 'selfless intervention', defined as the exercise of unilateral jurisdiction 'for the realization of cosmopolitanism, a political-philosophical notion that the international community has a shared morality and that members of this community – whether states or individuals – have rights and duties towards each other'.[128]

[122] *Nuclear Weapons* case (n 107) Declaration of Judge Bedjaoui, [13].

[123] ibid.

[124] *Island of Palmas (United States v The Netherlands)* (1928) II RIAA 829, 838: 'Sovereignty in the relations between States signifies independence. Independence in regard to a portion of the globe is the right to exercise therein, to the exclusion of any other State, the functions of a State.'

[125] See in particular C Voigt, 'Delineating the Common Interest in International Law' in W Benedek et al (eds), *The Common Interest in International Law* (Antwerp, Intersentia, 2014); and E Benvenisti, 'Sovereigns as Trustees of Humanity: On the Accountability of Sovereigns to Foreign Stakeholders' (2013) 107 *American Journal of International Law* 295, 305. See also *Tadic (Interlocutory Appeal on Jurisdiction)* IT-94-1 (2 October 1995) [97]: 'A State-sovereignty-oriented approach has been gradually supplanted by a human-being-oriented approach. Gradually the maxim of Roman law *hominum causa omne jus constitutum est* (all law is created for the benefit of human beings) has gained a firm foothold in the international community as well.'

[126] *Case concerning the Gabcikovo-Nagymaros Project (Hungary v Slovakia)* (Merits) [1997] ICJ Rep 88, Separate Opinion of Vice-President Weeramantry, 118.

[127] ibid 115.

[128] C Ryngaert, *Selfless Intervention: Exercising Jurisdiction in the Common Interest* (Oxford, Oxford University Press, 2020) 1–2. Notably, Ryngaert' s contribution draws on the results of the present study and those of fellow researchers in the UNIJURIS project on unilateral jurisdiction and global values, funded by the European Research Council (ERC Starting Grant 336230 – UNIJURIS) and the Dutch Organization for Scientific Research (VIDI Scheme, project number 452-12-002).

According to the author, where multilateral solutions are not forthcoming, and states with the strongest nexus fail to act, other states 'may in principle be allowed to exercise, unilateral jurisdiction in the common interest'.[129] Placed in the balancing scales, 'the reality of a perceived global urgency (eg a global public good risks going undersupplied or global justice risks not being delivered in the absence of unilateral action) may well trump "traditional" concerns over interference in other states' affairs'.[130] In order to prevent accusations of 'false cosmopolitanism', Ryngaert stresses the importance of a measure's 'embeddedness in international instruments recognizing a particular interest as indeed common to the international community'.[131] Indeed, the aim of protecting a common interest may support an individual state's 'substantial connection' with the subject matter, thus buttressing jurisdictional claims. As we have seen in chapter 8, this finds particular resonance in the rationale of the universality principle, which is premised upon a notion of states as 'agents' of the international community, competent, and arguably even obliged, to protect fundamental community values.[132]

It is argued here that community interests in fact also have a liming function. Respect for community interests namely requires *respect* and restraint from states when carrying out activities that may adversely affect those interests. As noted by Tarlock, this is especially evident in an environmental context, where the dilemma is clearest between maintaining the sovereign state as 'the basic juridic unit', while recognising that 'many internal exercises of national sovereignty are now understood to affect the entire planet'.[133] Such interests may then also limit the way in which states exercise their jurisdictional rights.

In terms of operationalisation, it is submitted that one could incorporate respect for common interests by requiring states to minimise any negative externalities of their activities on recognised concerns of the international community. These recognised concerns include, at the very least, common environmental concerns such climate change, recognised in international agreements. This finds support in general principles of environment law, in particular harm-prevention and precaution, which require states to act with due diligence in cases of potential environmental harm.[134] Following the logic of Judge Weeramantry, other common interests, particularly respect for fundamental human rights, may arguably have a similar limiting function. As will now be seen, this also aligns with more justice-oriented considerations that have been

[129] Ryngaert (n 128) 93.
[130] ibid 99.
[131] ibid 105.
[132] See chapter 8, section 6.
[133] D Tarlock, 'Stewardship Sovereignty: The Next Step in Former Prime Minister Palmer's Logic' (1992) 42 *Washington University Journal of Urban & Contemporary Law* 21, 24.
[134] See further chapter 2 on these general principles of international environment law.

recognised by international tribunals as being relevant to the delimitation of sovereign power in other fields.

4.2. Justice-Oriented Principles as Positive Jurisdictional Conditions

In addition to implied jurisdictional limitations deriving from state sovereignty, it has also been suggested that certain other justice-oriented principles may have a role to play in regulating the way in which states exercise their rights more generally.[135] Of particular relevance in a jurisdictional context are the principles of equity, good faith and non-abuse of rights, which may arguably influence both the design and the design process of states' prescriptive measures. These principles will now be considered in turn in sections 4.2.1 and 4.2.2.

4.2.1. Equity

Although its status as an independent principle remains contested, equity remains a well accepted part of international law.[136] Essentially equity is 'intended to reduce the gap between law and justice in a particular case'.[137] Depending on its function, equity can fill a lacuna in the law or inform the interpretation of formal legal rules, not 'as a principle endowed with autonomous normativity', 'but rather as a method for infusing elements of *reasonableness and "individualized" justice* whenever the applicable law leaves a margin of discretion to the court or tribunal which has to make the decision'.[138] In practice these different categories may greatly resemble each other, with some commentators questioning whether they can be meaningfully distinguished from international law at all.[139]

The ICJ has found interest-balancing to be a condition of the equitable delimitation of certain types of sovereign rights, particularly territory and natural resources. Looking at key examples, the considerations of the ICJ certainly have analogous potential in the context of prescriptive jurisdiction. Considering this issue, Ryngaert points to the *North Sea Continental Shelf* cases which he notes are comparable to jurisdiction in that that they 'address the basic question of how to delimit a state's power'.[140] There the ICJ held that, in the matter of maritime delimitation, opinio juris reflects the 'basic legal notions' that 'delimitation must be the object of agreement between the States concerned, and that

[135] See in particular Ryngaert (n 1) 157 et seq; Akehurst (n 4) 189.
[136] R Lapidoth, 'Equity in International Law' (1987) 22 *Israel Law Review* 161, 163.
[137] ibid 164, considering also the *Case Concerning the Diversion of Water from the Meuse (The Netherlands v Belgium)* PCIJ Rep Series A/B No 70, 76.
[138] F Francioni and R Wolfrum, 'Equity in International Law', *Max Planck Encyclopaedia of Public International Law*, online edn (Oxford, Oxford University Press, 2013) [7] (emphasis added).
[139] See eg V Lowe, 'The Role of Equity in International Law' (1988) 12 *Australian Year Book of International Law* 54.
[140] Ryngaert (n 1) 157.

such agreement must be arrived at in accordance with equitable principles'.[141] In this regard the ICJ held that:

> [T]here is no legal limit to the considerations which States may take account of for the purpose of making sure that they apply equitable procedures, and more often than not it is the balancing-up of all such considerations that will produce this result rather than reliance on one to the exclusion of all others. The problem of the relative weight to be accorded to different considerations naturally varies with the circumstances of the case.[142]

Broad interest-balancing was thus an integral part of an equitable delineation method.

Of particular relevance for this study is the ICJ's finding that 'equity does not necessarily imply equality'.[143] Special circumstances must be taken into account because it is possible that 'in a theoretical situation of equality within the same order, an inequity is created'.[144] In a climate change context, this 'corrective' aspect of equity is strongly reflected in the principle of common but differentiated responsibility and respective capabilities (CBDRRC). The CBDRRC principle seeks to incorporate capacity constraints into the regulatory responses to common environmental concerns, particularly climate change, and is discussed further in chapter 10.[145]

In the 1973 *Fisheries Jurisdiction* case, the ICJ once again considered interest-balancing to be an integral part of the equitable delimitation of sovereign rights, this time in relation to the apportionment of fishing resources between the UK and Iceland. There the ICJ noted that:

> [I]n order to reach an equitable solution of the present dispute it is necessary that the preferential fishing rights of Iceland, as a State specially dependent on coastal fisheries, be reconciled with the traditional fishing rights of the Applicant.[146]

The judgment's emphasis on the relativity of the competing rights is instructive here, the ICJ noting that:

> Due recognition must be given to the rights of both Parties, namely the rights of the United Kingdom to fish in the waters in dispute, and the preferential rights of Iceland. *Neither right is an absolute one*: the preferential rights of a coastal State are limited according to the *extent of its special dependence on the fisheries* and *by its obligation to take account of the rights of other States and the needs of conservation*; the established rights of other fishing States *are in turn limited* by reason of

[141] *North Sea Continental Shelf Cases (Fed Rep of Germany v Denmark; Fed Rep of Germany v Netherlands)* [1969] ICJ Rep 3 (*North Sea Continental Shelf* cases) [85].

[142] ibid 92–93. See also ICJ, *Case Concerning the Continental Shelf (Tunisia v Libya)* [1982] ICJ Rep 18, 50.

[143] *North Sea Continental Shelf* cases (n 141) [91].

[144] ibid.

[145] See further eg H Winkler and L Rajamani, 'CBDR&RC in a Regime Applicable to All' (2014) 14 *Climate Policy* 102.

[146] *Fisheries Jurisdiction (United Kingdom v Iceland)* (Merits) [1974] ICJ Rep 3 (*Fisheries Jurisdiction*) [71].

> the coastal State's special dependence on the fisheries and its own obligation to take account of the rights of other States, including the coastal State, and of the needs of conservation.[147]

The ICJ thus considered each party's rights to be limited not only by the rights of the other, but, more generally, by an obligation to take into account the rights of other states and the needs of conservation.

Reinforcing the function of interest-balancing in reaching an equitable solution based on international law, the Court continued that:

> In the fresh negotiations which are to take place on the basis of the present Judgment, the Parties will have the benefit of the above appraisal of their respective rights, and of certain guidelines defining their scope. The task before them will be to conduct their negotiations on the basis that each must in *good faith pay reasonable regard to the legal rights of the other* in the waters around Iceland outside the 12-mile limit, *thus bringing about an equitable apportionment of the fishing resources based on the facts of the particular situation*, and *having regard to the interests of other States* which have established fishing rights in the area.[148]

Thus, in order to achieve the result of 'equitable apportionment of fishing resources', states must negotiate in good faith and 'pay reasonable regard to the legal rights of others'. Good-faith negotiations may further be a portal through which to achieve more inclusive participation in the design of a measure. As noted by Ryngaert, this is necessary for extraterritorial measures, which do not generally allow for the participation of non-citizens.[149] That non-citizens are then bound by legal norms 'can only be legitimate if the norm-addressees (citizens) can adequately participate in relevant decision-making processes'.

It is interesting to project this balancing analysis over the delimitation of concurrent prescriptive jurisdiction. Reasoning by analogy, a state's jurisdiction would first be limited 'according to the extent of its special dependence' on the subject matter, which in the case of jurisdiction would be the existence and possibly strength of the 'substantial connection'. It is then further limited by a good-faith obligation to take into account the rights of other states, and any recognised community interest which may be affected by its jurisdictional assertion. In this way, the operationalisation of equity is interwoven with the principles of good faith and non-abuse of rights, the latter which will now be considered further.

4.2.2. *Good Faith and Non-abuse of Rights*

The good-faith principle is one of the most well-recognised and arguably most important general principles of international law.[150] A well-known expression

[147] ibid (emphasis added).
[148] ibid [78] (emphasis added).
[149] Ryngaert (n 128) 109–10.
[150] A prominent codification of the principle can be found in Art 2(2) of the UN Charter, which provides that: 'All Members, in order to ensure to all of them the rights and benefits resulting from

of this principle can be found in Article 26 VCLT, which provides that 'every treaty in force is binding upon the parties to it and must be performed by them in good faith'.[151]

Another clear and highly relevant manifestation of this principle can be found in the chapeau of Article XX GATT, which has been interpreted by the AB to require states to seriously attempt negotiations prior to resorting to unilateral action, and to ensure that the design of the measure is flexible enough to take into account specific conditions in different states.[152] This latter requirement aligns closely with the CBDRRC principle, discussed further in chapter 10.

In *The South China Sea Arbitration* (2016), an arbitral tribunal established under Annex VII of the LOSC considered the principle of good faith in the relations between states.[153] There the Philippines had argued that China's 'dredging, artificial island-building, and construction activities' in the South China Sea had 'acted to aggravate and extend the dispute between the Parties'.[154] In interpreting the applicable law, the Tribunal considered that 'there exists a duty on parties engaged in a dispute settlement procedure to refrain from aggravating or extending the dispute or disputes at issue during the pendency of the settlement process'.[155] According to the Tribunal, 'such a duty is inherent in the central role of good faith in the international legal relations between States'.[156] In support of this conclusion the Tribunal referred to Article 26 VCLT and Article 300 LOSC, the latter of which requires parties to 'fulfil in good faith the obligations assumed under this Convention and [to] exercise the rights, jurisdiction and freedoms recognized in this Convention in a manner which would not constitute an abuse of right'.[157]

Turning to non-abuse of rights, this doctrine prohibits states from exercising their rights so as to hinder another state in the exercise of its own rights, causing it to suffer injury.[158] It also prohibits the exercise of a right for a purpose other than for which the right has been created.[159] In his 1972 contribution

membership, shall fulfill in good faith the obligations assumed by them in accordance with the present Charter.'

[151] Vienna Convention on the Law of Treaties (adopted 23 May 1969, entered into force 27 January 1980) 1155 UNTS 331.

[152] WTO, *United States – Import Prohibition of Certain Shrimp and Shrimp Products – Report of the Appellate Body* (6 November 1998) WT/DS58/AB/R (*US–Shrimp*) [158]: 'The chapeau of Article XX is, in fact, but one expression of the principle of good faith. This principle, at once a general principle of law and a general principle of international law, controls the exercise of rights by states.' See further A Kiss, 'Abuse of Rights' in R Wolfrum (ed), *Max Planck Encyclopaedia of Public International Law*, online edn (Oxford, Oxford University Press, 2006) [1], [4].

[153] *South China Sea Arbitration (Philippines v China)* (Merits) Award of 12 July 2016, PCA Case No 2013-19; United Nations Convention on the Law of the Sea (adopted 10 December 1982, entered into force 16 November 1994) 1833 UNTS 3.

[154] ibid [1166].

[155] ibid [1169].

[156] ibid [1171].

[157] See further ibid [1172].

[158] Note, however, that there is some discussion on the independent value of the non-abuse of rights principle. See further Kiss (n 152) [10].

[159] ibid.

on 'Jurisdiction in International Law', Akehurst argued that '[e]ven when the content of legislation does not infringe a specific rule of international law, it may nevertheless be contrary to international law if it constitutes an abuse of rights'.[160] This will be the case if 'legislation is designed to produce mischief in another country without advancing any legitimate interest of the legislating State'. In this regard Ryngaert notes that, while the prohibition of abuse of rights 'appears related to the principle of good faith', 'it is unclear whether bad faith is actually required for the principle to be relied upon, or whether abuse of discretion (eg the wide margin of jurisdictional discretion that States enjoy under the *Lotus* judgment) suffices'.[161] In practice these two may end up being difficult to distinguish.[162] A clear example in the context of trade measures is disguised protectionism, which is explicitly prohibited as an abuse of right by the chapeau of Article XX GATT.[163]

Taken together, it is argued that 'positive' justice-oriented conditions may direct states to make best efforts to ensure that the way in which they exercise jurisdiction respects the interests and rights of other states and the international community. This entails genuine consideration of the individual conditions in the affected states during the design phase, where states may not use public policy measures as a guise for a protective agenda. What differentiates these justice-oriented principles from sovereign equality is that they do not pursue *equality* as an end in itself, and recognise situations where objectively equal treatment may nonetheless infringe the interests of other actors. As such they 'correct' the application of formal rules.[164]

5. PROPOSED REGULATORY TOOL: THE 'CONSIDERATE DESIGN' APPROACH

While the foregoing analyses remain explorative, they open different avenues through which to approach the legal conditions on states' prescriptive jurisdiction. As we have seen, this is an issue on which there is simply very little clarity in international law. Based on the above analysis of the literature and related case

[160] Akehurst (n 4) 189.

[161] Ryngaert (n 1) 161.

[162] For his part, Reinhold considers abuse of rights and abuse of discretion together, arguing that 'the aspect of abuse of right and the arbitrary exercise of a right are closely related and not clearly distinguishable'. S Reinhold, 'Good Faith and International Law' (2013) 2 *UCL Journal of Law and Jurisprudence* 40, 49.

[163] According to the Appellate Body in *US–Shrimp*, 'the doctrine of *abus de droit*, prohibits the abusive exercise of a state's rights and enjoins that whenever the assertion of a right "impinges on the field covered by [a] treaty obligation, it must be exercised bona fide, that is to say, reasonably"'. *US–Shrimp* (n 152) [158] (references omitted).

[164] This has strong roots in common law jurisdictions – for an older explanation, see Lord Kames, *Principles of Equity* (Edinburg, 1767) available under a creative commons licence (CC0 1.0) through University of Michigan Library: name.umdl.umich.edu/004841431.0001.000.

law in other fields, this section proposes an overarching limitations framework, integrating the different principles into a 'considerate design' tool.

To start with, the possible operationalisations of these principles can be summarised as follows:

1. *Non-interference and non-intervention* could be seen as requiring legislatures to avoid regulatory acts which result in true conflict with the laws of another state.
2. *Sovereign equality* could be seen as requiring legislatures to design measures so as to minimise the extent to which they encroach upon the broader regulatory freedom of other states. Such encroachment does not only occur in the case of true conflict but also conflict in the 'broader sense', 'where two rules or principles suggest different ways of dealing with a problem'.[165]
3. *Common interests* can be seen as requiring legislatures to avoid externalities resulting in the harm of recognised community interests, in particular common environmental concerns.
4. *Equity* could be seen to require states, when designing measures, to take into account different circumstances in affected states, granting differential treatment where this is needed for a just division of sovereign power. This 'corrects' the law in situations where the application of sovereign equality would otherwise lead to an inequitable outcome.
5. *Good faith and non-abuse of rights* are related to equity, and may be considered as requiring attempts to take into account the interests of others during the preparation phase are genuine and best-effort, where a measure may not be used as a guise to infringe the rights of other states (no mischief).

It is argued that these principles may inform the exercise of jurisdiction, steering regulators to design their measures 'considerately'. According to the 'considerate design' approach, legislatures, when designing measures must, in good faith, seek to minimise any encroachment on the regulatory freedom of other equal states and on recognised community interests, taking into account differences in circumstances which may require differential treatment. Where affected states have chosen not to subject their operators and suppliers to certain standards, legislating states must then limit the burdens imposed upon these actors. Admittedly, with regard to differential treatment, states may well be forced to walk something of a tightrope, as differential treatment risks violating non-discrimination requirements in other regimes, such as world trade law. This issue

[165] International Law Commission, 'Fragmentation of International Law: Difficulties Arising from the Diversification and Expansion of International Law', Report of the Study Group of the International Law Commission (13 April 2006), A/CN.4/L.682 [24], [25], discussed in the context of climate change by H van Asselt, 'Dealing with the Fragmentation of Global Climate Governance Legal and Political Approaches in Interplay Management' (Global Governance Working Paper No 30, 2007) 3.

will be discussed further in relation to the application of the considerate design approach to unilateral climate change measures in chapter 10.

6. CONCLUSION

In an increasingly interdependent world, it is very likely that more than one state will be able to claim a substantial connection to certain subject matter, leading to concurrent jurisdiction. Although this need not necessarily be problematic, a balance must be found between the regulatory freedoms of the acting states, bearing in mind the risk of overregulation from concurrent jurisdictional claims.

This chapter has argued that international law has a role to play in conditioning unilateral prescriptive jurisdiction with an extraterritorial element. To start with, as jurisdiction is itself a manifestation of sovereign power, principles limiting state sovereignty can be seen as 'negative' conditions on jurisdiction requiring self-restraint.[166] Key among them is clearly the principle of sovereign equality, although the derivative or 'foundational' principles of non-interference and non-intervention also have a role to play in situations of true conflict. In addition, the principles of equity, good faith and non-abuse of rights may serve as 'positive' conditions for the realisation of justice. These have a corrective function, pursuing equity rather than equality.

Drawing together these explorative strands, this chapter has proposed a 'considerate design' approach, according to which legislatures, when designing measures, must in good faith seek to minimise any encroachment on the regulatory freedom of other equal states and on recognised common interests, taking into account differences in circumstances which may require differential treatment. The 'considerate design' approach does not entail a completely open balancing exercise of all possible state interests, as was so criticised under the US Third Restatement.[167] Rather, it is primarily focused on maintaining a maximum simultaneous regulatory freedom, at least in the formal sense. This is desirable from both a practical and doctrinal perspective. As states are best placed to formulate and realise their own interests, the most effective way of protecting sovereign independence is to ensure mutual respect for each other's regulatory space from the outset, and not just when there is a direct conflict of laws. Although real-world power differences mean that some states will inevitably have more regulatory 'space' than others, the exercise of self-restraint can at least help to curb the imbalance.

From a doctrinal perspective, jurisdiction is concerned with the channelling of states' regulatory power to pursue their own interests, and not so much with

[166] See KM Meessen (n 70) 59: 'States accommodate countervailing interests of foreign States to the extent that this seems reasonable from their own perspective, and *they may be assumed to do so also at least on the ground of respecting foreign State sovereignty*' (emphasis added).
[167] See eg *Empagran* case (n 33) 167.

the substance of these interests, which is regulated by more specific regimes. Of course, state interests play a role as the object upon which a substantial connection is based. However, the law of jurisdiction does not specify a limitative list or hierarchy of permissible interests. Conditions on the exercise of jurisdictional rights must seek, as far as possible, to remain substance-neutral, forming a common denominator for the balancing of sovereign power more generally. It is of course possible that one or more of the individual rules could be developed into a more robust jurisdictional limitation on its own, and it remains to be seen to what extent the legal community will develop these norms. Whatever may be the eventual crystallisation, the increasing overlap of regulatory spheres calls for further clarification on how to protect sovereign equality and common interests in a jurisdictional context. These limitations remain an essential and underexamined component of the jurisdictional framework to date.

10

Applying the 'Considerate Design' Approach: Opportunities and Challenges

1. INTRODUCTION

THE PREVIOUS CHAPTER set out the theoretical framework for the proposed 'considerate design' approach as a tool to align the exercise of prescriptive jurisdiction with core norms of public international law. As it is derived from general principles, the considerate design approach is abstract in formulation. Questions then arise as to how it may be applied in the context of extraterritorial climate-protective measures. This chapter will explore some key opportunities and challenges for the application of the considerate design approach to the EU's unilateral measures.

While certainly interesting for further study, it goes beyond the scope of this chapter to conduct comprehensive assessments of the vast array of EU measures. Rather, a selection of key overarching issues on the 'negative' and 'positive' sides of considerate design will be addressed. Focusing on the negative aspect of considerate design, section 2 first examines the obligation of jurisdictional self-restraint in situations of conflicting and competing measures, reflecting normatively upon whether 'necessity' may legitimise diverging standards. Section 3 then turns to the 'positive' aspect of considerate design, focusing on the possible implementation of the principle of common but differentiated responsibilities and respective capabilities. Good faith and non-abuse of rights are intrinsic elements of genuine considerate design. As will be seen, these are infused within the various strategies considered throughout this chapter.

2. CONSIDERATE DESIGN AND JURISDICTIONAL RESTRAINT: RESPECT FOR COMPETING STANDARDS

As discussed in chapter 9, it is argued that jurisdiction, as an exercise of sovereignty, is negatively conditioned by the principles of non-intervention, non-interference and sovereign equality. These principles limit sovereignty in the interest of maintaining formal equality between states. In the context of unilateral measures with an extraterritorial element, sovereignty-limiting principles direct states to exercise self-restraint through respect for competing standards. The following sections will consider how to effectuate such respect, and the tensions which arise with maintaining states' policy autonomy.

2.1. Non-interference and Collective Inaction

The principles of non-intervention and non-interference have been considered in national case law as potential barriers to prescriptive measures giving rise to conflict in the stricter sense.[1] Although it is not entirely clear how 'strict' conflict needs to be, the threshold is in any event very high. Applying the definition of the ILC in its Report on Legal Fragmentation, the considerate design approach posits that the principles of non-interference and non-intervention require states to refrain from prescribing a competing standard that would make it impossible for an affected party to comply with both sets of rules.[2] These competing standards may be national or international. Notably, when considering a competing multilateral and unilateral standard, the former has a legitimacy advantage, as it is supported the 'pooled' sovereignty of multiple states.[3]

For the operationalisation of this approach, much hinges on when compliance with both schemes is impossible. In practice this threshold should be applied looking at factual realities on a case-by-case basis. Inevitably, bright-line standards will be difficult to draw, and it is argued that the obligation of jurisdictional self-restraint should be interpreted broadly. In other words, legislatures should seek to avoid designing measures that make it impossible for affected parties, in light of economic and other practical realities, to continue their operations while adhering to competing standards.

An example in EU policy where 'strict' conflict remains a possibility is that of aviation emissions. As discussed in chapter 6, at the time of writing, Article 28b(3) of the EU Aviation Directive instructs the Commission to provide a proposal to, 'where appropriate', 'amend, delete, extend or replace' the current derogations put in place to prepare to implement the global offsetting scheme (CORSIA).[4] This leaves open the option that the EU reverts to the original international scope of its ETS, depending on the Commission review of CORSIA's

[1] For case law, see eg Joined Cases C-89, 104, 114, 116, 117 and 125–129/85, *A Ahlström Osakeyhtiö v Commission* [1988] ECR 5193 (*Wood Pulp*) [20] and *Hartford Fire Insurance Co v California*, 509 US 764, 113 S Ct 2891 (1993) (*Hartford Fire*) [799].

[2] International Law Commission, 'Fragmentation of International Law: Difficulties Arising from the Diversification and Expansion of International Law', Report of the Study Group of the International Law Commission (13 April 2006) A/CN.4/L.682, 19.

[3] See also C Ryngaert, *Selfless Intervention: The Exercise of Jurisdiction in the Common Interest* (Oxford, Oxford University Press, 2020) 109, on participation as a condition for selfless intervention.

[4] Parliament and Council (EU) Regulation 2017/2392 of 13 December 2017 amending Directive 2003/87/EC to continue current limitations of scope for aviation activities and to prepare to implement a global market-based measure from 2021 [2017] OJ L350/7 ('Regulation 2017/2392').

environmental integrity. Much then depends on the extent to which the EU will align with CORSIA. If it extends the derogations to fully accept the offsetting scheme, then conflict may be avoided. However, if the Union maintains its ETS, even in its reduced scope, tensions arise. The latter scenario was envisioned by the Commission in its 2030 Climate Target Plan, where it noted that 'the EU should continue to regulate at least intra-EU aviation [and maritime] emissions in the EU ETS'.[5] Intra-EEA flights are considered 'international flights' under CORSIA, whereby these flights would be subject to both schemes.[6] As things currently stand, particularly in light of the ICAO's 'exclusivity clause', the credits and offsets would not be reciprocally recognised.[7] This would likely lead to emissions being counted twice, while costs of compliance with both schemes may well be prohibitive for some operators. At least in practical terms, this may well make it practically impossible for operators to comply with both schemes.

Concerns on this issue have been clearly expressed by operators in EU Member States, the French Aviation Industry Federation (FNAM), for example, arguing that 'uniform standards' must be implemented in all ICAO Member States to 'minimise market distortions'. 'CORSIA can't be implemented through EU-ETS.'[8] For its part, the EU appears to consider that simultaneous standards are possible, its 2020 Inception Impact Assessment considering all scenarios, including 'ETS-CORSIA "clean cut"', 'ETS-CORSIA "mix"', and 'ETS-CORSIA "mix" according to licence of aircraft operators'.[9] One could seriously question, however, whether this is a practical or merely theoretical possibility.

While non-intervention weighs in favour of jurisdictional restraint here, an inescapable question is whether this may be somewhat mitigated by the nature of climate change as a common concern of mankind.[10] In the aviation context, the EU's objective is to remain 'consistent with the Union economy-wide greenhouse

[5] Commission (EU), 'Stepping up Europe's 2030 climate ambition Investing in a climate-neutral future for the benefit of our people' (Communication) COM(2020) 562 final, 17 September 2020, 16.

[6] First Edition of Annex 16, Environmental Protection, Volume IV 'Carbon Offsetting and Reduction Scheme for International Aviation (CORSIA)' (adopted by the ICAO Council on 27 June 2018) (CORSIA SARPs) ch 2.1.1, applicable to 'international flights' as defined in ch 1.1.2. as 'the operation of an aircraft from take-off at the aerodrome of State or its territories, and landing at an aerodrome of another State or its territories'. See further UM Erling, 'International Aviation Emissions under International Civil Aviation Organization's Global Market Based Measure: Ready for Offsetting?' (2017) 42 *Air and Space Law* 1.

[7] ICAO Resolution A40-19, 'Consolidated statement of continuing ICAO policies and practices related to environmental protection – Carbon Offsetting and Reduction Scheme for International Aviation (CORSIA)' (adopted 40th Session of the ICAO Assembly, 24 September–4 October 2019) [18].

[8] Feedback from French Aviation Industry Federation (FNAM) to the European Commission, ref no F15999 (20 December 2018) ec.europa.eu/info/law/better-regulation/have-your-say/initiatives.

[9] Directorate General for Climate Action, 'Inception Impact Assessment Revision of the EU Emission Trading System Directive 2003/87/EC concerning aviation', Ref Ares (2020)3515933–03/07/2020, 4.

[10] cf the WTO necessity test in *Korea–Beef*, where the AB found that '[t]he more vital or important the common interests, the easier it would be to accept the measure as "necessary"'. WTO, *Korea – Measures Affecting Imports of Fresh, Chilled and Frozen Beef* – Appellate Body Report (10 January 2001) WT/DS161/AB/R (*Korea–Beef*).

gas emission reduction commitment for 2030 with the aim of preserving the environmental integrity and effectiveness of Union climate action'.[11] Indeed, the International Coalition for Sustainable Aviation went so far as to argue that replacement of the ETS with CORSIA would – given the latter's environmental weakness – 'constitute a *breach* of Europe's obligations under the Paris Agreement.[12] This raises a dilemma. On the one hand, prescribing conflicting legislation certainly 'interferes' with the regulatory space of other sovereigns. On the other hand, the competing regulations are arguably insufficient for the protection of the climate as a recognised common concern.

Conceptually speaking, balancing the common interest against sovereignty infringements risks returning to a rule-of-reason style analysis which does not find sufficient support in practice.[13] A key concern there is the capacity of domestic courts to solve conflicts of law through very broad interest-balancing. Arguably, however, in very exceptional circumstances a more narrow interest-balancing may be appropriate, particularly at the 'design' phase. In this regard, an analogy can be drawn with the customary rule of 'necessity' as a circumstance precluding wrongfulness under the law of state responsibility.[14] Notably, the role of 'necessity' in a jurisdictional context is different because it does not bear upon a violation of an obligation, but rather a tension raised with the principles of non-intervention and non-interference.[15] Of course, it is possible that these latter principles may crystallise into 'harder' jurisdictional limitations, the violation of which could rely on circumstances precluding wrongfulness. This is not yet the case, however.

Briefly exploring this analogy, Article 25(1) of the ILC Draft Articles on State Responsibility (DARS), provides that 'necessity' may only be invoked where it:

(a) is the only way for the State to safeguard an essential interest against a grave and imminent peril; and

[11] Parliament and Council (EC) Directive 2008/101 of 19 November 2008 amending Directive 2003/87/EC so as to include aviation activities in the scheme for greenhouse gas emission allowance trading within the Community [2008] OJ L8/3 ('Aviation Directive') Art 28(3)(b). *Korea–Beef* (n 10) [162].

[12] International Coalition for Sustainable Aviation, 'Letter: CORSIA & European Climate Ambition on Aviation' (Carbonmarketwatch.org, 12 September 2018) www.carbonmarketwatch.org/publications/letter-corsia-european-climate-ambition-on-aviation/ (emphasis added).

[13] *Restatement (Fourth) of the Foreign Relations Law of the United States* (St Paul. MN, American Law Institute Publishers, 2018) ('US Fourth Restatement').

[14] For some consideration for the necessity defence and climate change in civil disobedience cases, see LN Long and T Hamilton, 'The Climate Necessity Defense: Proof and Judicial Error in Climate Protest Cases' (2018) 38 *Stanford Environmental Law Journal* 57.

[15] Necessity was notably considered in a jurisdictional context in *M/V Saiga (No 2)*, where the International Tribunal for the Law of the Sea (ITLOS) assessed whether Guinea was precluded from applying its customs laws, to the *Saiga*, a ship registered to St Vincent and the Grenadines, when in its EEZ. Referring to *Gabcikovo Nagymaros*, ITLOS rejected this claim, finding that the 'considerable fiscal losses a developing country like Guinea is suffering from illegal off-shore bunkering in its exclusive economic zone' to be insufficient evidence of imminent peril. *M/V 'Saiga'* (No 2) (*Saint Vincent and the Grenadines v Guinea*) (Provisional Measures, Order of 11 March 1998) ITLOS Reports 1998 (*M/V 'Saiga'*) [130], [135].

(b) does not seriously impair an essential interest of the State or States towards which the obligation exists, or of the international community as a whole.[16]

In the *Gabcíkovo-Nagymaros* case, the ICJ considered whether Hungary's reliance on a state of 'ecological necessity' found support in international law.[17] There the Court had 'no difficulty in acknowledging that the concerns expressed by Hungary for its natural environment in the region affected by the Gabcikovo-Nagymaros Project related to an "essential interest" of that State'.[18] Referring to the ILC Commentary, it noted that 'safeguarding the ecological balance has come to be considered an "essential interest" of all States'.[19] As regards the requirement of 'grave and imminent peril', the Court found that '"peril" appearing in the long-term might be held to be "imminent" as soon as it is established, at the relevant point in time, that the realization of that peril, however far off it might be, is not thereby any less certain and inevitable'.[20] In that case, the Court did not enquire definitively into the scientific evidence regarding the existence of imminent peril because it found that it could not be demonstrated that the peril invoked by Hungary arose 'entirely out of the project', or that Hungary had no other means available to it, than to violate an international obligation.[21]

While these last considerations may pose obstacles in the present context, it is argued that this need not always be the case. As extensively discussed in chapter 8, climate change is recognised to cause grave harm to vital state interests. Scientific reports support the conclusion that such harm is 'imminent', with experts calculating less than ten years remaining before we exhaust the carbon budget, should emissions stay at their current levels.[22] Sectors where carbon emissions remain unbridled are then particularly problematic. For example, aviation emissions have been projected to contribute almost one-quarter of the remaining carbon budget by 2050.[23] Although the harm of climate change does not arise 'entirely out of' aviation emissions, these are projected to become such a key source of GHGs that failing to reduce them would arguably put unreasonable strain on remaining global mitigation options. As a regulatory tool, it

[16] ILC, 'Draft Articles on Responsibility of States for Internationally Wrongful Acts, with Commentaries', A/56/49 (Vol I)/Corr.4, Art 25(1).

[17] *Gabčikovo-Nagymaros Project (Hungary v Slovakia)* [Judgment] ICJ Rep 88 (*Gabčikovo-Nagymaros*).

[18] ibid [53].

[19] *M/V 'Saiga'* (n 15) [135].

[20] *Gabčikovo-Nagymaros* (n 17) [54].

[21] ibid [55].

[22] World Economic Forum, 'The Global Risks Report 2020' (Insight Report, 15th edn, 2020) 35; V Masson-Delmotte et al (eds), 'Summary for Policymakers', in *Global Warming of 1.5°C. An IPCC Special Report on the impacts of global warming of 1.5°C above pre-industrial levels and related global greenhouse gas emission pathways, in the context of strengthening the global response to the threat of climate change, sustainable development, and efforts to eradicate poverty* (2018).

[23] 'Aviation Could Consume a Quarter of 1.5C Carbon Budget by 2050' (Carbon Brief, 8 August 2016) www.carbonbrief.org/aviation-consume-quarter-carbon-budget.

is clear that a carbon-offsetting scheme simply does not provide the same level of protection as a cap-and-trade scheme which puts a ceiling on emissions.[24] The Climate Action Tracker assessed the 2030 goal of the ICAO as 'critically insufficient'.[25] CORSIA was considered unlikely to achieve the ICAO's goal of carbon-neutral growth by 2020, being projected to cover less than half of international emissions by 2035. In addition, the offset unit prices were critiqued as providing 'little or no incentive to roll out innovative zero carbon technology' and considered unlikely to stimulate investments in emission reduction measures.[26] In terms of negotiating an alternative, the EU's capacity is limited, not being a member of the ICAO. At the same time, EU Member States do not always vote in line with the Union's position, as demonstrated by their (implicit) acceptance of CORSIA's exclusivity clause.[27] Taken together, strong arguments can then be made in favour of a degree of infringement in the regulatory autonomy of states that underregulate a substantial source of carbon emissions which are known to threaten a vital shared interest.

That being said, in the bigger picture it is far more desirable for states to avoid rather than justify conflict with competing measures. In cases of dual regulatory schemes, unilateral measures should then be crafted to reduce burdens as much as possible. The following section will now look at how states may design measures with respect for the sovereign policy autonomy of other states.

2.2. Sovereign Equality: Reducing the Impact of a Dual Regulatory Burden

As discussed in chapter 9, it is argued that the principle of sovereign equality steers regulators to reduce the foreign-related impact of the measures they design. This lessens the 'interference' caused by unilateral standards made dependent on subject matter also falling within the purview of other states' sovereignty. This analysis focuses on different types of 'impact' corresponding with the types of extraterritorial element discussed in chapter 3.

To refresh the employed typology, 'type 1' extraterritorial elements concern requirements imposed as a hard condition of entry; 'type 2' extraterritorial elements are optional benefits made dependent on certain conduct. When applied to foreign operators, both types of measures will distort a home states'

[24] 'Corsia: The UN's Plan to "Offset" Growth in Aviation Emissions after 2020' (Carbon Brief, 4 February 2019) www.carbonbrief.org/corsia-un-plan-to-offset-growth-in-aviation-emissions-after-2020.

[25] 'International Shipping and Aviation Emissions Goals both "Critically Insufficient"' (Climate Action Tracker, 26 June 2020) www.climateactiontracker.org/press/international-shipping-and-aviation-emissions-goals-both-critically-insufficient/.

[26] ibid.

[27] As regards the latter, see 'ICIS Editorial, 'CORSIA Exclusivity Clause – Potential EU ETS Implications' (ICIS, 11 October 2019) www.icis.com/explore/resources/news/2019/10/11/10427666/corsia-exclusivity-clause-potential-eu-ets-implications.

own regulatory incentives. In principle, measures that confer a conditional voluntary benefit cause relatively less interference, as they do not bar market access altogether. Foreign operators then have a choice to forgo the benefit. In practice, however, such measures may restrict the amount of trade possible, with serious economic impacts. For example, energy suppliers that choose not to meet the Renewable Energy Directive sustainability criteria will likely have a lower market share in EU Member States.[28]

Alignment with competing legislation is a key strategy for reducing the foreign-related impact of unilateral measures. To craft less 'conduct-restrictive' measures, states should carefully assess whether a measure's design could leave more space for other states' policy. Here, it is helpful for states first to identify the countries most likely to be impacted by a certain measure. In a trade context, this can be done using an impact assessment based on factors such as the ratio of an exported good or service from a certain country to its GDP.[29] One could also consider the share of the regulated product in a trading partner's total exports.[30] Another relevant factor is the overall increase in costs of implementing the unilateral standard for actors in other countries. A variation of this can be found in the criteria for determining subsectors 'deemed to be exposed to a significant risk of carbon leakage' under the EU Carbon Leakage Directive.[31] The criteria used are the direct and indirect costs of implementation and the intensity of a sector's trade with third states.

Intuitively, it is clear that where measures overlap, the means by which they can be adhered to should be harmonised as much as possible. In reality, identifying opportunities for harmonising compliance standards is often complicated by perceived divergences in desired levels of protection. As the law of state jurisdiction would not, in principle, seem to limit state freedom to set policy objectives, delineating competing claims is a challenging exercise. An example here is the EU's maritime MRV scheme for international shipping emissions, which overlaps

[28] Parliament and Council (EC) Directive 2009/28/EC of 23 April 2009 on the promotion of the use of energy from renewable sources and amending and subsequently repealing Directives 2001/77/EC and 2003/30/EC [2009] OJ L140 ('Renewable Energy Directive').

[29] One could also consider the overall trade to GDP index, which measures the importance of international trade to the national economy. See further '% of GDP' (worldbank.org) www.data.worldbank.org/indicator/NE.TRD.GNFS.ZS.

[30] This is defined by the World Bank as: 'the share of each export product (at a chosen level of disaggregation) in the country's total exports'. See, 'Trade Indicators' (worldbank.org) www.wits.worldbank.org/wits/wits/witshelp/Content/Utilities/e1.trade_ indicators.htm.

[31] Parliament and Council (EC) Directive 2009/29 amending Directive 2003/87/EC so as to improve and extend the greenhouse gas emission allowance trading scheme of the Community [2009] OJ L140/63 ('Carbon Leakage Directive'), amending Parliament and Council (EC) Directive 2003/87 establishing a scheme for greenhouse gas emission allowance trading within the Community and amending Council Directive 96/61/EC [2003] OJ L275 ('ETS Directive') Art 10(a)(15). See also Commission (EU) delegated decision concerning the determination of sectors and subsectors deemed at risk of carbon leakage for the period 2021 to 2030 (Communication) COM(19) 930 final, 15 February 2019.

with the IMO's global DCS. As discussed in chapter 5, the EU has opted for only partial alignment. In its 2019 Impact Assessment, the Commission is very explicit about the weighing of compliance burdens against environmental protection when considering the various alignment scenarios.[32] Ultimately, 'streamlining' was chosen, with several points on which the Commission's proposed amendments do seek harmonisation with the IMO DCS.[33] 'High convergence' was, however, rejected because 'although this option might lead to more significant reduction in administrative burden', 'it would reduce or supress the incentives to overcome market barriers and get the efficiency improvements pursued through the EU MRV Regulation'.[34]

This example illustrates how, in practice, harmonisation may be rejected when a state feels that this would undermine its regulatory objective. To complicate matters further, it is not always easy to distinguish between a measure's objective and the means of implementation. This is a well-recognised issue under the law of the WTO, particularly under Article XX(b) GATT. As discussed in chapter 4, while recognising autonomy over environmental policy objectives, a refined 'necessity' test has been developed to assess the policy *instrument* itself.[35] A measure's necessity will depend on 'the importance of the interests or values at stake, the extent of the contribution to the achievement of the measure's objective, and its trade restrictiveness'.[36] Importantly, the WTO law necessity test cannot be applied analogically in a jurisdictional context. WTO law weighs one state's policy autonomy against trade-restrictive effects harming WTO members' rights under the Covered Agreements. Sovereign equality is focused on states' rights to interfere with each other's regulatory autonomy. That being said, WTO law does provide some useful guidelines for general alignment strategies, which will now be considered further.

As a first strategy, the acting state may consider whether another state's existing procedures could be recognised as equal or comparable. The analysis of 'comparable' or 'equivalent' protection should be based in good faith

[32] Commission Staff Working Document, Impact Assessment Accompanying the document 'Proposal for a regulation of the European Parliament and of the Council amending Regulation (EU) 2015/757 in order to take appropriate account of the global data collection system for ship fuel oil consumption data' SWD(2019) 10 final, 4 February 2019 ('Impact Assessment MRV Amendment') 23. These are: (1) a 'baseline' scenario with no alignment, (2) 'streamlining' with partial alignment and (3) 'high convergence' to 'harmonise all its technical aspects with the IMO DCS'.

[33] Proposal for a Regulation of the European Parliament and of the Council amending Regulation (EU) 2015/757 in order to take appropriate account of the global data collection system for ship fuel oil consumption data COM(2019) 38; Impact Assessment MRV Amendment (n 32) Art 1; Explanatory Memorandum to COM(2019)38 – Amendment of Regulation (EU) 2015/757 in order to take appropriate account of the global data collection system for ship fuel oil consumption data, 7.

[34] Impact Assessment MRV Amendment (n 32) 32–33.

[35] See further M Du, 'The Necessity Test in World Trade Law: What Now?' (2016) 15 *Chinese Journal of International Law* 817, 818.

[36] WTO, *Brazil – Measures Affecting Imports of Retreaded Tyres – Report of the Appellate Body* (17 December 2007) WT/DS332/AB/R (*Brazil–Retreaded Tyres*) [178].

on reliable data. This draws on the 'contribution' requirement of the GATT necessity test, which requires 'a genuine relationship of ends and means between the objective pursued and the measure at issue'.[37] Where 'a contribution is not "immediately observable" or where 'it may prove difficult to isolate the contribution' of one measure in its broader policy context, then necessity may be based on whether a measure is 'apt to produce a material contribution to the achievement of its objective'.[38] In *Brazil–Retreaded Tyres*, the AB found that '[t]his demonstration could consist of quantitative projections in the future, or qualitative reasoning based on a set of hypotheses that are tested and supported by sufficient evidence'.[39] A similarly constructed 'meaningful contribution' criterion has already featured in the jurisdictional analysis as a requirement for reliance on the effects-doctrine. It has broader value as a yardstick for not only for establishing an acting state's interest, but for *comparing* the contribution of different measures and the extent that unilateralism is truly needed. It goes without saying that such determination should be done in good faith.

As reflected in the *US–Shrimp* case, states should further engage in best-effort negotiations to reach an agreement before imposing unilateral standards, particularly regarding an environmental matter which 'demands concerted and cooperative efforts on the part of the many countries'.[40] In the 2020 case on the *Appeal Relating to the Jurisdiction of the ICAO Council under the International Air Services Transit Agreement (Bahrain, Egypt and United Arab Emirates v Qatar)*, the ICJ reiterated its recognition that 'a genuine attempt to negotiate can be made outside of bilateral diplomacy', where '[e]xchanges that take place in an international organization are also recognized as "established modes of international negotiation"'.[41]

In the case, for example, of the EU maritime MRV, the Union's insistence on third-party verification only, rather than accepting the IMO DCS approach of verification according to national rules, could be questioned.[42] The EU's concerns that this would undermine the 'reliability' and 'accuracy' of the system[43] could be ameliorated through dialogue and streamlining with other states in advance. Notably, the EU Forest Law Enforcement Governance and Trade (FLEGT) Scheme is a good example of where the EU and third states do

[37] ibid [210].
[38] ibid [151].
[39] ibid [151].
[40] WTO, *United States – Import Prohibition of Certain Shrimp and Shrimp Products – Report of the Appellate Body* (6 November 1998) WT/DS58/AB/R (*US–Shrimp*) [166] [168].
[41] *Appeal Relating to the Jurisdiction of the ICAO Council under Article II, Section 2, of the 1944 International Air Services Transit Agreement (Bahrain, Egypt and United Arab Emirates v Qatar)* ICAO, 4 July 2018 [91].
[42] Regulation 22A, 'Collection and reporting of ship fuel oil consumption data' (IMO MEPC.278(70)).
[43] Impact Assessment MRV Amendment (n 32) 29.

negotiate Voluntary Partnership Agreements in advance, the latter creating an exemption from the EU Timber Regulation.[44]

The reduction of unnecessary administrative requirements will also lessen a measure's foreign-related impact.[45] A well-recognised strategy is to exempt small-scale operators from full administrative requirements. To 'minimise the administrative burden', the revised RED II, for example, provides that EU sustainability and GHG emissions-saving criteria should only apply to electricity and heating from biomass fuels produced in installations with a minimum thermal input.[46] The EU Timber Regulation purports to 'avoid imposing any unnecessary administrative burden' through requiring 'only operators that place timber and timber products on the internal market for the first time' to comply with due diligence system.[47] In the same vein, 'operators already using systems or procedures which comply with the requirements of this Regulation should not be required to set up new systems'.[48] The due-diligence obligation was hailed by environmental group Client Earth as an 'appropriate tool' to 'strike the balance between the need for both flexibility and certainty'.[49]

A more contentious example is the EU requirements under its amended Monitoring and Reporting Regulation (MRR) for aviation emissions, which do not fully accommodate the simplified CORSIA CO_2 Estimation and Reporting Tool (CERT).[50] CERT is available for operators with annual emissions below 500,000 tonnes in the year 2019–20.[51] Rather than measuring the actual fuel consumption,

[44] Regulation 2173/2005 on the establishment of a FLEGT licensing scheme for imports of timber into the European Community [2005] OJ L347/1, Arts 1, 2.

[45] cf WTO, *US – Certain Country of Origin Labelling (COOL) Requirements* (23 July 2012) WT/DS384/AB/R, WT/DS386/AB/R (*US-COOL*) [347], where the AB examined the complex country of origin requirements for livestock set by the US. As this information was not 'communicated to consumers in an understandable manner', it constituted 'arbitrary and unjustifiable discrimination'.

[46] Directive (EU) 2018/2001 of the European Parliament and of the Council of 11 December 2018 on the promotion of the use of energy from renewable sources [2018] OJ L328 ('RED II') Art 104.

[47] Regulation (EU) No 995/2010 of the European Parliament and of the Council of 20 October 2010 laying down the obligations of operators who place timber and timber products on the market [2010] OJ L295 ('Timber Regulation') rec 15.

[48] ibid rec 18. This was supported by the International Chamber of Commerce considering the Timber Regulation as a model for the implementation of the Nagoya Protocol in the EU, 'Nagoya Protocol Implementation in the EU: Comments on a Possible Due Diligence System and the EU Timber Regulation' (ICC, 18 June 2012) www.iccwbo.org/content/uploads/sites/3/2012/06/Nagoya-Protocol-Implementation-in-the-EU-Comments-on-a-possible-due-diligence-system-and-the-EU-Timber-Regulation.pdf.

[49] 'The EU Timber Regulation Due Diligence Obligation: An Appropriate Tool' (Client Earth, November 2015) www.documents.clientearth.org/wp-content/uploads/library/2015-11-25-the-eu-timber-regulation-due-diligence-obligation-an-appropriate-tool-ce-en.pdf. For a more critical analysis, see, however, A Fishman and K Obidzinski, 'European Union Timber Regulation: Is It Legal?' (2014) 23 *Review of European, Comparative and International Environmental Law* 258, 270.

[50] Commission Implementing Regulation (EU) 2018/2066 of 19 December 2018 on the monitoring and reporting of greenhouse gas emissions pursuant to Directive 2003/87/EC of the European Parliament and of the Council and amending Commission Regulation (EU) No 601/2012 [2018] OJ L334 ('EU MRR').

[51] CORSIA SARPs (n 6) ch 2.2.2.

it is an estimate based on aircraft type and journey. Under the EU requirements, emitters of less than 25,000 tonnes of CO_2 per year (or annually flying less than 243 flights per consecutive four-month period) may make use of Eurocontrol's Small Emitters Tool (SET).[52] This still leaves a gap in protection for the in-between group, with operators in overseas territories likely to be hit particularly hard.[53]

Finally, heightened tensions may arise where a state, or the EU, makes the application of its measure dependent on the *policy choices* of other states (type 3 extraterritorial element). Such 'contingent unilateralism' is arguably more problematic because it speaks 'directly' to the sovereign in its policy autonomy.[54] Indeed, sovereign equality arguably precludes strict equivalency of *legislation* because other states are simply left with no freedom as to the means with which they wish to address the complex regulatory challenges posed by climate change. States should further exercise flexibility in relation to the policies which they consider eligible for exemption or differential treatment.[55] In *US–Shrimp*, the fact that the other states were required 'to adopt a regulatory program that is not merely comparable, but rather essentially the same' was criticised by the AB as a 'rigid and unbending standard'.[56] This 'coercive' effect was considered to constitute unjustifiable discrimination in violation of the chapeau of Article XX GATT. A better approach is contained in the EU Timber Regulation, which, in the absence of an internationally accepted definition, defines timber as 'legally harvested' when it is 'harvested in accordance with the applicable legislation in the country of harvest'.[57]

3. CONSIDERATE DESIGN AND EQUITY: COMMON BUT DIFFERENTIATED RESPONSIBILITIES AND RESPECTIVE CAPABILITIES

The considerate design approach steers states to take into account the 'positive' justice-oriented conditions of equity, good faith and non-abuse of rights when crafting unilateral measures. In doing so they must make genuine best efforts to ensure that the way in which they exercise jurisdiction respects the interests

[52] EU MRR (n 50) Art 55.

[53] For this criticism, see International Air Transport Association, 'Comments on the Commission's Draft Delegated Regulation on Reporting Measures to Implement CORSIA' (13 December 2018) ec.europa.eu/info/law/better-regulation/have-your-say/initiatives/2007-Appropriate-monitoring-reporting-and-verification-for-a-global-scheme-for-aviation-emissions/F15893.

[54] J Scott and L Rajamani, 'Contingent Unilateralism – International Aviation in the European Emissions Trading Scheme' in B Van Vooren, S Blockmans and J Wouters (eds), *The EU's Role in Global Governance* (Oxford, Oxford University Press, 2013) 209.

[55] J Scott and L Rajamani, 'EU Climate Change Unilateralism' (2012) 23 *European Journal of International Law* 469, 469.

[56] *US–Shrimp* (n 40) [164].

[57] Timber Regulation (n 47) Art 1(f).

and rights of other states and the international community. As discussed in the previous chapter, these principles may be applied to 'correct' the application of formal rules where objectively equal treatment leads to unjust outcomes. As seen throughout this chapter, good faith and non-abuse of rights are infused in all elements of the considerate design approach. They feature, for example, in the good-faith use of scientific evidence and best-effort negotiations when deciding upon standards. The present section will therefore focus on equity, which, in the context of climate change, is reflected in the cornerstone principle of CBDRRC. Section 3.1 will explore the contours of this norm and its relevance in a jurisdiction context. Section 3.2 then considers different design options for differentiation based on CBDRRC. Finally, section 3.3 touches briefly upon the challenge of incorporating CBDRRC in a manner compatible with the non-discrimination requirements found throughout the concurrently applicable *lex specialis* regimes discussed earlier in this book.

3.1. CBDRRC in the Context of Climate Change

In its essence CBDRRC requires that states, when 'pursuing a common goal, take on different obligations, depending on their socio-economic situation and their historical contribution to the environmental problem at stake'.[58] Analysing the norm in a climate-change context, Caney helpfully distinguishes between 'mitigation' and 'adaptation burdens'.[59] The former are the opportunity costs of not engaging in activities contributing to climate change, whereas the latter are 'the costs to persons of adopting measures which enable them and/or others to cope with the ill-effects of climate change'.[60]

In terms of formulation, Principle 7 of the 1992 Rio Declaration provides a helpful starting point, providing that:

> In view of the different contributions to global environmental degradation, States have common but differentiated responsibilities. The developed countries acknowledge the responsibility that they bear in the international pursuit of sustainable development in view of the pressures their societies place on the global environment and of the technologies and financial resources they command.[61]

[58] See further eg E Hey, 'Common but Differentiated Responsibilities' in R Wolfrum (ed), *Max Planck Encyclopaedia of Public International Law*, online edn (Oxford, Oxford University Press, 2011) [1]. For a detailed analysis, see L Rajamani, *Differential Treatment in International Environmental Law* (Oxford, Oxford University Press, 2006).

[59] S Caney, 'Cosmopolitan Justice, Climate Change and Responsibility' (2005) 18 *Leiden Journal of International Law* 749, 751–52.

[60] ibid.

[61] Principle 7 of the Rio Declaration on Environment and Development, in *Report of the UN Conference on Environment and Development* (12 August 1992) UN Doc A/CONF.151/26. See further Scott and Rajamani (n 55) 477.

This soft-law provision informed Article 3(1) UNFCCC which instructs the parties to

> protect the climate system for the benefit of present and future generations of humankind, on the basis of equity and in accordance with their common but differentiated responsibilities and respective capabilities. Accordingly, the developed country Parties should take the lead in combating climate change and the adverse effects thereof.

Importantly, this provision also refers to 'respective capabilities', extending the basis for differential treatment under the CBDR principle to states' respective capabilities (RC) as well as their past contribution to the problem.[62] Notably, the 2015 Paris Agreement made a further addition, Article 2(2) providing that the Agreement 'will be implemented to reflect equity and the principle of common but differentiated responsibilities and respective capabilities, *in the light of different national circumstances*'.[63]

These subtle changes in wording reflect intense underlying debates on the precise criteria according to which differentiation should be determined.[64] A particular issue here is the identification of degrees of economic development, initially encapsulated in the static classification of the UNFCCC Annexes. This move had an unintendedly painful legacy, resulting in a long-lasting deadlock between those supporting the 1992 categories and those insisting on a more up-to-date, dynamic approach.[65] According to Savaresi, the Paris Agreement's silence on the definitions of more and less developed countries, together with the addition of the phrase 'in the light of different national circumstances', may be interpreted as 'an expression of the drafters' will to move beyond the approach to differentiation embedded in the UNFCCC'.[66] This issue will be discussed further in section 3.2.

Although the CBDRRC principle appears explicitly and implicitly throughout the climate-change regime, its legal status remains debated. Given its entrenchment, Scott and Rajamani contend that:

> [E]ven if this principle does not assume the character of a legal obligation in itself, it is a fundamental part of the conceptual apparatus of the climate change regime, such that it forms the basis for the interpretation of existing obligations and the elaboration of future international legal obligations within the regime in question.[67]

[62] See further H Winkler and L Rajamani, 'CBDR&RC in a Regime Applicable to All' (2014) 14 *Climate Policy* 102.

[63] The Paris Agreement (adopted 15 December 2015, entered into force 4 November 2016) (2016) 55 ILM 740 ('Paris Agreement') Art 2(2) (emphasis added).

[64] See further on the positions of the parties during the Paris Agreement negotiations: 'Differentiation under the Paris Agreement – A Tough Fight' (Third World Network, 28 December 2015) www.twnetwork.org/climate-change/differentiation-under-paris-agreement-%E2%80%93-tough-fight.

[65] See further P Pauw et al, 'Different Perspectives on Differentiated Responsibilities: A State-of-the-Art Review of the Notion of Common but Differentiated Responsibilities in International Negotiations' (Dt Inst für Entwicklungspolitik 2014) 6/2014 1.

[66] A Savaresi, 'The Paris Agreement: A Rejoinder' (ejiltalk.org, 26 February 2016) www.ejiltalk.org/the-paris-agreement-a-rejoinder/.

[67] Scott and Rajamani (n 55) 477.

It is submitted that the principle also has interpretative value in relation to jurisdiction, as a specific application of equity to the way in which states exercise their legislative competence in the context of climate protection. The principle's relationship with equity is clearly visible in the definitions contained in both Article 3 UNFCCC and Article 2 of the Paris Agreement, and there is considerable support in the literature for CBDRRC as an operationalisation of equity in the context of climate change.[68] As seen in chapter 9, the premise that different circumstances may require formally different treatment is further in line with the ICJ's findings in the *North Sea Continental Shelf* cases, regarding the equitable delimitation of sovereign territory.[69]

3.2. How to Differentiate when Designing Unilateral Measures

While there is a general consensus that the CBDRRC principle requires differential treatment, difficult questions remain as to its appropriate basis and concrete application. To start with, following the approach of the climate regime, the principle should be considered in relation to states based on the location of where the emissions are produced (production-based 'system boundary').[70] While this is the current political choice, questions can be raised as to the appropriateness of production-based counting, given that a great proportion of goods and services are produced through GHG-emitting processes in less developed countries to be consumed in more developed countries. Indeed, it is the EU's unilateral attempts to circumvent the territorial system boundary that have given rise to these jurisdictional tensions in the first place.

In terms of application, Scott and Rajamani consider a role for the CBDRRC principle in relation to acts of contingent unilateralism, such as that of the Aviation Directive.[71] Equivalent protection clauses, in particular, inherently raise tensions with the requirement of differential treatment, as they impose higher standards without considering the affected state's capacity to bear the burden or its original contribution to the problem. For this reason, flexibility is required in relation to compliance, which can be integrated through extended compliance periods or lower protection thresholds.[72] These are examples of procedural and substantive means of implementing CBDRRC, respectively, and would appear equally valid for measures with type 1 and type 2 extraterritorial elements.

More generally, Romera and van Asselt provide a helpful analysis of the key categories of norms in international environmental agreement through which

[68] See eg Pauw et al (n 65) 3, referring for support to P Sands et al, *Principles of international environmental law*, 3rd edn (Cambridge, Cambridge University Press, 2012) 233.

[69] See further chapter 9, section 4.1.

[70] Pauw et al (n 55) 12; Scott and Rajamani (n 55) 475.

[71] Scott and Rajamani (n 55) 487.

[72] ibid 490.

CBDRRC may be put into action.[73] These are central obligations, provisions on implementation and provisions providing assistance, such as technology transfer.[74] This norm division is also of conceptual value for the design of unilateral climate protection measures with an extraterritorial element. Starting with central obligations, setting aside political likelihood, accepting a lower protection threshold from producers in developing countries may be a window for the application of CBDRRC. For example, GHG savings required for biofuels to be considered 'sustainable' could be adjusted according to a country's capacity and historical responsibility. Compositely, Mehling and others suggest that the smaller group of least developed countries (LDCs) may be exempted from a measure's scope.[75] According to the authors, this 'can be reconciled with the environmental objective' of such measures, as LDCs 'contribute only minimally to global emissions'. In a broader legal context, however, the feasibility of unilaterally differentiating substantive obligations will highly depend on the concurrently applicable rules in specific regimes. In particular, regulators must navigate the tensions with the non-discrimination requirements prominent in the WTO, IMO and ICAO rules.

Of course, it also remains the question whether a state wishes to differentiate the central obligations of a unilateral measure because this may undermine its level of protection. Furthermore, where measures pursue multiple policy objectives, states may have other health or safety reasons for desiring products or services to meet stricter equivalency standards. An example here is the EU Regulation 2019/631 setting CO_2 performance standards for new passenger cars, which is intended both 'to contribute both to the objectives of the Paris Agreement' and to reduce pollutants which 'significantly harm our health'.[76]

The second suggested strategy is to simplify the provisions on implementation for developing states. The Paris Agreement illustrates this in relation to the transparency framework, which according to Article 13, 'shall provide flexibility in the implementation of the provisions of this Article to those developing country Parties that need it in the light of their capacities'. An example of where the EU has been criticised on this point is its choice to restrict the permitted monitoring methods for aviation emissions under its ETS MRR.[77] The ETS MRR only recognises two methods for the monitoring of fuel consumption.[78] The CORSIA standards and operating procedures (SARPs) recognise three

[73] B Martinez Romera and H van Asselt, 'The International Regulation of Aviation Emissions: Putting Differential Treatment into Practice' (2015) 27 *Journal of Environmental Law* 259, 268.

[74] ibid.

[75] MA Mehling et al, 'Designing Border Carbon Adjustments for Enhanced Climate Action' (2019) 113 *American Journal of International Law* 433, 475.

[76] Regulation (EU) 2019/631 of the European Parliament and of the Council of 17 April 2019 setting CO2 emission performance standards for new passenger cars and for new light commercial vehicles, and repealing Regulations (EC) No 443/2009 and (EU) No 510/2011 [2019] OJ L111.

[77] EU MRR (n 50) Art 53.

[78] ibid Annex III, s 1.

additional fuel monitoring methods, which not only provide more flexibility, but are also argued to be simpler in execution.[79] The Union's position was that the impact of its measures would be minimal, as the great majority of operators were already subject to the (more restrictive) EU standards under the EU ETS.[80] There is, however, a new group here, namely operators based in EEA outermost regions, or dependencies and territories of EU Member States.[81] It has been argued that this group will be negatively affected, being required to adhere to the more complex monitoring methods in a very tight time frame.[82]

Compliance periods offer another recognised avenue for differentiation. Here, CORSIA may offer some inspiration, taking into account 'special circumstances and respective capabilities' through phased implementation, with voluntary participation for LDCs, Small Island Developing States (SIDS) and Landlocked Developing Countries (LLDCs).[83] As discussed, however, there is a risk that overly long implementation periods may undermine the effectiveness of a measure, particularly in light of the envisioned tipping point for global emissions.[84] An EU example is RED II, which implements a 'freeze' of high indirect land-use change (ILUC)-risk biofuels at 2019 levels, to be 'phased out' to zero by 2030.[85] Although not without controversy, in principle this aspect gives foreign suppliers, who in the case of palm oil are largely from developing countries, time to adjust to a complete ban.

Finally, technical and financial assistance provisions may be included to lower the burdens of compliance for developing states. This may go some way to alleviating the strain of a higher level of ambition in the substantive agreements.[86] In the 2030 Climate Target Plan, the Commission, for example, suggests that the envisioned expansion of the ETS should 'address distribution impacts', 'by using part of the corresponding auction revenues'.[87]

A fundamental remaining issue in applying CBDRRC is on what basis countries should be differentiated. One approach, promogulated, for example, by

[79] CORSIA SARPs (n 6) Appendix 2; for critique, see IATA Comments on CORSIA Implementation (n 53).

[80] Reflecting on this, see UK Department for Transport, 'Explanatory Memorandum on EU Legislation' (10 April 2019) 7252/19 C (2019) 1644 final, explaining that for this reason the EU considered it unnecessary to conduct an impact assessment.

[81] These operators are now included under Commission Delegated Regulation (EU) 2019/1603 of 18 July 2019 supplementing Directive 2003/87/EC of the European Parliament and of the Council as regards measures adopted by the International Civil Aviation Organisation for the monitoring, reporting and verification of aviation emissions for the purpose of implementing a global market-based measure [2019] OJ L250, Art 1(2)).

[82] IATA Comments on CORSIA Implementation (n 53) 3.

[83] CORSIA (6) [5].

[84] TL Lenten et al, 'Climate Tipping points – Too Risky to Bet Against' (*Nature*, 27 November 2019) www.nature.com/articles/d41586-019-03595-0.

[85] RED II (n 46) Art 26(2).

[86] Hey (n 58) [7].

[87] Commission 'Stepping up Europe's 2030 climate ambition, Investing in a climate-neutral future for the benefit of our people' (Communication) COM(2020) 562 final 15.

the Climate Action Network, is to divide the differentiation criteria into 'equity indicators' and 'raw indicators'.[88] The former are 'higher-level, ethically-inflected indicators' such as contribution to harm, whereas the latter are 'familiar, publicly available demographic or economic data' 'that can be taken "off the shelf"', such as GDP.[89] As discussed, these indicators are used to measure current respective capabilities and historic contribution to climate harm.[90] In this way, according to Hey, 'common but differentiated responsibilities can be understood as a translation of the concept of intra-generational equity to the inter-State level'.[91]

Questions remain, however, about the weight to be given to the various indicators. Firstly, the inclusion of states' historical contribution to environmental harm has been contested on ethical grounds because present citizens of developed countries bear no 'causal responsibility' for the emissions of their predecessors.[92] Shue counters this with the argument that 'current generations are, and future generations probably will be, continuing beneficiaries of earlier industrial activity'.[93] Others disagree, however, contending that later generations had no choice in the receipt of this benefit.[94] Nevertheless, as climate change occurs as the consequence of the accumulation of emissions over time, past emissions have undoubtedly made an important contribution to the present harm, and cannot be ignored entirely.[95]

There is also much debate on the appropriate 'raw indicators', which are particularly relevant for determining countries' 'respective capabilities'.[96] At the outset it would seem that it is no longer appropriate to follow the division set by the Annexes to the UNFCCC, as this was clearly not accepted by the parties to the Paris Agreement.[97] Rather, an individual, adjustable approach is needed.

[88] Climate Action Network, 'The Core Convention-Based Equity Indicators' (climatenetwork.org, September 2013) www.climate network.org/sites/default/files/can_convention-based_indicators_sept2013.pdf.

[89] ibid.

[90] Winkler and Rajamani (n 62) 3.

[91] Hey (n 58) [12]. See also, C Redgwell, 'Principles and Emerging Norms in International Law: Intra- and Intergenerational Equity' in KR Gray, R Tarasofsky and C Carlarne (eds), *The Oxford Handbook of International Climate Change Law* (Oxford, Oxford University Press, 2016) 186, 187.

[92] J Thompson, 'Historical Responsibility and Climate Change' in L Meyer and P Sanklecha (eds), *Climate Justice and Historical Emissions* (Cambridge, Cambridge University Press 2017) 48.

[93] H Shue, 'Global Environment and International Inequality'' (1999) 75 *International Affairs* 533, 536; discussed further in Caney (n 59) 753.

[94] J Thompson, 'Historical Responsibility and Climate Change' in L Meyer and P Sanklecha (eds), *Climate Justice and Historical Emissions* (Cambridge, Cambridge University Press, 2017) 48.

[95] E Page, 'Distributing the Burdens of Climate Change' (2008) 17 *Environmental Politics* 556, 559–60.

[96] See further B Müller, N Höhne and C Ellermann, 'Differentiating (Historic) Responsibilities for Climate Change' (2009) 9 *Climate Policy* 593, 594.

[97] For further legal analysis, see D Bodansky, J Brunnée and L Rajamani, *International Climate Change Law* (Oxford, Oxford University Press, 2017) 122, noting that the UNFCCC Annexes were compiled in haste at the closing of negotiations, with little consideration given to which countries were on which list.

Arguing in favour of criteria 'capable of being applied on the basis of data that are accessible and reliable', Scott and Rajamani suggest per capita GDP as a possible indicator.[98] Others argue that the Human Development Index (HDI) would be more appropriate, as it also measures social development.[99] According to the Climate Action Network, calculations of capability should include a state's 'development need', which is the 'shortfall between its current socio-economic profile and a future profile in which all its people have achieved some adequate level of economic development, however defined'.[100] This requires a 'development threshold' to indicate the space of development need, where '"development" is not reducible to poverty alleviation'.[101] National per capita income and emission averages are not considered 'in themselves serviceable indicators' because there is no universal correlation between income and other aspects of development.[102] It has also been noted that per capita calculations are themselves problematic as they do not reflect causal contribution.[103] On the other hand, however, aggregate calculations do not reflect population size, which is relevant to the notion of responsibility also embedded in the CBDRRC principle.[104]

As a concrete example, the CORSIA approach discussed above is based on UN country development categorisations, which have their own extensive assessment criteria. For instance, the identification of LDCs is based on income, human assets and economic vulnerability, which are calculated using a number of indicators including gross national income per capita and the Human Assets Index.[105] The list of countries is constantly reviewed and updated every three years.[106]

Ultimately, amidst these methodological conundrums, it will be up to individual states to choose which raw indicators they use. An element of arbitrariness appears inevitable, rendering procedural safeguards particularly important.[107] In this regard, Scott and Rajamani note the need for transparency and consistency when applying the measures as well as periodic review.[108] This would appear in keeping with the good-faith and non-abuse of rights principles.

[98] Scott and Rajamani (n 55) 488.
[99] Climate Action Network (n 88) 5.
[100] ibid.
[101] ibid.
[102] ibid.
[103] Müller (n 96) 597.
[104] ibid.
[105] 'LDC Identification Criteria and Indicators' (United Nations website, 2021) www.un.org/development/desa/dpad/least-developed-country-category/ldc-criteria.html.
[106] ibid. For a list of Small Island Developing States, see 'Small Island Development States' (United Nations website, 2021) sustainabledevelopment.un.org /topics/sids/list.
[107] Scott and Rajamani (n 55) 590.
[108] ibid 488, noting that: 'Needless to say, the selection of the applicable objective criteria will necessarily be a subjective and controversial exercise.'

3.3. Walking the Tightrope: CBDRRC and Non-discrimination

As alluded to above, the application of CBDRRC may raise tensions with the non-discrimination requirements found in the *lex specialis* regimes discussed earlier in this book. This will require a case-by-case analysis, involving complex questions of regime interaction.[109] Nonetheless, it is valuable to briefly consider some key points of friction which regulators will need to navigate when designing 'extraterritorial' climate protection measures.

To start with, in a trade law context, the interests of developing countries are protected though 'special and differential' (S&D) treatment provisions, as 'an integral part of the WTO Agreements'.[110] As noted by Larbprasertporn, S&D is not quite the same as CBDR(RC), as the former 'intends first and foremost to promote international trade' and not environmental protection.[111] Historical contribution to climate change is also not taken into account. More generally, WTO law does not contain a definition of 'developed' and 'developing' countries.[112] Although states are free to decide this for themselves, other states do not necessarily recognise these self-categorisations, and whether or not they benefit from developed members' schemes will depend on the giving country.

Under the GATT, key S&D requirements relevant for the design of climate-protection measures pertain to the flexibility and delayed implementation of certain commitments, and can be found in Article XXXVII.[113] This provision does not, however, form an exception to the NT and MFN requirements prohibiting differential treatment of like products and services from different countries of origin.[114] More solace is offered by the so-called 'enabling clause', providing a basis for preferential treatment for developing countries as an exception to the MFN requirement in Article I GATT.[115] This is the basis for the Generalized System of Preferences (GSP) granting preferential tariff treatment. The EU has implemented the system through its EU GSP and the GSP+ for sustainable

[109] For a comprehensive analysis, see eg RF Yearwood, *The Interaction between World Trade Organisation (WTO) Law and External International Law: The Constrained Openness of WTO Law (a Prologue to a Theory)* (Abingdon, Routledge, 2012).

[110] See WTO, Doha Ministerial Declaration (20 November 2001) WT/MIN(01)/DEC/1. See also WTO, 2005 Hong Kong Ministerial Declaration (18 December 2005) WT/MIN(05)/DEC, [35]–[37].

[111] P Larbprasertporn, 'The Interaction Between WTO Law and the Principle of Common but Differentiated Responsibilities in the Case of Climate-Related Border Tax Adjustment' (2014) 6 *Goettingen Journal of International Law* 145, 153.

[112] 'Who Are the Developing Countries in the WTO?' (WTO website, 2021) www.wto.org/english/tratop_e/devel_e/d1who_e.htm.

[113] See further Committee on Trade and Development, 'Special and Differential Treatment Provisions in WTO Agreements and Decisions' (Note by the Secretariat, 12 October 2018) WT/COMTD/W/239.

[114] Larbprasertporn (n 111) 152, referring to Panel Report, *EEC–Dessert Apples*, L/6491 [1989] BISD 36S/93 [12.31].

[115] GATT, Decision on Differential and More Favourable Treatment Reciprocity and Fuller Participation of Developing Countries (28 November 1979) L/4903 [1], [2(b)].

development and good governance.[116] Under the EU GSP, 'developing countries are automatically granted GSP if they … [a]re classified as having an income level below "upper middle income" by the World Bank' and are not already benefiting from another preferential market access arrangement.[117] An eligibility requirement for GSP+ is that vulnerable countries ratify certain 'relevant conventions', including the UNFCCC and the Kyoto Protocol.[118]

There remains, however, a high likelihood that differential product and production requirements will conflict with WTO law.[119] In this regard, Mehling and others suggest that, while 'desirable' to avoid disproportionate effects on developing countries, 'differentiation should be based on differences in the carbon content of products, not their country of origin'.[120] Foreign producers should have an opportunity qualify for differential treatment based on their product's 'actual climate performance'. However, even when constructed in an origin-neutral manner, as discussed in chapter 4, foreign carbon footprint measures are very likely to violate the NT and MFN requirements. In this regard, it has been suggested that the chapeau of the general exemptions provision, particularly under the GATT, may provide a window for the incorporation of CBDRRC in WTO law.[121] This would seem to follow from the AB's finding in *US–Shrimp* that:

> [D]iscrimination results not only when countries in which the same conditions prevail are differently treated, but also when the application of the measure at issue does not allow for any inquiry into the appropriateness of the regulatory program for the conditions prevailing in those exporting countries.[122]

While not uncontroversial, this view offers a window for prima facie GATT violations differentiating on the basis of CBDRRC to be saved by the chapeau of Article XX.[123]

Applied here, this could mean that where a developing state has, for capacity reasons, chosen to implement less stringent climate-protection standards, its measures should not be automatically rejected. An interesting case in this regard is that of the EU's criteria for determining ILUC-risk biofuels. At the

[116] Consolidated text: Regulation (EU) No 978/2012 of the European Parliament and of the Council of 25 October 2012 applying a scheme of generalised tariff preferences and repealing Council Regulation (EC) No 732/2008 [2012] OJ L303 ('Regulation 732/2008').

[117] ibid 4(1)(a).

[118] ibid Art 9(1)b and Annex VIII.

[119] See further S Davidson Ladly, 'Border Carbon Adjustments, WTO-Law and the Principle of Common but Differentiated Responsibilities' (2012) 12 *International Environmental Agreements* 63.

[120] Mehling et al (n 75) 475.

[121] See further eg Ladly (n 119); M Hertel, 'Climate-Change-Related Trade Measures and Article XX: Defining Discrimination in Light of the Principle of Common but Differentiated Responsibilities' (2011) 45 *Journal of World Trade* 653, 667.

[122] *US–Shrimp* (n 40) [165].

[123] For an alternative approach, see also L Reider, 'Art XX GATT 1994 – Climate Change and Disadvantaged Nations' (Völkerrechtsblog, 12 May 2020) www.voelkerrechtsblog.org/art-xx-gatt-1994-climate-change-and-disadvantaged-nations/.

time of writing in 2020, Indonesia had formally requested a Panel, arguing that the EU 'prepared and adopted these [ILUC] measures without taking into account circumstances specific to the developing countries' producing palm oil.[124] Compounding the problem, according to Indonesia, the measures further 'lack transparency and an objective basis'. In particular, Indonesia refers to the EU's own admission that 'the level of greenhouse gas emissions caused by indirect land-use change cannot be unequivocally determined with the level of precision required to be included in the greenhouse gas emission calculation methodology'.[125] Not only may these factors prove serious hurdles under WTO law, but the suggestion of arbitrariness and protectionism raises tensions with CBDRRC and the non-abuse of rights principle.

In the context of aviation and maritime emissions, the situation is complicated by the fact that separate multilateral agreements are being negotiated which balance non-discrimination with CBDRRC in their own ways. This is no mean feat. In the context of maritime emissions, there has been longstanding disagreement regarding the interaction of CBDRRC with the IMO principle of no more favourable treatment (NMFT).[126] In this regard Article 1(b) of the IMO Convention states as an objective:

> To encourage the removal of discriminatory action and unnecessary restrictions by Governments affecting shipping engaged in international trade so as to promote the availability of shipping services to the commerce of the world without discrimination.

Non-discrimination is also reflected in various provisions of the LOSC, Article 227 for example providing that:

> In exercising their rights and performing their duties under this Part, States shall not discriminate in form or in fact against vessels of any other State.

The friction between CBDRRC and NMFT was particularly clear in the IMO negotiations of the energy-efficiency standards for ships under MARPOL Annex IV. In their extensive analysis, Chircop, Doelle and Gauvin note the rejection of several proposals, including allowing for differentiated ship construction standards in developed and developing states.[127] As a more optimistic example of careful, if hard-fought, compromise, Kopela points to the IMO Resolution on

[124] WTO, *European Union – Certain Measures Concerning Palm Oil and Oil Palm Crop-Based Biofuels – Request for the Establishment of a Panel Indonesia* (24 March 2020) WT/DS593/9 (*EU–Palm Oil and Biofuels*) 5–6.

[125] See Red II (n 46) rec 81.

[126] S Kopela, 'Climate Change, Regime Interaction, and the Principle of Common but Differentiated Responsibility: The Experience of the International Maritime Organization' (2014) 24 *Yearbook of International Environmental Law* 70, 78.

[127] A Chidrop, M Doelle and R Gauvin, 'Shipping and Climate Change International Law and Policy Considerations – Special Report' (Centre for International Governance Innovation, 2018) www.cigionline.org/sites/default/files/documents/Shipping%27s%20contribution%20to%20climate%20change%202018web_0.pdf.

the Promotion of Technical Co-operation and Transfer of Technology.[128] The IMO Initial Strategy on emission reductions also reveals remaining tensions, Chircop noting 'a veritable "battle of principles"' during the negotiations of the shipping industry's mitigation target.[129] What resulted was a somewhat diluted 'guiding principle' on 'the need to be cognizant of' the non-discrimination and CBDRRC principles.[130] Leaving the matter open for longer-term policy, the IMO Initial Strategy provides that '[t]he impacts on States of a measure should be assessed and taken into account as appropriate before adoption of the measure', where '[p]articular attention should be paid to the needs of developing countries, especially small island developing States (SIDS) and least developed countries (LDCs)'.[131]

Non-discrimination has a similarly strong role on the field of aviation emissions. Key examples are Articles 11 and 44 of the Chicago Convention, the latter which notes as an 'aim and objective' of the ICAO to 'develop principles and techniques of international air navigation … so as to: (g) '[a]void discrimination between contracting States'. For CBDRRC, the preamble of the Resolution A 38-18 on the development of a market-based measure for emissions does 'acknowledg[e] the principles and provisions on common but differentiated responsibilities and respective capabilities … under the UNFCCC and the Kyoto Protocol'. It has been argued, however, that this soft wording was 'not a full embrace' of CBDRRC.[132]

The differentiation of burdens under the initial CORSIA design has been discussed throughout this chapter. In general, the ICAO appears to adopt an open and flexible attitude. Resolution A 39-2 'agrees' that the ICAO fuel efficiency improvement goals

> would not attribute specific obligations to individual States, and the different circumstances, respective capabilities and contribution of developing and developed States to the concentration of aviation GHG emissions in the atmosphere will determine how each State may voluntarily contribute to achieving the global aspirational goals.[133]

For parallel unilateral measures, these fast-developing multilateral schemes themselves raise tensions with CBDRRC. Even at the initial data collection phase, it remains problematic that operators from developing countries are faced

[128] Resolution MEPC 229(65), 'Promotion of technical cooperation and transfer of technology relating to the improvement of energy efficiency of ships' (adopted on 17 May 2013) MEPC 65/22, Annex 4, [3(1)].

[129] A Chircop, 'The IMO Initial Strategy for the Reduction of GHGs from International Shipping: A Commentary' (2019) 34 *International Journal of Marine and Coastal Law* 482, 494.

[130] Resolution MEPC 304(72)' Initial IMO Strategy on Reduction of GHG Emissions from Ships' (adopted on 13 April 2018) MEPC 72/17/Add.1, Annex 11 [3.2].

[131] ibid [4.10].

[132] Romera and van Asselt (n 73) 272.

[133] Assembly Resolution A 39-2, 'Consolidated statement of continuing ICAO policies and practices related to environmental protection – Climate change' (adopted at the 39th Session of the ICAO Assembly, 27 September–6 October 2016) [4]–[5].

with dual regulatory burdens, while having a lower capacity to bear the costs. Should the EU ultimately be unsatisfied with the ambition of both multilateral schemes, it is essential that the Union pay particular attention to the consideration of states' differentiated responsibilities and respective capabilities in the design of its measures.

4. CONCLUSION

This chapter has explored possible strategies with which regulators may design climate-protective measures to make them more 'considerate' of the interests of other equal sovereigns. As a jurisdictional tool, the aim of the considerate design approach is first and foremost to maximise states' respective regulatory space. Alignment stands out as a key means of reducing the foreign-related impact of a measure. This requires good-faith efforts of states to assess both the external impact of their measures, as well as the necessity and level of ambition of a chosen unilateral standard. Such assessment should have an objective scientific basis, and be complimented by dialogue with other regulators on recognised equivalent and comparable protection standards.

A remaining dilemma clearly illustrated in EU policy is that alignment may well be considered to undermine the desired level of protection. As climate change is a common concern of vital importance, this chapter has briefly reflected on whether necessity may legitimise a relaxation of the general duty to respect other states' sovereignty. Although explorative in nature, strong normative arguments can be made in favour of a limited exception to the requirement of jurisdictional restraint in a prescriptive context.

As a positive condition, consideration for states' common but differentiated responsibilities forms an essential but ever-challenging design requirement. The different realisation strategies recognised in the literature for central, implementation and assistance norms in multilateral environmental agreements are also helpful in a unilateral context. Here, however, acceptance of differentiated substantive requirements will largely depend on their compatibility with the rules of specific regimes. A particular obstacle is the tension arising between CBDRRC, the principle of non-discrimination, which features prominently in WTO, ICAO and IMO policy. As regards world trade law, the chapeau of Article XX GATT has been argued to provide an avenue for synergy between the competing norms of non-discrimination and CBDRRC. In the ICAO and IMO contexts, the delicate and undefined balance of interests is swiftly being negotiated. There the situation is arguably more problematic because the EU's 'extraterritorial' measures create a dual compliance burden, which also affects developing states. Should the EU choose to maintain higher unilateral standards, it is imperative that particular weight be given to a just differentiation of burdens.

11

Concluding Remarks

As the global regulatory space becomes ever more crowded, there is an acute need for development within the law of jurisdiction. Functionally speaking, state jurisdiction must play a 'meta' role, as a law to balance the reach of other laws. This balance was traditionally found along territorial lines. Today, however, it is clear that such an approach no longer answers the needs of modern society. This is particularly evident in the context of unilateral climate protection measures taken to achieve state obligations under international environmental law. The latter, comparatively younger legal field has evolved out of recognition of the realities of interdependence that classical jurisdictional doctrine often appears to ignore.

It is well recognised that the mechanics of international law make responsiveness an obstacle. As noted by Krisch:

> Like all law, international law is marked by a focus on the past: most of its sources refer to historical events, and in fact, many of its central elements have remained the same for a long time. This provides it with a particular stability and makes it a prime source of legitimacy, since it can claim century-long acceptance by international society.[1]

Yet this focus on the past also has its risks, as 'century-long acceptance' has less legitimising force when it is premised on a different practical reality. This is exacerbated by the fact that, as noted by Tarlock, '[t]raditional international law is designed to produce the lowest common denominator standards based on long-standing national practice because these are the only norms that can be accepted as law'.[2] Thus, where short-term costs reduce long-term ambitions, multilateral regimes may not adequately respond to pressing environmental needs.

That being said, international environmental law has seen a relatively swift crystallisation of norms that do respond to the challenges of interdependence, in particular the obligations of prevention and precaution. These consider the interests of other affected states and the international community, setting due-diligence standards to anticipate, prevent and mitigate environmental harm.

[1] N Krisch, 'International Law in Times of Hegemony: Unequal Power and the Shaping of the International Legal Order' (2005) 16 *European Journal of International Law* 369, 377.

[2] D Tarlock, 'Stewardship Sovereignty: The Next Step in Former Prime Minister Palmer's Logic' (1992) 42 *Washington University Journal of Urban & Contemporary Law* 21, 23.

It is argued here that it is high time for the law of state jurisdiction to adapt as well. As it has different objectives and must consider a broader spectrum of interests than international environmental law, there can be no direct correlation between these regimes. Nevertheless, it is clear that there are avenues for development throughout the jurisdictional analysis.

Fundamentally this book advocates for a more 'balanced' interest-balancing test, the elements of which form a golden thread throughout the various chapters. As a first step, the 'extraterritorial element' is recognised at the point when the interests of *affected* states are sufficiently engaged. As argued in part I of this book, this will be the case when a measure's operation is de facto dependent on foreign conduct or circumstances. In practice, this threshold then includes situations where one state's measures place the burden of compliance with environmental measures on foreign producers whose home states have chosen not to implement the same type of policy.

At this point, as a second step, the interests of the *acting* state may be considered, to determine whether it can claim a jurisdictional basis. Here one must first turn to the relevant *lex specialis* regimes which, as discussed in part II, impose their own web of conditions on unilateral climate related-trade measures. This book has focused on the fields of world trade law, international civil aviation law and the law of the sea. As uncertainties remain, the customary rules and general principles of state jurisdiction have an important gap-filling role as a *lex generalis*. As is well established in jurisdictional theory, here a jurisdictional basis will exist when a state has a 'substantial connection' to the subject matter it seeks to regulate.

Part III considers the 'substantial connection' requirement, and its application in the field of climate change. As they respond to a 'common concern of humankind', measures seeking to mitigate climate change find, at the very least, doctrinal support in the more normative universality principle. However, accepting 'climate change jurisdiction' based on universality alone would compromise the law's competence delineation function, and does not find support in state practice. In constructing the substantial connection, the effects-doctrine offers a more plausible window, its increasing acceptance in an economic context illustrating that the law of jurisdiction can and does respond to states' perceived need to regulate emerging issues which negatively impact on their national interests.

Of particular relevance to the effects-doctrine is the issue of non-linear cumulative causation, which does not fit well within the mould of the classic jurisdictional principles. It is argued that here the widely recognised and concurrently applicable norm of precaution should inform the jurisdictional analysis. In particular, precaution may buttress a broader interpretation of the effects-doctrine as providing a jurisdictional basis when a state can demonstrate that the conduct measurably contributes to an increase in the risk of reasonably foreseeable grave harm. More recent developments before higher domestic courts demonstrate a willingness to embrace an 'every bit of carbon counts' approach. Thus both the 2019 *Urgenda* case and the 2020 *Friends of the Irish Environment*

CLG cases recognized a 'consistent' and near 'linear relationship' between GHG emissions and global warming, already leading to a 'profound environmental and societal impact'.[3] Acknowledging the link between emission reduction measures and the prevention of harm aligns with the functional rationale of the effects doctrine, according to which states have jurisdiction to respond to firmly established causes of serious territorial harm.

Admittedly, this approach acknowledges quite a broad 'basis' for unilateral extraterritorial climate change jurisdiction. The way in which states exercise jurisdiction is then at least as relevant, as this will inevitably have a ripple effect on other actors. The dramatic change of stance on the role of 'reasonableness' in the Fourth US Restatement on Foreign Relations Law, however, illustrates the remaining uncertainty in legal discourse as to the nature and content of states' obligation to consider others in a prescriptive context.[4] In the case of the EU, it is in regard to this aspect that the greatest criticisms may be levied against its climate change measures. At the same time, this is also where the greatest potential lies for improvement.

Against this backdrop, part IV proposes a 'considerate design' approach, as a tool to assist regulators in crafting unilateral measures with an extraterritorial element. As jurisdiction is a manifestation of sovereign power, it is argued that principles limiting state sovereignty steer states to exercise jurisdictional restraint. The principle of sovereign equality is of particular importance here, as well as its 'derivative' principles of non-interference and non-intervention. Taking a broader perspective, the justice-oriented principles of equity, good faith and non-abuse of rights may positively condition the design of unilateral measures.

Difficult questions then arise as to the possible operationalisation of these principles in a prescriptive context. It is argued here that they may be most valuable when applied as conditions on a measure's design, so as to reduce potential conflicts of interests at the outset. As the law of jurisdiction is concerned with the channelling of states' regulatory power, the aim of this approach is primarily to maximise states' simultaneous regulatory freedom. States are, after all, best placed to formulate and realise their own interests. As such, it is argued that the most effective way of protecting states' sovereign equality is to ensure mutual respect for each other's regulatory space, at least in the formal sense. Indeed, while it is recognised that global realities may distort the achievement of material equality, a formal design requirement may go some way in restraining the

[3] *Friends of the Irish Environment CLG v Government of Ireland, Ireland and the Attorney General*, Appeal No 205/19 [2020] IESC 49 [3.3]; *Urgenda Foundation v Kingdom of the Netherlands*, Supreme Court (20 December 2019) ECLI:NL:HR:2019:2006 [2.1].

[4] *Restatement (Fourth) of the Foreign Relations Law of the United States* (St Paul, MN, American Law Institute Publishers, 2018). See also *Barcelona Traction, Light and Power Co, Ltd (Belgium v Spain)* [1970] ICJ Rep 3, 105.

influence of powerful actors. The application of these principles is therefore not restricted to dramatic situations of 'true conflict', and should rather be extended to the broader policy choices of other states. As mentioned, this includes states' choice not to act, for example through choosing not to burden their producers with the costs of environmental protection. In this way, the interests of private actors are relatedto the interests of their home states.

Applying the considerate design approach to climate-protection measures, a more specific challenge is the trade-off between states' autonomy to set their own desired level of environmental protection, and the foreign-related impacts of this policy choice. In the case of competing measures, maximum possible alignment may go quite some way in reducing a measure's foreign 'interference'. Yet dilemmas remain, when, based on reliable scientific evidence, a competing standard is simply not enough. This is arguably the case with CORSIA, which has been widely criticised for its lack of ambition. Normatively speaking, where a competing measure is demonstrably insufficient to achieve a reasonable share of the minimum internationally agreed level of protection, this may reduce the pressure to exercise jurisdictional restraint.

What then becomes essential is integration of CBDRRC. Accepted strategies for differentiation in substantive and procedural norms of multilateral environmental agreements may provide useful guidance in a unilateral context. These include exceptions for least-developed states, delayed implementation periods and simplified compliance requirements. Of course, such strategies face the many obstacles of compatibility with the applicable *lex specialis* regimes, in particular the pervasive non-discrimination requirement. While this remains a challenging task for regulators, the greatest efforts should be taken to effectuate CBDRRC, particularly where measures impose a dual regulatory burden on operators.

Despite the persistent obstacles, an optimist may see potential for the law of jurisdiction in an environmental context. Climate change simply cannot be ignored, and there is an increasingly strong call in the global community for adequate legal responses. Indeed, the explosion of climate change litigation is pushing the issue further into the broader legal arena, in particular in the fields of human rights protection and states' duty of care.[5] Furthermore, the developments in liability law regarding causation and climate change illustrate that, despite its relative novelty, measures concerning complex environmental harm can be integrated into existing legal frameworks. In light of this progress it is logical and necessary that the law of state jurisdiction should also move towards further responsiveness to climate change challenges. That it is capable of doing so is evidenced by the growing acceptance of the effects-doctrine across various newer fields of law, including data protection and international economic law.

[5] For a helpful overview of case law developments, see 'Climate Change Litigation Databases' (Sabin Center for Climate Change, Columbia University) climatecasechart.com.

The reception of the EU's proactive climate policy then provides an important 'space' to watch in the coming years.

Finally, from a utilitarian perspective, it is hoped that an adapted balancing approach would allow for more equitable burden sharing, with further recognition for the interests of developing states.[6] Thus the economic pressure often exerted by more powerful markets on developing countries should be considered relevant when determining the existence of 'extraterritoriality' at the outset. As these states are often the most vulnerable to climate change, recognition of environmental harm as legitimising preventative action may go some way to alleviating the harm suffered. Furthermore, integration of the CBDRRC principle into the jurisdictional conditions may help to balance the costs of compliance according to capability. Alongside these developments, legal discourse has an important role to play in catalysing and contextualising the regulatory debate. This will be greatly helped by increased coherence, and more holistic reflection on the different interest at stake, particularly the silent yet essential voice of our planet.

[6] On burden sharing in the context of climate change, see further S Caney, 'Cosmopolitan Justice, Climate Change and Responsibility' (2005) 18 *Leiden Journal of International Law* 749.

Selected Bibliography

Adenas, M and Zleptnig, S, 'Proportionality and Balancing in WTO Law: A Comparative Perspective' (2007) 20 *Cambridge Review of International Affairs* 71.

Ahmed, T and Butler, I, 'The European Union and Human Rights: An International Law Perspective' (2006) 17 *European Journal of International Law* 771.

Ajevski, M, 'Serious Breaches, the Draft Articles on State Responsibility and Universal Jurisdiction' (2008) 2 *European Journal of Legal Studies* 12.

Akehurst, M, 'Jurisdiction in International Law' (1973) 46 *British Yearbook of International Law* 145.

van Alsenoy, B and Koekkoek, M, 'Internet and Jurisdiction after Google Spain: The Extraterritorial Reach of the 'Right to Be Delisted'' (2015) 5 *International Data Privacy Law* 105.

Allott P, 'Power Sharing in the Law of the Sea' (1983) 77 *American Journal of International Law* 1.

Anderson, B, 'Unilateral Trade Measures and Environmental Policy' (1993) 66 *Temple Law Review* 751.

Ankersmit, L, *Green Trade and Fair Trade in and with the EU: Process-Based Measures within the EU Legal Order* (Cambridge, Cambridge University Press, 2017).

Ankersmit, L, Lawrence, J and Davies, G, 'Diverging EU and WTO Perspectives on Extraterritorial Process Regulation' (2012) 21 *Minnesota Journal of International Law online* 14.

Asselt, H van, Sindico, F and Mehling, MA, 'Global Climate Change and the Fragmentation of International Law' (2008) 30 *Law & Policy* 423.

Atwood, JR and Brewster, K, *Antitrust and American Business Abroad* (New York, Shepard's/McGraw-Hill, 1958).

Bae J, 'Review of the Dispute Settlement Mechanism under the International Civil Aviation Organization: Contradiction of Political Body Adjudication' (2013) 4 *Journal of International Dispute Settlement* 65.

Backes, C, *Law for a Circular Economy* (The Hague, Eleven International Publishing, 2017).

Bäckstrand, K and Elgström, O, 'The EU's Role in Climate Change Negotiations: From Leader to "Leadiator"' (2013) 20 *Journal of European Public Policy* 1369.

Banaszewska, DM, 'Lex Specialis' in R Wolfrum (ed), *Max Planck Encyclopedia of Public International Law*, online edn (Oxford, Oxford University Press, 2015).

Bartels, L, 'The Inclusion of Aviation in the EU ETS: WTO Law Considerations' (Issue Paper No 6, International Centre for Trade and Sustainable Development, 2012).

Bartels, L, 'Article XX of GATT and the Problem of Extraterritorial Jurisdiction – The Case of Trade Measures for the Protection of Human Rights' (2002) 36 *Journal of World Trade* 353.

Baslar, K, *The Concept of the Common Heritage of Mankind in International Law* (The Haque, Martinus Nijhoff, 1998).

Bassiouni, C, 'International Crimes: Jus Cogens and Obligations Erga Omnes' (1996) 59 *Law & Contemporary Problems* 63.

Bäuerle, T, 'Integrating Shipping into the EU Emissions Trading Scheme?' in HJ Koch, D König and J Sanden (eds), *Climate Change and Environmental Hazards Related to Shipping: An International Legal Framework, Proceedings of the Hamburg International Environmental Law Conference 2011* (Leiden, Nijhoff, 2013) 105–19.

Bäuerle, T, 'Integration of Marine Transport into the European Emissions Trading System – Environmental, Economic and Legal Analysis of Different Options' (Report No (UBA-FB) 001372, German Federal Environment Agency (Umweltbundesamt), 2010).

Benvenisti, E, 'Sovereigns as Trustees of Humanity: On the Accountability of Sovereigns to Foreign Stakeholders' (2013) 107 *American Journal of International Law* 295.

Berman, P, 'Global Legal Pluralism' (2007) 80 *Southern California Law Review* 1155.

Bernasconi-Osterwalder, N, et al, *Environment and Trade: A Guide to WTO Jurisprudence* (London, Earthscan, 2006).

Berners-Lee, M, *How Bad Are Bananas? The Carbon Footprint of Everything* (London, Profile Books, 2011).

Beyerlin, U, 'Different Types of Norms in International Environmental Law Policies, Principles and Rules' in D Bodansky, J Brunnée and E Hey (eds), *The Oxford Handbook of International Environment Law* (Oxford, Oxford University Press, 2008) 425–47.

Bianchi, A, 'Reply to Professor Maier' in KM Meessen (ed), *Extraterritorial Jurisdiction in Theory and Practice* (Alphen aan den Rijn, Kluwer Law International, 1996) 74–102.

Biermann, F, 'Common Concern of Humankind: The Emergence of a New Concept of International Environmental Law' (1996) 34 *Archiv des Völkerrechts* 426.

Biermann, F and Brohm, R, 'Implementing the Kyoto Protocol without the USA: The Strategic Role of Energy Tax Adjustments at the Border' (2004) 4 *Climate Policy* 289.

Bilder, R, 'The Role of Unilateral Action in Preventing International Environmental Injury' (1981) 14 *Vanderbilt Journal of Transnational Law* 51.

Bindoff, NL et al, 'Changing Ocean, Marine Ecosystems, and Dependent Communities' in H-O Pörtner et al (eds), *IPCC Special Report on the Ocean and Cryosphere in a Changing Climate* (2019) 448–587.

Bisset, M, 'Taxes and Charges under the Chicago Convention' in P Mendes de Leon (ed), *From Lowlands to High Skies: A Multilevel Jurisdictional Approach Towards Air Law* (Leiden, Brill, 2013) 67–76.

Blay, S, 'Territorial Integrity' in R Wolfrum (ed), *Max Planck Encyclopedia of Public International Law*, online edn (Oxford, Oxford University Press, 2010) 859–1091.

Bodansky, D, 'What's in a Concept? Global Public Goods, International Law and Legitimacy' (2012) 23 *European Journal of International Law* 651.

Bodansky, D, 'What's so Bad about Unilateral Action to Protect the Environment?' (2000) 11 *European Journal of International Law* 339.

Bodansky, D, 'Protecting the Marine Environment from Vessel-Source Pollution: UNCLOS III and Beyond' (1991) 18 *Ecology Law Quarterly* 719.

Bodansky, D, Brunnée, J and Rajamani, L, *International Climate Change Law* (Oxford, Oxford University Press, 2017).

Bodin, J, *Les Six Livres de La République* (Paris, Fayard, 1986).

Bogojević, S, 'Climate Change Law and Policy in the European Union' in KR Gray, R Tarasofsky and C Carlarne (eds), *The Oxford Handbook of International Climate Change Law* (Oxford, Oxford University Press, 2016) 674–91.

Boisson de Chazournes, L, 'Unilateralism and Environmental Protection: Issues of Perception and Reality of Issues' (2000) 11 *European Journal of International Law* 315.

Bossche, P van den, Schrijver, N and Faber, G, 'Unilateral Measures Addressing Non-Trade Concerns: A Study on WTO Consistency, Relevance of Other International Agreements, Economic Effectiveness and Impact on Developing Countries of Measures Concerning Non-Product-Related Processes and Production Methods' (Ministry of Foreign Affairs of the Netherlands, 2007).

Bossche, P van den and Zdouc, W, *The Law and Policy of the World Trade Organization* (Cambridge, Cambridge University Press, 2013).

Boyle A, 'Soft Law in International Law Making' in MD Evans (ed), *International Law*, 4th edn (Oxford, Oxford University Press, 2014) 118–36.

Boyle A, 'Law of the Sea Perspectives on Climate Change' in D Freestone (ed), *The 1982 Law of the Sea Convention at 30: Successes, Challenges and New Agendas* (Leiden, Brill, 2013) 157–64.

Bradford, A, *The Brussels Effect: How the European Union Rules the World* (Oxford, Oxford University Press, 2020).

Bradford, A, 'The Brussels Effect' (2012) 107 *Northwestern University Law Review* 1.

Bretherton, C and Vogler, J, *The European Union as a Global Actor* (New York, Routledge, 2006).

Brown, B, 'The Evolving Concept of Universal Jurisdiction' (2000) 35 *New England Law Review* 383.

Brownlie, I, *Principles of International Law*, 4th edn (Oxford, Clarendon Press, 1990).

Brunnée, J, 'Common Areas, Common Heritage and Common Concern' in D Bodansky, J Brunnée and E Hey (eds), *The Oxford Handbook of International Environment Law* (Oxford, Oxford University Press, 2008) 550–73.

Brunnée, J, '"Common Interest" – Echoes from an Empty Shell? Some Thoughts on Common Interests and International Environment Law' [1989] *Zeitschrift für Ausländisches Öffentliches Recht und Völkerrecht* 791.

Brunnée, J et al, 'Overview of Legal Issues Relevant to Climate Change' in R Lord et al (eds), *Climate Change Liability Transnational Law and Practice* (Cambridge, Cambridge University Press, 2011) 23–49.

Burr, S, 'The Application of US Antitrust Law to Foreign Conduct: Has Hartford Fire Extinguished Considerations of Comity?' (1994) 70 *University of Pennsylvania Journal of International Business Law* 221.

Cameron, J and Abouchar, J, 'The Status of the Precautionary Principle in International Law' in D Freestone and E Hey (eds), *The Precautionary Principle and International Law: The Challenge of Implementation* (Alphen aan den Rijn, Kluwer Law International, 1996) 29–52.

Caney, S, 'Cosmopolitan Justice, Climate Change and Responsibility' (2005) 18 *Leiden Journal of International Law* 749.

Capps, P, Evans, MD and Konstadinidis, P (eds), *Asserting Jurisdiction* (Oxford, Hart Publishing, 2003).

Cárdenas Castañeda, F, 'A Call for Rethinking the Sources of International Law: Soft Law and the Other Side of the Coin' (2013) XIII *Anuario Mexicano de Derecho* 355.

Cazorla, M and Toman, M, 'International Equity and Climate Change Policy' in M Toman (ed), *Climate Change Economics and Policy: An RFF Anthology* (Washington, DC, Resources for the Future, 2001) 235–47.

Charnovitz, S, 'The Law of Environmental PPMs in the WTO: Debunking the Myth of Illegality' (2002) 27 *Yale Journal of International Law* 59.

Charnovitz, S, 'The Moral Exception in Trade Policy' (1997) 38 *Virginia Journal of International Law* 689.

Cheng, B, *General Principles of Law Applied by International Courts and Tribunals* (London, Stevens, 1953).

Chircop, A, 'The IMO Initial Strategy for the Reduction of GHGs from International Shipping: A Commentary' (2019) 34 *International Journal of Marine and Coastal Law* 482.

Chicrop, A, Doelle, M and Gauvin, R, 'Shipping and Climate Change International Law and Policy Considerations – Special Report' (Centre for International Governance Innovation, 2018).

Churchill, R, 'Port State Jurisdiction Relating to the Safety of Shipping and Pollution from Ships – What Degree of Extra-Territoriality?' (2016) 31 *International Journal of Marine and Coastal Law* 442.

Churchill, R and Lowe, V, *The Law of the Sea*, 3rd edn (Manchester, Manchester University Press, 1999).

Clancy, E, 'The Tragedy of the Global Commons' (1998) 5 *Indiana Journal of Global Legal Studies* 601.

Colares, JF and Rode, A, 'Climate Change Mitigation and Trade Rules: The Opportunities and Limitations of Neutral Border Tariffs' (Working Paper, Energy Policy Institute at the University of Chicago, 2015).

Collins, R, 'The M/V "Norstar" Case (Panamav. Italy) (ITLOS)' 58 *International Legal Materials* (2019) 673.

Conrad, C, *Processes and Production Methods (PPMs) in WTO Law: Interfacing Trade and Social Goals* (Cambridge, Cambridge University Press, 2011).

Cooreman, B, *Addressing Global Environmental Concerns through Trade: Extraterritoriality under WTO Law from a Comparative Perspective* (PhD dissertation, Leiden University, 2016).

Cooreman, B, 'Addressing Environmental Concerns through Trade? A Case for Extraterritoriality' (2015) 65 *ICLQ* 229.

Cottier, T et al, 'The Principle of Common Concern and Climate Change' (2014) 52 *Archiv des Völkerrechts* 293.

Cottier, T et al, 'The Principle of Proportionality in International Law' (NCCR trade regulation 2012, Working Paper No 2012/38).

Craig, P, 'Competence and Member State Autonomy: Causality, Consequence and Legitimacy' in H Micklitz and B de Witte (eds), *The European Court and the Autonomy of Member States* (Cambridge, Intersentia, 2012) 9–34.

Crawford, J, *Brownlie's Principles of Public International Law*, 8th edn (Oxford, Oxford Univerity Press, 2012).

Cremona, M, 'The Union as a Global Actor: Roles, Models and Identity' (2004) 41 *CML Rev* 553.

Daugirdas, K, 'How and Why International Law Binds International Organizations' (2016) 57 *Harvard International Law* 325.

Deane, F, *Emissions Trading and WTO Law: A Global Analysis* (Cheltenham, Edward Elgar, 2015).

Davidson Ladly, S, 'Border Carbon Adjustments, WTO-Law and the Principle of Common but Differentiated Responsibilities' (2012) 12 *International Environmental Agreements* 63.

Delimatsis, P and Mavromati, D, 'GATS, Financial Services and Trade in Emission Reduction Certificates (RECs) – Just Another Market-Based Solution to Cope with the Tragedy of the Commons?' in T Cottier, O Nartova and SZ Bigdeli (eds), *International Trade Regulation and the Mitigation of Climate Change* (Cambridge, Cambridge University Press 2009) 231–58.

Demaret, P and Stewardson, R, 'Border Tax Adjustments under GATT and EC Law and General Implications for Environmental Taxes' (1994) 28 *Journal of World Trade* 5.

Dobson, NL, 'Article XX GATT as Guardian of the Environment', in P Delimatsis and L Reins (eds), *Encyclopedia of Environmental Law, Trade Law* (Cheltenham, Edward Elgar, forthcoming).

Dobson, NL, 'Competing Climate Responses: Reflections on EU Unilateral Regulation of International Transport Emissions in Light of Multilateral Developments' (2020) 67 *Netherlands International Law Review* 183.

Dobson, NL, 'Reflections on "Reasonableness" in the Restatement (Fourth) of US Foreign Relations Law' (2019) 62 *Questions of International Law Zoom-In* 19.

Dobson, NL, 'The EU's Conditioning of the "Extraterritorial" Carbon Footprint: A Call for an Integrated Approach in Trade Law Discourse' (2018) 27 *Review of European, Comparative and International Environmental Law* 75.

Dobson, NL and Ryngaert C, 'Provocative Climate Protection: EU "Extraterritorial" Regulation of Maritime Emissions' (2017) 66 *ICLQ* 295.

Dodge, W, 'Jurisdictional Reasonableness under Customary International Law: The Approach of the Restatement (Fourth) of US Foreign Relations Law' (2019) 2 *Questions of International Law Zoom-In* 4.

Dodge, W, 'International Comity in a Comparative Perspective' in C Bradley (ed), *The Oxford Handbook of Comparative Foreign Relations Law* (Oxford, Oxford University Press, 2018) 701–14.

Dodge, W, 'Jurisdiction in the Fourth Restatement of Foreign Relations Law' (2017) 18 *Yearbook of Private International Law* 143.

Du, M, 'Taking Stock: What Do We Know, and Do Not Know, about the National Treatment Obligation in the GATT/WTO Legal System?' (2015) 1 *Chinese Journal of Global Governance* 67.

Duffy, M, 'Climate Change Causation: Harmonizing Tort Law and Scientific Probability' (2009) 28 *Temple Journal of Science, Technology & Environmental Law* 185.

Dupuy, P, 'The Place and Role of Unilateralism in Contemporary International Law' (2000) 11 *European Journal of International Law* 19.

Dworkin, R, *Taking Rights Seriously* (Cambridge, MA, Harvard Univerity Press, 1977).

Eckes, C, 'International Rulings and the EU Legal Order: Autonomy as Legitimacy?' (CLEER Papers 2016/2, TMC Asser Institute, 2016).

Eeckhout, P, *EU External Relations Law*, 2nd edn (Oxford, Oxford University Press, 2011).

Erling, UM, 'How to Reconcile the European Union Emissions Trading System (EU ETS) for Aviation with the Carbon Offsetting and Reduction Scheme for International Aviation (CORSIA)?' (2018) 43 *Air and Space Law* 371.

Erling, UM, 'International Aviation Emissions Under International Civil Aviation Organization's Global Market Based Measure: Ready for Offsetting?' (2017) 42 *Air and Space Law* 1.

Erling, UM, 'The German Air Transport Tax: A Treaty Override of International Law' (2015) 10 *Florida International University Law Review* 467.

Faber J and Huigen T, 'A Study on Aviation Ticket Taxes' (CE Delft Report 18.7L14.149, November 2018) 19.

Falkner, R, 'The Paris Agreement and the New Logic of International Climate Politics' (2016) 92 *International Affairs* 1107.

Finke, J, 'Sovereign Immunity: Rule, Comity or Something Else?' (2010) 21 *European Journal of International Law* 853.

Fontanelli, F, 'Necessity Killed the GATT – Art XX GATT and the Misleading Rhetoric about "Weighing and Balancing"' (2013) 5 *European Journal of Legal Studies* 36.

Francioni, F, 'Equity in International Law' in R Wolfrum (ed), *Max Planck Encyclopaedia of Public International Law*, online edn (Oxford, Oxford Univeristy Press, 2013).

Francioni, F, 'Extraterritorial Application of Environment Law' in KM Meessen (ed), *Extraterritorial Jurisdiction in Theory and Practice* (Leiden, Brill, 1996) 122–46.

Friedmann, W, *The Changing Structure of International Law* (London, Steven & Sons, 1964).

Gans, BJ, 'Reasonableness as a Limit to Extraterritorial Jurisdiction' (1985) 62 *Washington University Law Quarterly* 681.

Gerrard, MB and Wannier, GR, 'United States of America' in R Lord et al (eds), *Climate Change Liability: Transnational Law and Practice* (Cambridge, Cambridge University Press, 2011) 556–604.

Giemulla, E and Weber, L, *International and EU Aviation Law – Selected Issues* (Alphen aan den Rijn, Kluwer Law International, 2011).

Gilioli, EL, 'Defining Jurisdictional Limits in International Antitrust: Should the EEC Adopt the Timberlane Approach?' (1981) 5 *Fordham International Law Journal* 469.

Guilfoyle, D, 'The High Seas' in D Rothwell et al (eds), *The Oxford Handbook of the Law of the Sea* (Oxford, Oxford University Press, 2015) 203–25.

Guzman, A, 'Choice of Law: New Foundations' (2001) 90 *Georgetown Law Journal* 883.

Hakimi, M, 'Unfriendly Unilateralism' (2014) 55 *Harvard International Law Journal* 105.

Hartmann, S, 'Comparing the National Treatment Obligations of the GATT and the TBT: Lessons Learned from the EC-Seal Products Dispute' (2014) 40 *North Carolina Journal of International Law and Commercial Regulation* 629.

Harvard Draft Convention on Jurisdiction with Respect to Crime, 'Article 3. Territorial Jurisdiction' (1935) 29 *American Journal of International Law Supplement: Research in International Law* 480.

Harvard Draft Convention on Jurisdiction with Respect to Crime, 'Article 5. Jurisdiction Over Nationals' (1935) 29 *American Journal of International Law Supplement: Research in International Law* 519.

Harvard Draft Convention on Jurisdiction with Respect to Crime, 'Article 7. Protection – Security of the State' (1935) 29 *American Journal of International Law Supplement: Research in International Law* 543.

Harvard Draft Convention on Jurisdiction with Respect to Crime, 'Article 10. Universality – Other Crimes' (1935) 29 *American Journal of International Law Supplement: Research in International Law* 573.

Havel, B and van Antwerpen, N, 'Dutch Ticket Tax and Article 15 of the Chicago Convention (Continued)' (2009) 34 *Air and Space Law* 447.

Havel, B and Mulligan, J, 'The Triumph of Politics: Reflections on the Judgment of the Court of Justice of the European Union Validating the Inclusion of Non-EU Airlines in the Emissions Trading Scheme' (2012) 37 *Air and Space Law* 3.

Havel, B and Sanchez, G, *The Principles and Practice of International Aviation Law* (Cambridge, Cambridge University Press, 2014).

Hermeling, C et al, 'Sailing into a Dilemma – An Economic and Legal Analysis of an EU Trading Scheme for Maritime Emissions' (Discussion Paper No 14-021, Centre for European Economic Research, 2014).

Hertel, M, 'Climate-Change-Related Trade Measures and Article XX: Defining Discrimination in Light of the Principle of Common but Differentiated Responsibilities' (2011) 45 *Journal of World Trade* 653.

Hertogen, A, 'Letting Lotus Bloom' (2016) 26 *European Journal of International Law* 901.

Hey, E, 'Common but Differentiated Responsibilities' in R Wolfrum (ed), *Max Planck Encyclopaedia of Public International Law*, online edn (Oxford, Oxford University Press, 2011).

Hey, E, 'Global Environmental Law: Common Interests and the Reconstruction of Public Space' (2009) 1 *Iustum Aequum Salutare* 41.

Hiesinger, S and Mavroidis, P, 'Planes, Trains, and Automobiles: The EU Legislation on Climate Change and the Question of Consistency with WTO Law' in C Bakker and F Francioni (eds), *The EU, the US and Global Climate Governance* (London, Routledge, 2014) 127–42.

Higgins, R, *Problems and Process: International Law and How We Use It* (Oxford, Oxford University Press, 1995).

Hobbe, S, 'Airspace' in R Wolfrum (ed), *Max Planck Encyclopaedia of Public International Law*, online edn (Oxford, Oxford University Press, 2008).

Holzer, K, *Carbon-Related Border Adjustment and WTO Law* (Cheltenham, Edward Elgar, 2014).

Honniball, A, 'The Exclusive Jurisdiction of Flag States: A Limitation on Pro-active Port States?' (2016) 31 *International Journal of Marine and Coastal Law* 499.

Horn, H and Mavroidis, P, 'To B(TA) or Not to B(TA)? On the Legality and Desirability of Border Tax Adjustments from a Trade Perspective' (2011) 34 *The World Economy* 1911.

Horn, H and Mavroidis, P, 'The Permissible Reach of National Environmental Policies' (2008) 42 *Journal of World Trade* 1107.

Howse, R and Regan, D, 'The Product/Process Distinction – An Illusory Basis for Disciplining unilateralism' in Trade Policy' (2000) 11 *European Journal of International Law* 249.

Howse, R, Langille, J and Sykes, K, 'Sealing the Deal: The WTO Appellate Body's Report in EC-Seal Products' (2014) 18 *American Society of International Law Insights*.

Human Rights Council (HRC), 'Report of the Independent Expert on the issue of Human Rights Obligations Relating to the Enjoyment of a Safe, Clean, Healthy and Sustainable Environment – Mapping Report' (Document A/HRC/25/53, Office of the United Nations High Commissioner for Human Rights, 2014).

Inazumi, M, *Universal Jurisdiction in Modern International Law: Expansion of National Jurisdiction for Prosecuting Serious Crimes under International Law* (Antwerp, Intersentia, 2005).

International Bar Association (IBA), 'Report of the Task Force on Extraterritorial Jurisdiction' (2009).

International Committee on the Legal Aspect of Extraterritorial Jurisdiction, 'Interim Report on Extra-territorial Jurisdiction and Export Control Law' (1990) 64 *International Law Association Reports of Conferences* 312.

International Law Commission (ILC), 'Report of the Study Group of the International Law Commission: Fragmentation of International Law – Difficulties arising from the Diversification and Expansion of International Law' (13 April 2006) UN Doc A/CN.4/L.682.

International Law Commission (ILC), 'Report of the International Law Commission on the Work of its 58th Session' (1 May–9 June and 3 July–11 August 2006) UN Doc A/61/10, Annex E: Extraterritorial Jurisdiction.

Jackson, J, 'Sovereignty-Modern: A New Approach to an Outdated Concept' (2003) 97 *American Journal of International Law* 782.

Jackson, J, 'Comments on Shrimp/Turtle and the Product/Process Distinction' (2000) 11 *European Journal of International Law* 303.

Jansen, B and Lugard, M, 'Some Considerations on Trade Barriers Erected for Non-Economic Reasons and WTO Obligations' (1999) 2 *Journal of International Economy Law* 530.

Jennings, R and Watts, A, *Oppenheim's International Law,* 9th edn (Oxford, Oxford University Press, 1992).

Jou, R and Chen, T, 'Willingness to Pay off Air Passengers for Carbon-Offset' (2015) 7 *Sustainability* 3071.

Kadish, SA, 'Comity and the International Application of the Sherman Act: Encouraging the Courts to Enter the Political Arena' (1982) 4 *Northwestern Journal of International Law & Business* 130.

Kamminga, M, 'Extraterritoriality' in R Wolfrum (ed), *Max Planck Encyclopaedia of Public International Law*, online edn (Oxford, Oxford University Press, 2011).

Kelemen, D, 'Globalizing European Union Environment Policy' (2010) 17 *Journal of European Public Policy* 335.

Kiss, A, 'Abuse of Rights' in R Wolfrum (ed), *Max Planck Encyclopaedia of Public International Law*, online edn (Oxford, Oxford University Press, 2006).

Klabbers, J, 'The Sources of International Organizations Law' in J d'Aspremont and Besson S (eds), *The Oxford Handbook of the Sources of International Law* (Oxford, Oxford University Press, 2017) 987–1006.

Kokott, J, 'States, Sovereign Equality' in R Wolfrum (ed), *Max Planck Encyclopaedia of Public International Law*, online edn (Oxford, Oxford University Press, 2011).

König, D, 'Flags of Ships' in R Wolfrum (ed), *Max Planck Encyclopaedia of Public International Law*, online edn (Oxford, Oxford University Press, 2009).

Kontorovich, E, 'The Piracy Analogy: Modern Universal Jurisdiction's Hollow Foundation' (2004) 45 *Harvard International Law Journal* 183.

Kopela, S, 'Climate Change, Regime Interaction, and the Principle of Common but Differentiated Responsibility: The Experience of the International Maritime Organization' (2014) 24 *Yearbook of International Environmental Law* 70.

Kopela, S, 'Making Ships Cleaner: Reducing Air Pollution from International Shipping' (2017) 26 *Review of European, Comparative and International Environmental Law* 231.

Kopela, S, 'Port-State Jurisdiction, Extraterritoriality, and the Protection of Global Commons' (2016) 47 *Ocean Development and International Law* 89.

Koskenniemi, M, 'What Use for Sovereignty Today?' (2011) 1 *Asian Journal of International Law* 61.

Krisch, N, 'International Law in Times of Hegemony: Unequal Power and the Shaping of the International Legal Order' (2005) 16 *European Journal of International Law* 369.

Krisch, N, 'The Decay of Consent, International Law in the Age of Global Public Goods' (2014) 108 *American Journal of International Law* 1.

Kunig, P, 'Intervention, Prohibition of' in R Wolfrum (ed), *Max Planck Encyclopaedia of Public International Law*, online edn (Oxford, Oxford University Press, 2008).

Lapidoth, R, 'Equity in International Law' (1987) 22 *Israel Law Review* 161.

Larbprasertporn, P, 'The Interaction Between WTO Law and the Principle of Common but Differentiated Responsibilities in the Case of Climate-Related Border Tax Adjustment' (2014) 6 *Göttingen Journal of International Law* 145.

Lawson, R, 'UK Air Passenger Duty Held to Be Consistent with the Chicago Convention' (2008) 33 *Air and Space Law* 3.

Leal-Arcas, R, Filis, A and Abu Gosh, E (eds), *International Energy Governance* (Cheltenham, Edward Elgar, 2014).

Lesnikowski, A, 'What Does the Paris Agreement Mean for Adaptation?' (2017) 17 *Climate Policy* 825.

Lowe, V, 'The Role of Equity in International Law' (1988) 12 *Australian Yearbook of International Law* 54.

Lowe, V, 'The Right of Entry into Maritime Ports in International Law' (1977) 14 *San Diego Law Review* 597.

Lowe, V and Staker, C, 'Jurisdiction' in MD Evans (ed), *International Law*, 3rd edn (Oxford, Oxford University Press, 2010) 313–39.

Lowenfeld, AF, 'Sovereignty, Jurisdiction, and Reasonableness: A Reply to AV Lowe' (1981) 75 *American Journal of International Law* 629.

Lowenfeld, AF, 'Public Law in the International Arena: Conflict of Laws, International Law, and Some Suggestions for Their Interaction' (1979) 163 *Collected Courses of the Hague Academy of International Law* 311.

Maier, HG, 'Extraterritorial Jurisdiction at a Crossroads: The Intersection Between Public and Private International Law' (1982) 76 *American Journal of International Law* 281.

Maier, HG, 'Interest Balancing and Extraterritorial Jurisdiction' (1983) 31 *American Journal of Comparative Law* 579.

Mann, FA, 'The Doctrine of International Jurisdiction Revisited after Twenty Years' (1984) 186 *Recueil des Cours* 9.

Mann, FA, 'The Doctrine of Jurisdiction in International Law' (1964) 111 *Recueil des Cours* 1.

Manners, I, 'Normative Power Europe: A Contradiction in Terms?' (2002) 40 *Journal of Common Market Studies* 235.

Marceau, G, 'The Interface Between the Trade Rules and Climate Change Actions' in Park DY (ed), *Legal Issues on Climate Change and International Trade Law* (Berlin, Springer, 2016) 3–39.

Marceau, G, 'A Comment on the Appellate Body Report in EC-Seal Products in the Context of the Trade and Environment Debate' (2014) 23 *Review of European, Comparative and International Environmental Law* 318.

Marten, B, 'Port State Jurisdiction over Vessel Information: Territoriality, Extra-Territoriality and the Future of Shipping Regulation' (2016) 31 *International Journal of Marine and Coastal Law* 470.

Marten, B, 'Port State Jurisdiction, International Conventions, and Extraterritoriality: An Expansive Interpretation' in H Ringbom (ed), *Jurisdiction over Ships: Post-UNCLOS Developments in the Law of the Sea* (Leiden, Brill, 2015) 105–39.

Marten, B, 'Port State Jurisdiction in New Zealand: The Problem with Sellers' (2013) 44 *Victoria University of Wellington Law Review* 559.

Martinez Romera, B, *Regime Interaction and Climate Change: The Case of International Aviation and Maritime Transport* (Abingdon, Routledge, 2017).

Martinez Romera, B, 'The Paris Agreement and the Regulation of International Bunker Fuels' (2016) 25 *Review of European, Comparative and International Environmental Law* 215.

Martinez Romera, B and van Asselt, H, 'The International Regulation of Aviation Emissions: Putting Differential Treatment into Practice' (2015) 27 *Journal of Environmental Law* 259.

Mayer, B, 'The Place of Customary Norms in Climate Law: A Reply to Zahar' (2018) 8 *Climate Law* 261.

Mayer, B, 'The Applicability of the Principle of Prevention to Climate Change: A Response to Zahar' (2015) 5 *Climate Law* 1.

McAdam, J, 'UNHCR Legal Protection and Policy Research Series – Climate Change Displacement and International Law: Complementary Protection Standards (PPLA/2011/03, May 2011).

McAusland, C and Najjar N, 'The WTO Consistency of Carbon Footprint Taxes' (2014) 46 *Georgia Journal of International Law* 765.

McDorman, T, 'Port State Enforcement: A Comment on Article 218 of the 1982 Law of the Sea Convention' (1997) 28 *Journal of Maritime Law and Commerce* 305.

Meessen, KM, 'Conflicts of Jurisdiction under the New Restatement' (1987) 50 *Law & Contemporary Problems* 47.

Meessen, KM, 'Antitrust Jurisdiction under Customary International Law' (1984) 78 *American Journal of International Law* 783.

Mehling, MA et al, 'Designing Border Carbon Adjustments for Enhanced Climate Action' (2019) 113 *American Journal of International Law* 433.

Meltzer, J, 'Climate Change and Trade – The EU Aviation Directive and the WTO' (2012) 15 *Journal of International Economic Law* 111.

Meng, W, *Extraterritoriale Jurisdiktion im Öffentlichen Wirtschaftsrecht* (New York, Springer, 1994).

de Mestral, A, 'Settlement of Disputes at the ICAO and Sustainable Development' in A de Mestral, P Paul Fitzgerald and Md Tanveer Ahmad (eds), *Sustainable Development, International Aviation, and Treaty Implementation* (Cambridge, Cambridge University Press, 2018) 199–214.

Mills, A, 'Rethinking Jurisdiction in International Law' (2014) 84 *British Yearbook of International Law* 187.

Mitchell, A and Merriman, D, 'Indonesia's WTO Challenge to the European Union's Renewable Energy Directive: Palm Oil & Indirect Land-Use Change' (2020) 12(2) *Trade, Law and Development* (forthcoming).

Molenaar, EJ, 'Port and Coastal States', in D Rothwell et al (eds), *The Oxford Handbook of the Law of the Sea* (Oxford, Oxford University Press, 2015) 280–303.

Molenaar, EJ, 'Port State Jurisdiction: Toward Comprehensive, Mandatory and Global Coverage' (2007) 38 *Ocean Development ant International Law* 225.

Molenaar, EJ, *Coastal State Jurisdiction over Vessel-Source Pollution* (Alphen aan den Rijn, Kluwer Law International, 1998).

Molenaar, EJ, 'Residual Jurisdiction under IMO Regulatory Conventions' in Ringbom H (ed), *Competing Norms in the Law of Marine Environmental Protection: Focus on Ship Safety and Pollution Prevention* (London, Kluwer Law International, 1997) 201–16.

Morgera, E and Marín Durán, G, *Environmental Integration in the EU's External Relations – Beyond Multilateral Dimensions* (Oxford, Hart Publishing, 2012).

Morosini, F, 'Trade and Climate Change: Unveiling the Principle of Common but Differentiated Responsibilities from the WTO Agreements' (2010) 42 *George Washington Law Review* 713.

Müller, B, Höhne, N and Ellermann, C, 'Differentiating (Historic) Responsibilities for Climate Change' (2009) 9 *Climate Policy* 593.

Müller, B and Michaelowa, A, 'How to Operationalize Accounting under Article 6 Market Mechanisms of the Paris Agreement' (2019) 19 *Climate Policy* 812.

Nedeski, N, *Shared Obligations in International Law* (Doctoral thesis, University of Amsterdam, 2017).

Nollkaemper, A, 'Unilateralism/Multilateralism' in R Wolfrum (ed), *Max Planck Encyclopaedia of Public International Law*, online edn (Oxford, Oxford University Press, 2011).

Nollkaemper, A, 'Rethinking States' Rights to Promote Extra-Territorial Environmental Values' in F Weiss, E Denters and P de Waart (eds), *International Economic Law with a Human Face* (The Hague, Kluwer Law International, 1998) 175–201.

O'Keefe, R, 'Universal Jurisdiction Clarifying the Basic Concept' (2004) 2 *Journal of International Criminal Justice* 735.

Oberthür, S, 'Climate Change Regime, Interactions with ICAO, IMO and the EU Burden Sharing Agreement' in S Oberthür and T Gehring (eds), *Global Environmental Governance: Synergy and Conflict among International and EU Policies* (Cambridge, MA, MIT Press, 2006) 53–78.

OECD, 'Processes And Production Methods (PPMs): Conceptual Framework and Considerations on Use Of PPM-Based Trade Measures' (document number OCDE/GD(97)137, Organisation for Economic Co-operation and Development, 1997).

Osofsky, HM, 'The Intersection of Scale, Science, and Law in Massachusetts v EPA' in WCG Burns and HM Osofsky (eds), *Adjudicating Climate Change* (Cambridge, Cambridge University Press, 2009) 129–44.

Oxman, B, 'Jurisdiction of States' in R Wolfrum (ed), *Max Planck Encyclopaedia of Public International Law*, online edn (Oxford, Oxford University Press, 2007).

Paepcke, F von, *Statehood in Times of Climate Change: Impacts of Sea Level Rise on the Concept of States* (Bern, Peter Lang, 2014).

Page, E, 'Distributing the Burdens of Climate Change' (2008) 17 *Environmental Politics* 556.

Paul, J, 'Comity in International Law' (1991) 32 *Harvard International Law Journal* 1.

Pauw, P et al, 'Different Perspectives on Differentiated Responsibilities: A State-of-the-Art Review of the Notion of Common but Differentiated Responsibilities in International Negotiations' (6/2014, Deutsche Institut für Entwicklungspolitik, 2014).

Pauwelyn, J, 'Carbon Leakage Measures and Border Tax Adjustments under WTO Law' in D Prévost and G van Calster (eds), *Research Handbook on Environment, Health and the WTO* (Cheltenham, Edward Elgar, 2012) 448–506.

Pauwelyn, J, 'US Federal Climate Policy and Competitiveness Concerns: The Limits and Options of International Trade Law' (Working Paper NI WP 07-02, Nicholas Institute for Environmental Policy Solutions, Duke University, 2007).

Pauwelyn, J, 'Recent Books on Trade and Environment: GATT Phantoms Still Haunt the WTO' (2004) 15 *European Journal of International Law* 575.

Pauwelyn, J, *Conflict of Norms in Public International Law: How WTO Law Relates to Other Rules of International Law* (Cambridge, Cambridge, University Press, 2003).

Peel, J, 'Climate Change' in A Nollkaemper and I Plakokefalos (eds), *The Practice of Shared Responsibility in International Law* (Cambridge, Cambridge University Press, 2016) 1009–1050.

Perrez, F, *Cooperative Sovereignty: From Independence to Interdependence in the Structure of International Environmental Law* (New York, Springer, 2000).

Petersmann, E, 'State Sovereignty, Popular Sovereignty and Individual Sovereignty: From Constitutional Nationalism to Multilevel Constitutionalism in International Economic Law?' (EUI Working Paper 2006/45, 2006).

Petersmann, E, 'International Trade Law and International Environmental Law' (1993) 27 *Journal of World Trade* 34.

Picone, P, 'The Distinction between Jus Cogens and Obligations Erga Omnes' in E Cannizzaro (ed), *The law of treaties beyond the Vienna Convention* (Oxford, Oxford University Press, 2011) 411–24.

Porges, A and Trachtman, J, 'Robert Hudec and Domestic Regulation: The Resurrection of Aim and Effects' (2003) 37 *Journal of World Trade* 783.

Potts, J, 'The Legality of PPMs under the GATT: Challenges and Opportunities for Sustainable Trade Policy' (International Institute for Sustainable Development, 2008).

Pulkowski, D, *The Law and Politics of International Regime Conflict* (Oxford, Oxford University Press, 2014).

Quiggin, J, 'Complexity, Climate Change and the Precautionary Principle' (Climate Change Working Paper C07:3, Risk and Sustainable Management Group, University of Queensland, 2007).

Rajamani, L, 'Ambition and Differentiation in the 2015 Paris Agreement: Interpretative Possibilities and Underlying Politics' (2016) 65 *ICLQ* 493.

Rajamani, L, 'The 2015 Paris Agreement: Interplay Between Hard, Soft and Non-Obligations' (2016) 28 *Journal of Environmental Law* 337.

Rajamani, L, 'The Warsaw Climate Negotiations: Emerging Understandings and Battle Lines on the Road to the 2015 Climate Agreement (2014) 63 *ICLQ* 721.

Rajamani, L, The Durban Platform for Enhanced Action and the Future of the Climate Regime. (2012) 61 *ICLQ* 501.

Rajamani, L, *Differential Treatment in International Environmental Law* (Oxford, Oxford University Press, 2006).

Randall, KC, 'Universal Jurisdiction under International Law' (1987) 66 *Texas Law Review* 785.

Rayfuse, R, *Non-Flag State Enforcement in High Seas Fisheries* (The Hague, Martinus Nijhoff, 2004).

Redgwell, C, 'Principles and Emerging Norms in International Law: Intra- and Intergenerational Equity' in KR Gray, R Tarasofsky and C Carlarne (eds), *The Oxford Handbook of International Climate Change Law* (Oxford, Oxford University Press, 2016) 185–201.

Redgwell, C, 'UNCLOS and Climate Change' (2012) 106 *American Society of International Law Proceedings* 406.

Regan, D, 'How to Think about PPMs (and Climate Change)' in Th Cottier, O Nartova and SZ Bigdeli (eds), *International Trade Regulation and the Mitigation of Climate Change: World Trade Forum* (Cambridge, Cambridge University Press, 2009) 97–123.

Regan, D, 'Regulatory Purpose and Like Products in Article III:4 of the GATT (With Additional Remarks on Article III:2)' (2002) 36 *Journal of World Trade* 443.

Reinisch, A, 'Sources of International Organizations' Law: Why Custom and General Principles Are Crucial' in J d'Aspremont and S Besson (eds) *The Oxford Handbook of the Sources of International Law* (Oxford, Oxford University Press, 2017) 1007–1024.

Reisman, M, 'Unilateral Action and the Transformations of the World Constitutive Process: The Special Problem of Humanitarian Intervention' (2000) 11 *European Journal of International Law* 3.

Restatement (Fourth) of the Foreign Relations Law of the United States (St Paul, MN, American Law Institute Publishers, 2018).

Restatement (Third) of the Foreign Relations Law of the United States (St Paul, MN, American Law Institute Publishers, 1987).

Reydams, L, 'The Rise and Fall of Universal Jurisdiction' (KU Leuven Working Paper no 36, 2010).

Reydams, L, *Universal Jurisdiction – International and Municipal Legal Perspectives* (Cambridge, Cambridge University Press, 2003).

Ringbom, H, 'Global Problem – Regional Solution? International Law Reflections on an EU CO_2 Emissions Trading Scheme for Ships' (2011) 26 *International Journal of Marine and Coastal Law* 613.

Ringbom, H, *The EU Maritime Safety Policy and International Law* (The Hague, Martinus Nijhoff, 2008).

Ryngaert, C, *Selfless intervention: The Exercise of Jurisdiction in the Common Interest* (Oxford, Oxford University Press, 2020).

Ryngaert, C, *Jurisdiction in International Law*, 2nd edn (Oxford, Oxford University Press, 2015).

Ryngaert, C, *Jurisdiction over Antitrust Violations in International Law* (Antwerp, Intersentia, 2008).

Ryngaert, C and Ringbom, H, 'Introduction: Port State Jurisdiction: Challenges and Potential' (2016) 31 *International Journal of Marine and Coastal Law* 379.

Sánchez-Tabernero, S, 'For Whom the Bell Tolls: The EU ETS in Aviation under the TBT Agreement' (2015) 49 *Journal of World Trade* 781.

Sadeleer, N, 'Climate Change, Uncertainties and the Precautionary Principle' (Jean Monnet Working Paper Series – Environment and Internal Market, vol 16/1, 2016).

Sands, P, *Principles of International Environmental Law*, 3rd edn (Cambridge, Cambridge University Press, 2012).

Sands, P, '"Unilateralism", Values, and International Law' (2000) 11 *European Journal of International Law* 291.

Scheipers, S and Sicurelli, D, 'Normative Power Europe: A Credible Utopia?' (2007) 45 *Journal of Common Market Studies* 435.

Schermers, H and Blokker, N, *International Institutional Law: Unity within Diversity* (Leiden, Brill, 2011).

Schreurs, MA and Tiberghien, Y, 'Multilevel Reinforcement: Explaining European Union Leadership in Climate Change Mitigation' (2007) 7 *Global Environmental Politics* 19.

Schwarze, G, 'Including Aviation into the European Union's Emissions Trading Scheme' (2007) 16 *European Energy and Environmental Law Review* 10.

Scott, J, 'Extraterritoriality and Territorial Extension in EU Law' (2014) 62 *American Journal of International Law* 87.

Scott, J, 'The New EU Extraterritoriality' (2014) 51 *CML Rev* 1343.

Scott, J and Rajamani, L, 'Contingent Unilateralism – International Aviation in the European Emissions Trading Scheme' in B Van Vooren, S Blockmans and J Wouters (eds), *The EU's Role in Global Governance* (Oxford, Oxford University Press, 2013) 209–23.

Scott, J and Rajamani, L, 'EU Climate Change Unilateralism' (2012) 23 *European Journal of International Law* 469.

Shaw M, *International Law*, 7th edn (Cambridge, Cambridge University Press, 2014).

Shelton, D, 'Common Concern of Humanity' (2009) 1 *Iustum Aequum Salutare* 33.

Shue, H, 'Global Environment and International Inequality' (1999) 75 *International Affairs* 533.

Silveira, LDO and Obersteiner, T, 'The Scope of the TBT Agreement in Light of Recent WTO Case Law' (2013) 8 *Global Trade and Customs Journal* 112.

Smitherman, C, *Transatlantic Merger Cases: United States–European Community Merger Review Cooperation* (London, Cameron May, 2007).

Soltau, F, 'Common Concern of Humankind' in KR Gray, R Tarasofsky, and C Carlarne (eds), *The Oxford Handbook of International Climate Change Law* (Oxford, Oxford University Press, 2016) 202–12.

Spier, J and Magnus, U (eds), *Climate Change Remedies: Injunctive Relief and Criminal Law Responses* (The Hague, Eleven International Publishing, 2014).

Stallard, H, 'Turning up the Heat on Tuvalu: An Assessment of Compensation for Climate Change Damage in Accordance with State Responsibility Under International Law' (2009) 15 *Canterbury Law Review* 163.

Stec, S, 'Humanitarian Limits to Sovereignty: Common Concern and Common Heritage Approaches to Natural Resources and Environment' (2010) 12 *International Community Law Review* 361.

Stigall, DE, 'International Law and Limitations on the Exercise of Extraterritorial Jurisdiction in US Domestic Law' (2012) 35 *Hastings International and Comparative Law Review* 323.

Svantesson, DJB, 'A New Jurisprudential Framework for Jurisdiction: Beyond the Harvard Draft' (2015) 109 *American Journal of International Law Unbound* 69.

Switzer, S and McMahon, JA, 'EU Biofuels Policy – Raising the Question of WTO Compatibility' (2011) 60 *ICLQ* 713.

Tanaka, Y, *International Law of the Sea* (Cambridge, Cambridge University Press, 2012).

Taylor, M, 'The EU's Human Rights Obligations in Relation to its Data Protection Laws with Extraterritorial Effect' (2015) 5 *International Data Privacy Law* 426.

Thompson, J, 'Historical Responsibility and Climate Change' in L Meyer and P Sanklecha (eds), *Climate Justice and Historical Emissions* (Cambridge, Cambridge University Press, 2017) 46–60.

Trachtman, JP, 'Trade and … Problems, Cost–Benefit Analysis and Subsidiarity' (1998) 9 *European Journal of International Law* 32.

Trachtman, JP, 'Externalities and Extraterritoriality, the Law and Economics of Prescriptive Jurisdiction' in J Bhandari and A Sykes (eds), *Economic Dimensions in International Law: Comparative and Empirical Perspectives* (Cambridge, Cambridge University Press, 1997) 642–83.

Trebilcock, M and Howse, R, *The Regulation of International Trade*, 3rd edn (London, Routledge, 2005).

Treves, T, 'Historical Development of the Law of the Sea' in D Rothwell et al (eds), *The Oxford Handbook of the Law of the Sea* (Oxford, Oxford University Press, 2015) 1–24.

Tzanakopoulos, A, 'Principles on the Engagement of Domestic Courts with International Law' (ILA Preliminary Report, 2012).

Verheyen, R, *Climate Change Damage and International Law: Prevention, Duties and State Responsibility* (Leiden, Brill, 2005).

Verheyen, R and Zengerling, C, 'International Dispute Settlement' in KR Gray, R Tarasofsky, and C Carlarne (eds), *The Oxford Handbook of International Climate Change Law* (Oxford, Oxford University Press 2016) 417–40.

Vogelenzang, P, 'Foreign Sovereign Compulsion in American Antitrust Law' (1980) 33 *Standford Law Review* 131.

Vogler, J and Stephan, HR, 'The European Union in Global Environmental Governance: Leadership in the Making?' (2007) 7 *International Environmental Agreements: Politics, Law and Economics* 389.

Voigt, C, 'Delineating the Common Interest in International Law' in W Benedek et al (eds), *The Common Interest in International Law* (Antwerp, Intersentia, 2014) 9–27.

Voigt, C, 'State Responsibility for Climate Change Damages' (2008) 77 *Nordic Journal of International Law* 1.

Vranes, E, 'Carbon Taxes, PPMs and the GATT' in P Delimatsis (ed), *Research Handbook on Climate Change and Trade Law* (Cheltenham, Edward Elgar, 2016) 77–108.

Vranes, E, 'Climate Change and the WTO: EU Emission Trading and the WTO Disciplines on Trade in Goods, Services and Investment Protection' (2009) 43 *Journal of World Trade* 707.

Weiler, JHH, 'Law, Culture, and Values in the WTO – Gazing into the Crystal Ball' in D Bethlehem et al (eds), *The Oxford Handbook of International Trade Law* (Oxford, Oxford University Press, 2009) 749–58.

Werksman, D, 'Could a Small Island Successfully Sue a Big Emitter? Pursuing a Legal Theory and a Venue for Climate Justice' in MB Gerrard and GB Wannier (eds), *Threatened Island Nations* (Cambridge, Cambridge University Press, 2015) 409–32.

Wewerinke-Singh, M, *State Responsibility, Climate Change and Human Rights under International Law* (Oxford, Hart Publishing, 2019).

Wiener, J, 'Precaution' in D Bodansky, J Brunnée and E Hey (eds), *The Oxford Handbook of International Environment Law* (Oxford, Oxford University Press, 2008) 597–612.

Williams, P, 'Law and Lawyers in the Multilateral Trading System: Back to the Future' in G Marceau (ed), *A History of Law and Lawyers in the GATT/WTO* (Cambridge, Cambridge University Press, 2015) 85–108.

Winkler, H and Rajamani, L, 'CBDR&RC in a Regime Applicable to All' (2014) 14 *Climate Policy* 102.

Wolfrum, R, 'International Law of Cooperation' in R Wolfrum (ed), *Max Planck Encyclopaedia of Public International Law*, online edn (Oxford, Oxford University Press, 2008).

Yee, S, 'Universal Jurisdiction: Concept, Logic, and Reality' (2011) 10 *Chicago Journal of International Law* 503.

Young, M, 'Trade Measures to Address Environmental Concerns in Faraway Places: Jurisdictional Issues' (2014) 23 *Review of European, Comparative and International Environmental Law* 302.

Zacharias, D, 'Part I Scope and Definition' in R Wolfrum, PT Stoll and C Feinäugle (eds), *Max Planck Commentaries on World Trade Law – General Agreement on Trade in Services (GATS)* (Leiden, Brill, 2008) 31–69.

Zagalis, P, 'Hartford Fire Insurance Company v California: Reassessing the Application of the McCarran–Ferguson Act to Foreign Reinsurers' (1994) 27 *Cornell International Law Journal* 241.

Zahar, A, 'Collective Obligation and Individual Ambition in the Paris Agreement' (2019) 9 *Transnational Environmental Law* 165.

Zahar, A, 'The Contested Core of Climate Law' (2018) 8 *Climate Law* 244.

Ziegler, Z, 'The Relationship between EU Law and International law' (Research Paper 15-04, University of Leicester School of Law, 2015).

Zimmerman, A, 'Violations of Fundamental Norms of International Law and the Exercise of Universal Jurisdiction in Criminal Matters' in JM Thouvenin and C Tomuschat (eds), *The Fundamental Rules of the International Legal Order – Jus Cogens and Erga Omnes Violations* (Leiden, Martinus Nijhoff, 2006) 335–53.

Zito, AR, 'The European Union as an Environmental Leader in a Global Environment' (2005) 2 *Globalizations* 363.

Index

www.ingramcontent.com/pod-product-compliance
Lightning Source LLC
Chambersburg PA
CBHW071302180926
51613CB00001B/110
* 9 7 8 1 5 0 9 9 3 5 8 2 6 *